Related Books of Interest

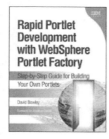

Rapid Portlet Development with WebSphere Portlet Factory
Step-by-Step Guide for Building Your Own Portlets

by David Bowley

ISBN: 0-13-713446-0

Expert developer David Bowley walks you through several of today's most common portlet development scenarios, demonstrating how to create powerful, robust portlets quickly and cost-effectively. Each walkthrough contains all the step-by-step instructions, detailed guidance, fast answers, and working sample code you need to get tangible results immediately.

As the best resource available on WebSphere Portlet Factory, this book reflects Bowley's unsurpassed experience constructing large enterprise portals. Bowley covers everything from back-end integration to user interface and AJAX techniques, helping you choose the right builder tool for each task and define high-level instructions that generate superior code artifacts. His example projects are simple enough to understand easily, but sophisticated enough to be valuable in real-world development.

WebSphere Business Integration Primer
Process Server, BPEL, SCA, and SOA

by Ashok Iyengar, Vinod Jessani, and Michele Chilanti

ISBN: 0-13-224831-X

Using WebSphere® Business Integration (WBI) technology, you can build an enterprise-wide Business Integration (BI) infrastructure that makes it easier to connect any business resources and functions, so you can adapt more quickly to the demands of customers and partners. Now there's an introductory guide to creating standards-based process and data integration solutions with WBI.

WebSphere Business Integration Primer thoroughly explains Service Component Architecture (SCA), basic business processes, and complex long-running business flows, and guides you to choose the right process integration architecture for your requirements. Next, it introduces the key components of a WBI solution and shows how to make them work together rapidly and efficiently. This book will help developers, technical professionals, or managers understand today's key BI issues and technologies, and streamline business processes by combining BI with Service Oriented Architecture (SOA).

Sign up for the monthly IBM Press newsletter at
ibmpressbooks/newsletters

Related Books of Interest

The New Language of Business
SOA & Web 2.0

By Sandy Carter
ISBN: 0-13-195654-X

In *The New Language of Business*, senior IBM executive Sandy Carter demonstrates how to leverage SOA, Web 2.0, and related technologies to drive new levels of operational excellence and business innovation.

Writing for executives and business leaders inside and outside IT, Carter explains why flexibility and responsiveness are now even more crucial to success — and why services-based strategies offer the greatest promise for achieving them.

You'll learn how to organize your business into reusable process components — and support them with cost-effective IT services that adapt quickly and easily to change. Then, using extensive examples — including a detailed case study describing IBM's own experience — Carter identifies best practices, pitfalls, and practical starting points for success.

 Listen to the author's podcast at:
ibmpressbooks.com/podcasts

Executing SOA
A Practical Guide for the Service-Oriented Architect

by Norbert Bieberstein, Robert G. Laird, Dr. Keith Jones, and Tilak Mitra
ISBN: 0-13-235374-1

In *Executing SOA*, four experienced SOA implementers share realistic, proven, "from-the-trenches" guidance for successfully delivering the largest and most complex SOA initiative.

This book follows up where the authors' bestselling *Service-Oriented Architecture Compass* left off, showing how to overcome key obstacles to successful SOA implementation and identifying best practices for all facets of execution—technical, organizational, and human. Among the issues it addresses include introducing a services discipline that supports collaboration and information process sharing; integrating services with preexisting technology assets and strategies; choosing the right roles for new tools; shifting culture, governance, and architecture; and bringing greater agility to the entire organizational lifecycle, not just isolated projects.

 Listen to the author's podcast at:
ibmpressbooks.com/podcasts

IBM
Press™

Visit ibmpressbooks.com
for all product information

Related Books of Interest

Service-Oriented Architecture (SOA) Compass
Business Value, Planning, and Enterprise Roadmap

by Norbert Bieberstein, Sanjay Bose,
Marc Fiammante, Keith Jones, and Rawn Shah
ISBN: 0-13-187002-5

In this book, IBM® Enterprise Integration Team experts present a start-to-finish guide to planning, implementing, and managing Service-Oriented Architecture. Drawing on their extensive experience helping enterprise customers migrate to SOA, the authors share hard-earned lessons and best practices for architects, project managers, and software development leaders alike.

Well-written and practical, *Service-Oriented Architecture Compass* offers the perfect blend of principles and "how-to" guidance for transitioning your infrastructure to SOA. The authors clearly explain what SOA is, the opportunities it offers, and how it differs from earlier approaches. Using detailed examples from IBM consulting engagements, they show how to deploy SOA solutions that tightly integrate with your processes and operations, delivering maximum flexibility and value. With detailed coverage of topics ranging from policy-based management to workflow implementation, no other SOA book offers comparable value to working IT professionals.

IBM WebSphere and Lotus
Lamb, Laskey, Indurkhya
ISBN: 0-13-144330-5

Enterprise Messaging Using JMS and IBM WebSphere
Yusuf
ISBN: 0-13-146863-4

IBM WebSphere System Administration
Williamson, Chan, Cundiff, Lauzon, Mitchell
ISBN: 0-13-144604-5

Outside-in Software Development
Kessler, Sweitzer
ISBN: 0-13-157551-1

Enterprise Master Data Management
Dreibelbis, Hechler, Milman, Oberhofer, van Run, Wolfson
ISBN: 0-13-236625-8

Enterprise Java Programming with IBM WebSphere, Second Edition
Brown, Craig, Hester, Pitt, Stinehour, Weitzel, Amsden, Jakab, Berg
ISBN: 0-321-18579-X

WebSphere®
Engineering

WebSphere®
Engineering

A Practical Guide for WebSphere Support Managers and Senior Consultants

Ying Ding

IBM Press
Pearson plc
Upper Saddle River, NJ • Boston • Indianapolis • San Francisco
New York • Toronto • Montreal • London • Munich • Paris • Madrid
Cape Town • Sydney • Tokyo • Singapore • Mexico City

Ibmpressbooks.com

IBM Press Program Managers: Tara Woodman, Ellice Uffer

Cover design: IBM Corporation

Associate Publisher: Greg Wiegand

Marketing Manager: Kourtnaye Sturgeon

Acquisitions Editor: Katherine Bull

Publicist: Heather Fox

Development Editor: Julie Bess

Managing Editor: Kristy Hart

Designer: Alan Clements

Project Editor: Jovana San Nicolas-Shirley

Copy Editor: Sheri Cain

Indexer: Lisa Stumpf

Compositor: Nonie Ratcliff

Proofreader: Seth Kerney

Manufacturing Buyer: Dan Uhrig

Published by Pearson plc

Publishing as IBM Press

IBM Press offers excellent discounts on this book when ordered in quantity for bulk purchases or special sales, which may include electronic versions and/or custom covers and content particular to your business, training goals, marketing focus, and branding interests. For more information, please contact:

U. S. Corporate and Government Sales
1-800-382-3419
corpsales@pearsontechgroup.com

For sales outside the U. S., please contact:

International Sales
international@pearsoned.com

The following terms are trademarks or registered trademarks of International Business Machines Corporation in the United States, other countries, or both: IBM, the IBM logo, IBM Press, AIX, CICS, ClearQuest, DataPower, DB2, Rational, Tivoli, Virtualization Engine, and WebSphere. Java and all Java-based trademarks are trademarks of Sun Microsystems, Inc. in the United States, other countries, or both. UNIX is a registered trademark of The Open Group in the United States and other countries. Other company, product, or service names may be trademarks or service marks of others.

Library of Congress Cataloging-in-Publication Data

Ding, Ying, 1955-

  WebSphere engineering : a practical guide for WebSphere support managers and senior consultants / Ying Ding.
    p. cm.
  ISBN-13: 978-0-13-714225-5 (hbk : alk. paper)
  ISBN-10: 0-13-714225-0 (hbk : alk. paper) 1. WebSphere--Handbooks, manuals, etc. I. International Business Machines Corporation. II. Title.
  TK5105.8885.W43D56 2008
  658'.054678--dc22

                    2008040607

Pearson Education, Inc.
Rights and Contracts Department
501 Boylston Street, Suite 900
Boston, MA 02116
Fax (617) 671 3447
ISBN-13: 978-0-13-714225-5
ISBN-10: 0-13-714225-0

Text printed in the United States on recycled paper at R.R. Donnelley in Crawfordsville, Indiana.

First printing December 2008

I dedicate this book to my father, Shuchun Ding, and my mother, Ximeng Wang. They taught me to take my responsibilities very seriously.

Contents

Chapter 9   Managing a Production Emergency   195

Acknowledgments

I want to thank Andrew Siwko, David Yao, Jing Zhang, and Robert Emery for working long, hard hours reviewing the drafts of this book and making highly valuable suggestions and comments.

I want to thank Development Editor, Julie Bess, and Pearson Education Acquisitions Editor, Katherine Bull, along with many others at Pearson Education, for working diligently with me to complete this book.

I especially express my appreciation and gratitude to my wife, Tiffany, and my son, Andy, for their encouragement and support. They made the successful completion of this project possible.

I also thank everyone who encouraged and helped me get through the long and challenging process of writing this book.

About the Author

Ying Ding is an IT veteran who has worked for IBM Global Technology Services as an e-business consultant to several major IBM energy and utilities customers.

Ying holds IBM certifications as a WebSphere System Expert, XML and related technologies expert, and e-business technologist. Ying writes and speaks frequently on WebSphere engineering topics, especially in the area of large system stability.

Ying is a graduate of one of China's largest and best universities, Jilin University at Changchun. Upon graduation, Ying was offered a lecturer position at the Graduate School of Jilin University. He studied at Brigham Young University, Hawaii Campus, as the first exchange student from China, and earned his M.S. in computer science from the engineering college of Lamar University at Texas.

Ying's primary research interests are in large IT infrastructure stability and resiliency, technical management of the IT engineering process, and IT infrastructure engineering methodology.

Ying lives with his wife and son in Charlotte, North Carolina. He can be reached at ying.ding@ymail.com.

Introduction

My experience in applying WebSphere® Application Server technologies has been a journey of making many mistakes and learning from them. This book, in a sense, is both a landmark of my journey and a systematic summary of a lifetime of learning opportunities.

WebSphere® Engineering: A Journey of Learning

In 1999, I started to work on WebSphere Application Server 3.0 as an IBM technical consultant. After braving a month-long intensive boot camp at a training facility covered by deep snow outside of Washington D.C., I was deployed to several large Texas energy companies. These engagements were great learning experiences. I was not only submerged in WebSphere technologies, but I also had a tremendous professional education that focused on customer satisfaction and depended on a tight team to deliver quality IT products and services.

In 2001, I joined a large financial services company and soon became a senior technical manager. Over the next five years, I stayed in the field of WebSphere Application Server engineering. I was close to the teams, the technologies, the systems, and the engineering processes. As a frontline practitioner, many years of technical and management engagements have been critical to building my expertise of WebSphere technologies. It allowed me to develop an incrementally well-rounded insight into the key aspects of WebSphere engineering. My work in the field exposed me to the full life cycle of WebSphere Application Server deployment and helped me increase my knowledge of WebSphere engineering.

After several years of achieving high WebSphere system stability for large and capable WebSphere Application Server systems, my first series of articles on WebSphere engineering were published in 2005. In my pursuit of 100 percent WebSphere system stability, I realized that the WebSphere technologies were stable, mature, and reliable; the technical skills of WebSphere engineers and consultants were good. However, a troubling and provoking question remained:

Why were there still so many production instabilities and so many stressful and demoralizing production fires in the industry? I struggled to understand this issue. Eventually, it dawned on me that WebSphere system instability was primarily a result of quality issues in product and service delivery. On further examination, I realized that these quality issues are directly related to the lack of rigorous system standards, consistent engineering processes, problems in hiring and training, and organization dynamics and stability issues. The challenges in WebSphere engineering practice and system stability had their root in the technical management of WebSphere Application Server engineering or, rather, the lack of it. This basic observation motivated me to document my thoughts and share them through publication. With continuous research, the concept of WebSphere engineering has become more defined and has led to this book. This book's intent is to identify where improvements in WebSphere engineering practice can be made and how to make these improvements. The chapters present various aspects of WebSphere engineering.

This Book's Organization

This book is a systematic introduction to WebSphere engineering. It provides an inclusive body of knowledge, best practices, and experienced insight as to where to make improvements. Its objective is to help WebSphere engineering support managers, senior WebSphere engineers, and consultants. This book covers the critical aspects of WebSphere Application Server infrastructure engineering work, from engagement to production operations.

This book is not a theoretical discussion of middleware engineering. Instead, it is based on industry experiences and, sometimes, the author's and technical reviewers' painful lessons of WebSphere Application Sever engineering practices.

Many chapters include a section that discusses lessons learned or critical issues pertaining to the chapter's main topics. This section may provide a systematic study of WebSphere engineering or useful references for on-the-spot solutions. Chapter 4 through Chapter 10 provides WebSphere engineering operations. These operations help ensure the quality delivery of WebSphere products and services.

Chapter 1, "Organization Models and Choices," discusses organization options and their pros and cons. These organization models provide references that help with organization design and redesign to achieve the optimal organization structure for your WebSphere support teams. This chapter defines WebSphere engineering tasks or operations. You must understand the classification of these operations because they are used in numerous important topics, such as engagement. This chapter explores the relationship between the organization model, organization stability, and WebSphere system stability.

Chapter 2, "Building a World-Class WebSphere Team Through Hiring and Training," focuses on technical skills. It discusses technical skills in four areas:

- A balanced approach to skills that include technical skills, technical project-management capabilities, and communication and teamwork experience

- Team building through structured and experienced hiring practices
- Focused technical training with different delivery models and maturity levels, and effective training methodologies and resources
- Technical training to grow the team's skills and serve as a morale booster for the team and as a relationship builder between the manager and the team

Chapter 3, "WebSphere Operations Framework," explores the core concept of WebSphere engineering and presents the WebSphere Operations Framework. Carefully read this chapter to understand WebSphere engineering and the WebSphere Operations Framework. This chapter expresses the intent to bring WebSphere Application Server work closer to a discipline of engineering that is characterized by tight standards and consistent processes.

Chapter 4, "Engagement Challenges," helps you secure adequate financial resources for your WebSphere team, both at the beginning and in the middle of a large project. This chapter discusses many systemic IT issues that make good engagement difficult to achieve. This chapter presents a service assignment and tracking system to quantitatively measure WebSphere services by appropriately using WebSphere engineering operation classification. It recommends a three-phased engagement process to manage large and challenging projects and an initial sizing and consulting engagement operation. This chapter shares experiences in managing dynamic and large projects, which cannot be well defined at the beginning of a project.

Chapter 5, "Server Build," discusses system-build issues and recommendations to deal with them. This chapter includes three operations: build planning, system design, and system build and configuration. This chapter also shows you how to validate your system build through testing. The descriptions of these operations conform to the WebSphere Operations Framework.

Chapter 6, "Functional and Integration Testing Environment Support," discusses major testing environment WebSphere support issues. This chapter explores the options to support testing environments, such as whether Java™ consulting needs to be provided or whether to use WebSphere Virtual Enterprise or WebSphere Application Server network deployment. This chapter also covers the Functional and Integration Testing WebSphere Support operation and resource and workload considerations.

Chapter 7, "Stress-Testing Environment Support," introduces the stress-testing WebSphere environment. This chapter uses the WebSphere Operations Framework to depict two WebSphere engineering operations: WebSphere Application Server configuration change support operation and WebSphere Application Server stress-testing support operation. This chapter emphasizes the importance of stress testing and explains the common problems resulting from insufficient stress testing. It discusses the major challenges of the stress-test environment for the WebSphere team. This chapter also explores the relationship between the production environment and stress-testing environment. Finally, this chapter sheds some light on the collaboration for stress-testing environment work and provides insight into the direction of the WebSphere stress-testing environment engineering support.

Chapter 8, "Production Environment Support," starts with lessons learned in maintaining WebSphere production system stability. These are practical insights into several areas of production support. Some experiences are counterintuitive, but nonetheless important. This chapter then offers important best-practice recommendations, such as empowering the production support team by sharing knowledge, system privilege, and tools. Finally, it describes the WebSphere Application Release Support Operation and the WebSphere Data Center Switch Support Operation.

Chapter 9, "Managing a Production Emergency," includes topics such as evaluating the severity of a problem and problem reporting, managing the WebSphere team during a production emergency, mitigating customer experience, and the all-important task of effective communication during high-impact and high-profile production problems. It also discusses how to build and strengthen your work relationship with IBM, as well as the formal process for further correcting, resolving, and preventing the problem from recurring (post-problem resolution). When you experience a production problem, read this chapter to obtain practical help to better manage your emergency.

Chapter 10, "WebSphere Application Server System Upgrade and Product Maintenance Management," first covers important system-upgrade challenges, such as obtaining approval, scheduling, adhering to standards, and not upgrading just for "upgrade's sake." This chapter discusses WebSphere Application Server planning engineering, process engineering, and build standards. Upgrade strategy communication is a major topic, especially from the aspect of gaining your business partner's support. This chapter also introduces the WebSphere Application Server Product Maintenance Operation.

Chapter 11, "Critical Work Relationships," covers the work relationship with the enterprise architecture team, the testing organization, application development and production support teams, and the capacity planning team. It also discusses nontraditional system resources, such as the web container thread and database connection pool.

Chapter 12, "Managing the Stability of Large Enterprise WebSphere Systems," stresses the need to intensely focus on and proactively manage the stability of large enterprise WebSphere systems. It provides insight and recommendations on achieving a balance between addressing immediate stability issues and long-term stability strategies. This chapter introduces ways to fundamentally improve large middleware system stability by forming the right financial incentive plans and organization structures. In addition, this chapter explores strategies to improve system stability for large enterprise WebSphere systems in interconnected change management.

Chapter 13, "WebSphere Engineering Going Forward," examines the future of WebSphere engineering. This chapter explores three new areas:

- WebSphere technologies that provide end-to-end IT infrastructure for SOA
- WebSphere Virtual Enterprise
- Service Science Management Engineering

Chapter 13 briefly introduces new WebSphere products and technologies, as well as the basic concept of Service Science Management Engineering. However, the focus is on technical skills, organization models, and engineering processes. This chapter purposely does not provide any definitive conclusions about WebSphere engineering's future, but asks intelligent questions that may lead to productive and systematic discussions of WebSphere engineering going forward.

How to Use This Book

This book can be read as a holistic study of WebSphere engineering or it can be a reference for on-the-spot solutions. For example, when you are in a production emergency, you may find practical help by reading Chapter 9. In addition, in Chapter 1, you may see a WebSphere organization model that makes sense to you when you are working through an organization redesign.

Although many chapters can be read independently, it helps if you read at least Chapter 1 through Chapter 3. These chapters familiarize you with the WebSphere engineering terminology and the basic ideas of WebSphere engineering organization, classification of operations, the contents of WebSphere engineering, and the WebSphere Operations Framework structure. As a result, it will become easier to read the rest of this book, even if you only read certain chapters.

I hope that this book provides you with helpful insights, recommendations, and references. If this book can help you better manage one problem in your WebSphere engineering practice, then my time writing this book is well spent.

CHAPTER 1

Organization Models and Choices

As a leader of WebSphere Application Server engineering, the first challenging task that you have is to either build a new WebSphere organization[1] or to streamline an existing one. Then, you need to choose a suitable organization model.

This is a tough job because the stakes are high. An unsuitable organization model can lead to an inferior WebSphere organization. Depending on the model that you choose, the WebSphere organization will either be well organized or intrinsically flawed. For example, a WebSphere organization with many unnecessary layers of escalation for production support won't be able to address production problems in a timely manner. In addition, unmerited division of engineering tasks, such as the separation of the project interface and system build into different teams, can cause serious relationship issues within the WebSphere organization because of resource contention and team priority differences.

The choice of organization model affects the stability and availability of your enterprise WebSphere systems.[2] In addition, you may have to make your model choice and implement it while mergers, acquisitions, and other business changes take place.

This chapter explores different models of a WebSphere organization, including the following:

---

1. A *WebSphere organization* is a shorter way of saying a WebSphere Application Server engineering organization. It is responsible for the design, build, and operation of the critical WebSphere infrastructure of a large company.
2. A *WebSphere system* is the short form of WebSphere Application Server system. This term emphasizes the WebSphere Application Server system software installed and configured for a specific target JEE application or application suite. "WebSphere system" as a technical term or concept does not include the JEE application or the JEE application suite that executes in the containers provided by the WebSphere system.

- Dedicated WebSphere organization
- Line of business (LOB)[3]-based support model
- WebSphere organization with separate engineering function
- Global WebSphere workforce
- WebSphere support of multiple levels
- WebSphere support for large projects with multigenerational plans
- WebSphere Center of Excellence

Dedicated WebSphere Application Server Engineering Support Organization

Before getting into a detailed discussion of a dedicated WebSphere organization, we need to define some terms: product-based support model and dedicated WebSphere support organization.

A *product-based support model* refers to an organization structure used in an IT infrastructure engineering organization. This type of structure is responsible for the full life cycle of the product engineering for one given set of products and related technologies. For example, you have a product-based technical support team that is responsible for the engagement, design, build, operations, support, and decommission processes for WebSphere technologies such as WebSphere Application Server, WebSphere Process Server, WebSphere Enterprise Service Bus, and WebSphere Portal. This technical team would not work on databases, operating systems (OSs), messaging technologies, and so on.

The use of the word "dedicated" in *dedicated WebSphere support organization* has two meanings. First, the expression "dedicated" indicates a technical team that is specialized in WebSphere Application Server infrastructure engineering. In other words, WebSphere Application Server and related technologies need to be this team's only concern. For example, building and supporting JBOSS and WebLogic need not be the concerns of a dedicated WebSphere team.[4] In this perspective, a dedicated technical team belongs to the product-based support model.

The second dimension of the term "dedicated" refers to a WebSphere Application Server engineering team or WebSphere team that works only to support its assigned LOB. A key organizational difference for a dedicated WebSphere team is the reporting structure. These WebSphere teams may belong to one large system-wide WebSphere organization, or these teams may have no horizontal organization connections. They report respectively to different IT divisions working for different LOBs.

---

3. *Line of business (LOB)* frequently refers to a highly connected group of products and services and business organizations that provide such products and services. For example, the consumer banking organization of a large international bank would be such a LOB. A large LOB may have many large business divisions, and each such business division may have a dedicated WebSphere engineering support team. A consumer online banking division of a large bank is a good example of large business division under a LOB.
4. *WebSphere team* is short for WebSphere Application Server engineering support team. The WebSphere team belongs to a WebSphere organization.

Separation of Teams and Classification of Tasks

A WebSphere organization must be divided into planning, process, and service teams. The planning team provides product strategy; the process team works on standards and engineering processes; and the service team delivers WebSphere products and services.[5]

The WebSphere engineering tasks are classified into three categories that have detailed operations. These categories are as follows:

WebSphere Planning Engineering (Plans and Strategies)

- Evaluate target legacy systems and form conversion strategies and plans.
- Evaluate existing WebSphere systems and devise migration strategies, plans, and roadmaps.
- Evaluate industry trends and emerging technologies and form introduction strategies and plans for the approved emerging technologies.
- Evaluate Java Enterprise Edition (JEE) standards development and give advice on migration strategies and plans.

WebSphere Process Engineering (Standards and Processes)

- Server build planning
- Server build
- Security
- Design naming convention
- Documentation
- System certification and validation
- WebSphere design and configuration
- WebSphere application deployment
- Integration methodology
- Development methodology
- Scripting and automation
- WebSphere best practices

---

5. Jorge Diaz, "Improving the WebSphere Support Process," (IBM Redbooks, 2003), 7–9.

ENGINEERING TASKS ARE DIFFERENT BETWEEN TEAMS

Many tasks for WebSphere process engineering and WebSphere service engineering may have the same names (for example, server build). However, the "server build" operation is a different task to different WebSphere teams. A team focusing on WebSphere process engineering is concerned with the WebSphere server build standards, the server build process, and process automation. A WebSphere service engineering team applies the WebSphere server build process and automation programs to build, configure, and deliver the WebSphere servers.

WebSphere service engineering (service delivery) has many similar tasks as WebSphere process engineering, but different contents. Here are the engineering tasks specific to service engineering:

- Security enabling
- On-call assistance
- Implement naming convention
- Troubleshooting and problem resolution
- Performance tuning and testing
- Development support
- WebSphere consulting
- JEE consulting

Categorizing WebSphere Application Server engineering functions helps conceive and design the structures of a WebSphere organization. The enumeration of engineering tasks makes it easier to think through the convergence of WebSphere Application Server engineering support life cycles, WebSphere Application Server environments and their components, and the product and service delivery.

This category of engineering function and the classification of engineering tasks are necessary elements that comprise an engineering framework. They make it possible to systematically deal with WebSphere Application Server engineering tasks in concrete terms. Chapter 3, "WebSphere Operations Framework," introduces the WebSphere engineering framework.

Although planning engineering and process engineering functions have different engineering tasks, they do have one similarity. These WebSphere Application Server engineering functions have no direct contacts with the customers. WebSphere teams serving these functions do not deliver WebSphere products and services directly to business partners. This is why frequently one WebSphere team takes on the responsibilities of both WebSphere planning engineering and WebSphere process engineering. However, from time to time, it is necessary to use senior planning and processing engineers to assist with high-impact production problems or difficult technical problems, working directly with the customers.

Dedicated WebSphere Organization of a Product-Based Support Model

A large, dedicated WebSphere organization that conforms to a product-based support model has many benefits. This organization is dedicated to WebSphere Application Server and related technologies. Figure 1.1 describes this organization model. A high level of communication helps achieve the standardization of systems and consistent engineering practices. A central leadership can effectively enforce the engineering processes and procedures across the WebSphere organization. A common document repository, a focused Web site, and a consistent documentation process contribute to successful knowledge management practice.

A service-oriented and project-focused approach can help with potential organization inflexibility associated with adopting a product-based support model. A project-oriented performance management needs to be considered as part of the complete solution of a dedicated WebSphere support organization.

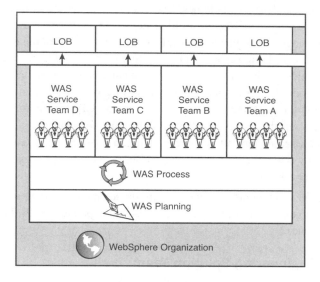

Figure 1.1 Dedicated WebSphere support organization built on a product-based support model

For a mature IT organization with an effective engagement process and a transparent IT infrastructure engineering cost model, use a dedicated WebSphere Application Server engineering support organization built on a product-based support model. This organization model works particularly well if your company has mature project management practice and large interconnected information systems.

However, a product-based support model may not work well if your engagement process is still evolving. A large technical organization dedicated to WebSphere Application Server and related technology may not be flexible enough to adapt to the fast-changing business needs of many projects. For example, it may be a challenge to quickly redeploy engineers to respond to the sudden surge of resource needs for a highly dynamic project. In addition, this support model works better if you have a sophisticated and transparent cost model. A large centralized Web-Sphere organization adds another layer to an already opaque financial metric. It is more challenging to depict a clear picture to your customer of WebSphere Application Server engineering costs.

Therefore, other important organization models deserve proper consideration (for example, the LOB-based support model).

LOB-Based Support Model

There are two different ways to implement a LOB-based WebSphere Application Server engineering support model. The first way is to build a technical team that supports multiple technologies and products for one LOB or a large business division. For example, you can build an infrastructure engineering team that supports WebSphere Application Server and other middleware products, the OSs, and the database technologies. Let's call this model the infrastructure engineering solution team, or to be more concise, the solution support team, because it is the convergence of many different technologies to engineer an IT infrastructure solution for the customer.

The other choice is to build separate infrastructure engineering teams that are dedicated to WebSphere technologies, but belong to different technical organizations that support one LOB or a large business division. For example, you may have one WebSphere team that supports an IT division working for the customer relation management (CRM) department. You may have another WebSphere team that is dedicated to the IT group for your sales and service division. These two WebSphere teams report to different IT organizations in your company. They do not belong to a company-wide WebSphere organization. There are no organization connections between these WebSphere teams.

These two organization models share some similar advantages and disadvantages. However, because there are enough differences, they are discussed separately with the similarities compared from time to time.

Infrastructure Engineering Solution Team

The major advantages of this organization model are flexibility, streamlined support, and ease of doing business for business partners and customers. The major disadvantages are that this form of organization is less developed and it needs work and time to grow and mature.

Advantages of a Support Team of Multiple Products

The relatively smaller infrastructure engineering organization is agile and flexible. In comparison, because of its size and complexity, a large IT infrastructure engineering organization may not be able to plan and implement changes as nimbly. A relatively smaller infrastructure engineering solution team may be able to adapt faster to changing business drivers; therefore, it may be able to do a better job of serving the business. The same goes for a small, separate WebSphere team dedicated to a LOB. Figure 1.2 depicts this support model.

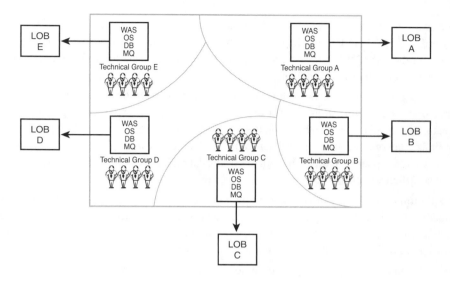

Figure 1.2   Engineering support team of multiple products

Better coordination is also an advantage of the infrastructure engineering solution team. For a product-based support model, you need special teams to coordinate the work of many product-based technical teams. For example, you need dedicated change coordination and environment coordination teams to ensure that the technical teams work together seamlessly. This is especially important during critical system changes, when a good transition between technical teams is critical.

ENVIRONMENT CHANGE COORDINATION TEAM

For a large technical environment in which many technical teams work together to perform complex changes, the environment change coordination team (also called the technical environment coordination team) leads the planning, scheduling, and coordinating of the changes through development and testing pipelines. This team plays a critical function that is indispensable for high quality and efficient change execution. For example, this team can help with the important communication work between technical teams. After an OS upgrade, this team can help certify the OS change and then inform the WebSphere team that it can commence its change. Without this team, timely communication and coordination may not consistently happen, which, as a result, may cause delays, quality issues, and even system production outages.

Good coordination is essential in managing large and complex technical environment. When you choose to build dedicated technical teams for each core technology, you want to establish a coordination function to help the technical teams work together. For any of these technical teams, doing a good job as an individual team is not good enough.

For example, during a major system upgrade that takes a long time, if the UNIX® team fails to inform the WebSphere team to begin WebSphere configuration changes as soon as it finishes an AIX® upgrade, the WebSphere team may not have enough time to perform a complex WebSphere system reconfiguration as planned.

An infrastructure engineering solution team can better deal with work coordination. For this support model, the system engineers for different core infrastructure technologies belong to the same team, and the coordination between them becomes substantially easier. In addition, for such a team it is unavoidable that one system engineer supports multiple core technologies. For example, the WebSphere engineer[6] may also serve as the UNIX system administrator. Then there won't be coordination difficulties.

In addition to better coordination, a single point of contact is highly desirable for good work relationships with your business partners and customers. It makes working with your team easier. Remember, from their perspective, the situation when multiple contacts to the infrastructure engineering organization have to be made for technical assistance must never arise.

For example, your application development team may feel burdened if it has to contact the WebSphere team, the database team, the operating system team, the load balancer team, the DMZ team, and the security server team separately to get an application code release planned and executed. A small support team of multiple products can better provide a single point of contact that helps simplifying the engagement process for technical services, and therefore is a major advantage of this support model.

Last, but not least important, is the transparency of cost. It is easier to define a financial relationship with one infrastructure engineering team. When the cost of infrastructure engineering has to come from many product-based support teams, it is substantially more difficult for the customer to maintain a satisfactory performance management metric that leads to a transparent financial relationship.

Clearly, the infrastructure engineering solution model has the merit of simplicity and the advantages associated with a simple structure. However, with its strengths also lies its major drawbacks. The possible problems of this organization model range from technical training pains to major difficulties in managing large and complex projects.

Disadvantages of a Support Team of Multiple Products

Technical training is a big hurdle for a support team working on multiple core technologies and products.

---

6. *WebSphere engineer* is short for WebSphere Application Server system engineer. A WebSphere engineer is an IT system professional who specializes in the design, build, and operation of middleware infrastructures built with the WebSphere Application Server and related WebSphere infrastructure technologies. WebSphere engineers often perform the initial WebSphere system configuration and the ongoing system configuration changes.

Managing the technical training for WebSphere technologies and products alone is a tough job. Managing the technical training well for many core technologies (for example, the WebSphere Application Server, databases, messaging systems, and numerous operating systems) poses a dire challenge for both the WebSphere manager[7] and engineers. For example, the technical manager of the team may not have the kind of knowledge and experience to determine the merits of a large variety of training programs proposed for the group. In addition, there is a limit on how many large sets of complex technologies and products that one system engineer can learn.

Another consideration is training budget. Instructor-led classes are arguably the most effective form of technical training, but this is costly. Such instructor-led training is more cost effective to organize for a large WebSphere organization with teams of WebSphere engineers at strategic locations. Usually, such large classes are charged a fixed fee regardless of the number of students, as long as there are no more than 12 to 15 students. Therefore, they are usually substantially cheaper than sending individual students to different classes. A large WebSphere team can reap the full benefits of the efficiency of large classes and the reduction in travel expenditure. For a smaller team, you may have to send individual engineers to classes at differing locations. You have to pay the full class fee and full travel expense.

As a final point, the size of a large WebSphere organization allows several WebSphere engineers to engage in formal instructor-led technical training together. Such training usually takes a week. For smaller teams, it is much harder to afford the time for technical training. It is not surprising that smaller LOB-based support teams can go for years without any formal technical training.

The technical competence of a smaller engineering organization may become questionable. In addition, this is not only a technical training issue. Focused engineering practice and real-world technical experience are vital in building technical competence. WebSphere technologies, as a subset of JEE specifications, are sizable and complex. Therefore, it is a great challenge from a knowledge acquisition and experience accumulation perspective to learn WebSphere technologies alone, to say nothing of learning many such large and challenging technologies at the same time.

If your engineers have to support WebSphere Application Server, operating systems, databases and messaging systems, the technical competence of your team comes into question because of a lack of focus. Your team may become an organization that can skillfully do entry-level system administration chores, but it is powerless when confronted with difficult system and application problems. Being a junior system administrator in today's highly competitive IT marketplace may not be an ideal position. Your business partners, your customers, and your senior management are more likely to respect and value a highly technical team that can help them survive a difficult IT job.

---

7. A *WebSphere manager* is a technical manager of a WebSphere Application Server engineering support team.

Finally, recruiting takes more time and is more costly. To hire a good WebSphere engineer is a tremendous challenge anywhere in the world because of the enormous success of WebSphere technologies. The attempt to hire a system engineer who's good at multiple core technologies, including WebSphere technologies, certainly complicates your hiring strategy, if it's feasible at all.

Separate WebSphere Teams

As previously mentioned, the other choice for a LOB-based support model is to build separate infrastructure engineering teams that are dedicated to WebSphere technologies, but belong to different technical organizations that support one LOB or a large business division (see Figure 1.3.) Separate WebSphere teams belonging to different IT organizations are a step up from the rather undeveloped solution-based support model. It can better deal with technical training, develop in-depth technical expertise, and grow advanced project management capabilities. This section describes some advantages and disadvantages of building separate WebSphere teams.

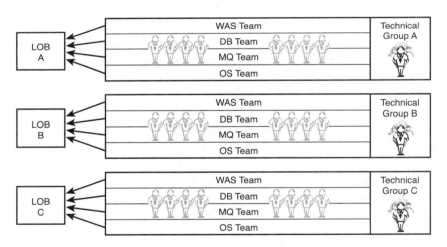

Figure 1.3   Separate WebSphere engineering support teams

Advantages of Separate WebSphere Teams

A better understanding of the systems and application of the LOB is an advantage that is also true for a solution-based support model. A separate WebSphere team dedicated to one LOB, over time, can develop a better understanding and acquire in-depth knowledge of both the IT infrastructure and the applications. This is because of better focus and less personnel change between the WebSphere teams of a large WebSphere organization.

These organization models make it relatively easier to develop strong work relationships with business partners and the customer. WebSphere engineering is never merely a technical job.

Complex and tough work relationship issues constantly challenge you. As a result, your success is determined not only by how well your team does a set of technical jobs, but also how well you manage your critical work relationships. A support team of multiple products or a separate WebSphere team dedicated to one LOB allows for better opportunities to build good work relationships. The engineers on different teams have an abundance of opportunities to better understand each other working together over a long period of time.

Disadvantages of Separate WebSphere Teams

When you decide to build separate WebSphere teams that report to different IT divisions, you have to consider the development stage of your enterprise IT systems. More specifically, you have to ask yourself what is the scale and the speed with which you are interconnecting your mission-critical enterprise IT systems. If your enterprise IT systems are increasingly interconnected, the LOB-based support model may lead to serious issues. This is especially true in the area of practice differences and system inconsistencies. The flaw of this model is the difference in standards and practices. By adopting this model, there may be different WebSphere systems developed and supported by different teams. This is particularly true if you don't have a centralized WebSphere planning engineering and process engineering function to make the WebSphere Application Server engineering practice consistent. What's more, it is extremely difficult and costly to correct such engineering differences and the system inconsistencies that have accumulated.

It is costly to support many WebSphere Application Server systems that are fundamentally different. For example, without a centralized WebSphere organization to enforce consistent system standards, different teams design and develop different engineering processes and automation programs for all the different systems. This can lead to enormous redundancy and inefficiency. Differences in practices, processes, and artifacts become established and entrenched with the development of a business division as well as the growth of its IT systems. As a result, it may be costly if your company decides to carry out any process and system consistency effort.

If you decide to correct these differences by introducing system-wide changes (for example, introducing consistent configuration automation), these differences are likely to derail your effort and may result in serious operation errors and production outages.

For example, one WebSphere team may use the same configuration automation program to make WebSphere system configuration changes for all WebSphere environments,[8] including development, testing, and production. However, another WebSphere team may do manual configuration in development and the testing environment while using a configuration automation program to make system configuration changes in the production environment. Thus, using the same WebSphere configuration automation program that your company has decided to deploy to all WebSphere systems, different WebSphere teams may have different experiences and results. The

---

8. A *WebSphere environment* is a complete set of WebSphere Application Server systems built for a specific purpose. For example, WebSphere production environments are WebSphere Application Server systems built for production operations.

team that uses manual configuration in development and the testing environment may not catch the problems with the configuration automation program. This is because of its established engineering process of not using automation in the testing and development environment. This may likely allow a configuration problem go undetected, slip into the production environment, and cause a serious unscheduled system outage.

These engineering practices differences and system inconsistencies make system integration and system interconnection extremely difficult. System standards, such as server naming conventions, can become deeply rooted second nature for WebSphere engineers after years of usage. Therefore, system inconsistencies, such as different WebSphere Application naming conventions and the different assignment of transport ports, can become serious system stability traps and challenges to integrated or interconnected systems. For instance, in a worst-case scenario, production traffic can be sent to the incorrect destinations because of port assignment standard differences.

WebSphere strategy and process work demand significant resources. A small separate WebSphere team may not be able to afford such resources. The lack of resources to work on critical WebSphere engineering tasks such as standards and processes have a far-reaching impact on the quality of product and service delivery for the WebSphere work in your company. In addition, this lack of enterprise-wide guidance in standards and processes in turn makes the system standard inconsistency and process difference problems become worse and more entrenched, thus enabling a negative cycle of deterioration. It is difficult for a small WebSphere team to support the overhead of planning and process engineering.

Summary of LOB Support Models

For an IT organization of a moderately sized company, both WebSphere organization models may work. However, the significant disadvantages of these models may become overwhelming for large IT organizations.

Typically, large IT organizations are more likely to extensively use WebSphere technologies for critical enterprise IT infrastructure. In addition, these large IT organizations have a stronger need to integrate and interconnect their critical enterprise systems. For this kind of IT organizations, a large and unified WebSphere organization with multiple parallel WebSphere teams dedicated to major LOBs may work better. This is especially true if the overall IT organization is relatively mature with sophisticated project management capabilities, established technology delivery practices, transparent cost model, and experienced technical service delivery management.

WebSphere Organization with Separate Engineering and Service Delivery Functions

For a large WebSphere organization, it is essential to have further specializations. There are natural groupings of talent in the WebSphere organization. Some engineers have the aptitude and gravitate to planning engineering and process engineering work. You can extract planning engineering and process engineering from the actual service delivery. Thus, you have an engineering team and a service delivery team. For these two teams, there are further choices to make.

WebSphere Engineering Team

For a WebSphere engineering team responsible for product strategy and process excellence, you have to decide if this team also works on the engineering work of other middleware products (for example, WebLogic Application Server). There is always pressure to do more with less. Given a limited budget for engineering work, do you want one middleware engineering team that takes on WebLogic, JBOSS, and so on, along with WebSphere technologies? The second question is whether to have a single engineering team that works on both planning engineering and process engineering, or have two separate teams.

Pros and Cons of One Team

The primary benefit of using one team to engineer multiple middleware products clearly is the cost savings. The possible disadvantages of this arrangement can be the lack of focus, competition for resources, and likely delays of key engineering deliverables.

WebSphere product strategy and process engineering are sometimes perceived as "soft" jobs. For example, building product road maps and WebSphere Application Server standards may not be considered as critical or as solid as WebSphere Application Server build or production support. This perception is incorrect. Without top-notch WebSphere talents focusing on an upgrade strategy, WebSphere Application Server standards, and process engineering, your WebSphere organization suffers.

For example, if your WebSphere planning engineer fails to deliver a product road map for your company in a timely fashion, there is no effective guidance in managing a WebSphere Application Server product upgrade. As a result, your product currency program fails. WebSphere Application Server system configuration automation is another example testifying to the importance of WebSphere process engineering. The WebSphere Application Server system configuration is a resource-intensive and error-prone job if done manually because of the existence of many WebSphere configurable items. However, if the process engineers provide the service engineers with a good configuration automation program, the WebSphere configuration work that could have taken days to do can be accomplished in a few hours, if not minutes. For the planners to do the best job possible, a feedback system needs to be built in to the WebSphere organization. Thus, the WebSphere planning engineers aren't working in a vacuum, but working shoulder to shoulder with service engineers who deliver on the plan.

Virtual Team

The best way to organize a WebSphere engineering team is to have one team dedicated to WebSphere technologies. If this is impossible and your engineering team must support multiple middleware products, encourage your engineering team to build virtual teams with members from the service engineering teams of various middleware products.

This serves two purposes. First, your engineering team has more resources to work on the engineering work for many middleware products. Secondly, it is more likely that the service engineers are more enthusiastic to adopt the standards and processes delivered because they have been part of the work and consider these the results of their own work. Actually, the virtual team approach may be a good idea even if you have one engineering team dedicated to only WebSphere Application Server technology.

One Engineering Team

Conceptually, WebSphere planning engineering and the WebSphere process engineering need to be considered separately. In engineering practice, it makes sense to have one WebSphere engineering team that do both. This team needs to have no direct production support responsibilities, but it is in charge of WebSphere planning and process engineering deliverables.

WebSphere Service Engineering Team

For the WebSphere service engineering team, you have to deal with whether you want to have separate technical teams to manage system design and system build. At the same time, do you want many parallel service teams responsible for production operations and project work for different LOBs? The project work for these service teams includes planning a build, managing changes, scheduling application code releases, and supporting testing and development environments. Therefore, you can divide WebSphere service engineering function into three teams:

- **Design team**. Responsible for working with the application architect and infrastructure architect to deliver WebSphere topology and configuration design documents.
- **System team**. Responsible for building the WebSphere system and performing system changes and upgrades.
- **Project support team**. Works with the project directly and takes charge of planning, change control, coordination, and WebSphere technical support for production, testing, and development environments.

It is possible to have one WebSphere design team and one WebSphere system team, but multiple parallel WebSphere project support teams for different LOBs.

Should you choose one WebSphere service engineering team that is responsible for the full life cycle of WebSphere product and service delivery? Or will you be better off having separate design, build, project support, and operations functions? When should you have a separate system team and when should you not? The following discussion answers these questions.

Separate WebSphere System Design Team

Having a separate system design team is a great gain for system consistency. It is easier to consistently deliver WebSphere topology and configuration design documents conforming to the WebSphere standards of your company. In addition, a dedicated system design team helps by steadily recommending and influencing best practices in WebSphere systems and JEE application. For example, the system design team may consistently recommend and produce a WebSphere topology that supports redundancy and failover for a critical WebSphere Application Server infrastructure in order to achieve high resiliency.

A possible problem of this team structure is that the system design team does not have to "eat its own dog food." This team designs a WebSphere system, but it does not have to live with it. In WebSphere engineering, it is mandatory to strive for a balance between conceptual elegance and technical practicality. When the design team does not have to bear the consequences of design flaws, engineering feasibility may become a secondary consideration. Therefore, a separate system design team may deliver something that looks terrific on paper, but is hard to implement in the real world and difficult to support in production operation. A separate system design team may deliver seemingly brilliant WebSphere designs burdened with excessive complexity that is not only difficult to build and support, but is also fragile. In the most devastating cases, the WebSphere system architecture delivered by a dedicated system design team may work so badly in production operation that it has to be replaced by a working WebSphere system via rebuild. This situation becomes worse when the responsibilities of the team are not clear, accountability is not enforced, and feedback between teams is not consistently done.

One of the ways to overcome this disadvantage is to devise the right incentive plan for the system design team to encourage the right behavior. The incentive plan must be linked to the performance of the design. The design team performance could be linked to the following:

- Feedback from the WebSphere system team and the service teams
- Metrics of unscheduled system outages caused by WebSphere system design flaws
- Evaluation of the WebSphere system performance and resilience features against design objectives and requirements

However, having one team provide performance feedback for another team is tricky because it involves the job of managing the sensitive peer work relationship, arguably one of the most challenging relationships in the corporate workplace. In addition, it is not easy to determine that a WebSphere Application Server outage is purely an issue of system design flaws. Often, WebSphere Application Server problems are complex with many contributing factors. Finally, evaluating performance against design goals is easy to say, but it is difficult to do because some of the major WebSphere Application Server design objectives and requirements are not easy to quantify. For example, it is difficult to provide the criteria of WebSphere system stability as a quantitative and measurable design goal. When the designers are not directly involved in fixing the resulting problems, it is hard for them to clearly understand the design issues and the resulting difficulties that the service engineers have to overcome.

Separate WebSphere System Team for Large Shared WebSphere Environments

By and large, it is good to have a separate WebSphere system team for large shared WebSphere environments. This team needs to take all of the system work, including system build, configuration change, system documentation, server security, and server recycling. This approach is especially appropriate for mainframe WebSphere system work because high system consistency is important for the stability and availability of these large enterprise servers. Yes, there are sophisticated problem insulation and dynamic system resource management capabilities available on the mainframe (for example, logical partition [LPAR] and workload manager [WLM]). However, serious WebSphere Application Server problems can still cause wide spread stability and availability issues and affect a large number of applications sharing mainframe system resources. Therefore, centralized WebSphere Application Server system work is necessary to enhance accountability, minimize operation errors, and achieve high system consistency for the mainframe.

The process is easy to follow. The WebSphere project team plans system changes and system upgrades and manages the change-control process. However, the project team won't directly make system changes. Instead, The WebSphere engineers from the project team request system changes through the system team. The WebSphere system team reviews, documents, executes, and certifies the system change. Thus, only one WebSphere team, the WebSphere system team, makes changes to the large shared WebSphere environments and is held responsible for the changes made. This is infinitely safer from a system stability perspective than having multiple WebSphere technical teams work on the same large shared WebSphere environments.

For large shared environments, it is critical that, at any given time, one WebSphere team has a comprehensive view of the entire WebSphere systems and is accountable for system consistency. Without such a centralized authority in WebSphere system work for large shared environments, it is difficult to maintain system consistency. As a result, your system is not stable. This is especially true for large WebSphere systems hosted on enterprise servers, such as mainframe servers.

Mainframe technical training and technical skill considerations support the arrangement of a separate WebSphere system team. You could have a small group of mainframe system experts to form a WebSphere system team. Meanwhile, many WebSphere engineers with JEE exposure and project management capabilities could comprise WebSphere project teams. This organization model makes your teams more effective and technical training easier.

Sure enough, there will be communication, cooperation, and collaboration issues between the WebSphere system team and the WebSphere project teams. From time to time, there will be a need for all the WebSphere teams to focus on improving teamwork and learn how to better work together on these large shared WebSphere environments. However, this is a necessary price to pay. Considering the system consistency and the stability advantage of this organization model, this is a balanced approach for these important large shared environments.

However, for large WebSphere environments built on a distributed platform that is dedicated to a single large and complex IT project, it is altogether a different issue.

Separate WebSphere System Team for Dedicated Environment on Distributed Platforms

A separate system team can be a good organization choice for a large shared environment, such as mainframe WebSphere Application Server systems. For WebSphere systems built on distributed platforms for large and complex IT projects belonging to one LOB, a separate WebSphere system team may not be necessary. For example, for the mainframe, the WebSphere Application

Server build requires specific system knowledge of the mainframe that takes years to learn. Therefore, a dedicated team that has the right staff can do a better job at a system build. For distributed platforms, a system build is a straightforward job that an average WebSphere engineer can perform.

This separation of system work may add an extra layer of service delivery dependency for the WebSphere service team. Your project team now has to take on the extra coordination with the system team to deliver any system work without extra benefits:

- The WebSphere project team is completely able to build servers.
- This is not a large shared environment where tight control of the system is necessary to provide system stability for many applications, but a dedicated environment.
- There is only one WebSphere team working in this environment.

Assigning a separate WebSphere system team to do system work on the distributed platform, you may have to deal with some issues.

The lack of clear division of labor may become the first troublesome area. Division of labor can easily become an issue between your WebSphere system team and your WebSphere project teams. They all belong to your WebSphere organization with a shared budget, workload, and human resource distribution across teams, but which team should be responsible for what tasks? Should the system team deliver a completely functional WebSphere Application Server to the service team? If there are any system issues during a major upgrade, should the system team be held accountable to fix the problems? It is critical that the division of labor between teams be one of the first decisions made so that everyone is on the same page.

Delays in system work are not uncommon. This is because there is one WebSphere system team with many WebSphere project teams competing for its resources and priority, as well as the resulting scheduling and coordinating challenges. Chapter 10, "System Upgrade and Product Maintenance Management," provides detailed discussion on the difficulties in competing for resources and scheduling for system work.

For distributed platforms, this model of separating system work from the project teams may cause problems between the WebSphere teams involved. This type of relationship issue within the same WebSphere organization is typically tough to deal with, even for experienced WebSphere managers and senior consultants.

Is this a core organization issue or a challenge to the management of technical teams? Will the benefit of centralized system control, consistent system build, and a high level of system consistency that typically comes from a separate system team justify the extra overhead, coordination, and organizational issues? Can a separate system achieve a higher level of automation? Different WebSphere professionals with different experiences and backgrounds may have different opinions. This book does not advocate one organization model against another. Rather, it is an experienced observation coming from long years of hands-on WebSphere engineering practice. Even for experienced practitioners, it is important to keep an open mind, be ready to adapt to the changes of business drivers, embrace positive changes, and design and implement technical organization according to the business actuality of your company.

Of course, nowadays, any discussion of building a high quality WebSphere organization is not complete without figuring out integration strategies and the support models of global deployment.

Building a Global WebSphere Workforce

An open mind and a positive attitude are needed to address the substantial disparity between financial resources available and the quantity and quality of work required for large IT infrastructure engineering organizations worldwide. Determined efficiency and productivity drive help, but they do not alter the resource-intensive nature of IT. IT is still in its infancy. It will take time before IT matures to an adequate level of industrial strength standardization and engineering process automation. Only then can the IT industry significantly reduce its dependency on high human resource consumption. Developing a global technical workforce has been one of the responses to financial and quality challenges. Globalization is a fundamental sourcing strategy, as well as an attempt at product quality and service delivery improvement.

Integrated Team Model

The integrated team model, or mirror team model, implements the concept of global teams incorporating onshore and offshore technical and management resources as each team sees fit in terms of the nature of the work, as well as time and location.

The blanket offshoring approach that hollows out the technical work of a large IT division seems more suitable for application development. Instead, the integrated team model for building a global technical team seems more appropriate for an organization responsible for enterprise infrastructure technology, such as WebSphere Application Server engineering.

The management and technical talents of a large enterprise infrastructure engineering organization belong to the core assets of a large company that has sizable and complex IT infrastructure essential to the continued success and prosperity of the company. The stability of the infrastructure engineering teams, such as support for critical WebSphere Application Server technology, has a direct relationship to the stability of the company's key IT infrastructure.

The integrated team model approach presents the least disruption to the WebSphere organization and the critical WebSphere Application Server infrastructure. It is important to have minimum organizational and functional disruption while building a global technical force. IT infrastructure engineering and system operations are different from application development. The infrastructure problems tend to be more direct, immediate, and pervasive. As far as application development is concerned, there are usually rigorous testing activities between development and production. Testing, especially stress testing, uncovers and eliminates application code and system configuration defects. Normally, no application code directly migrates to production environment without testing. However, there is nothing standing between your most critical production WebSphere Application Server systems and system operations that your WebSphere engineers perform. For example, the accidental launch of a WebSphere configuration program can incorrectly reconfigure one of your major WebSphere production systems, render it completely unusable, and cause a tremendous enterprise-wide outage. For enterprise infrastructure, especially for large and key technical environments, any disruption is instant, widespread, and serious. The integrated team model helps minimize such problems.

For the offshore WebSphere engineers and managers to be successful, it is critical to help them do a good job at technical training, learn the environments, and know the business partners. One of the best ways to achieve these objectives is to assign them to different WebSphere teams and work with the team for an extended period of time—the minimum needs to be one year. When they know the WebSphere systems, applications, engineering processes, and various technical teams and business partners, it is the right time to reconsider their assignment by fine-tuning the global organization. The integrated team model allows the best opportunity to train offshore WebSphere teammates and give them the best chance to be successful.

This integrated team model gives a WebSphere organization better control and flexibility over sourcing options, as stated here:

- An organization has total control over the scope and degree of this practice and can grow and downsize either onshore or offshore components of the WebSphere organization promptly according to the change in business drivers.

- In addition, this approach gives a better opportunity to directly manage the quality of WebSphere engineers both onshore and offshore via established hiring practices and professional and technical training mechanisms and channels.

- This model allows maximum control over the assignment of the roles and responsibilities of a global team with its onshore and offshore team members.

Long-Term Sourcing Strategy

Building a global workforce must not be taken only as a convenient means of labor arbitrage. Offshore resources will play an increasingly indispensable role in balancing labor costs, accessing rare skills, improving service quality, and reducing service latency.

For example, it is unlikely that all global locations will have exactly the same economic cycles. During a boom time in the U.S., less expensive and relatively more readily available WebSphere resources at offshore locations may be employed at greater numbers to reduce the overall labor costs for your WebSphere organization. In difficult moments of grave budgetary constraints, substantially more WebSphere engineering services can be performed at low cost by hiring more workers with good WebSphere skills at offshore locations. The offshore operations must play a balancing function in the overall WebSphere infrastructure[9] business.

---

9. *WebSphere infrastructure* refers to WebSphere technologies centered on IT infrastructure. These WebSphere technologies primarily include WebSphere Application Server, WebSphere Enterprise Service Broker or WebSphere Data Power, and others. WebSphere infrastructure specifically refers to the physical servers, network connectivity, load-balancing devices, security mechanisms, operating systems, and WebSphere system software installed, among other infrastructure components.

As a long-term strategy, the cost savings of offshore labor should be secondary. The focus of building a global WebSphere Application Server engineering organization should have other more sustainable objectives. The gaps in salary for onshore and offshore staff and will rapidly disappear. With the extra cost of managing a sizable offshore staff, there could be more costs rather than savings.

As a long-term benefit of globalization, a 24/7 support model is certainly worth exploring. A global WebSphere team and its members at different geographical locations are complementary to each other in engineering support and system operations. For example, China and India have different time zones from those of the U.S. with an 8- to 13-hour difference, depending on the time zones chosen for comparison. This time difference enables a true 24/7 nonstop support system operation, thus reducing human errors frequently associated with late-hour technical support. This helps cut down unscheduled system outage and improves the overall quality of service. The time difference can also reduce overtime payment that a company must make to be compliant with various state and federal labor laws and regulations at applicable locations and further reduce the cost of operations.

Building a local IT organization at strategic high growth locations, such as India and China, can be advantageous, too. This lays the necessary technical organization foundation to support the global growth visions of the company.

In the long run, managing project work and accommodating the real-time nature of infrastructure engineering support is key to the success of a WebSphere team of global workforce.

The WebSphere Application Server engineer has a project management perspective. A majority of change-management meetings, project meetings, and team huddles often occur during normal business hours. The primary WebSphere engineer must attend these meetings. It remains to be seen how this type of work can be effectively managed by global resources.

What's more, to be an effective primary WebSphere engineer, being able to perform real-time engineering or operations support is critical. The majority of such operations are during normal business hours, rather than at night.

Organizing global resources to support the above mentioned project work and real-time engineering activities and operations eventually determines the size of the global WebSphere team and the amount of assignments for the global team. One obvious solution is to get two or three shifts for the offshore teams to rotate into project work, real-time engineering support, and system operations during local night time. However, hiring and retaining WebSphere engineers anywhere in the world is becoming a great challenge. For some strategic global sites, such as India and China, the competition for WebSphere engineers is white hot. Beijing recruiters have even reached out to the U.S. market for senior WebSphere talents. Any WebSphere manager of global teams knows too well how difficult it is for hiring and retaining WebSphere engineers anywhere in the world. In a tough marketplace for hiring and retaining WebSphere engineers, requesting team members to take night shifts may not be the best way to build and keep a global WebSphere team.

From the perspective of building and managing global teams, there are many interesting and significant organization questions: how far an IT infrastructure engineering team must go to expand a global workforce, what the right balance of onshore, nearshore, and offshore teams should be, and how to distribute the project, engineering, and system support work across the globe.

Although there are no cookie-cutter approaches and there is no one-size-fits-all solution, it is critical that a global WebSphere team be able to engage in end-to-end WebSphere Application Server engineering support, from engagement and design to production operation and decommissioning.

One approach to overcome the difficulty of globalizing a WebSphere organization is to abolish the model in which the WebSphere team assigns a primary WebSphere engineer and secondary engineer to a large project during the full engineering life cycles of the project, and assign a service request system that reaches out to a pool of WebSphere engineers for support. Modern IT projects involving WebSphere Application Server are typically large and complex. Engineering reality is the best test bed for any organizational approach. It remains to be seen if such a pooled WebSphere engineer structure will meet the needs for the timely delivery of quality WebSphere Application Server products and services.

Engineering Support with a Three-Level Approach

A technical support model with a three-level structure has been popular with application development and support organizations. This technical support organization model has also been adopted by some technical teams supporting IT infrastructure. For example, some operating system support organizations may adopt a three-level resource pool support structure. However, what makes sense for some IT infrastructure engineering groups may not make sense for the WebSphere organization. This is because WebSphere technology is a part of JEE specifications. This relationship ties the WebSphere Application Server system tightly with the JEE applications that execute within WebSphere JEE containers. This close interdependency between the WebSphere Application Server system and WebSphere applications[10] makes it necessary for the WebSphere team to carefully consider the impact of its support structure and organization choice over the application teams, especially the application support teams.[11]

The shared responsibility of the WebSphere team and the application support team for supporting the WebSphere application and the initial uncertainty of the team responsible for the root cause of a production problem requires that the two teams work well together.

10. A *WebSphere application* is a JEE application designed and developed to execute within a WebSphere Application Server.

11. The *application support team* is also called the production support team. This technical support team ensures that the application is in stable production operation. This team has expert knowledge of the application operations. It works closely with all the technical teams, such as the WebSphere team, application development team, and testing team. The application support team is the first line of defense against possible stability problems. During production problem resolution, the application support team usually plays a leadership role.

Level 1 Technical Support

The application support team plays a pivotal role in both production application support and system stability. The application support team is the first line of defense against system stability issues. It has in-depth knowledge of the complex mission-critical application for which the WebSphere team provides a production execution environment. It also has limited WebSphere Application Server system privileges to expedite application production support chores.

For example, the application support team may have operator system privileges for the WebSphere Application Server. As a practical consideration, the WebSphere team most likely would want to grant operator privileges to the application support team because this reduces the WebSphere team participation in production issues that the production support team[12] is fully capable of managing. (It is not unusual to see the WebSphere team provide or share WebSphere technical training opportunities with the application support teams. Chapter 11, "Critical Work Relationships," discusses this topic.)

In this situation, the application support team calls in the WebSphere team when it has a difficult problem that demands expert-level WebSphere Application Server knowledge and skills, and the WebSphere team plays the role of Subject Matter Expert (SME), consultant, and senior-level technical support.

If the application support team is already playing the limited function of WebSphere technical support, installing a WebSphere Level 1 technical support role most likely creates a parallel or overlapping function with the application production team.

First, the WebSphere Level 1 support team may not have the necessary application knowledge to tell whether there is an application issue or a WebSphere system problem.

Second, when there is a difficult WebSphere system problem for which the production support team needs to call in WebSphere technical support, the WebSphere Level 1 team support may not be able to provide the senior-level WebSphere technical expertise needed. The WebSphere Level 1 support team may have to pass it on to the next level without adding value.

A third concern is the speed with which the right kind of WebSphere technical assistance is reached. When the company suffers a production issue, the application production support team does not have the patience to call in WebSphere Level 1 technical support when the only assistance provided may be sending out a page to WebSphere Level 2 support, who are capable of providing the kind of WebSphere technical assistance needed. When the WebSphere team is called upon to help, it is usually a serious and difficult problem that needs immediate attention. During a production emergency, it may be irritating to all the technical teams involved if there are any delays engaging the right WebSphere expert.

---

12. Also called the application support team or production support team, the *application production support team* provides advanced technical support for applications. This team has in-depth understanding of applications. It is the first line of defense for the system stability and smooth operation of the application. This team coordinates triage and problem resolutions when a production problem occurs, and it works with application development teams and other technical teams to provide a permanent fix for production problems. This team may have limited WebSphere administration privileges, which usually include recycling JVM instances and browsing WebSphere log files.

A large company may have thousands of large and complex WebSphere Application Server systems from different business divisions. It takes time to learn only a subset of these systems and become effective in providing support. A large IT organization is seldom a perfect world of ideal process optimization and flawless system consistency. Instead, large and complex WebSphere Application Server systems have a long history of evolution through mergers, acquisitions, business changes, and organization dynamics, and as a result, system differences and process inconsistencies exist. The WebSphere team must work in such reality. Therefore, the fourth area of concern is the difficulty in learning a large number of complex systems. In such a challenging environment, it is difficult for each engineer to provide WebSphere technical support for all the WebSphere systems and applications of a large company. This approach has pronounced technical training difficulties. It may not be possible for one WebSphere engineer to learn a large number of complex WebSphere Application Server systems.

Level 2 Technical Support

WebSphere Level 2 support has a solid set of WebSphere Application Server engineering tasks to perform, such as, deep dive performance tuning, troubleshooting, and high-impact and high-visibility production problem resolution. This job can cover the complete category of WebSphere Application Server engineering and it is a stable, visible, and desirable position.

If you have a WebSphere Level 2 technical support role, the best practice needs to be building a technical Level 2 support team with team members at each of the major geographical locations. This allows you to build a truly global WebSphere team that can provide the best WebSphere support around the clock. For example, you have the best engineering support around the clock if you have WebSphere Level 2 support around the world rather than concentrating on one geographic location. In addition, even global talent distribution makes it easier to build a local career path and mentoring opportunities for the WebSphere organization.

Level 3 Technical Support

The WebSphere Level 3 technical support role may have an overlapping role in terms of its function, especially for difficult production problems with several teams, and poses additional management issues. For example, if the WebSphere Level 3 support team works on application code to isolate defects, is that a service defined in a service level agreement (SLA) and, if not, what is the financial arrangement between organizations? If the WebSphere Level 3 support team provides application code improvements to fix a problem, who should be responsible for production instability introduced by the defects in the code improvements provided?

Another case is how to escalate and engage the IBM WebSphere Technical Support Organization when you have production problems and WebSphere Level 3 technical support. If a WebSphere Level 3 technical support role is set up, it is necessary to define the work relationship of the Level 3 support with IBM technical support, and how to engage IBM for technical support. The following exercise may help determine whether a WebSphere Level 3 technical support role is required.

As an established practice, IBM WebSphere Support and Java Support Organizations usually play the role of advanced WebSphere technical support. As with obtaining any technical support, there is an overhead cost in engaging IBM WebSphere and Java support. An IBM Problem Management Request (PMR) has to be opened with a detailed description of the technical problem that is occurring. Then, depending on the severity and difficulty of the problem, many technical discussions with IBM Level 1 or Level 2 WebSphere support or IBM Java support (or both) will likely take place.

If you have three levels of WebSphere technical support, it is an interesting question as to when and who needs to open an IBM PMR to secure IBM technical support. Let's assume that the Level 1 WebSphere support won't bypass Level 2 and Level 3 WebSphere support and therefore the Level 1 WebSphere support does not open an IBM PMR to seek IBM technical support. Let's say that the Level 2 WebSphere support engineer looks into the problem, but determines that more advanced WebSphere technical support is needed. Then, what does the Level 2 WebSphere support engineer do for an urgent production problem? Escalate to the WebSphere Level 3 support or open a PMR and seek technical support from IBM? Say that the technical support process stipulates that your Level 2 WebSphere support must escalate to the WebSphere Level 3 support, and the Level 2 support follows the process and escalates the problem to Level 3. In that case, the urgent production issue has already traversed, at this point, through three layers of technical support within a WebSphere organization. With each layer of technical support hand-off, there is a time-consuming burden of communicating a complex technical problem. Note that this is at a moment when the WebSphere engineers need to focus on solving a tough technical problem under the pressure to stabilize the WebSphere Application Server system and restore production operation. If the Level 3 WebSphere support decides to seek IBM WebSphere support, the WebSphere Level 3 support has to spend time both opening a PMR and discussing the problem with IBM Level 1 or Level 2 technical support. Figure 1.4 describes this support model.

Of course, to avoid a WebSphere technical support request traveling through five layers of engagement and communication process in order to loop in all WebSphere experts, and more importantly, to solve the production problem as soon as possible, the WebSphere Level 1 support and the application production support can immediately engage both the WebSphere Level 2 and IBM WebSphere support, as well as the WebSphere Level 3 support. Then, should this structure of three levels of WebSphere technical support be flattened? Does the WebSphere Level 3 support function overlap with IBM WebSphere support, the same as the WebSphere Level 1 support function overlaps with that of the application production support?

In the tough world of WebSphere engineering, where production problems urgently demand many technical teams promptly working together for a timely solution, an organization structure with many layers of laborious support escalation process is cumbersome and impractical.

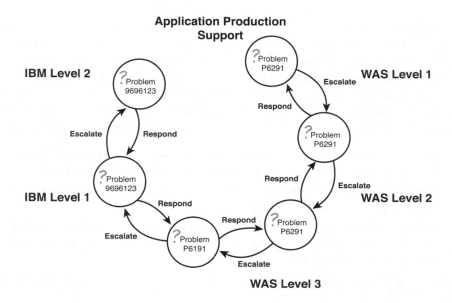

Application Production Support

IBM Level 2

? Problem 9696123

WAS Level 1

? Problem P6291

Escalate

Respond

Escalate   Respond

Respond

? Problem P6291

? Problem 9696123

Respond   Escalate

IBM Level 1

Respond

WAS Level 2

Escalate

Respond

? Problem P6191

? Problem P6291

Escalate

WAS Level 3

Figure 1.4   Three-level structure of WebSphere technical support

JEE experts in the application development organization need to also be considered. Because WebSphere technology is an implementation of a subset of JEE specifications, it is helpful to have assistance from senior JEE experts. This is especially true when there are production emergencies and there is a need to better understand the JEE application. WebSphere Level 3 support must have solid JEE experience. However, senior JEE developers and application architects in the application development organization can and should play the role of JEE application consulting during a production emergency.

The JEE experts on the WebSphere team are focused on the infrastructure side of the middleware work while the JEE developers and architects spend more time on the JEE applications. The developers and architects of the JEE application certainly know more of their application design philosophy and the technical details of their application code.

In addition, in terms of the overall IT organization, it is more efficient and cheaper to build a temporary task force to solve a serious technical problem, rather than training, retaining, and paying for WebSphere Level 3 support engineers for their advanced JEE application development expertise, which is not heavily used.

WebSphere plan engineers and process engineers are usually senior WebSphere professionals. They can be mobilized to participate in difficult technical problem resolution as part of a task force during a high-severity production incident. This is a more resourceful organization approach than keeping a pool of senior WebSphere engineers as Level 3 WebSphere support.

WebSphere technical support with three dedicated levels of expertise may look elegant and sound logical. It may look like a good way to organize because it has clear-cut divisions according to the skill levels. It could appear to be a logical way to separate WebSphere production support work based on its perceived efficiency of using the right talent for the right job. However, this three-level resource pool support model will most likely be unable to endure the test of time and engineering practice to provide unified support for a large company with a sizable WebSphere Application Server installation base that holds numerous complex WebSphere applications:

- There are technical training difficulties with learning a large number of complex WebSphere systems, practically all the WebSphere applications and infrastructure that a company has. This is especially true for a large company with a large number of WebSphere Application Server systems.
- Possible overlapping responsibilities and redundant roles with production support and IBM technical organization when the roles and responsibility, as well as engagement model, are not well defined.
- Reduced speed in production service restoration and production problem resolution, especially when the engagement and escalation process is not optimized.

It helps to have a flattened team structure with normal on-call rotation for every WebSphere engineer. This allows all the technical talents, including IBM, the WebSphere engineers, and the application development team, work shoulder to shoulder as an effective technical force to resolve tough problems together.

Nevertheless, a carefully defined process and a clear division of roles and responsibilities may help mitigate the risk of a layered support model. For example, problems can be classified according to difficulty and severity. For low-severity and relatively less difficult problems, Level 1 support can work independently. For high-severity problems, Level 2 and Level 3 need to be informed of the problem and provide leadership and guidance to Level 1, or participate directly in the problem resolution when appropriate. Therefore, the Level 1 WebSphere support performs the usual support chores, such as recycling the server, collecting and uploading data for IBM, opening a PMR, documenting the problem, and providing a report to senior management. The Level 2 and Level 3 support can play the leadership role in problem resolution and work as consultants and mentors to Level 1 WebSphere support. A flexible tiered structure of a virtual team and rotation may also work. For example, senior WebSphere planning engineers and process engineers can serve as Level 2 and Level 3 support when needed. For example, when the WebSphere team fights through a major production emergency, senior WebSphere engineers can be pulled in to help Level 1 WebSphere support engineers and work together as a virtual team.

A leveled resource pool model may be suitable for supporting a moderate number of WebSphere Application Server systems because it is possible for the WebSphere team members to learn a reasonable number of large systems, such as, supporting the WebSphere Application Server systems of one business division.

This model works well if the WebSphere Application Systems are standardized and the Web-Sphere applications are consistent in terms of architecture and operations. For example, a shared environment that holds many WebSphere applications belongs to one business division.

Technical Support for Very Large IT Projects with Multigenerational Plans

WebSphere Application Server technology is typically used to host powerful but complex JEE applications. Some of these large IT projects have multigenerational plans. There will most likely be active new initiatives for years. To support such large IT projects, a level of support personnel stability is necessary. This helps your team deal with complex technical details, maintain project management continuity, and build work relationships with peer technical teams and business partners.

Let's look at what you can do to best assist the previously mentioned large IT projects.

Building a Small Subteam

These large IT projects are the manifestation of senior management's determination and the financial commitment of an IT organization for top priority as well as strategic business initiatives. Besides, these are difficult projects because of size, complexity, and visibility. You want to carefully choose those who are most suitable to be the members of a small, but elite, WebSphere subteam.

Of course, you want to use your best and most experienced WebSphere engineers for the most important WebSphere projects. However, they are scarce resources. You may also want to pair off senior WebSphere engineers or consultants with junior team members. This allows your senior WebSphere engineer or top consultant to delegate entry-level technical or project management tasks to junior team members. This allows your senior team members to focus on complex and difficult work and add more value. Your junior engineers have an opportunity to learn to do a job, build confidence, and gradually take on more challenges under the guidance of senior team members. This arrangement also helps you to better deal with possible staff turnover and provide continued quality support for your strategic projects.

Separate WebSphere Support

For the WebSphere engineering support of a very large IT project, you have the following two distinct areas of focus:

- Production environments
- Testing and development environments

It is important to understand the specific requirements for each area and assign the right kind of WebSphere engineers and consultants.

For production environment support, the WebSphere engineer or consultant selected must have good technical skills. However, equally important, if not more critical, are good communication skills and project management capabilities.

For the selected WebSphere engineer to lead the WebSphere work in a large production environment, she must be able to communicate clearly and powerfully. A factual, considerate, and assertive manner is highly desired. Key communication capability is particularly important when working with the production support team on resolving differences during production emergencies.

The second attribute of the role is the ability to have both a great sense of urgency to get the job done while keeping a calm and professional demeanor. For example, the team members must focus on resolving a nagging production problem and restoring the service of an important production system while confidently and professionally interacting with the team and management.

Last, but not least, is project management capabilities. The candidate for this senior WebSphere engineer position must understand the value of carefully managing a large WebSphere project. She needs to be familiar with the practices and mechanisms of project planning, change management, job scheduling, quality assurance, and progress management. For example, the candidate must be able to lead the subteam to deliver many servers within deadline. The candidate must have an appreciation of quality control (for example, diligently following established server build and validation processes). The candidate must have the enthusiasm to perform a large number of difficult project management jobs. For example, she must have the patience to participate in lengthy change-control meetings, and must fight through planning sessions for the right window to perform a critical change. Without technical project management skills and enthusiasm, success is elusive for the candidate.

The next area of focus needs to be the testing and development environment support, including the critical stress-testing environment, which requires a different type of WebSphere engineer. Some of the attributes for this role include JEE development background, enthusiasm for deep diving into technical niceties of tough problems, and the patience of combing through large amounts of testing data to reach recommendations for solving tough system problems or complex performance issues.

JEE development experience comes in handy for collaborating and conversing with testers, developers, and architects to resolve difficult technical problems uncovered during testing—especially stress testing.

Curiosity and interest in understanding and tackling tough technical problems are essential for this role. The WebSphere engineer assigned to this job must not be someone who only has the technical knowledge and skills needed to do the job. A suitable candidate must truly enjoy solving tough technical problems and be proud and excited to provide excellent solutions.

Patience for combing through a large amount of testing data is important. The WebSphere engineer must have the patience to work with testers to analyze and research testing results. The

WebSphere engineer must have the perseverance to participate in repeated tests and analysis to seek optimal system configurations.

The candidate must have exposure to a broad set of technologies. This helps her develop an end-to-end view of a large WebSphere Application Server-centered IT system with many integrated components and interconnected systems. In particular, this is important for optimizing WebSphere Application Server systems in problem avoidance and performance enhancement. For example, from a traffic and load perspective, an end-to-end view from the customer browser, geographical load balancer, Web server, security server, and application server, all the way to the backend enterprise data store helps in constructing a fine-tuned traffic pipeline that minimizes system problems and maximizes system performance.

Ensure Standards and Practice Consistency

Over time, a large IT project can evolve into different system standards and engineering practice. In the long run, such differences are costly to correct, if possible at all. Therefore, you need special countermeasures against possible consistency problems for large projects. Both organization adjustments and engineering processes can help reduce the inconsistencies.

System Consistency Challenge

Having a small team engaged on a large WebSphere project for an extended period of time may present unique challenges. One of the challenges is deviations from WebSphere Application Server standards, which would then cause inconsistencies in engineering practices. For example, to expedite a WebSphere Application Server build to suit an application, the WebSphere engineer engaged may define the resources, such as Java Database Connectivity (JDBC), at server level rather than at node level, as your enterprise WebSphere Application Server build standard recommends. This may lead to a problem when a different WebSphere engineer updates the resource definition. He may be unaware that a nonstandard resource definition was used. As a result, the change in resource definition may be made at the node level rather than server level. This causes the application to fail when it tries to find the resource definition, and an unscheduled production outage occurs. It also causes automation problems that are to be used to audit enterprise systems.

Team WebSphere System Architect

To prevent such inconsistency problems, you can assign a senior WebSphere engineer with both WebSphere Application Server system experience and JEE expertise to work with all the projects as the team system architect. The primary role of the team system architect is not to design every possible WebSphere Application Server topology and configuration document for all the projects for which your team is responsible. (Of course, the team system architect can always provide input for WebSphere Application Server architecture issues.) However, his primary function is to review every WebSphere Application Server topology and configuration document that your WebSphere team delivers to ensure that the documents conform to the enterprise WebSphere standards and generally accepted WebSphere engineering practice.

System Audit

Another effective means to ensure WebSphere Application Server system consistency is to periodically conduct a system audit. This audit can be done using an automated program and, when necessary, a manual process. For example, a quarterly WebSphere system audit can be done. You need to also perform a spot check of the system as an ad-hoc quality assurance. Any problems uncovered during the system audit need to be corrected. WebSphere system audits without rigorous follow-up are useless.

Rotation and System Stability Considerations

A reasonable partial rotation of WebSphere engineers for large and important IT projects can help achieve high WebSphere Application Server system consistency and standardized engineering practices. However, this rotation may also destabilize your critical WebSphere Application Server systems and disrupt work relationships. These large IT projects need organization stability to be successful. Therefore, you have to carefully weigh the pros and cons and reach a balanced solution to any intended rotation as a correction to possible system inconsistencies. Of course, there are always many organizational considerations, business objectives, and project imperatives that you need to consider with personnel changes.

WebSphere Center of Excellence

The WebSphere Center of Excellence (WCoE) can be a virtual organization that is used as a forum for WebSphere technology discussions to help build consensus in your IT organization. WCoE can also be a full-scale technical organization with a clear emphasis on consulting rather than direct product or service delivery to the customers. Either way, a good WCoE is useful and valuable.

Virtual Organization

When a WCoE functions as a virtual organization of WebSphere Application Server technology, its function is similar to that of WebSphere planning engineering. However, it has a different emphasis on providing a forum for technology discussion in order to build consensus. In addition, the members can work together to review and approve product strategies, plans, and roadmaps. For appropriate cases, WCoE can make infrastructure technology recommendations, such as the following, to the senior management for approval:

- Evaluate and approve target legacy systems and form conversion strategies.
- Evaluate and approve migration strategies, plans, and roadmaps for WebSphere technologies.
- Evaluate emerging technologies and make recommendations on introduction strategies and plans.
- Evaluate JEE standards development and approve migration strategies and plans.

As far as existing products (for example, WebSphere Application Server), WCoE needs to be able to discuss and approve product strategies, plans, and roadmaps. For new products, such as WebSphere Process Server, WCoE can facilitate discussions and make recommendations to the enterprise infrastructure architectural authority for approval or disapproval about the use of the technology in a company. In other words, the WCoE needs to be an ongoing meeting that is a forum for stakeholders to review new technology and best practices.

This kind of WCoE is a critical organization where you can exercise influence over the technological future of the WebSphere technologies in your company. WCoE's work can shape the future for your WebSphere teams. You want to lead and participate in making key decisions working with the other WCoE members.

This is a virtual team that you want to be part of. This is a forum that you do not want to miss.

Full-Scale WebSphere Engineering Organization

WCoE can be a full-sized WebSphere Application Server engineering organization with an emphasis on WebSphere consulting rather than direct product and service delivery. As seen in Figure 1.5, WCoE has a unique organization structure:

- JEE standards and framework
- WebSphere performance testing and monitoring
- WebSphere operations excellence

WCoE needs to be staffed with experienced WebSphere engineers whose job is to help other WebSphere engineers be more successful. These senior WebSphere engineers do not directly provide WebSphere Application Server products and service to the customers. Instead, they provide engineering artifacts, such as monitoring strategy for performance testing and automation scripts for system audit. They are also pulled into production emergencies to help solve tough technical problems, or are otherwise engaged to assist in resolving for difficult technical problems. However, WCoE does not have day-to-day production on-call responsibilities.

JEE Standards and Framework

Senior JEE developers and architects will be part of WCoE. They will work with the application development organization to deliver JEE application standards and JEE application best practices. They will be responsible for the design and implementation of JEE application framework. All JEE applications with WebSphere as the target deployment environment must use the framework in application development.

These JEE experts provide consulting services for JEE standards, application framework, and WebSphere application best practices. This consulting service is not only for other WebSphere engineers, but also for enterprise architects, application developers, and software vendors. If this WCoE team does a good job upfront, many potential application and system problems are eliminated in preemption (for example, before the software defects have a chance to be programmed into the applications).

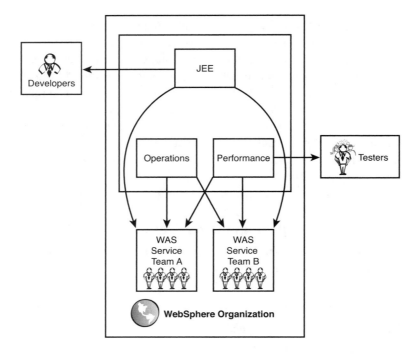

Figure 1.5   WCoE

WebSphere Performance Testing and Monitoring

WebSphere performance testing and monitoring strategies are critical to the quality and stability of the systems delivered and managed. Consultants who focus on performance and monitoring work are both WebSphere infrastructure and IT infrastructure experts. These WebSphere performance and monitoring consultants have extensive knowledge of the IT infrastructure of a company. They know how many enterprise applications are interconnected or integrated through the system capabilities provided by the infrastructure.

Thanks to their extensive infrastructure and application knowledge, WebSphere performance and monitoring consultants know where, how, and what to monitor in production and performance testing environments. They know how to retrieve detailed performance data in target areas. They use these precious performance data to help the testing organization form highly effective testing strategies and plans. In other words, they are the experts of the powerful methodology of selectively monitoring production systems. They retrieve relevant performance data to guide corresponding performance testing. They know how to use the performance data harvested in testing systems to further hone the production environment. In addition, they have the low-level technical skills to help them perform their job and achieve their technical vision. For example, they know how to create or use system tools to monitor various infrastructure components, such as networks, OSs, JVM, and Java applications.

This team is the high-strength glue that powerfully connects production and testing. These WebSphere performance and monitoring experts are fearsome warriors who neutralize system and application defects with deadly accurate "smart bombs." They are mighty defenders of your WebSphere system stability and availability, working with your testing organization and application support team.

WebSphere Operations Excellence

WebSphere operation excellence is all about quality automation that is tested and well controlled. This is presided over by WebSphere engineering process and automation experts. They are operations specialists whose job is to help the service engineers reach a high level of productivity and delivery quality through process automation. Their charge is to design process automation programs and apply script programming skills to develop the automation programs.

These WebSphere engineers also provide process automation consulting and help the service engineers customize the automation programs. The team helps to substantially improve the productivity of a team while reducing many human errors in system operations.

Production support refers to participating in production-related engineering and operations support, such as providing production with on-call support. WCoE engineers must have no direct production on-call support responsibilities, but can be engaged for difficult and critical problems as SMEs.

WCoE, as a full-blown WebSphere engineering organization, can belong both to a product-based support model or solution-oriented support model. WCoE can be the engineering division of a large WebSphere organization, or provide support to solutions-based teams.

WebSphere service engineering teams assigned to different LOBs can collectively function as a peer organization to WCoE. WCoE and WebSphere service engineering teams work together on WebSphere planning engineering through a virtual team led by WCoE.

Summary

Building a WebSphere organization for a large company is an exceedingly complex job, especially in today's challenging business environment of globalization amid fast-changing technologies and constant business dynamics. There always seems to be a large number of seemingly contradictory and competing factors and objectives.

For example, for a technical organization to be highly effective and competitive in WebSphere technologies, it needs to build a product-based WebSphere organization for technology focus and technical specialization. However, product-based support models present engagement and coordination challenges, such as the lack of a single point of contact and the need for a specialized team to help with system maintenance and change coordination among technical teams.

Another example is the separation of WebSphere planning engineering and process engineering from WebSphere service engineering. If an organization has this separation of WebSphere engineering functions, the WebSphere planning engineers and WebSphere process engineers are not distracted by daily production concerns; therefore, they can focus on delivering important WebSphere engineering artifacts. However, this separation, if not managed appropriately, may lead to the creation of WebSphere standards and processes not usable in real-world WebSphere engineering practice.

Most importantly, you must consider your overall IT organization and the engineering and process reality of a company. No WebSphere organization model can solve the systemic issues of an IT organization. You have to understand how far you can go and what you can do within your company's specific situation.

However you choose to organize your WebSphere organization, the bottom line is clear: It must help build a highly technical engineering team, enhancing accountability, and improving the quality of WebSphere products and service delivery.

Sun Tzu said, "Anciently the skillful warriors first made themselves invincible and waited for the enemy's moment of vulnerability." This quote reveals the intent of this chapter: optimally organize a WebSphere organization, preferably a large infrastructure engineering support organization dedicated to WebSphere technologies. By doing so, an organization positions its WebSphere teams in a winning alignment.

Now you have an organization framework with which you can start building a world-class WebSphere technical force of unsurpassed performance, a topic that is discussed in Chapter 2, "Building a World-Class WebSphere Team Through Hiring and Training."

CHAPTER 2

Building a World-Class WebSphere Team Through Hiring and Training

There are three decisive factors for the success of a large WebSphere organization: people, technology, and process. The WebSphere Application Server products and underlying Java Enterprise Edition (JEE) technologies are rapidly maturing. Process excellence is actually a manifestation of your WebSphere team's quality. Therefore, among the three factors, people are arguably the most critical link.

The collective knowledge level, attitude, experience, teamwork, and communication skills of your WebSphere engineers are the decisive factors for your team's success. For example, if a WebSphere engineer does not fully understand the technical details of Java Message Service (JMS), he won't realize that it is difficult to use JMS to integrate a WebSphere application with a legacy application that has a socket-based communication protocol. Such integration engagement takes much research and experimentation, and it tends to be time consuming. As a result, the financial resource analysis that the WebSphere engineer provides and the project plan that the WebSphere engineer commits to may be inaccurate or unsupportable.

Attitude is also important. The WebSphere team manages critical IT infrastructure, which demands a WebSphere engineer with a high sense of responsibility. Sometimes, all the WebSphere engineer has to do is to push a button (for example, to recycle a WebSphere server). However, to push exactly the right button at 2 AM on a Saturday after closely following a predefined operation sequence is not a job that everyone can flawlessly perform. When this seemingly trivial job is not done correctly, serious consequences can result, including high-severity production outages, high-visibility customer impact, and significant financial damage to your company.

Good knowledge and the right attitude are not enough to be a good WebSphere engineer. The WebSphere team works with many peer teams on large and complex projects. Teamwork skills and communication capabilities are critical. For example, one WebSphere engineer can clearly communicate the root cause analysis of a production problem to a peer team responsible for the

41

problem while improving the work relationship with the peer team through skillful teamwork and experienced communication. A less experienced WebSphere engineer who tries to communicate the same root cause analysis can get into a stressful confrontation with the peer team and damage the work relationship.

This chapter tackles how to excel in identifying and hiring the right middleware technical professionals for the right jobs. It discusses the options, priorities, and balance in hiring Web-Sphere Application Server engineering talent.

Hiring quality WebSphere Application Server practitioners is half of your team-building success story. You also need to focus on technical training for your WebSphere team so that your engineers are constantly gaining new knowledge and renewing skills to remain competitive.

This chapter covers two major topics: building an outstanding and highly competent Web-Sphere team through hiring as well as technical training.

Many technical training topics are covered in this chapter. First, this chapter discusses the importance of JEE exposure, system expertise, project management capability, and communication and teamwork. It explores hiring differences between contractors and employees, a strategy for hiring in a tough market, and how to conduct a structured interview. It compares centralized technical training for the entire WebSphere organization and decentralized technical training for each WebSphere team. This chapter introduces a technical training methodology: a guided flexible training program for each WebSphere engineer. It gives recommended strategies for technical training when you do not have technical training funding. This chapter discusses many practices and considerations, such as rotating WebSphere engineers, internal projects, team metabolism, stability, and balanced formal technical training. Finally, it points out technical training as a motivator and relationship builder.

Hiring to Build a World-Class WebSphere Team

This section explains the mix of technical skills and professional experience you need to look for to build a balanced WebSphere team. It discusses what kind of communication and teamwork skills are needed. It also covers important topics, such as interviews, hiring contractors, and what you can do when you're hiring WebSphere Application Server engineering professionals in a difficult market.

A computer science education or the equivalent must be a candidate's prerequisite. General work experience in designing, building, and operating WebSphere Application Server infrastructure is also required. This is because WebSphere engineering work is Category 1 IT Work, according to the U.S. National Academies.[1]

---

1. Computer Science and Telecommunications Board (CSTB). "Building a Workforce for the Information Economy," (National Academy Press, Washington DC, 2001) 2.2.4, 7.1.

The U.S. National Academies define Category 1 IT Work and Category 2 IT work as the following:

- Category 1 IT Work involves the specification, design, build, and testing of an IT artifact. It also involves IT research. Such work requires conceiving of and initial design of a computer system that leads to new approaches.
- Category 2 IT Work involves the application and operation of IT products or services designed or developed by others. In general, Category 2 IT Work requires the ability to support technical systems and communicate with both vendors and system users.

The U.S. National Academies research asserts that a four-year formal computer science education is required for Category 1 IT workers, because of the need to effectively deal with computing problems of many variables and a high degree of complexity, as well as problems that involve processing large amounts of data and scalability issues. A formal computer science education or equivalent nurtures an IT worker with the professionalism required for the success of large and complex projects. Finally, a formal computer science education helps the IT worker develop a better understanding of the underlying mechanisms to resolve complex problems. The U.S. National Academies conclude, "When business requirements and problems involve more complex or larger solutions, individuals with formal computer science education become more valuable."

Let's look at the planning, process, and service delivery aspects of WebSphere engineering and determine which category of IT work WebSphere engineering belongs to and if a formal four-year computer science education or equivalent is needed.

WebSphere planning engineering (plans and strategies) is primarily Category 1 IT Work because of the research required, innovative solutions needed, and the complex project management nature of the work involved. Forming conversion plans, migration strategies, and adopting the right JEE artifacts and the right technologies demands in-depth research and highly educated evaluation work, leading to new and innovative approaches to complex and capable construction of hardware and software combinations: enterprise WebSphere systems.

WebSphere process engineering (standards and processes) is charged with designing and forming standards and processes. This area focuses on conceiving and testing new processes and standards. WebSphere process engineering belongs to Category 1 IT Work. The scripting and automation efforts for large systems involve a sizable design, coding, and testing efforts where serious software disciplines, such as good documentation and component-based development, are required.

WebSphere service engineering (service delivery) involves tasks belonging to Category 1 IT Work, with some tasks having a possible dual identity. System certification and validation for large and complex WebSphere production infrastructure systems is more of an elaborate exercise to figure out integration issues, and, therefore, needs to be categorized as a Category 1 task. However, when only a simple certification process is involved, certification work can be Category 2.

Among the multitude of WebSphere system tuning tasks, several tasks, such as system parameters tuning for performance enhancement, system parameters tuning for problem avoidance, system queue adjusting, and data source tuning against a database, directly affect system integration. Security can be complicated in terms of integrating with LDAP servers and mainframe security. Therefore, both performance tuning and WebSphere security are Category 1 Work. As previously seen, most WebSphere service engineering tasks belong to Category 1 IT Work.

In general, a WebSphere engineer with a formal computer science degree or equivalent tends to be a suitable candidate.

After making sure that your candidate has a solid foundation in computer science, you must examine a candidate's strength in the following areas:

- JEE expertise
- Technical project management
- System experience
- Communication and teamwork

JEE

JEE expertise is important. For a permanent position, if possible, consider a candidate with good exposure to JEE application development, because WebSphere Application Server is an implementation of a subset of JEE specifications. JEE knowledge helps the WebSphere engineer do a better job. What's more, senior JEE expertise on your team can empower the team to deal with application problems. WebSphere Application Server provides the execution environment for the JEE application. However, the border between a JEE application and WebSphere Application Server is not always clear cut. The WebSphere engineer has to work closely with the application architect and developer to make the overall WebSphere system, including the JEE application, function as designed. In addition, JEE capability gives your team an enhanced troubleshooting capability that your business partners respect, because problems encountered in a WebSphere environment can have a root cause in both the system and the application, and it is frequently difficult to isolate at the onset of the problem. Particularly, if your WebSphere organization includes a JEE consulting team, you need to hire senior-level JEE experts to provide consulting services to the application development team.

From a training perspective, it is relatively easier to train IT professionals with JEE expertise in the role of WebSphere Application Server system engineers because the JEE expertise helps with understanding WebSphere Application Server technologies. For example, it is easier for a WebSphere engineer with JEE exposure to better understand the WebSphere Application Server implementation of the Enterprise JavaBeans (EJB) container.

A JEE-biased hiring strategy is easy to understand. But should every member of the WebSphere team be a JEE expert? Is this a balanced approach for hiring WebSphere engineers? The answer is no. There are diverse talent needs for building a strong WebSphere team. It takes three kinds of technical talents to build a powerful WebSphere team: technical project specialists, JEE experts, and system gurus. Of course, the WebSphere team members, though having different focuses and specialization, must all have good knowledge and solid experience in WebSphere Application Server and related technologies.

Now, it's time to look at the skills needed to build a WebSphere team, especially project management capabilities and system expertise.

WebSphere Project Management

Among the many WebSphere Application Server engineering tasks listed in Chapter 1, "Organization Models and Choices," WebSphere Application Server project management tasks are conspicuously missing. This is because project management tasks are common to all IT infrastructure technologies. However, project management performance by your team is a key factor for your team's overall success. Your WebSphere team has a lot of critical project management work to do. You need WebSphere engineers that are good at managing large and complex infrastructure projects. Of course, all WebSphere engineers need to have an in-depth knowledge of WebSphere Application Server technologies.

All large IT projects have professional project managers who allocate and manage financial resources, provide overall leadership in planning and progress management, and perform the critical coordination between technical teams. IT project managers, though, work at a much higher level than the WebSphere team does to provide indispensable project leadership under which all the technical teams, including the WebSphere team, perform their work for large IT projects. For example, the IT project manager is in charge of an infrastructure project plan in which the WebSphere Application Server system build is a high-level task that is associated with a deadline. It usually does not and should not contain details as to, when, where, and how to build a WebSphere Application Server system, or which engineer will do so. Instead, it has the high-level information of the server build. The WebSphere team needs to work on a technical details-oriented plan for the WebSphere Application Server build job. For example, the WebSphere team has to plan, prepare, and assign engineers to do the following details that the IT project manager does not really need to be concerned with:

- Stage the WebSphere Application Server binary.
- Prepare the build automation.
- Specify the system configuration.
- Build the server.
- Configure the server.

- Perform system validation and certification.
- Deliver the server to project management.

In addition, the WebSphere team has to perform critical communications and coordination at a technical level with the other technical teams to successfully accomplish the server build. For example, the WebSphere team communicates to the operating system team about the WebSphere system security setup so that the operating system administrator can implement proper file system-level security for the WebSphere system to be built.

WebSphere Application Server engineering for a large company is never purely a technical job. Good technical project management capabilities and communication skills are necessary for the team to perform its normal functions. The WebSphere Application Server technical project management includes, but is not limited to, the following tasks.

WebSphere Project Resource Estimate

The success or failure of a large WebSphere project is decided before the first WebSphere Application Server environment is designed and built. Without adequate resources, especially human resources (HR), your WebSphere project may have a rough road. Therefore, a good resource estimate upfront is pivotal to properly starting a WebSphere project.

It is not a simple job to perform a good resource estimate because there are many complex factors to consider. Some of these are easier to quantify (for example, the number of servers, WebSphere Application Server system redundancy and failover, and service level agreements ([SLA]). Yet, some elements in resource estimates are not as easy to quantify. A new application development team may have more code quality issues, causing high workloads for the WebSphere team. However, can you quantify the maturity of the development team and estimate the corresponding resource impact on the WebSphere team? How do you measure the consistency of application architecture to enterprise WebSphere Application Server build standards and the resulting WebSphere team resource consumption? It demands considerable WebSphere project experience, knowledge of WebSphere Application Server technology, understanding of WebSphere engineering processes, and the business acumen to do a good job at resource estimation.

Of course, the WebSphere engineer or consultant won't be successful if he only does a good job at resource estimations. He also needs good communication skills. There almost always is work to do to convince your customer or business partner of your resource needs.

WebSphere Project Planning

Without solid planning, a WebSphere project won't succeed. From system design to production code migration, a carefully made, and faithfully executed plan adjusted in a timely manner ensures the quality and the consistency of WebSphere Application Server product and service delivery. Impromptu operations and an improvised approach only lead to disappointment.

What's more, the WebSphere Application Server engineering work plan, when integrated with your change-management process and assignment scheduling mechanism, provides a desirable work rhythm for your team. This makes your team stand out among technical support teams, many of which are mostly "interrupt driven." Your team is in a mode to provide service when there is a need of service. For example, the WebSphere engineers working for a team with excellent planning practices know exactly when to perform a job for each system. Therefore, they can better organize their work and time, prepare well, and deliver a service of predictable quality.

Change Planning, Scheduling, and Coordination

WebSphere Application Server environments are usually large and complex. For many technical teams working well together, good change management is indispensable. Change-control processes and emergency change-control processes need to be rigidly followed all the time. Otherwise, there won't be a stable WebSphere system. However, change management is not easy. It demands both time and energy. For example, sitting through many long change-control meetings is required, and so is documenting, updating, and seeking approval for numerous change-control requests.

Managing change control well demands attention to detail, patience, and good communication skills. For example, you have to meticulously document changes in the format of change-control requests. You have to understand the context of the change (for example, get the big picture by attending change-control meetings where you provide further details and obtain necessary approvals). Then, you have to carefully communicate the change to the team or concerned members of the team. Of course, you have to figure out how to connect your scheduling system with the change-management system because this helps the assigned team members perform the approved changes at the appropriate times. Finally, the assigned engineers have to coordinate with other technical teams to make the approved WebSphere system changes at the designated time on the authorized server in the right sequence. The ability to plan, schedule, and coordinate is important to do a good job as a WebSphere engineer.

System Expertise

It is essential to have solid JEE expertise on the team. However, you also need expertise that focuses on infrastructure systems, such as networks, firewalls, and load balancers. System expertise is as important as JEE exposure to the overall technical potency of the WebSphere team. A systems expert who does not have a JEE development and consulting background is by all means capable of performing advanced WebSphere engineering functions (for example, troubleshooting a difficult and elusive WebSphere system problem that has complex relationships to the network, DMZ, and load balancer). System expertise is valuable and having experienced system experts is vital to the WebSphere team.

It is common to see WebSphere technologies at the center of large integrated systems. For example, WebSphere Application Server is the central piece that ties together multiple components, such as load balancers, security servers, system automation, operating systems (OSs), demilitarized zones (DMZs), networks, monitoring systems, reporting systems, databases, enterprise systems, and others. Therefore, the WebSphere team needs system expertise that helps with integration and solving problems between WebSphere Application Server and its integrated components and systems. There are dedicated technical teams in these areas (for example, the network team). The WebSphere team does work with these teams to address issues. However, a system expert with WebSphere knowledge and experience can see complex technical problems from the WebSphere technologies' perspective, and as a result, he can provide valuable input and service. System expertise includes the following.

In-Depth Knowledge of Web Servers

Web servers are important to WebSphere engineering, even Web servers that have no applications using Java containers. The Web server is the focal point of integrating or interfacing with many infrastructure components and systems—for example, load balancers, DMZ, security servers, third-party software, and the interface with the WebSphere Application Server through a plug-in. A significant number of problems that the WebSphere team must deal with are Web server-related. Therefore, Web server expertise helps the WebSphere team do a better job of understanding and solving these problems. For example, a good understanding of IBM HTTP Server (IHS) architecture and its process management features help the team better understand the root cause of many IHS processes clogging the OS native memory space.

Load Balancers

WebSphere engineers who have good exposure to load balancers help the WebSphere team do a good job in designing and implementing Web server topology, as well as Web server integration with load balancers. This expertise is also imperative in Web server-related problem isolation, as well as in designing, consulting, and implementing Web server automation, such as failover.

Networks and DMZs

Networks and DMZs are important to WebSphere Application Server. DMZs can be considered a special network. Because of security concerns, the Web servers of an Internet-facing application may be located in a DMZ. In this situation, there is the possibility that the WebSphere team may have to manage the DMZ involved, especially when your company does not have a dedicated DMZ team. Even if the WebSphere team does not directly manage the DMZ, your

WebSphere engineers have to understand how the Web server interacts with firewalls and the network-related aspects of the DMZ to work effectively in such an environment. For example, during production emergencies, in-depth knowledge of networks and DMZs helps isolate the root cause and quickly identify the right direction for troubleshooting efforts. In addition, you have to be aware that firewall issues are common in the setup of a WebSphere application with DMZ components.

Scripting and Automation

Scripting and automation are indispensable capabilities to any system administration job. The same goes for WebSphere engineering. WebSphere teams have a significant set of system administration jobs to do. Fortunately, all the previously mentioned areas of expertise, such as networks and DMZs, contribute to a WebSphere engineer's technical capability in scripting and automation.

Operating Systems

OS knowledge and the skills that come with a formal computer science education, as well as industry practice, are vital to a WebSphere engineer's technical competence. A number of WebSphere system problems may either share a resemblance to a network problem, or have relationships to network issues. For example, an intermittent network connection between the WebSphere Application Server and the database server may cause a Java Database Connectivity (JDBC) connection pool saturation. OS knowledge helps you understand what OS-level tools to use to test the connectivity between the WebSphere Application Server and the database server. OS knowledge helps the WebSphere team focus its efforts in the right direction when dealing with a difficult problem. It is critical to work in the right direction to quickly solve a tough problem. The harder you work along the wrong path, the worse the problem becomes. This is especially true when you are under pressure to stabilize your critical WebSphere system and you do not have a lot of time to lose.

Both practical OS skills and theoretical OS knowledge can help your WebSphere engineers. A modern OS is the central piece of a computer system. For example, with a good understanding of how an OS manages memory, controls processes, and allocates CPU, the WebSphere engineer can connect the dots between the various components of a computer system to develop a dynamic view of computing, rather than having only a static picture. A good grasp of OSs helps the WebSphere engineer better appreciate what is happening under the hood and gives him a better feel for the right direction to problem resolution. Because OS theories are in the collegiate computer science education curriculum, here again, the need for a formal college education or equivalent in computer science is obvious. Figure 2.1 shows the balanced skills of the WebSphere team.

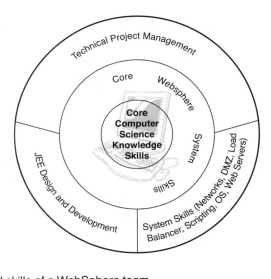

Figure 2.1   Balanced skills of a WebSphere team

General Communication Skills

WebSphere engineering work for a large IT organization is not suitable for everyone. It can be challenging or even painful for those who have inadequate communication and teamwork skills. A good candidate for WebSphere engineering support needs to always have excellent technical skills. However, without good communication and teamwork, it is difficult to do a good job as a WebSphere professional, who has to work with many technical teams and is frequently right in the middle of a conflux of important changes and critical events.

These are some of the general communication skills and teamwork capabilities that the hiring manager needs to look for; later, this chapter discusses the specific communication skills needed.

Listening

One of the most important communication skills is listening. Candidates need unusual patience and focus when listening, especially when the topics involve a large amount of technical details that sometimes are seemingly unrelated. This capability is necessary when working with a large technical team from different areas to solve a tough technical problem. Second, you want to determine the degree of intensity with which the candidate listens. Listening is effective only if it is with intensity. Otherwise, the candidate misses the key messages. When dealing with a critical production mission, a WebSphere engineer cannot afford to miss a key message. Third, give more consideration to a candidate who knows how to fully understand what is being discussed by asking the right questions. A good listener asks questions to better understand the topic being discussed, and a good communicator exercises effective influence by asking good questions. An experienced WebSphere manager or senior consultant can evaluate the listening skills of a candidate during interviews, especially a face-to-face interview. For example, you can observe if the candidate listens tentatively while others talk. A good listener asks good questions to fully understand the topic. You have to see if the candidate is interested in carefully listening to, and is willing to try to understand, different opinions.

Speak with Confidence and Authority

Listening and asking questions are important ways to communicate. However, when it is needed, your WebSphere engineer must speak with confidence and authority. For example, if a WebSphere engineer makes an important recommendation to fix a production problem while speaking feebly, it may be interpreted that the WebSphere team is not sure about the proposed solution. Because of such perceived lack of confidence, critical and worthy suggestions during a production emergency from the WebSphere team may be dropped without consideration.

Speaking with confidence and authority is not easy. For example, if you are not prepared for an important meeting, it is difficult to talk about complex issues with confidence. Nevertheless, it is frustrating to have a good WebSphere engineer whose public demeanor and mannerisms do not inspire technical confidence and professional respect. This is a serious issue. The WebSphere team may lose a critical opportunity to help shape the right decisions. In addition, highly visible behaviors cast a shadow on the business reputation of the WebSphere team. Therefore, when possible, look for those articulate WebSphere engineers who can speak with confidence and authority.[2] Of course, thorough knowledge of the topic and preparation before attending a meeting can inspire confidence. However, it can be a problem for the image and influence of the WebSphere team when knowledgeable and skillful team members do not speak in a way that conveys confidence and authority.

Direct but Professional

In the workplace of a large corporation, the ability to discuss sensitive issues professionally is critical. Dealing with serious production problems must not be an exception. On the other hand, being crisp, expressive, and convincing when talking about complex business problems and difficult technical issues is equally important. You can evaluate the candidate in this regard during a face-to-face interview.

Positive

For the WebSphere team, there never seems to be a lack of trying moments when it is easy to become negative. In addition, people who are positive in outlook may have a communication

2. S. Scott and G. Walsham. *The Broadening Spectrum of Reputation Risk in Organization: Banking on Risk and Trust Relationship*, (London: Department of Information Systems, London School of Economics and Political Science, 2004).

style that appears negative. This can be a liability in a crisis. You want your WebSphere engineers to be positive and constructive in their communication, either with business partners or within the team. There are two sides to everything. An ideal candidate focuses on the positive. You want a candidate who focuses on the constructive prospects of a difficult issue (for example, what opportunities come with the challenge, what positive solutions can be achieved, what compromises and agreements are possible between those who have different opinions, and what helpful facts and new information can be uncovered by sharing open and honest discussions). A constructive attitude makes winning possible for the team because it infuses much positive energy into your team.

Sensitivity to Work Relationships

Ask your candidate about work relationships. Discuss the concept of "constantly improving work relationships." Learn what the candidate wants to do to achieve this important objective. For example, you can ask for her opinion about a message to large audiences on the root cause of a serious production problem, assuming that the production support manager, a key business partner, disagrees with the WebSphere team on the root cause analysis. If the candidate's message to the production manager clearly addresses accountability while being diplomatic, positive, and considerate in the spirit of sharing credit and taking responsibility, that is a candidate that you want. If your candidate provides a message that is factual, but blunt, inconsiderate, or blaming (explicitly or implicitly), that is not a candidate that you want.

Write Concisely

Often, the WebSphere team has to communicate sensitive and complex problems in writing. For example, your team may have to provide a report on problems of severe production outages to senior management. This report can contain a lot of information, such as the problem statement, root cause analysis, corrective actions taken, and any remaining issues. Of course, it takes a lot of work to write a long report full of technical details. However, it takes more effort and time to do a write-up that is concise and clear, and is therefore more suitable for senior management consumption. No, you won't be looking for literary talent with Pulitzer Prize potential. However, if your WebSphere engineers can write concisely and with clarity, your life as the WebSphere manager or senior consultant is much easier, and your WebSphere team becomes more effective.

Special Communication Skills

There are two major areas of special communication skills that you are looking for: major technical issue communication and critical situation communication. Your candidate needs to have fundamentally sound communication skills. Given training, coaching, and practice, the candidate must have the potential to eventually perform these critical types of communication.

Complex Technical Issue Communication

A common mistake in communicating complex technical issues is not to think through what you are going to say from the perspective of the target audience. An update to the senior management over a critical issue about Java Virtual Machine (JVM) memory saturation is not helpful if it includes exhaustive heap parameter settings descriptions and Java garbage-collection characteristics. Senior managers are interested in the high level status of the issue—the big picture of the situation, not technical details. In addition, providing many technical details force senior management to wade through a long document to get to what they need to know. This is not a good practice.

Communication about complex technical issues, even those intended for technical staff, can contain an overwhelming amount of detail. This is the second common mistake: too much information. The quantity of communication does not equal the quality of communication. Worse, too much technical detail may drown out the key message that you are trying to convey. It is a tough job to crisply communicate a complex technical issue.

Lastly, sometimes there is repetition of the same content in an effort to explain a complex technical problem. Technical discussion is not a genre that always generates a tremendous amount of excitement. A difficult and long technical discussion challenges anyone's attention span. When characterized with frequent repetition, it can be downright tedious. Your hiring job is to identify that WebSphere engineer who can "say it once, and say it powerfully." A face-to-face interview allows an experienced manager to evaluate whether the candidate can communicate crisply. You may also find it effective to ask the candidate's manager or coworkers about her communication skills, especially if the candidate is verbose.

Critical Situation Communication

Some are better equipped in personality and temperament to thrive under the pressure of production emergencies, while others are not.

Yes, confidence can come from training and experience. However, some may be able to learn quickly how to perform the all-important communication job during critical situations, while others may learn slowly. Under the pressure of a critical situation, slow learners may appear to be irritated, snappish, and in a dreadful mood. You do not need anyone in a bad mood when you have a big problem to solve—this can become contagious. Demoralizing remarks spread quickly across the organization already under stress.

Communicating effectively is only possible when the WebSphere engineer is calm and confident. A good WebSphere professional can be as composed and as focused as a battle-hardened soldier. You can talk patiently about an important proposal to fix an urgent problem as long as you are secure in your technical capabilities and have faith in your WebSphere team.

Good communication skills are of paramount importance to the success of the WebSphere team. This is because the WebSphere team is right in the middle of many systems and many organizations. What's more, it is frequently in the spotlight during high-visibility production emergency. Try hard to hire the best possible communicators in the IT industry for your permanent and contract positions!

Hiring Contractors

For the IT industry, contractors have become a major part of the workforce. The following needs special consideration when hiring contractors.

Long-Term Contractors

For long-term contractors, there must be no difference in hiring criteria between contractors and permanent employees. Hire those who can learn new skills independently because you may not be able to provide technical training to contractors because of coemployment risks. In addition, the consulting companies providing contractors usually do not want to provide training for their contractors because of high turnover in IT consulting businesses. The contractor can negotiate with the consulting company on technical training or depend on his private funding to get the needed technical training done.

Short-Term Contractors

Short-term contractors do not require comprehensive skills. Instead, focus on the area needed to do the specific job that the contactor is hired for; for example, the system build. To hire a contractor to build a large number of WebSphere Application Servers, you do not have to consider advanced WebSphere project management capabilities or JEE expertise. Important areas for consideration are OS skills, experience in building servers, and the ability to use automation and to work with other technical teams. A senior WebSphere engineer can work with the contractor and provide guidance when needed.

Project Management

Unless you are hiring a contractor to lead a large project, WebSphere project management skills may not be as critical as when hiring a permanent employee. Usually, you want an employee to lead WebSphere projects. However, sometimes, for various reasons, you may have no choice but to use a contactor to lead a large project. In this case, technical project management skills become a consideration for hiring contactors. For example, when you have more new projects than employees to work on them, if you need a primary WebSphere support engineer and you cannot hire permanent employees, you have to use contractors to manage new WebSphere projects.

Hit the Ground Running

You want the contractor to hit the ground running with minimum technical training. As a coemployment risk consideration, you may not want to provide technical training for a contractor. The only training possible is to allow time for the contractor to get familiarized with the particulars of the assigned WebSphere project. As a best practice, hire as experienced a contractor as possible. Corporate WebSphere standards, established engineering processes, and well-documented procedures help in reducing the company-specific training needs. However, these documents cannot replace professional experience and advanced technical skills that take years to build and mature.

Tough IT Middleware Market for Hiring

The middleware market is an increasingly tough market for hiring WebSphere engineering professionals. It is not impossible to hire an experienced WebSphere engineer, but it is difficult. What can you do to build a top-notch WebSphere team through hiring? The following are some pointers.

Proactive Hiring

Because of the tremendous popularity of WebSphere technologies, it is difficult to hire an experienced WebSphere engineer anywhere in the world. To do a good job at hiring, be proactive. If you simply sit there waiting for the normal HR process to run its course, your requisition may take forever to be filled. First, work closely with your HR representative. Check the requisition status at least once a week. Your HR representative has many positions to fill; therefore, her attention to your requisition will help get your position filled quickly. Second, do your own search on the Internet, through your IT organization, and with the help of your peer managers. Get help from WebSphere professional organizations and put an advertisement on your WebSphere Global User Group Web site. Finally, you may want to see whether there are employees with WebSphere engineering experience within your IT organization who want to make a change. Sometimes, you can trade your requisition for a WebSphere engineer already working for your company. Training system engineers with other JEE application servers experience can be a good practice as well.

Convert Contractors

Converting a proven contractor is a good idea. The contractor has worked on your team for a while and knows the systems, the people, and the processes; therefore, he is likely to work out as an employee. The contractor is proven; therefore, he is likely to be a safe bet. The consulting company that provides the contractor usually requires one year of service from the contractor before allowing such a conversion.

Hiring Entry-Level Candidates

If your choice is between hiring an entry-level candidate and losing the opening, hire an entry-level candidate. You can always provide technical training. In addition, a good WebSphere team needs a mixture of entry-level, intermediate, and experienced technical professionals. Any WebSphere team has low level repetitive engineering chores that are ideal for providing training for entry-level team members. Thus, the senior WebSphere engineers can focus on more value added tasks.

However, you cannot have too many entry-level WebSphere engineers. Otherwise, your team's capability in solving difficult technical problems and coping with advanced WebSphere project management tasks dwindles. As a result, your WebSphere team's business reputation suffers.

Build a Relationship and Retain Your Key Talents

Lots of turnover in the workplace can contribute to the dissatisfaction of an employee with his direct manager. Building a relationship with your team needs to be the highest priority on your to-do list. Money is important. For many employees, being treated well is equally important. Work hard to build a relationship with your team and try everything possible to retain the key talents. It's the best thing that you can do to build a world-class WebSphere team.

Structured Interview

To gain consistent results, use a structured interview process. A structured interview includes a technical interview, an engagement interview, checking references, verifying qualifications, and building interview expertise.

Technical Interview

The technical interview needs to be both a comprehensive examination of the candidate's technical skills and a verification of the work experiences specified in the resume. For a large WebSphere organization, it may not be the best idea to have a written technical interview questionnaire because its content may be shared among candidates.

It is important to systematically verify that the candidate has the technical skills claimed in the resume. This is for technical skills validation as well as integrity verification. The WebSphere team has critical production responsibilities and access to key IT systems. Professional integrity and personal honesty are important.

For example, if a candidate claims to have work experience in JMS, but cannot answer questions on JMS listener, the candidate is not being truthful. Do you think that he will tell you the truth about his error that caused a high-severity production problem?

A technical interview can be equally effective if conducted via telephone or in a face-to-face meeting. In addition, a one-on-one technical interview is better than a group interview. The evaluation of the candidate is free of the work relationship considerations between peers. It can be sensitive when one senior consultant likes the candidate for his technical skills, but a manager new to WebSphere technologies has strong but unqualified differences of opinion. Of course, the interviewers can work out their differences and reach a hiring decision. However, this costs time and effort, and the outcome sometimes can be surprising.

Engagement Interview

A face-to-face engagement interview is more effective than using the phone. Besides, a group interview may be more appropriate for the engagement interview, because it allows an opportunity for the candidate to interact with more team members.

Engagement interviews must be conducted after the technical interview, after confirming that the candidate has the technical skills to do the job.

During the engagement interview, observe how the candidate behaves and what the candidate says to determine whether the candidate has the appropriate communication and teamwork skills. In addition, you want to make sure that this individual is someone that you want to work with. Look for behaviors that belong to a good listener. You're looking for statements of diligence and enthusiasm, and a commitment to quality, and respect for teammates.

You can ask questions about occasional overtime during production emergencies. You can inquire about doing a careful and responsible job. You can explore with the candidate how to build work relationships.

A high-performance WebSphere team has good team chemistry. It does not really matter how strong a candidate is technically; if you have good reasons to believe that he won't work well with the team, the job offer needs to go to another qualified professional. Yes, a truly strong technician is difficult to find and can be highly valuable in troubleshooting and challenging consulting engagements. However, times have changed. Gone are the days when a single technical guru could accomplish a complex technical task alone. Nowadays, IT work is so large and multifaceted that any significant accomplishment is truly the result of teamwork. A candidate who is strong technically but indulges in behaviors detrimental to the coherent spirit of a team working together won't be a good team member. You have to depend on the team to get the job done, not on one individual, regardless of her technical strength. Harmonious work relationships within your team are critical to your success; you cannot afford to jeopardize it by introducing any cacophonous members to the team. Face-to-face interviews with several team members may allow an opportunity to observe the candidate's teamwork skills. Talking to her former managers and coworkers is an effective way to check out the candidate's teamwork skills. Questions about taking responsibility, sharing credit, and managing work relationships with peers, managers, and senior management usually help you get to know the teamwork aptitude of a candidate. Your life as the manager becomes easier and your team becomes substantially better if you can avoid a candidate who has a big ego, shows no awareness of maintaining and improving work relationships, and displays an inappropriate desire for constant attention from senior management.

Check References on Technical Work Performance

It is a best practice to check credible references for technical and engagement issues, especially those that surface during the interviews. Discuss these questions with the manager or a colleague of the candidate. This is different from what the HR department does. Your intention is to discuss the technical skills of the candidate with a fellow professional who knows the candidate rather than verifying the candidate's professional qualifications.

Verify Qualifications: Character Is as Important as Technical Skills

Do you have a team member who holds a master's degree in computer science from Leland Stanford Junior University? If you do, do you know that Leland Stanford Junior University is the full name of Stanford University? If you do not, you have not verified the academic qualifications of this team member before hiring him. If you are certain that your HR department has a solid process for verifying qualifications, you are fine. Otherwise, verify qualifications yourself. This is not only a way to ensure that you hire quality employees, but it also prevents you from hiring people with character flaws and integrity issues. WebSphere engineering is a critical area for your company, and you cannot afford to hire people who are dishonest. A face-to-face interview is important because you can verify later that the candidate walking in the door is the one you interviewed.

Build Interview Expertise

Unfortunately, conducting interviews is sometimes considered a soft task. This could not be more wrong. Good interviewing is not only challenging, but it's critical for the WebSphere team. It demands practice and experience.

You do not have a job opening every day. To gain competence in conducting interviews for the team, you may want to designate one or two senior engineers to be the interviewer for the team. This is especially good for the technical interview. You may want to do the engagement interview yourself along with the team members who did the technical interview.

Building a strong WebSphere team through hiring is not painless. You get better with practice. Your next important task is building a WebSphere team into a highly competitive technical force for your company through technical training.

Building a Strong Team by Focusing on WebSphere Technical Training

The performance of a WebSphere team, as well as that of its leadership, can be clearly measured by the intensity of its technical training. A poorly managed WebSphere team can go for years without any formal technical training. As a result, its capability as a technical organization is weakened. A WebSphere team in need of training tends to show less confidence in tackling difficult problems. Such a team may not be able to provide effective technical solutions, especially under the pressure of a production emergency. Of course, the lack of technical training and the resulting weakened technical capability does not help in building a strong business reputation. It is important to have a strong business reputation because it has a direct relationship to the prosperity of any technical organization.

An inadequately trained WebSphere team may suffer more WebSphere system stability issues. Also, it is more likely to fall into the vicious circle of constant production fires. The team becomes so exhausted from being constantly engaged in production emergencies that it has no time to spare for either technical training or process excellence. Then, the WebSphere team suffers not only from technical inadequacy, but also inconsistent service delivery as a consequence of impromptu operations and improvised approaches. It is unlikely that a WebSphere team in need of technical training can design, build, and operate WebSphere systems of high stability and availability.

Without good technical training, the morale of the WebSphere team becomes an issue. WebSphere engineers have an important but challenging job. They have to work with a set of powerful, large, and complex technologies to build a WebSphere Application Server-centered, mission-critical IT system. They need all the help they can get. They need to constantly renew their knowledge and skills to do a good job. Insensitivity or indifference to the team's training needs sends a strong negative message to the team. Inability or inaction in providing technical training affects the team morale, its perception of its leaders, and its employee satisfaction.

However, managing technical training well is not easy. You need a suitable training strategy. This section introduces three different WebSphere training approaches:

- Centrally plan, fund, and execute training for the entire WebSphere organization.
- Each WebSphere team does its own training.
- Develop technical training initiatives for each WebSphere engineer.

Centralized Technical Training

Centralized technical training means using one training plan for the entire WebSphere organization. All the WebSphere engineers, regardless of specialization, participate in the same uniform set of technical training programs. For example, you have two courses in your training plan for the year: a WebSphere Application Server system administration class and a WebSphere Application Server system optimization class. All of your WebSphere engineers (for example, process engineers and service engineers) take these two classes as their required technical training for the year.

The ease of management is the primary benefit for this training strategy. For example, you only have to do training planning and funding work once for the entire organization.

The second advantage is cost reduction. You can conduct technical classes at strategic locations with the highest concentration of WebSphere engineers. Thus, you can put 12 to 15 engineers into one class to maximize cost benefits. This arrangement also significantly reduces travel expenses.

TECHNICAL TRAINING CLASSES

Twelve to fifteen engineers is usually the maximum number of students for a hands-on technical class on WebSphere Application Server. Too many students prevent the instructor from adequately answering questions or addressing issues that students may have during labs. At the same time, during the course of a class, students benefit from learning from each other. When the class is too small, discussions among students are fewer and the opportunities for students to learn from each other diminish. In addition, when the class is too small, you may not be able to take advantage of the size of the operation and get the most out of your training dollars.

Some WebSphere managers are more focused on technical training, while others may have different priorities. Centralized technical training can be the common denominator of technical training for all the WebSphere teams. As a result, technical training is done consistently across the WebSphere organization.

The major drawback of centralized technical training is the lack of differentiated training programs for different WebSphere teams. Different teams have different training needs. For example, the training needs of a WebSphere team working on a WebSphere process server differ from that of a team working on a WebSphere portal server. Technical training is business driven. A WebSphere team's training needs are decided by its projects. For a large WebSphere organization with a variety of WebSphere projects, successfully applying a centralized technical training strategy is difficult.

Still, it is commendable to have a technical training plan, even a centralized one. It is a lot better than having no training program at all, which unfortunately may be true for many WebSphere organizations.

WebSphere engineers have different levels of technical maturity. Therefore, they need different levels of training. For example, if the team needs highly advanced training, but you have a group of new engineers, they may be out of place in advanced training. On the other hand, intermediate-level training may not interest the senior members of the team. Later, this chapter introduces a customized training strategy called the guided flexible training program, which can address the different needs for technical training of your team.

Decentralized Technical Training

Decentralized technical training is a strategy that allows each of your WebSphere teams to manage their own training, planning, funding, and scheduling. The benefits of this training strategy include positive competition between teams, easier training schedules, and better alignment of training to projects.

Decentralized technical training introduces positive competition between WebSphere teams. It encourages teams to compete to do a better job at training. This strategy is particularly effective if your company has a "first come, first serve" policy for training funding. This is actually a fair policy. It ensures that those teams in need of technical training get the funding if they work hard and early on a training plan. Meanwhile, it discourages unnecessary training spending, which is not totally unavoidable for the cookie-cutter sort of centralized training approach.

It is easier to schedule training for one WebSphere team rather than for the entire WebSphere organization. For the centralized training approach, it is difficult and time consuming to coordinate the training schedules for many WebSphere teams with different project deadlines. Thus, cancellations and low attendance are common. Decentralized training helps a team better manage training scheduling, because it has a much smaller set of projects to consider.

Most importantly, decentralized training helps better align your technical training with your WebSphere projects. You can focus on your team's projects and the business needs of these projects in deciding what technical training to take. This is possible because you are free from the complicated job of considering other WebSphere teams, their projects, and the necessary compromises. Avoid unnecessary occasions where you have to deal with the sensitive peer relationship if possible. Decentralized training can help you focus on getting the training for your team, rather than coping with office politics.

Decentralized training advocates a team-based training strategy. Its major advantages are recognizing the complexity and diversity of WebSphere engineering work of large corporations and the varied technical training needs for different WebSphere teams. However, decentralized training is not able to adequately deal with the different ways people learn. To require all the WebSphere engineers to train exactly the same way may not be the best solution. Therefore, there is the need for more advanced technical training.

The next section introduces guided flexible training programs focusing on planning and funding efforts for each individual WebSphere engineer.

Guided Flexible Training Program

WebSphere engineers are different and learn differently. Some learn by reading technical books and journals. They enjoy and can concentrate for a long stretch of time on reading technical literature. They appreciate this form of learning because it allows them time to reflect on the technical information, and reread if necessary. Others may not like to read technical books because they become bored.

Some engineers prefer instructor-led hands-on classes where they can ask questions and learn by doing labs, talking to the instructor, and working with fellow students. Others may find fast-paced labs difficult to follow.

Some engineers love to go to large technical conferences. They like to interact with fellow WebSphere professionals from other companies and learn how other engineers do their job. They like keynote speeches and seminars, and they regard them as great ways to learn. Others may feel that technical conferences do not offer enough depth on topics that they are interested in.

Last, but not least, if you have a thriving team with a range of WebSphere engineers from entry level to senior level, there are requirements for many levels of technical training.

A guided flexible training program fully recognizes that different people learn differently, and allows a WebSphere engineer to choose her own best method of learning. In addition, a guided flexible training program provides a link between the team training objectives and the individual training objectives for a WebSphere engineer. A guided flexible training program also uses required technical certification to ensure consistent training results for those engineers who choose not to take formal instructor-led technical classes.

Technical training is not cheap. Two instructor-led WebSphere Application Server technology courses may cost up to $5,000. A conservative estimate of the training budget per WebSphere engineer per year, including some travel allowance, could go as high as $7,000.

A guided flexible training program allocates a technical training budget for each engineer. For example, you can earmark $7,000 for technical training for one engineer for the year. You can work with your engineer to set technical training targets (for example, WebSphere Application Server 7 system administration and performance-testing support). The WebSphere engineer can decide what to do to with the budget, with your approval. Here are a few examples of what he can do:

1. Use his budget to take the following courses: IBM WebSphere Application Server Administration 7 and IBM WebSphere V7 Performance Testing and Monitoring.

2. Choose to go to IBM Impact 2009 and attend another testing conference, such as one of the worthy software-testing conferences available.

3. Go to IBM Impact 2009 and purchase several WebSphere Application Server testing books and professional journals. Technical literature can be expensive, so this allowance is helpful.

4. Take a complete set of preparatory classes for intermediate IBM technical certification and advanced IBM technical certification on WebSphere Application Servers.

Management guidance ensures that his choice of technical training is consistent with the technical training target set for him. For example, management won't approve his training request if the chosen class is for WebSphere portal server, which has nothing to do with his assigned projects.

To ensure the quality of training, WebSphere engineers who choose not to take formal instructor-led classes in their target area of technical expertise are required to take and pass the appropriate IBM technical certification. This requirement becomes part of those engineers' performance objective documentation.

Using the guided flexible training program, WebSphere engineers have the maximum possible flexibility and freedom to configure their technical training. Management works with the engineers on what to learn, but not how to learn. This is a form of personalized technical training that allows engineers more effective use of their training budgets and helps them achieve the highest possible satisfaction from technical training.

A guided flexible training program is built on the fundamental belief that, given freedom, the majority of people choose to do the right thing. Given flexibility, freedom, and proper guidance, WebSphere engineers do an outstanding job in directly managing their own technical training and make the right decisions for greater shareholder values, stronger customer delight, and their own satisfaction.

What to Do if You Have No Funding

If you have no funding for training, figure out a way to get what your team needs. When you do not have a budget (or have a limited budget), be resourceful and find practical ways to get your team trained without spending money. The following are some training considerations.

IBM Free Training

IBM offers many free technical training courses on selected topics. These courses are usually free, but the students are responsible for travel expenses. Figure 2.2 and Figure 2.3 show examples of IBM's free training courses.

Figure 2.2   IBM free training 1

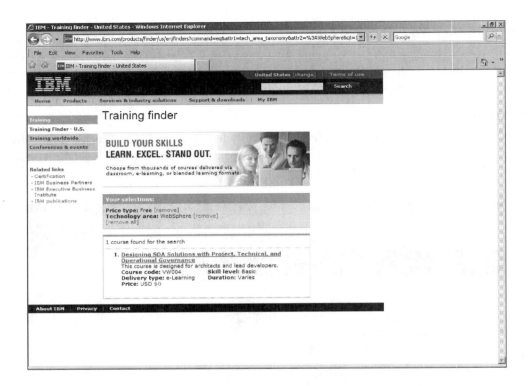

Figure 2.3   IBM free training 2

IBM Proof of Technology Programs

Proof of Technology programs are a good opportunity to learn new technologies. Many have hands-on labs and experienced instructors to explain the new technologies, lead discussions, and answer questions. The program is free and usually lasts two or three days. Proof of Technology programs expose new technologies to senior IT professionals, such as senior WebSphere engineers or WebSphere managers. You can participate in an IBM Proof of Technology program in your area by talking to the IBM Software Group representative in your company.

IBM Education Assistant

IBM Education Assistant is a free technical training resource (see Figure 2.4). Just Google "IBM Education Assistant" for more information. It is a large aggregation of high-quality multimedia classes with the following features:

- A comprehensive presentation collection of WebSphere Application Server and related technologies that is animated with audio; it provides in-depth exploration of WebSphere Application Server products.

- Instructions for accomplishing a particular technical task, along with background education about the technical details "under the hood."

- Tutorials with carefully developed labs and files assist and reinforce what you learn.

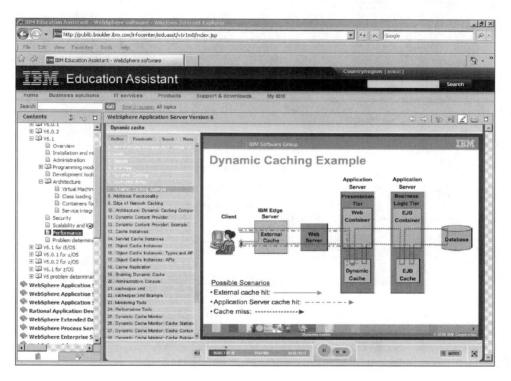

Figure 2.4 IBM Education Assistant

Use Your Resident IBM Team for Technical Expertise

Using IBM technical expertise within your company can be a good way to give your team free technical training. For example, to educate your team on Service Oriented Architecture (SOA), invite a senior IBM application architect to conduct a workshop for your team. An IBM mainframe system expert on the IBM team in your company can help you train your team on mainframe productivity tools such as ISO/ISPF.

Technical Exchange Webcasts

IBM WebSphere support uses technical exchange webcasts to share technical information with the user community (see Figure 2.5). IBM technical experts do not only share their technical expertise with you, but they also answer your questions. This is an excellent form of high quality, interactive, free technical education.

Figure 2.5   WebSphere support technical exchange webcasts

Many training resources, including WebSphere technical exchange webcasts and the WebSphere Education Assistant, can be found at an IBM Web site. You may just want to Google "WebSphere Support – Self-Assist Resources and Tools" (see Figure 2.6).

This Web page has a link to a helpful one-page document called the IBM Self-Assist Guide (see Figure 2.7). You may want to keep a copy of this document handy, because it can serve as a quick reference to self-assist resources and tools.

Figure 2.6   WebSphere support – Self-Assistant Resources and Tools

Make the Best Use of Your Staff Meetings

Staff meetings sometimes can be a real challenge. Many times, there are meaningful agenda items to discuss at staff meetings. However, from time to time, there is nothing important to justify an hour-long meeting for the entire team. Rather than cancel the staff meetings that are difficult to schedule, use that time for technical training. You can use the time for two different kinds of technical training:

- **Focused technical topic**. For example, you can ask a team member to prepare a series of presentations on the WebSphere Virtual Enterprise workload management features.
- **Application walkthrough**. Your team may have many large and complex WebSphere applications. It is not an easy job to provide WebSphere engineering support for such applications. To help your team to consistently deliver high quality support, ask the primary WebSphere engineer of a large application to make a presentation about the application. The primary WebSphere engineer for the application can use the time to walk the

team through some of the system differences and application peculiarities. This application walkthrough, when done consistently, can be a good form of technical training for your team.

- **Technical presentation.** You can use part of your staff meeting to invite technical experts to make presentations about subjects to which your team needs exposure. For example, you can invite a SOA expert to talk to your team about your company's SOA strategy and how she perceives how the WebSphere team can help.

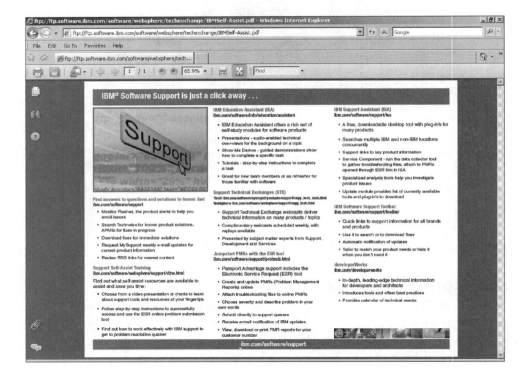

Figure 2.7   IBM Self-Assist Guide

Rotation of Roles and Responsibilities

Rotate the roles and responsibilities of your WebSphere engineers to provide technical training. Periodically rotating engineers from one role to another broadens the collective skill set of the team while growing the technical competence of the WebSphere engineers involved.

Rotation of Primary and Secondary WebSphere Engineers

This rotation of roles can be used as a means of challenging the secondary WebSphere engineer on the greater responsibilities for an application, especially in the area of project management. The secondary engineer has a chance to do more work in planning, coordination, and communication. Thus, the secondary WebSphere engineer becomes prepared to take full charge of a large and difficult project with the help of the primary WebSphere engineer. Then, when the secondary engineer is ready to take over, the primary WebSphere engineer can disengage and lead a new project.

Rotation of Production Support and Testing Support

The rotation of production environment support and testing environment support for a large WebSphere project can help both WebSphere engineers do a better job in both roles. The production support WebSphere engineer may develop ideas on where testing strategies need to be improved after working for a long time in the production environment that bears the direct impact of testing results. For example, if rigorous testing work has been done, the production environment tends to be stable. When there are issues in testing, the stability of the production environment and those WebSphere engineers supporting the production environment tends to suffer. The testing environment support engineer may know when and how to better monitor testing status. Based on a given set of testing results and status, the testing support engineer may have a better feel for what to expect in production.

The production support WebSphere engineer and the testing support WebSphere engineer need to work together closely to ensure the stability and availability of the production systems. Maintaining a good relationship between the two is not always easy. Switching roles help develop a renewed appreciation for the challenges and efforts of the other. This mutual understanding helps with work relationships and teamwork.

Rotation of WebSphere Engineers Within the Same WebSphere Team

As the saying goes, variety is the spice of life. Rotating WebSphere engineers within the same team gives the engineers something new to do, they get to know a different business division, and they have the opportunity to learn a new set of WebSphere applications. If you are able to do your project in your sleep, it may be time for you to do something different. New projects bring new technical challenges, and therefore new skills. This also helps the engineers become familiar with many projects with which the team is engaged. This helps the engineers perform their on-call duties when they have to support any of the team's projects.

Rotation and Team Stability

Although rotating roles is a helpful way of technical training, it does bring significant changes to your team. Stable WebSphere teams are indispensable to stable WebSphere systems. There is an intrinsic relationship between organization stability and system stability because of the relatively long learning curve needed to become proficient for large WebSphere Application Server systems. In addition, it takes time to build internal and external work relationships. These work relationships are also important to system stability.

Rotations, even within the same project, must be prudently planned. Before making any moves, you have to consider technical training, employee satisfaction, team morale, and business needs. You must be cautious in making rotations. Otherwise, your indiscretion will surely throw both your WebSphere teams and your WebSphere systems off.

Balanced Formal Technical Training

Instructor-led formal WebSphere technical training is an effective and desirable form of technical training. With budget constraints and limited possible hours to take training, you have to figure out the right content and the right amount of technical training for your WebSphere team. Therefore, it is important to form a balanced technical training strategy and policy.

The content of the technical training for a specific WebSphere engineer can be achieved by performing a training needs assessment (TNA).[3] This allows you to evaluate gaps in technical skills needed for the position and upcoming projects.

Training needs can also be conducted at a team level using a Team Training Needs Assessment Document. Although the results of a TNA can be different, there are four types of WebSphere technical training to consider.

Foundation

The foundation is the minimum formal technical training that a WebSphere engineer needs to take. A WebSphere Application Server Administration class for a specific platform, such as AIX or Linux®, must be the minimum required technical training for the entire WebSphere team. This training needs to be conducted for each major WebSphere Application Server upgrade (for example, from WebSphere Application Server 6.0 to WebSphere Application Server 7.0).

Core

The right amount of WebSphere technical training could be derived from the number of core WebSphere technologies that the engineer supports. For example, say that the engineers support the following core technologies:

- Rational® Application Developer
- WebSphere Application Server for Linux
- WebSphere Portal Server

---

3. Gregory E. Huszczo, *Tools for Team Excellence*, (Davies-Black Publishing, 1996).

Three formal instructor-led technical courses should then be required along with peer training, on-the-job training, and studying self-paced technical training materials in the format of Computer Based Training (CBT), Digital Visual Library (DVL), and online classes:

- IBM WebSphere Application Server Administration
- EJB Development Using Rational Application Developer
- IBM WebSphere Portal Administration

It is difficult for one WebSphere engineer to take on more than three core technologies. Providing competent engineering support is hard because there is too much to learn. More than 15 days of formal technical training a year may be too much in terms of budget, work scheduling, and resource consumption.

Concentration

Again, TNA must be used to figure out the right amount of formal technical training for a WebSphere engineer who works in a specialized area. Here are a few examples:

- WebSphere service engineers supporting large stress-testing environments may take the IBM WebSphere V7 Performance Testing and Monitoring Tools for Administrators class.
- WebSphere process engineers working on automation may take the IBM WebSphere Application Server V7 Scripting and Automation (Remote Class) class.
- WebSphere service engineers supporting critical production environments may take the IBM WebSphere Application Server V7 Problem Determination class.
- WebSphere service engineers providing JEE consulting services may take the Web Services Development for WebSphere Application Server V7 with IBM RAD V7 class.

Special Training Needs for Special Projects

Sometimes, you may have important but unusual projects that involve a large technical training undertaking. For these projects, extra training planning and special funding must be secured before your team can be successfully engaged in training activities.

For example, you have a large project moving a critical application suite from a distributed platform to the mainframe platform. Most of your engineers have no mainframe exposure and must be systematically trained to do a WebSphere engineering job on the mainframe. There are as many as 11 mainframe foundational courses and mainframe classes to take.

- IBM z900 and z990 Architecture
- Introduction to z/OS Environment
- Fundamental System Skills in z/OS

- Introduction to Parallel SysPlex
- Introduction to SysPlex Distributor
- z/OS System Services Structure
- Introduction to z/OS WLM
- Introduction to z/OS Security/RACF
- z/OS Facilities and Tools
- WebSphere Application Server Administration for z/OS
- Security Workshop: WebSphere Application Server for z/OS

For such massive training projects, you have to carefully exclude them from your usual training plans that are inadequate to manage technical training for special projects. In other words, special training shouldn't be included in normal technical training, as it is only appropriate for the special project, and special training is funded differently. Vigorously seek special funding from your IT division or from the sponsor of the project upfront before you make a commitment to the special project. Special training is frequently needed for a project that adopts a nonstandard technical architecture. While making sure that the WebSphere team needs special funding for special training, make it clear that nonstandard technical environments are more costly to design, build, and operate. Therefore, it represents higher costs for your company.

Technical Training as a Morale Booster and Relationship Builder

Technical training provides more benefits for your team outside of the opportunities to learn new skills. It is a powerful motivator and potent relationship builder between the team and its management. An inexperienced manager uses job security threats as the motivator and a good manager builds relationships with the team through technical training.

Sometimes people are ignorant of the most obvious and basic facts. For example, you do not always remember that technical people depend on their technical skills to make a living. Structured training efforts have an immense impact on WebSphere team morale because they help with growing technical skills.

Words are powerful, but deeds speak louder. Your efforts to get your team technical training helps build a strong relationship between you and the team. You are more likely to be identified as a helpful leader, not a whip-cracking boss with an accelerated ambition to advance to the corner office.

Your work to bring about technical training for the team may not always be successful. Your skills and techniques in managing training may not be perfect and may not always work. That is fine and the team understands, as long as you really try.

There are many techniques for managing technical training. However, the key for performance is not just techniques. If you want to get your team technical training, find a way. By the same token, nothing can help you if you do not genuinely care for the professional growth and technical maturity of your team. Doing a good job at training demands that your heart be in the right place. People are intelligent, and with time, they understand who you are and if you want to help.

Summary

Hiring directly affects the success of a large company's WebSphere engineering strategy. A desirable candidate for a WebSphere engineering position needs to have sound WebSphere technology knowledge and skills. In addition, JEE development experience, extensive systems skills, and advanced project management capabilities are important hiring considerations. Communication skills and teamwork are critical attributes for a candidate.

WebSphere engineering support is a fast-growing area that brings an abundance of promising career opportunities for talented WebSphere engineers. It is also a tough market to hire in, which forces WebSphere managers to be proactive and creative in hiring and retaining engineers.

This chapter introduced a guided flexible training program to allow different engineers to learn in different ways. It is possible to get training even when you do not have the proper funding. Training is not only a means of learning new technical skills; it is also a powerful way to motivate and build relationships within your team. Rotating roles is an important way to train, but be mindful not to destabilize your team and your WebSphere systems.

Chapter 1 examined WebSphere engineering organization choices. This chapter investigated ways to build a strong WebSphere engineering support team. Chapter 3, "WebSphere Operations Framework," describes WebSphere engineering and the WebSphere Operations Framework. It lays the foundation for the discussion about WebSphere engineering operations and life cycles explained in the rest of this book.

WebSphere Operations Framework

This important chapter provides critical information about a systematic approach to WebSphere Application Server engineering work: the WebSphere Operations Framework. This chapter carefully defines the WebSphere Operations Framework, which is a major component of WebSphere engineering.

Each of the concrete WebSphere engineering operations introduced in later chapters is consistent to the WebSphere Operations Framework. The WebSphere Operations Framework provides a general structure and reference. Each WebSphere engineering operation provides the actual implementation of the framework. Carefully reading this chapter will help you better use the information provided in many of the later chapters, where the WebSphere Operations Framework is systematically implemented to describe WebSphere engineering operations.

The WebSphere Operations Framework's primary intention is to bring WebSphere Application Server work into a discipline of engineering with consistent processes and tight standards. The goal of this approach is to help WebSphere products and service delivery become more predictable and consistent. It intends to introduce major improvements to the technical management of WebSphere technology, and it attempts to transform the work relationships between the WebSphere team and other technical teams.

This chapter provides an engineering reference model and a complete framework. This model's application and the use of the framework helps make life easier for WebSphere managers, engineers, and consultants. Along with the application of the model and framework, this chapter offers experience-based discussions for each WebSphere engineering life cycle and its associated operations. This chapter is neither an academic discussion of IT management theory nor an extension of any documented IT engineering methodology. Instead, it is an original, experience-based, and practical guide for WebSphere managers, senior engineers, and consultants.

This chapter explores the following topics:

- Introduction to WebSphere engineering
- Objectives and terminology of the WebSphere Operations Framework
- The WebSphere Operations Framework's technological components and technical environments
- The WebSphere Operations Framework's technical teams
- The WebSphere Operations Framework's support life cycles
- The WebSphere Operations Framework's operations attributes

This book systematically applies both the WebSphere engineering life cycle concept and the WebSphere Operations Framework. It consistently uses the WebSphere Operations Framework to completely describe each operation specification. In a given chapter, if an operation has been explained in a previous chapter, this operation is mentioned only in the chapter with a reference to the previous chapter. An operation's complete description is not repeated.

This book briefly explains the important artifacts and processes used in WebSphere operations. However, it does not give detailed processes or artifact examples for any given operations, as that is beyond the time and space limitation of this book. In addition, detailed engineering processes and supporting artifacts derived from the WebSphere Operations Framework should find different implementations and manifestations for different companies. This is necessary to manage different infrastructures. You can apply the framework to fit your particular engineering practices and derive tailored and useful engineering process deliverables for your business environment.

WebSphere Engineering

Detailed WebSphere engineering tasks are categorized. This categorization is significant to forming the core concept of WebSphere engineering, because it establishes the technical tasks and necessary prerequisites of WebSphere engineering.

The enumeration of the WebSphere engineering tasks is intended to facilitate the discussion of building a WebSphere organization. The WebSphere engineering tasks identified also help form strategies for WebSphere technical training. In addition, these WebSphere engineering tasks help form the foundation for a practical and useful engagement system and process. Both the WebSphere organization model and WebSphere technical training are important areas of WebSphere engineering.

Definition of WebSphere Engineering

First, it's time to further define WebSphere engineering. In this book, the terms *WebSphere Application Server engineering* and *WebSphere engineering* are interchangeable. These terms refer to the IT engineering work to design, build, and operate WebSphere Application Server infrastructure. (*WebSphere engineering* is sometimes used for the ease of reading.)

WebSphere engineering is a disciplined IT methodology, a systematic quality control, and test metric for engineering practices and technical processes pertaining to WebSphere Application Server deployment. WebSphere engineering focuses on rigorous system standards and consistent engineering processes to achieve stable, resilient, and capable WebSphere Application Server centered IT infrastructure for enterprise applications of Service Oriented Architecture (SOA).

Here are the attributes of WebSphere engineering:

- It provides a collection of referential organization models, choices, and best practices in building an optimal WebSphere engineering support organization through educated organization design or redesign, structured and balanced skills assessment in hiring, and focused and continuous technical training.
- It is a carefully documented set of WebSphere engineering operation classifications and engineering task enumerations that forms a necessary foundation for the development of engagement tools and engineering framework.
- It intends to be an advanced engineering approach to ensure the engagement, design, build, operations, and support of high performance yet stable enterprise WebSphere Application Server systems.
- It introduces a complete WebSphere Operations Framework that covers each phase of the engineering activities to ensure the completeness and quality of WebSphere products and service delivery.

WebSphere engineering emphasizes the following set of critical technical management objectives:

- Achieving high WebSphere system stability through standardization, process excellence, operation quality assurance, and system anomaly prevention
- Optimizing strategies in dealing with production problems, high-impact emergencies, and critical situations
- Promoting a team approach to middleware infrastructure engineering by building, maintaining, and improving critical work relationships through skillful collaboration and experienced communication
- Implementing quantitative measurement of technical services and objective evaluation of WebSphere system operations performance

As previously mentioned, this chapter focuses on the WebSphere Operations Framework.

Lessons Learned from Managing a WebSphere Team

The WebSphere Operations Framework does not come from IT management methodology literature, and it does not refer to an established IT engineering theory. Rather, its origin is in the industry practice and real-world engineering experience in the WebSphere Application Server. It is a methodical and rigorous summary of a journey of learning.

In the past ten years, I have witnessed the rapid maturing of both WebSphere technology and its practitioners. My first large and complex WebSphere project involved many production emergencies—or production fires, so to speak. Production fires are stressful; they require a team to work day and night as a fire squad. Emergencies in critical pre-production environments are just as bad; showstoppers in a critical stress-testing environment often demand immediate attention and timely solutions. In the business of IT, we all have to fight fires. However, constant firefighting allows little time for technical training, system management improvement, and engineering process development.

What I learned from the WebSphere engagement was that certain tasks need to be completed to have a successful WebSphere project:

- Apply the right model to organize an effective WebSphere team.
- Develop a disciplined hiring practice and aggregate the best WebSphere professionals.
- Remain focused on technical training.
- Perform regular documentation (for example, a system tracking document that provides the system information for your WebSphere infrastructure).
- Develop and improve key WebSphere engineering processes.
- Constantly grow critical work relationships between technical teams, such as between the WebSphere team and the enterprise architecture team. Chapter 11, "Critical Work Relationships," discusses work relationships.

Achieving WebSphere Stability and Availability

Much time has passed since the early days of my WebSphere experiences. WebSphere Application Server 7 is definitely different from WebSphere Application Server 3.5 or 4. The WebSphere technologies are mature, and WebSphere teams worldwide are making progress. It seems that the WebSphere infrastructure should be resilient and reliable. With all the powerful WebSphere technologies available (for instance, horizontal and vertical clustering and the dynamic operation features of WebSphere Virtual Enterprise), 100 percent stability and availability should be common. Unfortunately, it is still a tough challenge to reach high stability and availably for both large and small WebSphere systems. In addition, WebSphere teams still work in a complex and difficult environment. So, although much has improved, WebSphere teams must still continue to learn.

WebSphere technology maturity alone does not guarantee that you achieve a stable WebSphere infrastructure. The individual technical excellence of WebSphere engineers also does not ensure high availability. The stability and availability of your WebSphere Application Server system depends on many critical factors (such as the engineering rigor of your team and your team's work relationships with key business partners). For example, if you suffer from relationship issues with your testing organization, you may find it difficult to collaborate with your testing teams to form the right testing strategy that uncovers and addresses WebSphere system and application defects. As a result, your system availability and stability suffer.

Your WebSphere team must do a good job during all the critical phases of the WebSphere engineering life cycle: the design, build, operation, and support phases. What's more, the WebSphere team has to deliver quality products and service while working in a complex and dynamic environment.

In a modern IT organization, the success of any job is achieved through collective effort. Without good work relationships with critical business partners, such as the testing organization, the application production team, and enterprise architects, you cannot achieve high WebSphere system stability.

The WebSphere team does not have an easy responsibility. The WebSphere Application Server is usually a central integration point for many critical components and systems, such as load balancers, databases, messaging systems, security software, and other enterprise applications. The mission-critical Java Enterprise Edition (JEE) applications execute in WebSphere containers. All of these components make WebSphere the hub of large IT projects. The WebSphere systems interface with many other systems, so the WebSphere team must work closely with many peer technical teams.

Consequently, the WebSphere team must deal with a high degree of complexity. Typically, the WebSphere team works with a powerful, complex, and dynamic WebSphere technology, in a large, complex, and constantly changing IT organization for large, complex, and challenging IT projects.

It is definitely a challenging job to work in these complex areas while trying to flawlessly design, build, operate, and support a capable and stable WebSphere Application Server-centered IT infrastructure.

Lack of a Systematic WebSphere Technical Management Framework

As an IT practitioner, you always have to pay attention to technology. You must be sensitive to new technological directions and work hard to learn new technical details. However, in WebSphere's case, the main obstacle of achieving a higher level of engineering excellence and system stability and availability is not a technical issue. The main hurdle for the IT industry to move forward is neither the maturity of the WebSphere technology nor the skill level of individual WebSphere technical professionals. Rather, what slows the advancement of WebSphere engineering maturity is the inadequate technical management methodology and framework for applying the WebSphere technology in the IT infrastructure.

For all WebSphere managers, senior engineers, and consultants in the industry, a systematic body of knowledge in WebSphere engineering helps push the WebSphere application to the next level of sophistication and achievement. You need to build effective and efficient WebSphere organizations. You must hire the best and keep them trained. You need to pay more attention to the engineering process. You need to understand that the WebSphere Application Server technical management is difficult and frequently counter-intuitive. You want to be aware that the Web-Sphere Application Server technical management is a learned skill and acquired capability that demands training, practice, and shared industry-strength experience. You need a systematic methodology to guide WebSphere engineering activities. You need a consistent framework to deliver quality WebSphere products and services. You need a comprehensive way to measure the completeness and quality of your deliverables. WebSphere engineering is exactly such a methodical body of knowledge and skills and a rigorous effort to systematically address the technical management of WebSphere Application Server infrastructure work.

The following sections explain the WebSphere Operations Framework, which is a subset of WebSphere engineering.

Objectives and Terminology of the WebSphere Operations Framework

The primary objectives of the WebSphere Operations Framework are quality WebSphere products and service delivery and high WebSphere system stability and availability.

From a bird's eye view, the WebSphere Operations Framework is primarily a mapping between the WebSphere technology components and technical environments, technical teams, and dynamic WebSphere engineering life cycles. Examples of the WebSphere technology components include a WebSphere server cluster or Web servers fronting the WebSphere Application Servers. An example of a WebSphere technical environment would be a group of WebSphere systems built for stress testing. An example of a WebSphere technical team is an operating system support team that works with the WebSphere team. A dynamic WebSphere engineering life cycle example is a WebSphere topology design and then another WebSphere production server build.

The mapping results are a complete set of clearly defined tasks or operations. These operations conform to a consistent engineering framework that guides WebSphere engineering work and measures the quality and completeness of the deliverables.

In other words, this engineering framework establishes guidelines that ensure a consistent, efficient, repeatable, and complete WebSphere engineering support practice. Any distinct aspects of a particular application or environment must be captured and documented as a unique set of operations. The entire WebSphere engineering support process needs to reference this common framework. It is the actual implementation of a major component of WebSphere engineering.

More specifically, the WebSphere Operations Framework is a mapping among these three elements:

- Technology components and technical environments
- Technical teams that use and support WebSphere environments
- WebSphere engineering life cycle phases

A detailed explanation for each WebSphere Operations Framework element is provided later in this chapter. Table 3.1 outlines some examples of each component.

Table 3.1 Elements of WebSphere Operations Framework

Technology Components and Technical Environments	Technical Teams	WebSphere Engineering Life Cycle Phases
Messaging system	WebSphere MQ engineering support team	Service engagement
Database connectivity software	Enterprise architecture team	WebSphere topology design
WebSphere Application Server clusters	Testing teams	WebSphere server build
WebSphere systems built for production operations	Application production support team	Production code migration

WebSphere Operations Framework Objectives

WebSphere Operations Framework objectives are challenging and diverse. They include the following:

- Ensure quality technical consultation to engagement representatives who are responsible for interfacing with the customer and the technical teams in the engagement phase of the project, and with business partners during the requirements gathering, business requirements definition, and resource allocation phase of a project.

- Provide quality technical consultation to technical and nontechnical teams during the high level and low level design phases of a project.

- Implement high performing, secure, reliable WebSphere environments based on business requirements, application architecture, and overall infrastructure design.

- Ensure the integrity of a WebSphere environment that operates according to its design intent.

- Make sure that the day-to-day WebSphere environment performance adheres to the service level agreement (SLA) with your business partners or customers.

- Ensure that the WebSphere products operate at the supported and optimal level as defined, recommended, or required by IBM.

- Ensure that the WebSphere Application Servers are configured and maintained at current build levels recommended by IBM.

- Ensure that the application code development and deployment confirm to enterprise JEE and WebSphere Application Server standards and best practices.

- Maintain proficiency in operating and deploying technologies that integrate and connect with the WebSphere Application Server, including authentication software, messaging software, operating system software, deep dive diagnostics software, and monitoring software.

WebSphere Operations Framework Terminology

You need to appropriately understand this book's terminology to describe the WebSphere Operations Framework. You need to know the following terms:

- **Operation**. Service provided by the WebSphere team. Each service can be represented by a complete unit of work. Typical services include WebSphere server build, system and application stress testing, high level or low level design consulting, JEE application troubleshooting, or system problem resolution.

- **Operation specification**. The interface or contract between the system professional executing the operation and the target for the actual operation. Specifically, this covers what needs to be done, how it must be done, success criteria, and notification requirements.

- **Activities**. Actions taken to complete an operation. Can be executed sequentially or in parallel.

- **Activity diagram**. Describes a list of activities that accomplish an operation. These diagrams can be powerful visualizations that describe the order and path the activities need to take. This is optional because not all activities need an activity diagram to describe.

- **WebSphere Engineering Support Life Cycle**. Classification of different phases of WebSphere Application Server engineering support. A life cycle is end-to-end engineering support that starts with a technical service engagement, moves to server build, and then application production migration. It ends with the WebSphere environment decommission. Each life cycle phase requires one or more distinct operation. An operation can be executed exactly once or repeated in multiple life cycle phases.

WebSphere Operations Framework Components and Environments

The WebSphere Operations Framework is a complete solution that consists of the following technological components and technical environments:

- Hardware platform, including operating systems and network components

- Extensive set of load balancers

- Major infrastructure components, such as proxy servers, firewalls, Domain Name Servers (DNS), and directory services that integrate with the WebSphere Application Servers

- Web servers
- WebSphere Application Server software
- JEE applications executing within WebSphere
- Third-party software integrated into the WebSphere Application Server
- Enterprise information systems, external systems, and business components that are interconnected through WebSphere
- Enterprise database systems

The WebSphere Application Server auxiliary components include the following:

- Software tools that perform system monitoring, troubleshooting, runtime diagnostics, customer-experience monitoring, data gathering, and operation automation.
- Engineering support processes that specify particular aspects of support and operations. This includes various documents and artifacts associated with these technical processes.
- An interconnected ticket dispatch system that includes searchable documentation that serves as a central problem-management repository.
- A system record that documents system that serves as the major knowledge-management system for the WebSphere organization.

The WebSphere Operations Framework technical environments characteristically include the following WebSphere environments. Different companies may have different technical environments and different names:

- **Development environment**. It is possible but not necessary to have multiple development environments for one large WebSphere project in order to simultaneously work on multiple releases of the application code.
- **Unit testing environment**. Occasionally referred to as component testing environment or functional testing environment. It is possible but not necessary to have multiple unit testing environments for one large WebSphere project in order to simultaneously test multiple releases of the application code.
- **System testing environment**. Sometimes called the integration testing environment. It is possible but not necessary to have multiple system testing environments for one large WebSphere project in order to simultaneously test multiple releases of the application code.
- **Stress-testing environment**. Sometimes used for performance-testing purposes. This environment frequently has a heavy system load. Stress testing and performance testing are time consuming and difficult. It is frequently necessary to have multiple WebSphere stress-testing environments in order to simultaneously test multiple releases of the application code.

- **Environment for break and fix**. For highly critical applications, this dedicated Web-Sphere system keeps an application code base and the relevant WebSphere configuration identical to production environment. Application code fixes and configuration changes are tested in this environment before being introduced to the production environment.

- **Training environment**. Could be considered a production environment if your company uses this environment to train external users on new application releases.

- **Pre-production environment**. Also called the quality assurance environment. This environment is the final staging environment before the migration of an application release to the production environment.

- **Production environment**. Usually a heavily clustered environment with both local server redundancy within one data center and geographical server redundancy between data centers.

Depending on the WebSphere organization model that you adopt, you may have more than one WebSphere team. Assume that a dedicated product-based support organization model is in place. Therefore, there is one WebSphere team for a line of business (LOB). The WebSphere team conducts technical service engagement, system design, system build, day-to-day operations, and project support.

The WebSphere team is a WebSphere service engineering support team that participates in WebSphere planning, engineering, and process work, collaborating with WebSphere planning engineers and WebSphere process engineers.

There are numerous business partners, collaborating technical teams, and peer infrastructure engineering support teams.

There are also application and system support teams for integrated business components or interconnected information systems. For example, your WebSphere system may be integrated to a large customer-care system. Then, from time to time, you need to work with the application support team of the customer-care system.

SOA is a major direction of information technology. WebSphere technologies provide comprehensive infrastructure support to SOA. Chapter 13, "WebSphere Engineering Going Forward," discusses SOA and WebSphere support for SOA.

Some JEE applications executing in WebSphere Application Server are not designed and developed by your company's application architects and application developers. Instead, they are purchased software packages. The WebSphere team has many opportunities to work with the vendor representatives on issues such as the WebSphere Application Server standards and JEE best practices.

The following is a list of technical teams: (Some companies may have more teams than what are listed here.)

- WebSphere team
- Application production support team
- Application development team
- Business components or information system support teams
- IBM WebSphere and Java technical support organizations
- Sun Microsystems Java technical support organizations
- Vendor representatives for software packages
- Monitoring, command and control, and systems management teams
- Testing teams, especially the performance-testing or stress-testing teams
- Enterprise architects and application architects
- Infrastructure architects and infrastructure design engineers
- Capacity planning and runtime performance analysis teams
- Infrastructure engineering support teams, such as database, messaging, security, operating systems, load balancing, Demilitarized Zone (DMZ), and networking
- Technical service engagement team
- Service delivery managers and LOB technology managers
- Change management team
- Project managers

Figure 3.1 outlines the technological components, the technical environments, the technical teams, and their relationships and interactions.

Figure 3.1 describes how a WebSphere team works. The WebSphere team uses its knowledge management system, such as an application support manual. It collaborates with other technical teams, such as external teams. It takes advantage of tools such as deep dive diagnostics, such as Introscope. All these activities serve to perform a specific engineering operation to accomplish the design, build, operation, and support of a stable and capable WebSphere Application Server system.

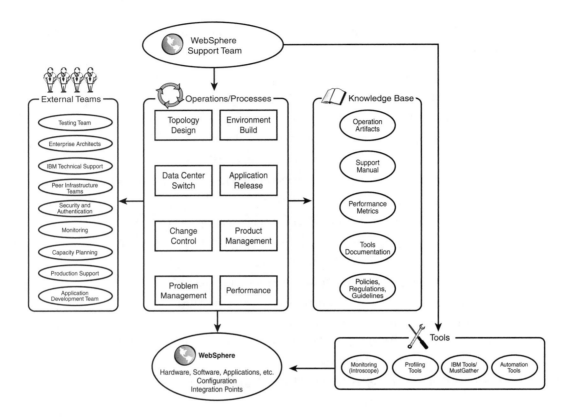

Figure 3.1   WebSphere environment interaction

WebSphere Engineering Support Life Cycles

A WebSphere operating environment is dynamic. It has distinct tasks for each phase in the Web-Sphere Engineering Support Life Cycle. These tasks are categorized as operations. This section outlines the life cycle phases and their descriptions. Each life cycle phase is covered throughout the remaining chapters, as are other important areas, such as production emergency management and critical work relationship management.

WebSphere Initial Sizing and Consulting Engagement

The WebSphere Initial Sizing and Consulting Engagement phase is the beginning of the Web-Sphere Engineering Support Life Cycle for a WebSphere project. The WebSphere team provides WebSphere technical consulting services to enterprise architects. The WebSphere team performs initial sizing of the initiative in resources consumption. The WebSphere team helps the solution provider, either internal or external, with technical information needed about the enterprise Web-Sphere Application Server system standards and engineering practices of your company. During the engagement life cycle, you want to advocate the adoption of a good Proof of Concept (POC) pilot project, especially for large and complex solutions.

WebSphere Server Build

The WebSphere Application Server build includes three distinct subphases: WebSphere server build planning, topology design, and server build.

The WebSphere Application Server build planning also includes Web server work. Web server build planning is a critical subphase of the server build. This cycle includes important engagement, design, and resource estimate tasks. The assigned Subject Matter Expert (SME) must thoroughly understand the resource estimates and tools needed to perform the all-important resource estimate work. Usually, a senior WebSphere engineer and technical lead with good project management skills is suitable for resource estimate work. A WebSphere engineer with only technical skills may not do a good job at resource estimate work. The resource estimate work may include WebSphere environment sizing revisions or updates based on newly available information. Other critical tasks include collecting and processing infrastructure requirements to make numerous decisions, such as the number of development and testing environment pipelines. The requirements of the JEE application are also important. The WebSphere team drafts, discusses, and finalizes a SLA with the client. The support level defined in the SLA usually directly affects the resource consumptions of the WebSphere team; therefore, SLA work is also important during this subphase.

The second subphase is the WebSphere topology design. The WebSphere team does the WebSphere topology design in collaboration with the infrastructure design team. A senior Web-Sphere engineer and topology expert work with the lead infrastructure design consultant to develop a detailed WebSphere topology, which usually includes the Web server topology. The WebSphere topology is based on the application architecture and business requirements. The WebSphere topology design also inputs the technical details of the target WebSphere system and JEE application integration and deployment. WebSphere and Web server topology design decides the configuration details of the WebSphere system, including the Web servers.

The actual Web server and WebSphere Application Server build includes a server build, server configuration, and build validation. This is the most visible and tangible part of building the WebSphere Application Server. Senior management, the client, and the technical community may mistakenly conclude that this is all that must be done for a WebSphere server build job. They may not see the huge amount of intangible work that must be done before you can perform the physical act of building the WebSphere Application Servers. For example, they may overlook that the WebSphere team works on engagement, planning, design, server build coordination, configuration preparation, and other items before the WebSphere server is built. A full understanding of what the WebSphere team has to do to build a server helps you allocate adequate financial and human resources to get the build done correctly.

Functional and Integration Testing

WebSphere Functional and Integration Testing is crucial for a stable, available, and high-performance production environment.

The WebSphere Application Server environments for this engineering life cycle typically include development, functional testing, system testing, and occasionally quality assurance. Sometimes, quality assurance is classified as part of the production environment, along with the WebSphere systems for user training, especially when external customers use these systems. You can have many functional and integration environment pipelines, depending on the business drivers. These environments must conform to the same WebSphere Application Server build standard and configuration, even though they are different in purpose, capacity, and overall infrastructure design. Consistent environments ensure functionalities and reduce problem-resolution efforts at different levels.

The first job is to keep the WebSphere systems up and running so that the application development team and testing teams can do their jobs. This is also a WebSphere environment where you conduct WebSphere consulting, JEE best practices consulting, and design integration resolutions to other systems and third-party software. You must ensure upfront that the application design and coding practices conform to WebSphere Application Server standards and your company's JEE best practices.

Stress Testing

Before any application code can be migrated to the production WebSphere environment and go live for production operation, there must be sufficient load testing or stress testing in a stress-testing environment. The results produced from these rigorous tests must be validated and signed off by various responsible teams.

The stress-testing environment must be, to a reasonable degree and as much as possible, identical to or representative of the real production environment in configuration, capacity, and upstream and downstream component configuration. The same must be true for backend system integration. WebSphere topology, application deployments, and user loads (total concurrent users) for both production systems and the stress-testing environments must be identical or as similar as possible for optimal results, if not more stringent in testing environments. Considering budget constraints and business requirements, the stress-testing environment may be proportional to production, and performance data must be extrapolated to represent real performance data.

The stress-testing environment is where you uncover application and system issues, resolve them, and stop them from migrating to your production systems. This is usually your last defense for instability issues, especially defects in application code and critical system configuration settings errors. This is the part of the life cycle where you stop these error conditions before they affect your production systems.

Application Migration and Deployment

After successful function, integration, stress and performance testing through the entire environment pipeline, it is time to reconfigure or start building the production environment. Then, you are ready to deploy the application code into the WebSphere JEE containers. The WebSphere system changes are made based on the new overall infrastructure design and refreshed WebSphere topology and configuration design. The WebSphere topology and configuration are often updated and revised based on testing results, especially stress-testing results. This complex process involves multiple technical teams. (Chapter 8, "Production Environment Support," details these teams and the migration process.) Your code migration strategy and division of labor decide the coordination among technical teams. For example, if you do not have a dedicated code migration function, then your WebSphere team must work with the application support team to perform the production code migration and deployment.

Production Support

After a successful production WebSphere environment update, build, and application code deployment, you need to implement daily support operations to ensure the integrity and performance of the production WebSphere environment. Many activities take place in this stage; for example, you need to implement scheduled application releases, application maintenance, and troubleshooting activities, WebSphere system patches and fixes application, performance monitoring, system assurance, and other routine tasks.

WebSphere Upgrade

WebSphere Application Server upgrade management includes planning and process engineering and service delivery. The major tasks are forming conversion and migration strategies and plans, devising standards and baselines, and developing engineering processes and automation facilities. WebSphere application best practices must be introduced, and WebSphere topology gold standards must also be introduced as a best practice.

Figure 3.2 outlines the relationships between the engineering support life cycles, the operations, and the operation specifications.

For each project, you can map each WebSphere engineering support life cycle with many operations. This mapping translates into a consistent set of operation specifications that ensures the quality and completeness of the engineering operation.

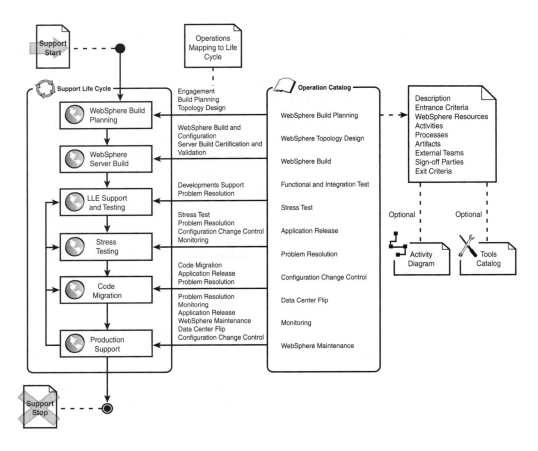

Figure 3.2   WebSphere Engineering Support Life Cycle

WebSphere Operations Framework: Operations Attributes

This section defines the attributes of operations involved in WebSphere Application Server engineering support. The operations are basic units of work that can be repeated and reused in the phases of the WebSphere Application Server engineering support life cycles. The WebSphere Application Server operations are at the core of WebSphere engineering because these operations provide a basic reference and framework to ensure that the products and services can be delivered in a consistent and predictable manner. Systematic auditing of the WebSphere Operations Framework application can be an interesting quality assurance mechanism.

Each operation has the following attributes as a structured description of the operation:

- **Description**. Operation description
- **Entrance Criteria**. Set of prerequisites that need to be met
- **WebSphere Resource**. WebSphere professionals
- **Activities**. List of activities
- **Processes**. Processes to be used
- **Artifacts**. Primarily documents generated, referenced, or used
- **Tools**. Tools that the operation uses
- **External Teams**. External teams with which to interact
- **Sign-Off Parties**. Teams that sign off on the operation
- **Exit Criteria**. Criteria to be met to complete the operation

Summary

This chapter provides a full description of the essential concept of WebSphere engineering.

It has explained the origin and objectives of WebSphere engineering. It has given the definitions of WebSphere engineering and the WebSphere Operations Framework, a subset of WebSphere engineering.

It has presented the WebSphere Operations Framework, its structures and terminologies, such as operations and environments, as well as a complete set of WebSphere engineering support life cycles.

This chapter has also explained how the WebSphere Operations Framework will be used in the rest of the book.

In Chapter 4, "Engagement Challenges," you will learn how to manage WebSphere project engagement challenges and how to use the WebSphere Operations Framework to define and describe a new engagement process.

Engagement Challenges

Money is the ultimate leverage for most IT projects. Without adequate financial resources, your WebSphere team won't be successful in providing quality engineering support for your projects. Without adequately dealing with engagement issues upfront and securing proper financial resources for a project, the subsequent WebSphere work will not have a strong foundation. Therefore, the engagement work is critically important to the WebSphere team.

To the WebSphere team, a good engagement process covers two critical areas: human resource estimates and high-level infrastructure design. Specifically, one of the engagement objectives for the WebSphere team is to ensure that it has adequate financial resources to work on the assigned WebSphere projects. The other objective is to collaborate with infrastructure design engineers and other technical teams, such as the application architecture team, to do high level design (HLD) of the WebSphere-centered IT infrastructure for the project. The design work affects the resource estimation because it decides the size and complexity of the WebSphere infrastructure; thus, the differences in resource needs.

The infrastructure design work during engagement—regardless of whether it is called high level design, low level design (LLD), or detailed design—is relatively high level and rough grained design compared to the detailed WebSphere topology and configuration design that is to be delivered based on the high level overall infrastructure specifications.[1, 2]

As an important part of the engagement process, you estimate the WebSphere hosting charges for the project. Fortunately, although the estimate and allocation of hosting charges is

1. Jalote, Pankaj. *An Integrated Approach to Software Engineering*, Third Edition. Springer, 2005, Chapter 1, "Introduction."
2. Leon, Alexis. *Software Configuration Management Handbook*, Second Edition. Artech House, 2005, Chapter 2, "The Software Development Process."

important, it is often relatively straightforward when human resources are not part of the equation. Therefore, hosting charges without considering human resources is not a difficult issue, and it is not discussed here. Instead, this chapter focuses on the complex challenges, such as the financial estimation of WebSphere services. The WebSphere team plays a supporting role in testing, so the WebSphere services that support testing are also considered.

This chapter focuses on the root causes for engagement challenges, especially systemic ones. You must understand the IT environmental issues with which you work. Understanding these systemic issues helps you identify your strengths, options, and limitations under your environmental constraints.

To be knowledgeable about these systemic issues, you need to know how to best perform your WebSphere engineering work, but you also need to gain knowledge as to why some engineering practices are best within a defined IT financial context. Knowledge is power. An enterprise view of systemic strengths and constraints allows you to examine your daily engineering challenges with a new insight and helps you choose what to focus on now (and what to tackle later). You do not want to engage in a futile fight on impossible missions.

This chapter proposes recommendations for a better engagement experience. It introduces a Service Request, Assignment, and Tracking System and details a practical engagement process.

Finally, this chapter explains how to manage engagement for a large but fast-changing WebSphere project with a significant portion of its infrastructure and applications unknown upfront when you design and build the WebSphere infrastructure. This is a challenging situation in which your large WebSphere projects may be sidelined into the trap of repeated delays and budget overruns.

Systemic Issues of IT Services and Engagement Difficulties

Engagement process challenges exist in many areas, as Figure 4.1 shows. This section examines this multifaceted problem in each area and discusses possible solutions. If such solutions are not possible, at least through these discussions, you will gain a better insight into some of the systemic issues confronting IT today. From here, you can make informed decisions for your WebSphere infrastructure engineering work.

Many of the difficulties in engagement work are rooted in the lack of practical means to quantitatively measure IT services. This section explains why quantitatively measuring IT services is difficult and why such measurements are critical for your engagement process to work well. This section also discusses what you can do now to improve your team's engagement experiences.

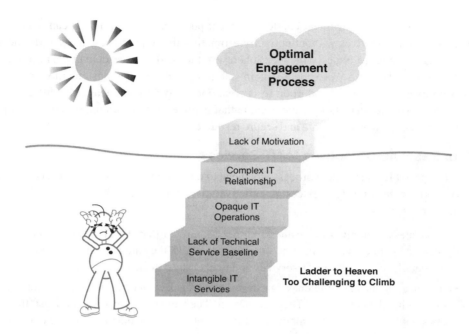

Figure 4.1   Ladder to the optimal engagement process—a challenging climb

Intangible Nature of IT Services

During the engagement phase, the most difficult job is securing adequate financial resources, especially for hiring human resources to do the job. The WebSphere manager or senior consultant needs to determine and allocate resources for a given WebSphere project. To achieve this objective, it is important to derive fact-based, quantitatively accurate information about the cost of WebSphere services. However, services—especially IT services—are a challenge to measure quantitatively.

For large companies, this human resource estimate and allocation challenge tends to be more pronounced because of the organization's complexity, the operation size, and the wide range of technologies involved. It is natural that people tend to better understand tangible and concrete objects. The intangible nature of IT services sometimes leads even experienced IT professionals to underestimate, or completely overlook, the service portion of an IT initiative, and instead focus on servers built, software installed, and systems delivered. Of course, the tangible result of a physical server build as a concrete deliverable is easier to comprehend and identify. However, not everyone fully appreciates the services delivered, such as attending a large number of design sessions, coordinating the technical teams, and managing change control.

Because of these engagement challenges, WebSphere engineering teams can make commitments for large initiatives without correctly estimating the required resources to do the job. This may lead to quality issues with WebSphere product and service delivery. These quality issues usually translate into WebSphere system stability problems that consume more resources for the WebSphere team already short on resources. For the WebSphere team, the difficulty getting adequate resources can start a vicious cycle that is not easily broken unless you develop an effective way to objectively estimate and secure resources.

Lack of Baseline Objectives for IT Services

To have a respectable engagement process, you need to quantitatively measure the costs of IT services. However, measuring IT services quantitatively is challenging, if it's even possible. Here are some examples:

- If business executives or business partners complain that the IT infrastructure service charges include no information of the charge details, they are correct. They do not know the details of the costs of IT services and neither does the team.

- If management has efficiency questions, they suspect that the team does not exactly know what they are doing. They are correct. The team does not know. At least, the team does not know exactly the amount of time spent on a particular WebSphere engineering task for a project performed by the managed team.

- Whenever a new initiative is assigned to a team, nobody knows how many human resources are needed because of the lack of practical metrics to estimate human resource needs. Worse, there may not be an established financial mechanism to secure the resources. As a result, a WebSphere team can suffer chronic resource shortage. Resource issues can be a constant burden and distraction to the WebSphere manager and senior consultants. It may prevent these technical leaders and the technical team from focusing on a technical job.

- It is almost impossible to compare the quality and performance of IT services between different companies or within the same IT organization.

- For the WebSphere engagement process, the lack of a quantitative mechanism to provide fact-based human resource analysis and estimates seriously hinders quality service delivery. The estimate of resource consumption is often experience-based with great variation and inconsistencies. For example, an experienced WebSphere consultant may produce an estimate for a large WebSphere system build that is substantially higher than that of a new project manager. However, the senior WebSphere consultant may not have much to refer to other than prior WebSphere project experience, which is valuable, but not as convincing as solid WebSphere engineering metrics. This may lead to perception issues regarding the efficiency of the WebSphere team and its resource management practices. Furthermore, necessary WebSphere engineering hours are frequently underestimated; this negatively affects the initiative momentum and project progress.

The lack of accurate measurement of WebSphere engineering services is a complex problem. There are efforts to manage the problem—for example, calculating the resource consumption primarily by the number of Java Virtual Machine (JVM) instances. Will this methodology solve our problem?

Counting the Number of Java Virtual Machine Instances

Making decisions on resource needs by counting JVM instances sounds like a far better approach than making a purely experience-based estimate. This approach is apparently better than an arbitrary resource needs statement, especially when there is no better solution. After all, it does provide resource consumption projections and decisions that are based on a quantitative measurement: the number of JVM instances. However, this approach is fundamentally flawed and can be highly misleading for the following reasons:

- It is true that large applications tend to use more JVM instances; however, many significant factors make a difference in resource consumption for WebSphere systems with similar numbers of JVM instances. For example, application size must be taken into consideration. If the size of the WebSphere application or application suite is not considered, you get an inaccurate resource estimate when only counting the number of JVM instances. The size of the WebSphere application can significantly change the resource needs for the WebSphere team. For example, your enterprise customer-relationship management system that is used by tens of thousands of employees and hundreds of interconnected systems needs more WebSphere technical support than an authorized vendor lookup application used by internal teams, no matter how many JVM instances each system uses.

- The quality of the design, coding, and implementation of the WebSphere application can substantially affect which WebSphere technical service is needed. A WebSphere application that has frequent code quality-induced production fires consumes a huge amount of WebSphere engineering hours, regardless of the number of JVM instances installed.

- The number of changes to the application and the infrastructure is one of the deciding factors for resource consumption. A highly dynamic system with weekly system changes, biweekly maintenance releases, and monthly major code updates is more resource intensive than a less dynamic WebSphere system that has more JVM instances, but only one or two changes a year and no new application releases for several years.

- Technical project management maturity is critical to the overall technical service quality. Therefore, it will affect cost in terms of resource consumption. For example, a well-coordinated WebSphere change reduces the need for rework. Sophisticated WebSphere system work planning makes WebSphere products and service delivery less expensive because of the work quality and predictable nature of the engagement. Well-prepared WebSphere engineers do a better job.

A seemingly workable way to support the WebSphere technical service resource consumption estimate by counting JVM instances is to create a set of complex factors or weights. For example, classify a WebSphere application into a dynamic factor system of 1 to 5 (with 1 as the most static and 5 as the most dynamic). You can create the weight system by performing statistical analysis of change tickets. However, some factors are difficult to measure because of their fuzzy nature or other considerations (for example, teamwork or the maturity of WebSphere technical project management). The collaboration between teams is critical, but not easy to objectively measure. Another example is the difficulty measuring the maturity of project planning. Also, some weight factors can be sensitive to classification. For instance, it is tremendously challenging to work relationship management for anyone to assess and classify WebSphere application design and coding quality. Of course, you can always analyze the number and root cause of stability problems and clearly identify the low site variations of code quality. However, this is a sensitive and difficult job. Just imagine the reactions if you tell your application development executive that his application has been classified as having severe quality issues and you need more financial resources to support the application.

The complexity factor is a sensitive topic; still, it is possible to develop an institutionalized approach (for example, documenting your complexity factor metrics upfront and the change control processes that are triggered for certain WebSphere application stability performance issues). It is possible to develop a complexity factor metrics system, although such a system is difficult to develop and more difficult to implement if it has to be objective, straightforward, and easy to understand. To develop such a system demands work and collaboration by both the WebSphere application development team and the WebSphere infrastructure engineering support team.

The key issue is that these weights, including the number of JVM instances, firstly must not be the primary means of resource estimation. Secondly, they must be derived from viable data to be viable objective methods. The number of JVM instances must be one of the complexity factors rather than the primary WebSphere engineering service measurement, because the number of JVM instances does affect the WebSphere team's workload, but it is far from being the primary factor of WebSphere engineering services.

The factual measuring of WebSphere engineering services is especially challenging when you must deal with a corporate IT culture that may or may not fully support objective and quantitative IT resource evaluation.

Corporate IT Culture

IT culture is a significant factor in the lack of factual IT services measurement. IT organizations for large companies are all about keeping the infrastructure available and delivering the applications on schedule amid constant and drastic changes in technology, business, processes, and organization. To optimally support business drivers in this demanding environment, flexibility and some opportunities for improvising are necessary to get the job done.

The problem is that IT processes may not always be followed; sometimes, they are even compromised. Granted, there are many difficulties in following established processes. IT processes themselves sometimes have quality issues. The teams may not do a good job at process adoption and implementation. There may be constant organizational changes that do not allow the time needed for existing processes to mature. There may be pressure from the business to move projects around IT processes. The combination of all these issues constitutes a culture and general business atmosphere in which following established processes can be inconsistent. For example, some WebSphere teams may have rigid change-management processes that must be followed, whereas others may promote the release of application code directly into critical production WebSphere infrastructure without following any established process.

Today, on one hand, the IT culture is slowly evolving into one that supports the notion that IT should be an engineering discipline with consistent processes and tight standards. On the other hand, practitioners still see numerous management behaviors and operation practices that richly reward improvisation and firefighting rather than encouraging process excellence and engineering discipline. Proof is aplenty. How many times have you seen large and critical systems entering production prematurely, when everyone knows that the systems are not ready for smooth production operation? How many IT managers have been promoted after fighting fires that started in their own departments because of a lack of process and standards? This kind of IT culture encourages a CMM Level 1 and 2 sort of immaturity, and it discourages IT practice from growing into a discipline of engineering.[3]

Many large corporations have adopted Six Sigma methodology in IT project management, especially through the use of the Six Sigma submethodology DMAIC (define, measure, analyze, improve, control). Using DMAIC to control the quality and financial aspects of a project is a good process- and data-driven methodology. Often, the WebSphere team covers every phase of the project, starting with define and measure, but has more engineering work to do in the analyze, improve, and control phases. These three project phases coincide with the design, build, and operate phases of WebSphere engineering life cycles. However, using DMAIC methodology alone to evaluate, assess, and measure WebSphere engineering services is difficult and inadequate, because it does not provide engineering details to substantiate the data captured for each phase. For example, if you explain to your customer that the define phase of a project takes 3,000 hours without presenting the WebSphere engineering services details involved, or without explaining the metrics for time accounting used in resource assessment, your customer may have questions about the validity of your estimate. DMAIC is a good methodology that performs best with the support of WebSphere engineering. A solution is given later in this chapter to support the DMAIC WebSphere project management approach with solid resource estimates and assessments.

Without standards and processes, the accurate and objective quantitative measurment of IT services is impossible. It is delightful to see that significant progress is being made to address many systemic issues. With IT culture maturing into one that supports rigorous IT methodology, such as WebSphere engineering, it is a small wonder that the engagement process is not bypassed and regarded as an ineffective bureaucratic procedure or an unnecessary inconvenience.

---

3. Persse, James R. *Implementing the Capability Maturity Model*. John Wiley & Sons, 2001, Chapter 1, "Overview of the Capability Maturity Model."

IT Organization

Considerable efforts are being made to address systemic issues. This book is one of the examples of finding a way to incorporate these processes into the WebSphere engineering practice. At the same time, awareness and cognizance of the available opportunities is necessary. We must be aware that incremental steps can be taken to overcome the systemic issues in a gradual and evolutionary fashion.

Motivation

First and foremost, IT organizations as a whole may start to feel an urgent need to quantitatively measure IT services. Of course, reaching a high level of maturity in IT project management and its operations is not only a huge effort, but poses a lingering question about what desirable results it can bring about for an IT organization. Should IT invest in designing and implementing strong service measurement? The answer is a resounding *yes*. IT must have strong motivation to measure IT services with quantitative accuracy. An accurate measurement of IT services gives IT organizations more freedom in operations—for example, more IT leverage in priority setting—because the business better understands the value and the needs of IT and may therefore allocate greater resources for urgent IT priorities that align well with the business drivers. It also results in increased accountability to IT and performance measurement clarity because the business accountability and transparency are of paramount importance in building world-class IT project management and operations. IT needs to be motivated to improve IT service accounting. An IT organization wants to go through the effort to attain precise IT service cost measurements. Indeed, it is a difficult job, with pockets of resistance in the IT infrastructure organization to fundamental service measurement improvements. This is because it is a sizeable job with many difficult facets.

Complexity and Size of Large IT Organizations

Another challenge of quantitative WebSphere services estimation is the footprint of the operation and the size of the organization in which WebSphere technologies are used. A large corporation's IT organization has to deal with a complex set of financial relationships within and outside of the organization. Systems, technologies, teams, and processes become an interconnected and interrelated techno-social ecosystem of complicated contexts and histories.

Understandably, providing a consistent set of quantitative tools for IT service cost estimates covering all the financial relationships is a difficult undertaking. As a result, it is difficult to develop a practical engagement process that applies to all these financial relationships.

Fortunately, it is possible to design practical solutions for one supported technology at a time. A useful solution does not need to be an enterprise-wide initiative to be successful. A bottom-up evolutionary approach with top-down support and guidance may provide fundamental, but gradual, corrections for these systemic issues. It is possible to design and implement solid, fact-based, quantitatively sound WebSphere service measurement tools and engagement processes.

Before such a process can be designed and implemented, you need to form a conceptual and technical foundation for WebSphere services cost estimates and measurement. This necessary foundation has two parts:

- WebSphere technical service classification
- A technical system that captures WebSphere engineering hours according to the WebSphere technical service classification

Recommendations for Quantitatively Measuring WebSphere Services

The first step to quantitative WebSphere service measurement is the proper classification of WebSphere technical service or WebSphere engineering operations. When you have a practical category with a reasonable number of WebSphere services, it is then possible for you to capture the engineering hours that the WebSphere team spends for each engineering operation. In other words, it is easier for the practitioners of WebSphere engineering services to determine where their time accounting fits on an ongoing basis. This forms the foundation to translate WebSphere engineering tasks into accurate IT service costs for these technical services in exact dollar amounts. It also makes it possible to build meaningful WebSphere service benchmarks in guiding the all-important resource estimate during the WebSphere engagement operation.

Recommendation 1: Service Request, Assignment, and Tracking System

Accurate quantitative measurement of IT services demands the categorization of WebSphere engineering operations. As previously mentioned, the usual Six Sigma-style IT project hour capturing is useful at the IT project management level, but it is powerless in understanding exactly what technical service the time allocated is spent on.

For example, if a WebSphere engineer records 20 define-phase hours for a WebSphere project, this information helps the project manager capture the overall WebSphere service cost for the project. However, it does not provide any information regarding what WebSphere technical service was provided for the 20 hours charged by a senior WebSphere engineer.

The availability of an effective, but simple, Service Request, Assignment, and Tracking System makes it possible to capture the engineering hours associated with a given WebSphere engineering operation, which therefore builds a meaningful baseline of WebSphere services. For example, useful information about the WebSphere server build baseline may become a reference point for accurate resource estimate and objective performance evaluation.

WebSphere Engineering Task Classification

In addition to all the normal time tracking or project-related billing capabilities and functions, the Service Request, Assignment, and Tracking System must have product-based engineering operations or task classification. This engineering operation classification needs to have appropriate granularity to facilitate charging time on a daily basis. On one hand, it must be detailed enough to capture meaningful data that differentiates one basic WebSphere engineering task from another. On the other hand, it must not be too detailed with numerous WebSphere engineering categories to make the system a burden.

For example, a WebSphere service engineer charges two hours to an e-commerce project. He can choose any of the following WebSphere service engineering categories to charge the two hours.

- WebSphere design and configuration
- WebSphere consulting
- JEE consulting
- Server build
- On-call assistance
- Documentation
- Code and design reviews
- Development support
- WebSphere application deployment
- Performance tuning and testing
- Application troubleshooting and problem resolution
- System troubleshooting and problem resolution
- System maintenance

There are only 13 WebSphere engineering categories listed. Therefore, the WebSphere engineer does not wade though hundreds of WebSphere engineering categories to charge his time. Another example is a WebSphere service engineer charging four hours to an e-commerce project for "on-call assistance." For a WebSphere engineer, logging into the system and entering his time should not take more than a few minutes.

The engineering categories in the Service Request, Assignment, and Tracking System, if limited to a reasonable number, won't become a burden for a WebSphere engineer to perform as a daily billing time entry duty.

This methodology is not contradictory to Six Sigma; rather, it provides powerful support to a Six Sigma-based IT project management practice. For example, the WebSphere engineering hours captured can provide solid data for DMAIC as shown in Table 4.1.

Table 4.1 Six Sigma Project Methodology and WebSphere Engineering

WebSphere Engineering Tasks provide WebSphere Service Details

Define	Measure	Analyze	Improve	Control
WebSphere consulting	WebSphere consulting	WebSphere design and configuration	Server build	Application troubleshooting and problem resolution
	JEE consulting	Code and design reviews	Development support	System troubleshooting and problem resolution
		Documentation	WebSphere application deployment	System maintenance
			Performance tuning and testing	On-call assistance
				Documentation

Weight Consideration for WebSphere Services

After an initial data accumulation and aggregation, this billing information, with a proper granularity of WebSphere engineering categories, can be analyzed against the following:

- Number of WebSphere instances
- Level of complexity of the WebSphere infrastructure
- Application code quality
- Intensity of testing and stress testing
- Application code release frequency
- Level of support as defined by the service level agreement (SLA)

It is now easy to understand the details of resource consumption for a certain given WebSphere engineering task with these factors taken into consideration. This system also helps derive averages and form reasonable baselines. You can classify your WebSphere systems based on these factors. For example, you can develop a classification system based on the number of WebSphere system configuration change tickets implemented per month to determine how dynamic the WebSphere system is. Another example is to measure the number of code fixes and major releases that occur during a predefined period as a weight of how active the business drivers for the WebSphere application are. With these weight indicator-based classification systems and the concrete WebSphere engineering hours, it is possible to better understand WebSphere engineering team resource consumption. This powerful tool reveals many previously hidden facts. For example, if the "Application troubleshooting and problem resolution" task alone for a WebSphere system exceeds 100 hours a week, application code quality issues are adding significantly more cost to WebSphere engineering support. With this newly gained knowledge, you can better address your resource concerns with senior management.

You Are Enabled

Suddenly, you find yourself armed with a new ability. You can analyze the data and derive accurate facts on WebSphere services. This information forms the basis for your WebSphere service estimate and measurement. Besides, this information should be interesting to your business leaders and business partners who use and depend on the technical service that the WebSphere team provides.

For example, for the e-commerce project mentioned previously, based on the reports from your Service Request, Assignment, and Tracking System, you know that 95 percent of the engineering hours of three WebSphere engineers were used on the "Application troubleshooting and problem resolution" engineering task. Further analysis may uncover that these were mostly stability issues caused by application code defects because of a recent change in application development sourcing. This fact helps you estimate and communicate the required WebSphere resources[4] for this and other initiatives of similar situations. For example, this information is a reference when you estimate the resource needs for a WebSphere project with similar infrastructure layout and an application development team that has been recently outsourced to a new consulting company.

The availability of the Service Request, Assignment, and Tracking System, as shown in Figure 4.2, provides a solid foundation for better resource estimates during the engagement process. This also provides a necessary groundwork for monetizing WebSphere services and providing benchmark baselines.

Recommendation 2: WebSphere Service Monetization and Benchmark Baseline

Now it is possible to accomplish the following two critical steps in accurate WebSphere service cost measurement and estimation:

- Translate WebSphere service into dollar amounts
- Use the large amount of WebSphere service performance data tracked and captured to form benchmark baselines

---

4. In IT industry speak, "WebSphere resources" means the WebSphere engineers needed for a given project and the funding needed to hire those engineers.

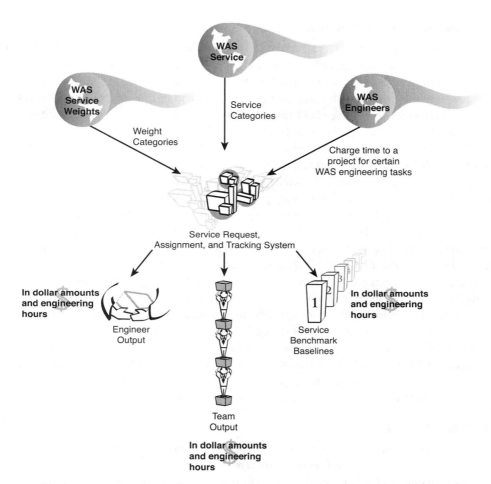

Figure 4.2 Using the Service Request, Assignment, and Tracking System to capture and provide WebSphere service benchmark baselines and WebSphere team or individual engineer service output in dollar amounts

Translating the WebSphere service hours recorded into a standard charge in dollar amounts is powerful, useful, and straightforward: It is the hours spent multiplied by the standard hourly cost of labor and organization operations overhead.

The measurement and estimation of WebSphere technical service can be further divided into two different categories for the convenience of benchmarking baselines: new project initiative and WebSphere hosting. This useful approach helps you better separate the new initiative phase and the production hosting phase of a large project. Some large WebSphere projects have many new initiatives, either in a sequential or parallel manner.

New WebSphere Project Initiative

New initiative resource estimation is all about a new WebSphere project. It includes engagement, consulting, design, build, testing, certification, and production migration. The most critical areas are design, build, and testing. The final result of the new initiative is the WebSphere system in normal production operation with functional development and testing environments delivered. The performance metrics need to be built around the total service output in terms of quality deliverables within the budget and project deadlines.

Globalization brings new opportunities and new challenges. There are great learning opportunities for WebSphere managers and senior consultants to skillfully manage global resources. For example, if you assign an offshore WebSphere engineer to be the primary WebSphere support engineer of a large initiative that has many project meetings, design sessions, and "interrupt driven" service requests (like, responding to a request for resolving a testing problem during normal U.S. business hours), how will you help the offshore WebSphere engineer succeed at her duties as the primary WebSphere support engineer for the project? Can you form a subteam that has an on-shore team member, a near-shore team member, and an off-shore team member working to provide true 24/7 engineering support for the large WebSphere project? Will innovative use of communication and collaboration technologies help? Can an important discussion be attended by team members at different times in a media-rich environment? In a technical work environment, will videos, audio, and text be conveniently shared among team members and decisions and agreements effectively achieved? Can a virtual team collaboration space be established in which a task can seamlessly pass between team members at different locations to work on the task in a nonstop fashion? Clearly, there are more questions than answers. However, this is an exciting area of WebSphere resource work in which you'll want to focus your learning activities.

WebSphere Hosting

WebSphere hosting with resource estimates focuses on production operations, system maintenance, on-call services, troubleshooting, problem resolution, and development and testing support for dynamic WebSphere applications. Hosting resource consumption has a direct relationship to application code quality and the frequency of new releases. Here the WebSphere hosting charge discussion is about human resources, not hardware and software license costs.

If the application code is characterized with a large memory footprint, unbounded data structures, and ill designed thread synchronization, among other inexperienced application development practices, you may have a purple alert production outage every week. JEE application as such can cost the infrastructure support teams, including the WebSphere team, a lot of money. For some large systems, the infrastructure teams can spend over a million dollars a year to support resolving application code issues alone.

More dynamic WebSphere environments need more technical support. For example, if you only have one new application release a year, you have dramatically fewer resource needs than if you have one new application code migration every month. There can be four sets of triggers that can be used to measure and classify a WebSphere application in terms of dynamism. Please refer to Table 4.2:

Table 4.2   Triggers for Resource Consumption Change

Measuring and Classifying WebSphere Applications in Terms of Dynamism

Dynamic Factors	Low	Medium	High	Very High
Total number of changes (system and application)	Less than or equal to 1 (sample trigger)	2–12 (sample trigger)	12–24 (sample trigger)	24–48 (sample trigger)
Total number of code releases (new releases and maintenance releases)	0 (sample trigger)	1–2 (sample trigger)	3 (sample trigger)	4–6 (sample trigger)
Total number of production problems (system and application)	Less than or equal to 10 low severity problems (sample trigger)	10–30 mostly low severity problems (sample trigger)	31–100 (sample trigger)	101–250 (sample trigger)
Total number of non-production problems (system and application)	Less than or equal to 1 (sample trigger)	10–30 (sample trigger)	31–100 (sample trigger)	101–250 (sample trigger)

Time measurement unit: per quarter

It may not be possible to estimate the dynamism of a WebSphere application while evaluating hosting charges at the define phase of the project; much of the data to be measured is not yet available. However, it is important to socialize these triggers to the business or the customer so that they fully understand the possible resource needs changes going forward. In addition, it is appropriate to include language in the SLA to enact change control to properly adjust the resource needs for hosting the WebSphere application when it is in production operation. It is possible that a large WebSphere project has multiple sequential or parallel new initiatives. For this kind of project, you need to clearly separate each new initiative and measure its new initiative phase and production hosting phase separately.

Other factors, such as the maturity of the application production support team and the conformity of the WebSphere application to enterprise WebSphere and JEE standards, also affect WebSphere resource consumption.

The ultimate measurement of WebSphere hosting quality is the stability and availability of the WebSphere production systems.

Revolutionary Impact on the Industry

The capability to quantitatively measure WebSphere services is a step forward. Take the WebSphere server build as an example. It seems only a small step forward to be able to measure a WebSphere server build in dollar amounts. However, it is a great qualitative leap forward in WebSphere engineering and will bring revolutionary changes.

Now it is possible to measure the efficiency and quality of a WebSphere build against a company benchmark. This capability eventually leads to high operation transparency. Your business leaders will know exactly what service and quality they're paying for. Therefore, they will develop more empathy and support for the WebSphere team because they know exactly where the WebSphere team is going and how they are doing.

It is possible to evaluate WebSphere service as an industry output. Now you can powerfully answer performance questions. What is the total output of the technical services of a WebSphere team per year? Is it below, above, or equal to your company benchmark? You now have answers that are accurate, fact-based, and convincing.

Pay for Performance (PFP) introduces healthy competition between employees and teams. However, when quantitative measurement of WebSphere services is not possible, a WebSphere team may direct its competitive energy in the wrong direction. IT is invisible when it is done right. However, if there are no effective ways to objectively measure WebSphere engineering service performance, WebSphere professionals may vie for visibility assignments to get noticed. Fortunately, the need to compete for visibility is no longer necessary. If your WebSphere team provided $10 million of quality IT service in 2007, and your peer teams mostly provided $6 million in WebSphere service, you do not need to compete for visibility. Visibility, reward, and recognition compete for you. PFP will no longer be a crude and cruel popularity contest or a masterful display of showmanship. You are soley measured by the contribution that you made for your company.

In addition, this helps managers pay attention to what is important to the company and themselves. This capability of exact technical service measurement and objective performance evaluation better aligns to company objectives and those of a WebSphere manager. For example, a WebSphere manager is strongly encouraged to hire highly skilled and qualified WebSphere engineers rather than building a tribe filled with loyal followers of questionable technical skills and enthusiasm. Loyalty is precious, but highly skilled employees with the right attitude get the job done. Remember that your performance is accurately measured by the quality output of your team. The managers are motivated to focus on doing the right thing for the team. For example, intensified technical training efforts may replace sophisticated political maneuvering.

Objective, quantitative, and accurate WebSphere service measurement will fundamentally transform your WebSphere organization.

Recommendation 3: Three-Staged Engagement Process

This section does not review the normal HLD and LLD processes that are relatively well-defined, better understood, and established engineering tasks.

HIGH LEVEL DESIGN AND LOW LEVEL DESIGN

High level design (HLD) is software and infrastructure design activity that focuses on architecture rather than detailed design. During the HLD process, the high level relationship of WebSphere Application Servers and other components are defined.

Low level design (LLD) delivers the details of the topology and configuration of the WebSphere system. During the LLD process, the WebSphere team delivers the WebSphere topology diagram and design document to define and describe the detailed layout of the WebSphere Application Server system and its configuration specifications. The overall LLD is still a high level design process to the WebSphere team. The detailed WebSphere topology and configuration design is a distinct sub-process of LLD and a specific engagement stage for the WebSphere team.

This section focuses on an extra phase of engagement process before a normal HLD starts. This extra phase is called initial sizing and consulting. This results in a three-staged engagement process:

- Initial sizing and consulting
- HLD and LLD
- Detailed WebSphere topology and configuration design

Use this extra phase to better manage engagement for large initiatives, especially those with major software components purchased from software vendors.[5]
The initial sizing and consulting engagement operation accomplishes three objectives.

Influence on WebSphere Standards Upfront

Before major business agreements are made, the WebSphere team must fully evaluate the solutions against enterprise WebSphere standards, roadmaps, policies, and guidelines. For example, the enterprise architect who is responsible for infrastructure deployment and management may work better if the WebSphere consultants can provide the information regarding your company's enterprise policy over WebSphere global security and JEE security. This enables your enterprise architect team do a better job in creating good Request for Proposal (RFP) and Request for Information (RFI) documents.

Promote Proof of Concept

With large and complex IT initiatives, the HLD workload can be significant. This extra phase before HLD begins allows the WebSphere team to provide initial sizing of the WebSphere infrastructure to determine the resource needs for HLD and Proof of Concept (POC) effort.

---

5. Cunico, Hernan, et al. *WebSphere Application Server V6 Planning and Design*. IBM Redbooks, 2005, Chapter 11.5.1, "Code Documentation."

HLD can involve many design meetings for the WebSphere team, and it can be a complex job for a Subject Matter Expert (SME) to accomplish. The resource consumption of tasks, such as consulting and attending many technical discussions, during this phase can be significant for the WebSphere team, and it is often underestimated.

A POC is arguably the best way to effectively explore the vendor application before buying. Without having a good POC in place before signing an agreement with technology vendors, you may take on significantly greater risk. As a result, technological surprises occur, frequently in nonfunctional areas such as scalability, failover, and transactional capacity. The WebSphere team needs to enthusiastically promote and participate in POC. The initial sizing and consulting phase helps with the advocacy and sizing of POC.

Ideally, a POC delivers the following:

- Proves that the solution works in your company's technical environment without comprising major engineering standards and processes
- Proves that the solution meets your company's resiliency and stability requirements
- Proves that the solution meets the performance objectives with a reasonable layout of infrastructure
- Provides initial sizing of the infrastructure

After a rigorous POC, you know the feasibility of the solution proposed, its supportability, the size of the effort, and the initial estimate of resource needs.

Best Practices

Providing the vendor with technical details about your company's WebSphere and JEE best practices is important. Doing this allows the vendor to obtain the level setting information that it needs to make its product compatible to the standard infrastructure and engineering practice of your company. Without this extra phase, either the vendor solution may not work within your company's normal IT infrastructure, or you may have to sacrifice your WebSphere infrastructure's quality and consistency. As a result, you may build an infrastructure anomaly to accommodate the proposed solution. This type of WebSphere system is practically unsupportable and leads to painful and costly problems. (A complete description of WebSphere initial sizing and consulting engagement operation is provided later in this chapter.)

Recommendation 4: Use the Engagement Process to Manage a Fast-Changing Large WebSphere Project

You'll often run into large but fast-changing WebSphere projects. These projects are usually highly dynamic with many significant changes happening rapidly. Many large IT projects have their fair share of turbulence at the beginning during the normal "settle down" period. However, these large WebSphere projects are characterized by unpredictable changes throughout their duration. These changes are difficult to prepare for during the engagement and design phases of the project.

For example, a large company decides to consolidate all business-decision support-related applications into one common application suite sharing the same large WebSphere infrastructure. You do not know how many applications will be converted to JEE applications, how many will be sunset, and how many will come into this WebSphere infrastructure at which timeframe. To make it worse, no one knows the answers to these critical questions. You have to design and build a WebSphere infrastructure for a large number of applications of which you have limited upfront knowledge. With these kinds of WebSphere applications, you often find yourself shooting at a fast-moving target.

Tough Issues

If you use the regular engagement process, even with its change control mechanisms, things may quickly get difficult. You may encounter grave issues in the following areas:

- Many significant WebSphere topology design changes are needed while the WebSphere systems are already in production operation. Changing WebSphere topology in production is difficult and risky. Chapter 5, "Server Build," discusses WebSphere topology design and the problems resulting from WebSphere topology changes in production.

- The WebSphere team may have inadequate or even no financial resources to work on the constant additions, expansions, and application and system changes. This results in budget overruns or even complete resource depletion.

- Most importantly, because of the lack of resources, the change of topology, and the constant onslaught of additional work, you may fail to achieve major milestones and deliverables. You may not be able to meet project schedules. Therefore, you may delay the project or cause its complete failure.

Although some project management professionals may deny it, large and fast-changing complex IT projects with a large undefined portion are not well understood. Misconceptions are grossly misleading about such projects. The following are some of the most popular, but harmful, beliefs:

- The WebSphere infrastructure has been built. You are only moving applications into the infrastructure, which should not be too resource intensive. Why do you still need many WebSphere resources?

- We carefully estimated the financials at the beginning of the project for the WebSphere team. Why have the allocated resources been depleted? Can I look at how the WebSphere resources have been managed?

- We all agreed to the project management documents, including schedules and work plans. Why are you consistently late? You need to find more efficient ways to complete the WebSphere work.

You may find yourself in a tight corner. Your large and critical WebSphere project is grossly late. You have no financial resources to finish the job. Still, you have a tremendous amount of work piling up. Worse, you are sort of under investigation. While you are busy working to finish the WebSphere engineering job, you have to spend time compiling documents and statistics to defend your WebSphere resource management and your WebSphere project management practices. Meanwhile, you have to do some serious pleading for more WebSphere resources. Figure 4.3 shows a normal flow for managing new applications in an operating WebSphere system. Contrast this to Figure 4.4, which shows what happens when change control and engagement processes are bypassed.

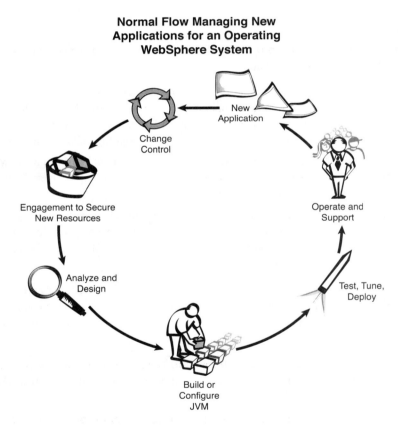

Figure 4.3   Normal flow managing new applications for an operating WebSphere system

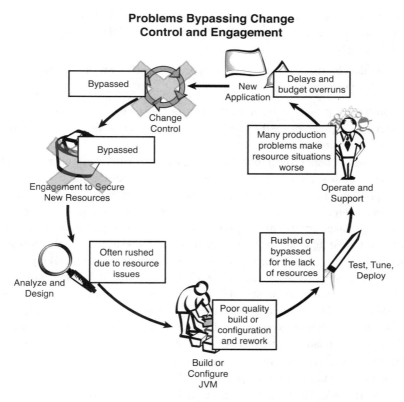

Figure 4.4   Problems occur when the change control and engagement processes are bypassed in managing new applications for an operating WebSphere system

Education Is Key

If you do not want to end up in the middle of a mess, the most critical task for you to perform is education.

You have to educate your project executive and your business partner on WebSphere engineering. You must give them a basic understanding of the WebSphere operations and tasks that your team must perform for each new application coming into the shared WebSphere infrastructure. You want them to fully understand the following facts about WebSphere service:

• Time-consuming project management work for each new application coming into the WebSphere infrastructure will affect resource needs.

- The physical WebSphere server build is not all that the WebSphere team does for each new application. Even though the WebSphere server build has been done, there are still a large number of tasks needing resources.

- Intense development and testing support for each new application requires extra WebSphere resources.

Time-consuming project management work is substantial. WebSphere project work is needed for each new application, and it can be divided into three areas: project planning, change management, and coordination.

For a large WebSphere project, planning requires much work. Your team must attend many planning meetings. Your team has to spend time reading and contributing to many project documents, such as project plans, system build plans, and business requirement specifications.

Change management involves documenting change details, requesting approvals for your changes, attending change control meetings, planning and assigning changes to appropriate team members, and coordinating changes with other teams and updating any system tracking documents or mechanisms that your organization uses (for example, a project tracking system).

Gone are the days when significant IT work was done by individuals and isolated small teams. Regardless of your IT organization's model, tight teamwork, close collaboration, and seamless coordination are necessary to execute any nontrivial work. For example, building a WebSphere Application Server system involves more than simply launching an automation script. It requires coordination work between the WebSphere team and the operating system team, the database team, and the network team, to name only a few.

There is a substantial amount of project work for each new application coming into an operating and existing WebSphere infrastructure, and this project work consumes resources.

The physical WebSphere Application Server build is only a small fraction of the overall WebSphere Engineering Support Life Cycle. System requirement engineering, WebSphere topology and configuration design, and WebSphere build planning and coordination are time-consuming but important tasks.

Again, it helps if you break the intuitive focus on tangible objects, such as a cluster of physical WebSphere server delivered. You are better off in negotiating resources if your business partners and line of business (LOB) managers appreciate the nature of WebSphere operations and activities as time-consuming technical services. If they are not educated, they may not be able to see the intangible IT services. Their intuition leads them to what they think the WebSphere team does: merely putting JEE applications into WebSphere containers that are already built. This misconception leads to gross underestimation of the resources needed by the WebSphere team.

Business partners and LOB managers should understand that, for every application coming into the WebSphere infrastructure, the WebSphere team has to go through the full engineering life cycle: from designing topology and configuration updates and building out application servers, to supporting development and testing and resolving many problems in testing and integration. There is intense WebSphere development and testing support work for each application.

WebSphere engineering support covers WebSphere production servers, WebSphere testing environments, and development with multiple pipelines. Before any new application can come into the WebSphere production infrastructure, there are intense WebSphere engineering support activities in development and testing environments in the following areas:

- Troubleshooting and problem resolution
- Performance tuning and testing
- Development support
- Code and design review
- WebSphere consulting
- JEE consulting
- Prototyping support
- System integration
- Third-party software integration

The time needed to accomplish these tasks depends on application code quality and the complexity of the integration needed. If these new applications have not been part of the original WebSphere resource estimate and allocation during the engagement process, it is easy to see why the WebSphere resources allocated may soon be depleted. In addition, it is easy to see why such WebSphere projects are frequently late.

Best Practices to Manage Large and Dynamic WebSphere Projects

It is a challenging job to manage large and fast-changing WebSphere projects with numerous undefined future applications. Although it is a complex situation, the solution is simple. By applying the following best practices, you should be able to effectively deal with each new application coming into the WebSphere infrastructure that has already been built with a number of applications having been deployed in the production operation:

- Any significant change to the WebSphere infrastructure requires an engagement process in the form of a service request. The engagement team evaluates the service request and conducts appropriate engagement work in design and resource estimation and allocation.
- Any new or additional applications not included in the original project documents involve change control and must go through the normal engagement process.
- Any significant application changes that require Web server or WebSphere Application Server rebuild or reconfiguration go through the normal engagement process, starting with a service request to the engagement team.
- The WebSphere team reserves the right to require more financial resources when the size of the application, its complexity, code quality, and the level of testing needed become more defined and are substantially different from the original agreement. At the point of engagement, the WebSphere team makes a resource estimate based on the level

of application details available at the time. When more application details are available, the WebSphere team re-evaluates the resource need and revises the resource estimate. This more effective resource estimate will be implemented as a change control item.

- The reservation must be documented and agreed upon by the project management, the application development executive, and the technical service delivery manager.
- The WebSphere team needs to make the specific requirement that each application coming into the WebSphere infrastructure must follow an established engagement process. In addition, the applications must provide a complete set of documentation required for the WebSphere team to understand the application in order to perform the infrastructure design and resource estimate and allocation work.

This process is simple, but effective. It ensures that checks and balances are established. This mechanism ensures that good design and resource estimate processes are followed. It helps with project schedule rearrangements, setting the right expectations, and allocating the right amount of resources needed to do a good job for large and fast-changing WebSphere projects. The process is especially useful when you do not know upfront what is coming into these critical and large WebSphere infrastructures.

Still, this type of large and fast-changing WebSphere project remains a huge challenge in project management and technical infrastructure support. For example, it is highly risky and difficult to significantly change WebSphere topology and configuration when the WebSphere system is in production. However, the recommended process allows the time and resources to perform a rigorous design and a careful implementation in case such need arises.

WebSphere Initial Sizing and Consulting Engagement Operation

The WebSphere Operations Framework provides a consistent and systematic methodology to describe a WebSphere engineering operation. The WebSphere engineering operations derived from applying the WebSphere Operations Framework can be used as a systematic reference and practical guide for your WebSphere engineering work. With these WebSphere operations, you have a system of solid measurements for your WebSphere engineering work, helping achieve a predictable quality of the WebSphere products and service delivered.

Operation Framework and Description

This section systematically describes the WebSphere initial sizing and consulting engagement operation applying the WebSphere Operations Framework.

Description

Initial sizing and consulting engagement may or may not be the start of the WebSphere Engineering Support Life Cycle, depending on the business decision reached during this process. The WebSphere team provides consulting services to enterprise architects, lead infrastructure design engineers, and other technical teams needing WebSphere consulting services. The WebSphere team performs the initial sizing of the initiative in resources consumption and infrastructure design. It also helps solution providers with technical information on enterprise WebSphere standards and practices. The WebSphere team advocates and provides sizing for POC, especially for large and complex solutions.

Entrance Criteria

- Approved project documents indicate sufficient funding for the WebSphere sizing and consulting work. Different companies may have different project documents, but the essence is the same: You have a written document that indicates the details and the official approval of project funding.
- Management approval of initial engagement and sizing engagement.
- A service request is approved and established for this project.
- Other SMEs, such as an operating system team representative, infrastructure design engineers, and project managers, are identified for consultation and collaboration.

WebSphere Resources

- WebSphere process engineers
- WebSphere manager

Activities

- Meet with the enterprise architect and lead infrastructure design engineer to understand the solution proposed.
- Communicate the WebSphere security baseline to the enterprise architect.
- Communicate the WebSphere server build standards to the enterprise architect and potential solution provider.
- Communicate the WebSphere best practices to the enterprise architect and potential solution provider.
- Estimate the initial WebSphere and Web server engineering resource needs for HLD.
- Estimate the initial WebSphere and Web server engineering resource needs for POC.
- Review the solution that the enterprise architect chose and provide WebSphere infrastructure related input.

Processes

- Resource and hosting estimate and sizing process
- Service request and work assignment process

Artifacts

- Request for Information Document (RFI) (external to WebSphere team)
- Request for Proposal Document (RFP) (external to WebSphere team)
- WebSphere security baseline
- WebSphere Application Server build standards
- WebSphere application best practices guidelines

Collaborating Teams

- Enterprise architecture team
- Infrastructure design and engineering team
- Peer infrastructure teams (OS, DB, MQ, security, and others)
- Capacity planning team

Sign-Off Parties

- Enterprise architecture team
- Engagement team
- Project management

Exit Criteria

- Enterprise architecture team provides final recommendation on the solution
- WebSphere team delivers the initial infrastructure sizing of the project and resource estimate for HLD

Key Processes and Artifacts Explained

This section explains the processes and artifacts used in the WebSphere Initial Sizing and Consulting Engagement Operation.

WebSphere Application Best Practices Guidelines

This technical document provides the software vendor or application development team with an enumeration of the technical details of the best practices in the context of your company's standard WebSphere infrastructure, and those that are discouraged.

WebSphere Security Baseline

Chapter 10, "WebSphere Application Server System Upgrade and Product Maintenance Management," covers the details of this document.

WebSphere Application Server Build Standards

Chapter 10 covers the details of this document.

Summary

This chapter discussed complex WebSphere engagement difficulties in the context of general corporate IT environment, where a number of systemic issues exist. These discussions intend to help you determine your strategy, develop an enterprise view of your options, and the limitations and constraints that you have to work with.

This chapter delved into the complex issue of quantitatively measuring IT services with regard to the intangible nature of IT services, corporate culture, and IT organizations. To help WebSphere engineering achieve service quantification, this chapter introduced a tripod solution.

The first leg is a Service Request, Assignment, and Tracking System. This system, with proper IT engineering task categories and appropriate environmental weights, provides the material foundation for quantitative measurement of WebSphere services. Therefore, it kicks off your systematic endeavor of deriving accurate and correct data for WebSphere engineering engagement process and performance measurement.

The second leg of the solution is a three-staged engagement engineering process focused on the first stage, initial sizing and consulting engagement operation. This operation alleviates a number of current engagement issues. This chapter used the WebSphere Operation Framework to describe the initial sizing and consulting engagement operation. The WebSphere team, as SMEs, are part of the initial sizing phase, the HLD and LLD phases, and the WebSphere topology and configuration design, which is a subphase of LLD.

The last section pertained to major issues of managing large, fast-changing, and unpredictable WebSphere projects.

Chapter 5 covers an important phase in the WebSphere Engineering Support Life Cycle, WebSphere server build.

Server Build

First, this chapter discusses the frequently seen problems in the WebSphere server build phase. Then, it presents the major operations in the WebSphere server build applying WebSphere engineering operations framework. The server build phase includes both system design and system build with the following four parts:

- WebSphere server build planning
- WebSphere topology design
- WebSphere server build and configuration
- WebSphere server build verification and validation

Stress-testing-based server verification and validation is intended only for large, complex, and critical production and pre-production environments.

This chapter discusses three operations in detail: WebSphere Server Build Planning Operation, WebSphere Application Server and Web Server Topology Design Operation, and WebSphere Server Build and Configuration Operation. But first, it covers some common server build issues.

WebSphere Server Build Phase Issues

In an unstructured IT infrastructure engineering practice environment, a large number of serious issues can occur during a WebSphere server build phase. This section describes some of these problems and offers ways to correct them. The WebSphere engineering operations framework can help you deal with these issues.

Engineering Issues

The biggest consequence of an unorganized engineering approach in a WebSphere server build is possible delays and substantially increased costs because of low-quality build work that often needs to be redone.

Informal WebSphere specifications requirement engineering is harmful to quality system builds, if not disastrous. An informal requirement engineering approach leads to quality inconsistencies in the delivered WebSphere systems. Rigorous interviewing processes and formal artifacts, such as a Business Requirement Form, a System Requirement Form, and a High-Level WebSphere Environment Specification Document, must be consistently used in systematic and rigorous requirement engineering efforts. These documents are briefly discussed in the section, "WebSphere Server Build Planning Operation."

Formal WebSphere topology and configuration design documents are important. The lack of rigorously documented WebSphere topology and configuration, in the form of design documents, often leads to unusable WebSphere environments. Interestingly, such WebSphere systems often suffer from a high level of unnecessary system complexity. A disciplined and structured design approach tends to lead to superior solutions blessed with the beauty of simple engineering. Improvised design methodology can be plagued with high complexity that is difficult to manage. Usually, this complexity renders the delivered WebSphere systems practically useless.

Design communication is critical. Fledgling WebSphere teams use unstructured documents, quick emails, and even verbal communications to convey a WebSphere server build request that contains many critical technical details in an inconsistent format. These haphazard build request communications result in confusion, a lack of accountability, and a greater chance for errors. For example, the WebSphere servers may be built on the wrong servers or even in the wrong data center.

Software incompatibility between Web servers and application servers—and other key components—may occur. This is especially true if you do not have an engineering framework and a set of tools to check on the completeness of compatibility of the various software components that must work together. In addition, you must ensure the compatibility between the WebSphere system and its execution environment, which is where the WebSphere Application Server will be built and operated. For example, you must make sure that the Java Development Kit (JDK), the operating system (OS), and a particular WebSphere Application Server build will be compatible and work together.

The production environment and pre-production environment system inconsistencies can sometimes cause serious production problems. When dealing with production issues, this is usually the first place that the application teams check. You hear the following question often when a production outage occurs: "We stress tested this application code release in the stress-testing environment, and it was all right. Do the WebSphere production and pre-production environments have the same configuration?"

There are hundreds of configurable items for one WebSphere Application Server. If manual configuration is the primary means to do the configuration job, human errors are impossible to avoid; as a result, costly production outages occur.

The lack of stress-testing-based system validation before a production code load makes it difficult to pinpoint WebSphere system issues, especially those sensitive to system load. Also, it is difficult to form a formal WebSphere system baseline to differentiate application performance issues from WebSphere system bottlenecks.

Business Partner Communication and Education

During a server build phase, inefficient practices may cause serious issues in business partner communication and education.

Because of the differences in roles, responsibilities, and current focuses, serious disagreements between infrastructure teams and application teams may develop. This is especially true with WebSphere server build standards and WebSphere security baseline implementation. You need to carefully prepare the communication and education of WebSphere build standards and the security baseline. Before meeting to discuss a difference in build standards, carefully review your company's build standard document and select appropriate contents to share either before or during the meeting with the key members of the application development team. In addition, explain that standard builds allow you to use the automation programs that significantly reduce the time needed to build and configure the WebSphere Application Server. For example, a manual configuration of a WebSphere Application Server may take days, while the automation takes only about an hour. You want the application development team to understand that building nonstandard WebSphere systems may delay the project, make the system less stable, and be difficult to support. You must seriously think through teamwork and work-relationship considerations, and careful preparation and patient explanations help retain good work relationships.

A server build is one of the most misunderstood WebSphere engineering tasks. Management and business partners frequently fail to realize that a WebSphere server build is more than the launching of a highly automated build script. Tell your management and business partners that a WebSphere server build phase includes a set of four complex engineering operations: planning, design, build and configuration, and rigorous build validation. The physical acts of launching an automation script and building the servers are only a small fraction of the server build phase engineering activities. Again, because of the intangible nature of IT services, people tend to see only the physical WebSphere Application Server. As the WebSphere manager or senior consultant, it's your job to educate people. Explain what the WebSphere team does and share these important operations of WebSphere engineering with management and your business partners. This way, your business partners and management will have a better understanding of the WebSphere engineering services that your team provides.

The application of WebSphere engineering—specifically the WebSphere Operations Framework—helps systematically prevent the problems just discussed. They also provide a set of powerful tools to manage these issues during the WebSphere server build phase of WebSphere Engineering Support Life Cycles.

WebSphere Server Build Planning Operation

Typically, WebSphere teams work on large and complex IT initiatives in a large and complex IT organization. The WebSphere Server Build Planning Operation needs the leadership of senior WebSphere consultants who know the IT organization landscape, have the right work relationships with peer engineering teams, are skilled in project management and technical environment coordination, and are effective in leading large WebSphere initiatives.

WebSphere technologies are powerful, but they are extensive and complex. Being a technical WebSphere expert is not easy. WebSphere engineering support for a large corporation demands more than just technical knowledge and skills. Good communication capabilities, excellent teamwork skills, and negotiation experience are indispensable for the WebSphere team during the WebSphere Server Build Planning Operation. Conflicting opinions and interests between the WebSphere teams and the application teams on issues such as WebSphere server build standards and WebSphere security baseline are common during the server build phase. The WebSphere team must exercise influence through education, information sharing, exception processing, and the use of management escalation as well as security exception escalation to manage these differences. The objective is to achieve a good balance between project progress and tight WebSphere standards and consistent engineering processes.

Operation Framework and Description

This section systematically describes the WebSphere Server Build Planning Operation applying the WebSphere Operations Framework.

Description

The WebSphere Server Build Planning Operation marks the start of the WebSphere server build, an important phase of the WebSphere Engineering Support Life Cycle. This high-level planning phase determines the number and the size of the needed WebSphere environments. During this phase, your team estimates the overall required resources and funding for hosting, according to the results of high level design (HLD). This important phase forms the basis of the subsequent engineering support operations. The assigned WebSphere process engineer, the primary WebSphere support engineer, and the WebSphere manager participate in the planning work.

Entrance Criteria

- Approved project documents indicate sufficient funding for the engineering work based on initial sizing and HLD documents.
- The WebSphere project, as part of the overall initiative, has gone through formal and official engagement processes.
- The service request has been approved and established for this project.
- Peer engineering teams, applications teams, and project management teams have been identified for coordination and collaboration throughout the full engineering support life cycle.

WebSphere Resources

- Primary WebSphere support engineers
- Web server support engineers

- WebSphere process engineers
- WebSphere manager

Activities

- Interview application team members and resources, including third-party software vendors, to identify the characteristics of the Java Enterprise Edition (JEE) application.
- Communicate WebSphere security baseline.
- Communicate WebSphere server build standards.
- Collaborate with enterprise architects, application architects, and infrastructure design engineers to collect infrastructure requirements.
- Based on the HLD, estimate or update the WebSphere and Web server engineering resources needed and hosting charges.
- Allocate WebSphere and Web server resources, including WebSphere process engineers, Web server process engineers (if you have a separate Web server support team), and designate primary and secondary WebSphere support engineers.
- Negotiate, review, and finalize a service level agreement (SLA) with application support teams.

Processes

- Resource and hosting estimates and sizing processes
- Service request and work assignment processes

Artifacts

- Business Requirement Form (external to WebSphere team)
- System Requirement Form (external to WebSphere team)
- WebSphere Security Baseline Document
- WebSphere Server Build Standards Document
- High-Level WebSphere Environment Specification Document
- WebSphere Admin Console Access Request Form
- WebSphere Admin Console Access Policy Statement Document
- WebSphere Resource Estimation and Hosting Charge Metrics Document
- SLA

Collaborating Teams

- Application production support team
- Application development team

- Infrastructure design team
- Peer infrastructure teams (OS, DB, MQ, and security, among others)
- Capacity planning team
- Environment change coordination team

Sign-Off Parties

- WebSphere manager
- Lead infrastructure design engineer
- Project management

Exit Criteria

- SLA is reached and agreed upon between the WebSphere support teams and application support teams.
- WebSphere Admin Console Access Policy Statement Document for the application support team is approved.
- WebSphere resource and hosting charge estimate or revision is delivered and approved.
- WebSphere project plan is finalized and approved.

Key Processes and Artifacts Explained

This section explains the processes and artifacts used in the WebSphere Server Build Planning Operation. The processes and artifacts differ from company to company. However, the general engineering objectives and functions are similar.

High-Level WebSphere Environment Specifications

The High-Level WebSphere Environment Specification Document includes high-level Web-Sphere server information divided by environments (production, stress testing, functional testing, system integration testing, and development). Its purpose is to facilitate design. For these technical environments, you need the following specifications:

- Number of environments
- Location
- Hardware specification
- OS platform
- WebSphere version
- High availability
- Support team (WebSphere team or application support team)
- Access requirements

WebSphere Admin Console Access Request Form

The WebSphere Admin Console Access Request Form is used to apply, approve, and track all security access to the WAS admin console.

WebSphere Admin Console Access Policy Statement Document

The WebSphere Admin Console Access Policy Statement Document provides policy-level guidance granting appropriate WebSphere admin console access to safeguard the company's critical testing and production WebSphere systems. This document explains policies, processes, and procedures that ensure orderly testing and production activities. If you have the document, granting or denying access request to the WebSphere admin console becomes a matter of following the established processes. Without these documents, granting or denying access requests depends on the WebSphere manager's discretion. As a result, reviewing and making decisions on access requests tends to be inconsistent, especially when the access request is denied; it can be more challenging to manage the work relationship with the requestors.

WebSphere Resource Estimation and Hosting Charge Metrics Document

The WebSphere Resource Estimation and Hosting Charge Metrics Document is usually a sophisticated spreadsheet that provides quantitative analysis in resource estimate and hosting charge calculations. The important factors are the number of instances, the degree of complexity of the WebSphere clusters, and the level of support needed. This is a complex work product. Filling in the document with proper information is a complex task that requires abundant experience. For example, it is not always possible to predict the application code quality. Low-quality code can significantly increase the troubleshooting workload of the WebSphere engineering support teams; they must open PMR with IBM, collect documents for IBM, coordinate triage activities, and communicate intermediate and final findings. Senior WebSphere engineers who have the experience and project insight should take these fuzzy aspects into consideration in their resource estimates.

WebSphere Application Server and Web Server Topology Design Operation

During the server build phase, the most critical element of engineering excellence is the WebSphere topology. WebSphere topology is the key element, not only because it's the layout of the WebSphere Application Server cluster, but also because it's the deciding factor of the overall quality of the WebSphere infrastructure you deliver. To a large degree, it also determines the resource consumption, capacity, hardware and software specifications, and most importantly, whether the WebSphere system you build will have the characteristics and features required to support the designated JEE application.

WebSphere topology is the foundation of a WebSphere application, just like the foundation of a house. You can't build a great house on a shaky foundation. After the house is built, it's difficult and costly to change the foundation. A defective WebSphere topology spells bad fortune for a WebSphere project. Changing WebSphere topology usually requires a complete rebuild of the

WebSphere system. Completely rebuilding a WebSphere system to reflect a new WebSphere topology during the production operation is difficult, costly, and risky.

It's misleading to think that all you have to do is carefully design the JEE and for the infrastructure, you can put it together quickly, and—no matter how large and complex it is—it will start working seamlessly by itself. That plan will not work; instead, consider the following guidelines:

- Conduct rigorous requirement engineering to formalize WebSphere system requirements.
- Give priority to the topology design.
- Work on the topology as early as possible.
- Provide multiple topology alternatives.
- Base the topology decisions on experience and experimental data.
- Topology design should be a team effort from both the infrastructure and application teams.

Often, the early availability of a stress-testing environment can provide a solid test bed for you to evaluate alternative topologies for performance and integration. Doing this forms a solid foundation for the system build phase of the project.

Operation Framework and Description

This section systematically describes the WebSphere Application Server and Web Server Topology Design Operation applying the WebSphere Operations Framework.

Description

During this operation, a detailed WebSphere and Web server topology is created. A WebSphere topology diagram (including Web server components) and a WebSphere Topology and Configuration Document is delivered, reviewed, and approved. The topology typically covers all the environments that need to be built and supported.

Entrance Criteria

- Specific data centers are identified to host the target WebSphere environments.
- The system specifications have been derived from nonfunctional requirements such as availability, redundancy, failover, capacity, scalability, and resiliency requirements, among others, balanced with budget constraints and technical infrastructureconsiderations.
- Project management and overall project plans are identified. Detailed project plans are developed for system design work.
- An infrastructure design consultant is assigned for HLD and low level design (LLD).
- WebSphere and Web server process engineers are assigned for WebSphere and Web server design responsibilities.

WebSphere Resources

- Primary WebSphere support engineer
- Web server engineer (if you have a separate Web server support team)

Activities

- Identify nonfunctional system requirements, such as application support requirements, availability, failover, performance, capacity, resiliency, and infrastructure system integration requirements.
- Identify hardware, software, third-party software components, and funding constraints that affect the design.
- Deliver the WebSphere topology diagram based on the infrastructure's HLD/LLD.
- Deliver the WebSphere Topology Design and Configuration Document based on the infrastructure's HLD/LLD.
- Review the WebSphere topology design check list.

Processes

- WebSphere Application Server topology design, review, and approval process
- Web server topology design, review, and approval process

Artifacts

- HLD document (external to WebSphere team)
- LLD document (external to WebSphere team)
- Capacity planning document (external to WebSphere team)
- Performance baseline document (external to WebSphere team)
- WebSphere topology design check list
- WebSphere topology design diagram
- WebSphere Topology Design and Configuration Document

Tool

- Visio (or a similar architecture drawing tool)

Sign-Off Parties

- Application production support team
- WebSphere team
- Infrastructure design engineer

Collaborating Teams

- Infrastructure design and engineering team
- Application development and application production support team
- Project management

Exit Criteria

- Successful delivery and sign-off of WebSphere Topology Design and Configuration Documents
- Successful delivery and sign-off of Web Server Topology Design and Configuration Design Documents

Key Processes and Artifacts Explained

This section explains the processes and artifacts used in the WebSphere Application Server and Web Server Topology Design Operation. The design check list can help ensure a well-rounded design. The WebSphere topology diagram and design document are complementing documents: The topology diagram presents the overall designs and the topology and design document explains the thoughts behind the delivered design.

WebSphere Topology Design Check List

The design considerations focus on the WebSphere topology's system characteristics, which is what the overall application infrastructure delivers:

- **Performance**. Application performance is determined by many factors, such as hardware, infrastructure, middleware, application architecture, and transaction volume. Designing for performance, you need the performance baseline testing conducted in a similar, if not identical, environment. For the WebSphere environment, you must ensure that sufficient traditional hardware resources, such as CPU, memory, disk space, and network bandwidth, are available.

- **Availability**. Availability, as a resiliency goal, is all about redundancy and the elimination of the single point of failure. For the WebSphere topology, horizontal and vertical clustering is highly recommended for critical applications. As another example, it is recommended that a Web server's front end reside on physical servers separate from the WebSphere servers.

- **Failover**. Automatic failover is highly recommended to reduce any server down time or service interruptions. The WebSphere session replication, database replication, and load-balancing features are also critical to failover features.

- **Load balancing**. Four layers of load balancing exist: geographical load balancing, IP sprayer, WebSphere plug-in to the WebSphere cluster members, and WebSphere Web container Object Request Broker (ORB) to WebSphere Enterprise JavaBeans (EJB) container. Consider each load-balancing method together with session affinity, transactions, and failovers.

- **Security**. For infrastructure security, consider HTTP and HTTPS, among other security protocols. For authentication and authorization, consider a flavor of Lightweight Directory Access Protocol (LDAP) service. The application may have its own authentication and authorization, such as Java Authentication and Authorization Service (JAAS) modules.

WebSphere Topology Design Diagram

The WebSphere Topology Design Diagram is commonly a Visio document with detailed diagrams on the WebSphere Server cluster layout. It includes Web servers and other infrastructure components, such as database and load balancers.

WebSphere Topology Design and Configuration Document

The WebSphere Topology Design and Configuration Document is a Microsoft Word document that explains the design and the specific details and rationales behind the WebSphere topology design. Regarding this particular WebSphere infrastructure built for a specific JEE application, it helps to describe some likely options for the WebSphere topology and explain what leads to your engineering decisions.

WebSphere Application Server and Web Server Build and Configuration Operation

During the system build phase, a fundamental change of attitude toward IT infrastructure should occur. The large IT infrastructures built today must have a rigorous test-based validation process. The WebSphere Application Server, as a commercial realization of a sizable JEE platform specification, is a powerful but complex technology. The WebSphere Application Server is also the integration point of an entire range of upper- and lower-stream components, such as load balancers, messaging systems, databases, third-party software, security components, and other enterprise systems, which adds to its magnitude of complexities. Building and delivering this powerful, capable, and complex infrastructure—free of defects without test-based validation—is difficult.

In my opinion, the quality of the test-based validation process is the key element for a system build's success. Often, you uncover and address system issues, especially at the integration points. Otherwise, they become system issues during the production operation. Conducting effective and practical end-to-end WebSphere system validation is a matter of implementation and could differ from company to company. The basic idea is simple: After the server build and before you load the application code, perform a stress-test-based validation to identify the integration defects or bottlenecks, and correct them. Thus, the system delivered is proven quantitatively free of defects and has the correctly designed characteristics, capacities, and features. Without this validation process, you often have unscheduled production outages, prolonged production problem resolution, and deteriorated work relationships between technical teams, most frequently during the production operation.

The WebSphere Server Build Verification and Validation Process, from an operation perspective, is a testing activity with a benchmark application, such as Trade 6, not the target JEE application.

Configuration during the build is all about good documentation and good automation. Without consistent WebSphere topology and configuration documents and formal server build documentation, you are not in a position to talk about WebSphere server build quality. Regarding good automation, the quality of your configuration automation affects both the system's stability and your team's productivity. For the WebSphere Application Server, there are hundreds of configurable items. Manual configuration should be a rare exception, because it is error prone and resource intensive. WebSphere configuration automation is at its best when your WebSphere systems are built to highly consistent enterprise WebSphere installation standards.

Operation Framework and Description

This section systematically describes the WebSphere Application Server and Web Server Build Operation applying the WebSphere Operations Framework.

Description
Build out the WebSphere environments, from installation, configuration, verification, and validation, all the way to application deployment. It is an end-to-end build out of the WebSphere environments.

Entrance Criteria

- The project has gone through official engagement services with solid resource estimate and HLD, LLD, and WebSphere system design.
- The environment is identified and the detailed specifications are well understood and available.
- HLD documents are approved and available.
- LLD documents are approved and available.
- The WebSphere Application Server and the Web server topology design and configuration documents are approved and available.
- The WebSphere and Web server build resource is allocated.
- The project plan for building the environment is developed.
- The peer infrastructure team resources are identified.
- The environment change coordination manager is identified.

Activities

- Become proficient in the WebSphere system work processes.
- Check and ensure that all dependencies are removed.

- Compile the environment-specific build document with the build details. Depending on the project, the environments may include development, functional testing, system integration testing, stress testing, quality assurance, and production environments with possible multiples of each environment. The build request document should be carefully filled out based on the WebSphere topology design, software, and hardware specifications. The version-controlled build request document should serve as the only WebSphere server build communication vehicle. Verbal or email communication with build specifications without the build document should NOT be accepted as build requests. It is important to exercise document version control for the build request document. This critical document is used by many teams, so a mistake can easily be made if one person uses an obsolete version of the document. It also helps to include the author's name and appropriate contact information. When a question arises, the author can be quickly contacted to address it.

- Ensure that the specific build request document template is available for a target version of the WebSphere Application Server and the Web server.

- When appropriate, follow your change-control process and open change-control tickets for the WebSphere environment build job.

- Update your WebSphere environment tracking document or automated systems immediately after the build activity.

- Schedule the server build in your service request system for your team members, and submit the completed build request document with specifications in your work assigning and tracking systems, such as the service request system.

- Prepare the system changes for the server build, including firewall rules, system administration, security, system monitoring, and any other required system setup according to your WebSphere work dependency check list.

- Execute the server build.

- Verify the server build. Verification of the server build includes the following work:
  - WebSphere product checking, including the version, WebSphere patch or fix pack version, and JDK version.
  - Web server product checking, including the version and the plug-ins (WebSphere, LDAP server, reporting software, and so on).
  - WebSphere functionality checking, including start, stop, and synchronization.
  - Web servers start and stop, log rotation, and functionalities of plug-ins, among others.
  - Global security.
  - Fill out your Server Build Acceptance Form.
  - Perform stress-test-based server build verification and validation. However, this level of verification and validation is only appropriate for highly complex and critical large production and pre-production environments.

- WebSphere configuration, including configuration and integration with other components (MQ, web services), backend information systems (database, CICS®), third-party vendor-specific products, and other interconnected applications.
- Make use of WebSphere configuration automation scripts and processes.
- Application deployment. Depending on the agreement with individual applications, the deployment can be handled by another infrastructure team, such as a Tivoli® team or the WebSphere team.
- Application testing. Conduct testing in a way that validates the applications, integrations, infrastructure, and so forth, but it may not be possible to test the full range of the application's functionalities.
- Environment build is signed off by both the application team and the WebSphere team.
- Update your knowledge management system and asset management system. For example, update your WebSphere Application Support Manual and WebSphere Environment Tracking Document, or any automated system cataloging or asset management system.

Processes

- WebSphere system work process
- WebSphere configuration automation process
- Change-control process

Artifacts

- WebSphere Server Build Standards Document
- WebSphere Security Baseline and Standard Document
- WebSphere Build Request Document
- Web Server Build Request Document
- WebSphere Server Build Acceptance Form
- Application Build and Deployment Document
- WebSphere Application Support Document
- WebSphere Environment Tracking Document
- Environment Certification and Acceptance Document

Tools

- Server build automation scripts
- Server configuration automation scripts
- Application deployment scripts

Collaborating Teams

- Application production support team
- OS system administration
- Security teams
- Networking teams
- Load balancing teams
- Directory services team

Exit Criteria

- WebSphere is built according to the WebSphere topology, and the following have successfully gone through a careful verification process:
  - Number of nodes and their relationship.
  - Signed off by application support team upon verification.
  - WebSphere is built according to the infrastructure design.
  - In the correct network zone.
  - With designated firewall rules.
  - On the targeted servers.
  - Signed off by the production application support team and WebSphere manager.
- The environment is certified by the application production support team in terms of application functionalities and all the integration points, as specified here:
  - Database
  - MQ
  - Web services interfaces
  - Third-party software integration
  - Inter-application connections

Key Processes and Artifacts Explained

This section explains the processes and artifacts used in the WebSphere Application Server and Web Server Build and Configuration Operation. You can take these processes and artifacts as references and develop your own. Proper documentation that is concise and relevant is your first step to a quality server build. It takes a lot of work to develop engineering processes. However, a documented process gives your team a good start in improving your work by optimizing your process.

WebSphere System Work Process

The WebSphere System Work Process demands careful design, piloting, and optimization. The quality of the WebSphere system work directly contributes to the overall stability of all of your WebSphere systems. You want to carefully manage the WebSphere system work. This document needs to provide details of the process for all the WebSphere Application Server system work, which includes the server build, server upgrade, fix and patch application, and JDK upgrade. The goal is to offer a standardized process and grow accountability, thus improving the consistency of your WebSphere systems, as well as the efficiency and accuracy of your WebSphere engineering support work. This process usually formalizes the following:

- Roles and responsibilities
- Server build request communication, certification, and configuration
- WebSphere system work scheduling
- Process for completing the Server Build Request Document
- Server maintenance and upgrade policy

WebSphere Configuration Automation Process

The purpose of the WebSphere Configuration Automation Process is to define a process for controlling WebSphere automation. The WebSphere automation program can be powerful and dangerous. This process ensures that the application of the WebSphere automation follows a series of predefined and rigid steps to ensure the quality of the work and reduce human errors. A powerful WebSphere automation program can instantly reconfigure your entire production WebSphere server suite; as a consequence, it can disable your production servers and cause a huge unscheduled outage. You need a tight process to control such powerful programs—the same as you would for powerful weapon systems.

WebSphere Build Request Document

The WebSphere Build Request Document is a critical communication and tracking mechanism that is used during the entire process of the WebSphere server build. This document collects all the information required to build the WebSphere instance on a target platform and track the server build requests. It includes the following areas:

- Author and author's contact information
- Version of the document
- Change history of the document
- Server build request
- Software requirements
- Hardware requirements
- Server security access requests

- OS requirements
- WebSphere installation specifications
- WebSphere global security requests
- JEE security-enabling specifications
- Web server specifications
- Server port assignments
- Infrastructure engineers assigned
- Change control information
- Monitoring requirements

Application Build and Deployment Document

The Application Build and Deployment Document records how you build and deploy your JEE application. This can differ from application to application. For example, this document can define the roles and responsibilities of different teams and the integration between tools used by different teams (if a Tivoli team is involved with JEE application code deployment).

WebSphere Application Support Document

The WebSphere Application Support Document is critically important. It contains all of your WebSphere infrastructures divided by the applications. This document is used to provide consistent engineering support for all of your applications. This document should be periodically audited and updated to keep it accurate. An inaccurate WebSphere Application Support Document can be harmful to both the quality of your engineering support work and the stability of your critical WebSphere systems. It can include the following:

- Description of the application
- Serve list with names and IP addresses
- WebSphere server specification
- OS specifications
- Monitoring and diagnostic tools information
- Web server specification
- JDK specification
- WebSphere topology
- Instruction on using specific system administration scripts
- Instructions for key events, such as failover and disaster recovery
- Key application contact list

Technical Environment Change Coordination

In the WebSphere server build phase, the key to success is to have a good WebSphere server build plan. Without a set of good WebSphere topology and configuration deliverables, you will not be successful in building a WebSphere server suite that has the desired systems characteristics required by the JEE application for its execution environment. However, a good WebSphere topology itself is not good enough, and with no exception, the WebSphere engineering support team has to work well with a large number of other technical teams to do their job well. During this phase, the WebSphere work's success also depends on the degree of collaboration and coordination between teams. If your IT organization has a technical environment change-coordination function that provides this critical coordination in planning and execution for large and complex technical environments, the infrastructure engineering teams may work better together.

The important technical environment change-coordination function provides an end-to-end view; therefore, it helps coordinate the work of technical teams. This technical environment change-coordination practice fits with a number of IT infrastructure engineering organization strategies: either a dedicated engineering team that supports WebSphere technologies only, or a team that supports multiple infrastructure products. These infrastructure engineering teams or sub-teams, such as WebSphere, MQ, DB2®, and UNIX, have deep knowledge of the products they support, and the technical environment change-coordination function provides leadership in planning, coordinating, and executing application and system changes. The technical teams from the IT infrastructure organization environment change-coordination teams frequently work shoulder-to-shoulder to implement these important changes. The change-coordination teams are the glue to all the other technical teams and their work; they help all the teams converge into a powerful and focused technical force, doing a quality job of providing your company with superior infrastructure engineering.

Technical environment change-coordination function needs to be present all the way from your critical production environment to your development and testing environment.

Summary

This chapter first discussed frequently seen issues during the WebSphere server build. Then, it introduced three WebSphere engineering operations using the WebSphere Operations Framework:

- WebSphere Server Build Planning Operation
- WebSphere Application Server and Web Server Topology Design Operation
- WebSphere Application Server and Web Server Build Operation

This chapter described many key processes and artifacts about server build, and it introduced the technical environment change coordination function.

In Chapter 6, "Functional and Integration Testing Environment Support," you work through WebSphere Functional and Integration Testing Environment support.

CHAPTER 6

Functional and Integration Testing Environment Support

The WebSphere Functional and Integration Testing Environment usually includes the development environment, functional-testing environment, and integration-testing environment.[1] Relative to the production and pre-production load-testing environments, the WebSphere engineering support for the Functional and Integration Testing Environment is not that stressful or exciting. However, the choices that you make for WebSphere support have a far-reaching effect on the WebSphere engineering support's overall quality for a given enterprise WebSphere application. These choices affect the quality and stability of your production and critical load-testing environments. This chapter explores the following topics:

- Major issues and lessons learned for the Functional and Integration Testing Environment WebSphere support
- Major engineering choices for the Functional and Integration Testing Environment WebSphere support
- WebSphere Functional and Integration Testing Support Operation
- Resources and workload considerations of the Functional and Integration Testing Environment
- A look at the future

---

1. For more information on structured testing, see "Structured Testing: A Testing Methodology Using the Cyclomatic Complexity Metric" by Arthur H. Watson, Thomas J. McCabe. Computer Systems Laboratory, National Institute of Standards and Technology, August 1996.

Major Issues and Lessons Learned for Functional and Integration Testing Environment WebSphere Support

For this testing environment, the first consideration of WebSphere engineering support is the support model: who handles WebSphere engineering support work and how it is to be done. Also, supporting a large number of parallel testing pipelines can pose unique challenges. Application deployment and system consistency, if not properly managed, can lead to complications. Let's look at these issues and share the experiences gained through some mistakes.

Functional and Integration Testing Environment Support Model

Different Functional and Integration Testing Environment support models may result in different engineering practices and standards between the WebSphere production environment, pre-production environment, and the WebSphere Functional and Integration Testing Environment. Occasionally, the application development and support organization may want to manage this environment, seemingly in a desire to gain maximum control. The arrangement can be such that the WebSphere engineering support team manages the WebSphere production environment and stress-testing environments, and the application teams control development and other testing WebSphere environments. The WebSphere engineering support team also consults the application development and support team.

The advantages of this arrangement are obvious. For the WebSphere team, it means that fewer resources are needed to support the WebSphere application. For the application teams, total control usually means more effective execution of its business objectives and priorities. Also, this lessens the need for communication and coordination between the application teams and the WebSphere team over the WebSphere Functional and Integration Testing Environment support. For a large IT organization, communication and coordination between these teams is not easy.

At the beginning, the disadvantages for this WebSphere support model are not obvious. It takes time for all teams to clearly see the drawbacks. Over time, the lack of communication and the differences in priorities of the application teams and the WebSphere team can lead to serious discrepancies in system consistency between Functional and Integration Testing Environment WebSphere systems and production and stress-testing WebSphere systems. Such gaps and differences can cause serious stability issues, and both teams must work to correct them.

As a best practice, the WebSphere engineering support team must support all WebSphere environments. If this is impossible for a given WebSphere application because of resource considerations or organizational issues, you may want to work with the application team responsible for the Functional and Integration Testing Environment WebSphere systems to schedule periodic system sync-up between these WebSphere systems. By doing so, you make the Functional and Integration Testing Environment WebSphere systems consistent with production and stress-testing environments before such differences cause production issues. Otherwise, the systems and practices become so different that it is impossible to correct them without significantly disrupting the development and testing activities.

In the case where the WebSphere team manages the Functional and Integration Testing Environments, for the development WebSphere environment, it may make sense to grant your application development team operator privileges as a self-help strategy. However, even for a development environment, the WebSphere team needs to reserve the configuration privilege as a skill-set consideration. Application developers rarely have in-depth knowledge of WebSphere configuration. If they randomly change a WebSphere configuration, it almost always results in numerous system issues that take considerable time to resolve. In the worst case, you may have to rebuild your development WebSphere environment. Not only does this add a tremendous amount of system work for your team, but it also slows the developers. Be diplomatic and professional; when you say no, be firm. Do not grant configuration privileges to testers and developers for any WebSphere environment.

Large Numbers of Functional and Integration Testing Pipelines

To speed your critical applications to market, it's useful to build a number of parallel Functional and Integration Testing WebSphere systems in the form of multiple development and testing pipelines. Building multiple parallel developments and testing WebSphere pipelines helps fill the gaps between fast-changing business needs and orderly IT engineering processes and procedures. Of course, you can incur substantial higher resource consumption for both a project's initiative phase and business-as-usual support. You must capture this resource need in the WebSphere project's engagement phase. Automating many of the WebSphere system administration tasks helps control resource consumption. Using the WebSphere Virtual Enterprise may lower the total cost of ownership. Still, given the WebSphere technology chosen and the automation level, more WebSphere environments need still more WebSphere engineers to support them. Eventually, you have to do more with more. Therefore, carefully evaluate the resource needs for more pipeline build out and systematically carry out support before you make commitments to your technology or business partners.

Third-Party Software Integration and Support

Before you introduce a third-party software into your organization, you need to engage a WebSphere team early; this ensures that the software meets your infrastructure requirements from a scalability and redundancy perspective. A series of questions or a requirements check list can be presented to the vendor for sign-off. After the vendor signs off, add that document to the contract. Third-party software integration and support can be challenging. For example, integrating third-party Web services software into a WebSphere application server may not be a huge technical issue. However, deciding the support model for the third-party Web services software may require careful thinking. The WebSphere engineering support team may not have the level of technical knowledge, training, and the vendor relationship to support the number of third-party software integrated into the WebSphere environment. One of the best approaches may be to leave the third-party software support and vendor-relationship management to the application support teams (or whoever has the most at stake in using the software). Regardless, the WebSphere team still must provide WebSphere consulting services to the team responsible for the third-party software support. The consulting work needs to be strictly related to WebSphere and the technical work to help the third-party software integrate with WebSphere. The WebSphere team can work with the teams responsible for the software to integrate it into the WebSphere Functional and Integration Testing Environment, the production environment, and stress-testing environments. However, to reiterate, do not take over the technical support for the third-party software.

System Consistency and Upgrade Strategy

In terms of basic configuration, it's necessary to maintain system consistency across different WebSphere environments—but not the overall WebSphere topology. WebSphere systems for the Functional and Integration Testing Environment may not have the level of redundancy, capacity, and failover features that the production and stress-testing environments have. Therefore, it is not necessary to keep the Functional and Integration Testing Environment consistent with the production and stress-testing environments in the WebSphere topology. However, the basic WebSphere configurations must be consistent.

All patches and upgrades must start with the WebSphere Functional and Integration Testing Environment and gradually migrate to upper environments. With many WebSphere pipelines for application development and testing, you must have a carefully coordinated WebSphere upgrade and patch strategy.

It is not proven yet if it is feasible to use WebSphere Virtual Enterprise at the Functional and Integration Testing Environment for a WebSphere project that has WebSphere Network Deployment-based production and stress-testing environments. Even if this is not a problematic strategy, it is wise to quickly adopt the WebSphere Virtual Enterprise technology into the production and stress-testing environments after you adopt the WebSphere Virtual Enterprise technology in the Functional and Integration Testing Environment. Using WebSphere Network Deployment at the production and stress-testing environments and the WebSphere Virtual Enterprise technology for the Functional and Integration Testing Environment for a long period of time may cause inconsistencies to occur in many areas. Problems may develop, such as inconsistent change control practices, different WebSphere automation programs, and separate WebSphere engineering processes.

Application Deployment

Application deployment can be a time-consuming, resource-intensive, and error-prone task. The best practice includes collaboration and teamwork with a dedicated team that specializes in building, packaging, and deploying application code and associated artifacts, such as property files, into various development, testing, pre-production, and production environments. It may take some time for this team to get it right. However, eventually it is a better engineering practice to relieve skilled WebSphere resources from this kind of application-level activity. It lets Web-Sphere system engineers focus on automating the deployment process, and it standardizes the process across the systems. It may take some effort for the WebSphere team to work well with the application deployment team; however, the saved WebSphere resources, the code deployment efficiency, and the quality gained are worth it. It is in the WebSphere team's best interest to help and support the application deployment team in doing its work better. (Chapter 10, "WebSphere Application Server System Upgrade and Product Maintenance Management," discusses this topic in more detail.)

Some application teams prefer coupling application-build and packaging automation with code-deployment automation. This is especially true if these application teams also, as a special arrangement, provide WebSphere engineering support for the Functional and Integration Testing Environment. Although this approach may appear to be the most optimal to the application teams, it is invariably resource intensive and inconsistent to the company-wide WebSphere engineering processes; therefore, it significantly hinders enforcing WebSphere standards and achieving engineering process automation. In real-world WebSphere engineering practice, using a dedicated application deployment team that has special tools and processes helps reduce resource consumption of code migration while increasing the quality of application code release. This saves your company money and makes your life as the WebSphere manager and the lives of your WebSphere engineers easier. Otherwise, your engineers must work late nights, especially during weekends, to migrate code, and you have to deal with the related resource consumption and manage the problems.

Major Choices for Functional and Integration Testing Environment WebSphere Support

You have many important choices to make in the area of WebSphere Functional and Integration Testing Environment support. These decisions significantly change this environment's direction and the quality of your WebSphere engineering support work. Therefore, make thoughtful and experienced choices in these areas:

- Provide development tooling support and development tooling-integration support.
- Offer Java Enterprise Edition (JEE) consulting.
- Use WebSphere Virtual Enterprise or WebSphere Network Deployment to build the WebSphere Functional and Integration Testing Environment.
- Put the WebSphere Functional and Integration Testing Environment under the control of change management.
- Employ a dedicated team to perform environment change coordination for the WebSphere Functional and Integration Testing Environment.

Development Tooling Support

Development tooling support includes supporting the development tool itself and integrating the development tool with the WebSphere testing environments. To effectively support the development tool, such as IBM Rational Application Developer for WebSphere, you must have WebSphere engineers who ideally have recent JEE application development experience using the newest development tool. (However, such talents may not always be available.) The application development team usually knows the development tool well and may know it better than the WebSphere team does. In addition, providing application development tool support may not be considered the WebSphere engineering team's core competence. The last consideration is the resource consumption of such support. An appropriate approach may be to only provide a reasonable level of development tool and testing environment integration support, unless the service level agreement (SLA) for a specific project includes development-tool support; thus, there are adequate financial arrangements and human resources to provide such support.

JEE Consulting

JEE consulting can include, but is not limited to, WebSphere-oriented JEE development training, code prototyping, and code review. WebSphere-oriented JEE training with simple code prototyping helps developers learn to develop WebSphere-friendly applications that fully use WebSphere features and enhancements to the JEE specification. However, like development-tooling support, this must be a funded activity consistent with a specific SLA and other project documents to ensure that the needed resources are allocated. Mission-critical JEE applications are large and complex. For large WebSphere applications, it is a resource-intensive task for the WebSphere team to review the design and actual coding of a large piece of JEE application code. JEE code review, although a best practice, belongs in the special needs category. It may not be practical for the WebSphere team to take it on without additional funding, especially for very large WebSphere applications.

Influencing and Enforcing WebSphere and JEE Best Practices

One major advantage of influencing and enforcing WebSphere and JEE best practices upfront is that you have fewer problems later. Occasionally, a JEE application can be built in a way that it is difficult to support within your company's standard WebSphere infrastructure. For example, the standard WebSphere topology for mission-critical and high-load applications at your company may be one that has horizontal and vertical clustering. However, if your application has a serialized messaging mechanism, it won't execute in a clustered WebSphere environment because it doesn't support clustering. As a result, your WebSphere system's capacity and scalability may suffer. Therefore, a key task for the WebSphere Functional and Integration Testing Environment engineering support is to ensure that the application follows a minimum set of JEE and WebSphere best practices. This helps you design and build a WebSphere system that conforms to the standards, that is free of intrinsic flaws, and that is consistent with your company's WebSphere engineering practices and processes. Building a supportable WebSphere system starts with JEE best practices consulting and WebSphere consulting in the following areas (working with your application architects and developers):

- **JEE**. Common best practices in JEE cover thread management, Enterprise JavaBeans Java Naming and Directory Interface (EJB JNDI) lookup, connection synchronization, and exception processing.

- **WebSphere resources**. Resource lookup, connection caching, messaging system choices, exception processing, and managing the JMS connection are important topics.

- **Vendor applications**. Clustering support is critical for redundancy, failover, and scalability, and for large and high volume WebSphere environments. You want to ensure that the application has nothing intrinsic in the design or coding that prevents clustering.

- **Packaging**. How does the application package? Are you going to use an Enterprise Archive (EAR) file or a Web Application Archive (WAR) file? Does it include application property files? All these questions can affect WebSphere engineering. Encourage and enforce consistent practices for packaging. For example, for environment-specific files such as property files, you may want to recommend not packaging them in the EAR file. This makes the EAR file exactly the same across all environments, thus reducing potential problems.

WebSphere Network Deployment or WebSphere Virtual Enterprise

For a relatively small WebSphere Functional and Integration Testing Environment, WebSphere Network Deployment suffices. A large WebSphere application can have as many as a dozen development and testing pipelines. For such a large WebSphere Functional and Integration Testing Environment with large numbers of WebSphere systems, WebSphere Virtual Enterprise is appropriate in terms of system administration, licensing costs, and hardware acquisition.

Change Control

If you put your Functional and Integration Testing Environment under the control of change management, it takes time to manage changes. However, the time that you save from carefully planning and orderly executing changes is worth following the formal change-control processes. For large and complex critical WebSphere systems, putting all WebSphere environments, including the Functional and Integration Testing Environment, under the control of change management is a best practice. It is a highly effective way to plan and implement changes for the WebSphere Functional and Integration Testing Environment. This is particularly true for large and critical WebSphere applications.

Environment Change Coordination

Whether your WebSphere Functional and Integration Testing Environment is large or small, your job becomes easier and the quality of your technical service improves if a dedicated team conducts environment change coordination. This dedicated environment change coordination team is covered in Chapter 5, "Server Build," and Chapter 11, "Critical Work Relationships."

WebSphere Functional and Integration Testing Support Operation

The most important task of the WebSphere Functional and Integration Testing Environment is to maintain high availability. You must keep your Functional and Integration Testing Environment up and running for developers and testers. Therefore, you must quickly deal with technical issues in WebSphere integration tasks (for example, configuring a data source to connect to the database on the mainframe or helping resolve roadblocks in a third-party software integration). The major WebSphere engineering operations at the Functional and Integration Testing Environment are supporting functional and integration testing and planning and implementing WebSphere configuration changes. Chapter 7, "Stress-Testing Environment Support," details WebSphere configuration change support.

Operation Framework and Description

This section systematically describes the WebSphere Functional and Integration Testing Support Operation applying the WebSphere Operations Framework.

Description

WebSphere engineering work in functional testing and integration testing support is to assist testing activities by providing WebSphere technical support in these environments. This technical support is based on an SLA for each individual project. The level of support differs from project to project. For example, you may only provide 8-to-5 technical support for Functional and Integration Testing Environments for one WebSphere application. However, for another project, WebSphere technical support may be provided on a 24/7 basis, according to a specific SLA. With increased focus on speed to market and building a global workforce, there is an increasing need to provide 24/7 WebSphere technical support in the Functional and Integration Testing Environment.

Entrance Criteria

- Ensure that the WebSphere technical support level being provided in the development and testing environments adheres to the SLA.
- Ensure that the target WebSphere environments have been built, certified, and are functional.

WebSphere Resources

- WebSphere system engineer (if you have a separate WebSphere system team)
- Primary WebSphere engineer for the project

- Secondary WebSphere engineer for the project
- WebSphere on-call engineers

Activities

- Plan, coordinate, and implement WebSphere application server and Web server-configuration changes for the environments.
- Update the WebSphere System Tracking Document after performing system changes.
- Update the WebSphere Application Support Manual after performing significant system changes.
- WebSphere administration activities, including start, stop, and synchronizing Web-Sphere application servers, as required by the SLA.
- Deploy application code, if required by the SLA.
- Collaborate and assist the application deployment team in planning and implementing code migration, as required by the SLA.
- Integrate third-party software into the WebSphere Application Server systems.
- Participate in the development and testing-problem troubleshooting, especially with issues related to WebSphere and Web servers.

Processes

- Configuration change process
- Defect tracking process (external to the WebSphere team)
- Change control process (external to the WebSphere team)

Artifacts

- WebSphere System Tracking Document
- Change Management Process Document (external to the WebSphere team)
- Problem Resolution Process Document
- Weekly testing status report (external to the WebSphere team)

External Teams

- Application support team
- Application deployment team
- Testing team
- Environment change coordination team

- IBM WebSphere and Java support team
- Other infrastructure support teams, such as MQ, DB2, operating systems

Sign-Off Parties

- Application support team
- WebSphere team
- Testing team
- Environment change coordination team
- Application deployment team

Exit Criteria

- Functional testing is performed and signed off.
- Integration testing is performed and signed off.

Key Processes and Artifacts Explained

This section explains the processes and artifacts used in the WebSphere Functional and Integration Testing Support Operation. These processes and artifacts vary from company to company, but the general engineering objectives and functions are similar.

Configuration Change Process

The configuration change process is an end-to-end process. It must not be a redundant or overlapping process to your company's overall change-management process. Rather, it is a low-level WebSphere engineering process. It needs to provide specific guidance in planning and executing the WebSphere configuration changes for your team. It may include the mechanisms that allow this low-level engineering process to hook up with the enterprise change-control process. It needs to detail how your team assigns configuration changes as tasks to team members, how to ensure the accuracy of a configuration change, and how to guarantee that configuration work is done accurately and as planned.

Defects Tracking Process

The defects tracking process usually provides guidelines on how the teams record, track, and resolve problems in development and testing. This process defines how to record the problem, the organization that generates the request for addressing problems, request dispatching, engagement of development resources, WebSphere resources, engagement of IBM technical support organization, and the tracking of defects in the end-to-end process of fixing those defects.

Change Management Process Document

The Change Management Process Document provides specific guidelines for processes, procedures, and mechanisms of your organization's change management practices. Every team member must fully understand this document and diligently follow your company's change-control processes and emergency change-management processes.

Weekly Testing Report

The weekly testing report is an important communication tool that your testing organization sends out to update the technical teams and management on the status of testing, including the status of issues, risks, and plans. This is a critical mechanism for quality control. If your testing organization does not have a weekly testing report, you can request a status from time to time. This is especially true when the WebSphere engineers assigned to the WebSphere Functional and Integration Testing Environment of the project report that testing problems are not being adequately addressed and corrected. You must ensure that adequate testing, especially stress testing, has been done and that the problems are satisfactorily addressed before the application code can migrate to the next level of WebSphere environment in the development and testing pipeline.

Resources and Workload Considerations of the Functional and Integration Testing Environment

One of the deciding factors with the Functional and Integration Testing Environment work for WebSphere engineers is a developer's technical maturity. Mature development teams have a good grasp of the WebSphere application development tool suite and need little support from the WebSphere engineering support team. Typically, a fledgling application development team usually needs more help, especially with integrating the development tool into the testing environment. Supporting a relatively new development team can be resource intensive. Therefore, appropriate resource estimates and allocation must be performed accordingly during the engagement phase of the project or as a change-control item in the financial documents of the project, when it is apparent that the original resource estimates and allocation are not adequate to support the development team.

Most large and complex WebSphere projects are dynamic, with many new code releases in the pipelines to deliver new business functions. The frequency of new releases and the assignment of code-deployment responsibilities are the two significant factors in WebSphere resource consumption. A WebSphere project that has a new major release every month needs far more WebSphere resources than an application that has a new major application release once a year. Frequently, people underestimate the resource needs for development and testing environments for an active WebSphere project that is in control mode. The WebSphere engineering support team has to work with the development team and testing team on every new release, starting from the Functional and Integration Testing Environment all the way to the production environment in managing changes and resolving technical issues. If the WebSphere team is responsible for code deployment, workload can increase substantially. Obtaining an accurate WebSphere resource estimate will be easier if you clearly understand the frequency of new application releases, the maturity of the development team, and release management or code deployment responsibilities upfront.

The size of the WebSphere Functional and Integration Testing Environment matters in resource estimates. One development and testing pipeline needs fewer resources than a massive WebSphere Functional and Integration Testing Environment of multiple parallel development and testing pipelines with intense development and testing activities. For such a large and dynamic WebSphere Functional and Integration Testing Environment, having a high degree of automation helps reduce resource consumption, as does using the WebSphere Virtual Enterprise.

A Look to the Future

In terms of CPU and memory, the Functional and Integration Testing Environment WebSphere infrastructure usually has a low level of utilization. The need for multiple pipelines arises from the simultaneous parallel development and testing work on many application releases, and from the need to separate these parallel release environments so they perform separate system changes as required by different releases. However, it is unlikely for all the development and testing pipelines to experience high system resource consumption at the same time. Also, the lack of testing load or traffic further reduces the need for the overall Functional and Integration Testing Environment system resources.

With its dynamic operations in resource allocation and highly intelligent quality of service, the WebSphere Virtual Enterprise is an ideal platform for the Functional and Integration Testing Environment. Also, its raw utilization data-capturing capability makes charging back to the business for WebSphere system usage more fact-based and transparent. However, before taking advantage of the WebSphere Virtual Enterprise for the Functional and Integration Testing Environment, there are challenges in the areas of the technical support organization model, WebSphere project-management maturity, corporate culture and communication practices, and the corporate IT funding model.

For example, say that you have a large customer-care application suite with six dedicated development and testing pipelines. It is supported by a WebSphere engineering support team, called WebSphere Team 1, which focuses in customer-care applications. Now, you are moving the Functional and Integration Testing Environment WebSphere Network Deployment-based systems to a large shared WebSphere Virtual Enterprise environment that is managed by a WebSphere engineering support team called WebSphere Team 2, which specializes in large shared environments. Before this large shared WebSphere Virtual Enterprise environment can operate smoothly, many decisions must be made:

- Which team will support the Functional and Integration Testing Environment for the customer-care applications? Does WebSphere Team 1 continue to support the WebSphere Functional and Integration Testing Environment for the customer-care application? If not, will the practice of using separate WebSphere teams supporting the same

large and complex WebSphere application at different environments create gaps, discon-
nects, and inconsistencies?

- Because of its multitude of environments in terms of planning and scheduling, Web-
Sphere upgrades can be difficult for any large WebSphere application. Will it be too big
of a task to coordinate many large WebSphere applications sharing the same WebSphere
infrastructure in the Functional and Integration Testing Environment? Planning and executing the system changes in many Functional and Integration Testing Environment
WebSphere systems for different applications, and synchronizing these changes with
WebSphere production and stress-testing environments of many applications, may
become too much to manage. In other words, can our WebSphere project-management
maturity level support such highly complex change management and environment-
change coordination?

- In large WebSphere Virtual Enterprise-based WebSphere environments, serious application or system problems for one application must be communicated to a much wider
audience. Major cultural and communication model changes are needed in corporate
tradition and information management practice to promote a more open, transparent,
horizontally connected environment.

- Currently, large IT projects can be funded separately by separate business divisions.
Appropriately funding critical IT projects through a large shared infrastructure may be a
big challenge for many companies, especially for a large IT project that has specific
auditing requirements as a mandate.

Before these critical questions find valid answers, the immediate solution is not to share a large
WebSphere Virtual Enterprise–based Functional and Integration Testing Environment across
many large enterprise applications that belong to many business divisions. Instead, a large dedicated WebSphere Virtual Enterprise–based Functional and Integration Testing Environment for
one large and complex WebSphere project that has many critical applications belonging to the
same business division may provide an immediate solution to high utilization of WebSphere system resources. It also helps initiate a new trend for building WebSphere Virtual Enterprise–based
WebSphere environments for dynamic operation for either the WebSphere Functional and Integration Testing Environment or a WebSphere stress-testing environment.

Summary

This chapter discussed the major WebSphere Functional and Integration Testing Environment
support issues and choices. It introduced the WebSphere Functional and Integration Testing Support Operation. This chapter also explored the resource and workload considerations, as well as
the future directions of WebSphere Functional and Integration Testing Environment engineering
support. The quality of WebSphere engineering support for this environment directly affects its
availability, the progress of the overall project, and the quality of the WebSphere stress-testing
environment. Chapter 7 discusses WebSphere stress-testing environment support.

Stress-Testing Environment Support

The quality of the WebSphere stress-testing environment support is arguably the most critical aspect necessary for maintaining and defending WebSphere production system stability; it is more important than the WebSphere engineering support work for the other testing environments. The WebSphere stress-testing environment and the stress tests performed in it are absolutely the last line of defense against significant defects in application code and system configuration. The experiences shared in the chapter are important to WebSphere managers or senior consultants who are in charge of critical enterprise WebSphere systems.

This chapter covers the following WebSphere stress-testing environment support topics:

- Defining the WebSphere stress-testing environment
- The WebSphere Configuration Change Support Operation
- The WebSphere Stress-Testing Support Operation
- Common problems that result from insufficient stress testing
- Major challenges for WebSphere stress-testing environment support
- WebSphere production system stability and stress testing
- A look at the future work of WebSphere stress-testing environment

WebSphere Stress-Testing Environment

A WebSphere stress-testing environment is usually a large WebSphere environment with possibly multiple separate WebSphere systems that accommodate multiple releases and testing pipelines built to perform stress testing in a parallel fashion to achieve time-to-market objectives. It usually is similar or identical in configuration, topology, and capacity to the WebSphere production environment. Some of the systems of the WebSphere stress-testing environment may have the same code release level as that of the WebSphere production environment. For example, there can be at least one WebSphere system with a code release that is the same as in production for a critical WebSphere system in order to recreate, test, and resolve production problems. However, most WebSphere systems may have different application code releases that are going through stress testing in a parallel fashion.

Having test backends with the capacity of production is ideal but rarely seen because of financial costs and technical complexity. Therefore, a major difference between WebSphere production systems and WebSphere stress-testing systems is frequently the backend test region capacity. This is a significant constraint for stress testing. As a result, it is often difficult to duplicate one or more complete backend systems of equal capacity to that of the production system for stress testing the WebSphere application and system. Not surprisingly, this limitation occasionally results in vulnerabilities and defects in the WebSphere application and system that aren't uncovered during stress testing because of backend capacity constraints. Therefore, some defects may slip through to critical production environments and cause production instabilities.

WebSphere stress-testing environment support includes almost all WebSphere engineering support operations, from code deployment to performance tuning and testing (regression testing, stress testing, and ad-hoc testing). This chapter focuses on the WebSphere Configuration Change Support Operation and the WebSphere Performance Tuning and Testing Support Operation.

This chapter explains the details of the WebSphere Configuration Change Support Operation and the WebSphere Stress-Testing Support Operation by applying the WebSphere Operation Framework to these operations.

WebSphere Configuration Change Support Operation

WebSphere has many configurable items. The engineering operation is frequently what makes or breaks the stability of large WebSphere systems. The objective of this operation is to ensure the quality of the system configuration work.

Operation Framework and Description

This section systematically describes the WebSphere Configuration Change Support Operation applying the WebSphere Operations Framework.

Description

Many teams can require WebSphere configuration changes (for example, the WebSphere team, the testing team, and application development team). However, it is essential that the WebSphere team reviews configuration changes and has the authority to raise issues for review before configuration changes are applied. In addition, the WebSphere team must reserve the privilege of executing WebSphere configuration changes. Any WebSphere configuration changes to stress-testing environments need to closely follow a rigorous change-control process.

Entrance Criteria

- WebSphere configuration changes are identified, proposed, and documented by the WebSphere team or application development team.

WebSphere Resources

- Primary WebSphere support engineer
- Secondary WebSphere support engineer or WebSphere on-call engineer when the scheduled change is during off hours and the change does not require the personal attention of the primary WebSphere engineer responsible for the project

Activities

- Open a change-control ticket for the change. The change-control ticket may cover multiple WebSphere environments in the same development and testing pipeline to plan and track the change and maintain the consistency of the change across various environments of a large system.
- Submit the change-control ticket for approval following the change-control process or the emergency change-control process.
- Schedule the change.
- To ensure quality, perform a walkthrough if the change won't be performed by the primary WebSphere support engineer of the WebSphere application. The primary support engineer knows the target environment and is less likely to make a mistake.
- Perform the change within the approved change window, collaborating with other engineering teams and working with the environment change coordination team.[1]
- Perform post-change peer reviews for the change.
- Participate in the certification of the WebSphere environment.

Processes

- Change-control process
- Emergency change-control process
- WebSphere system work process

Artifacts

- Configuration automation program
- Change-Control Process Document
- Post-Change Peer Review Document
- WebSphere System Tracking Document

---

1. For an explanation of the environment change-coordination team, please refer to Chapter 1, "Organization Models and Choices."

External Teams

- Change managers who review, approve, and coordinate changes
- Application production support team
- Environment change-coordination team
- Other infrastructure engineering teams

Sign-Off Parties

- WebSphere production support team
- Stress-testing team

Exit Criteria

- Configuration changes have been successfully implemented
- Post-Change Peer Review has been performed, documented, and filed
- Configuration changes have been certified
- Change tickets have been closed or updated
- Configuration changes have been signed off on

Key Processes and Artifacts Explained

This section explains the processes and artifacts used in the WebSphere Configuration Change Support Operation.

Emergency Change-Control Process

Different companies may have different emergency change-control processes. However, an emergency change request and approval must be recorded in written format. This minimizes confusion and errors during production emergencies. For example, you may send the change manager on duty a concise email in order to get a written approval in the format of an email. Verbal communication can be ambiguous and difficult to track; therefore, it's not the best practice for emergency change-control purposes.

Post-Change Peer Review Document

The Post-Change Peer Review Document needs to have the following information: the change ticket number, the time when the change is performed, the name of the primary WebSphere engineer who makes the change, the name of the secondary WebSphere engineer who peer reviews the change, and the verbiage of the due diligence and sharing of the responsibility for the change performed. For example, you can include the following verbiage in this document:

We, the primary WebSphere engineer and the backup WebSphere engineer, diligently executed this authorized system change, and we carefully verified that the change made is accurate and free of errors. We agree to share responsibility for correctly performing this critical system change.

This document ensures change quality and accountability.

WebSphere System Tracking Document

The WebSphere System Tracking Document records and tracks your large WebSphere environments (for example, the server name, the IP address, version, its physical location, the project name, and other pertinent information). It is important to have a process in place in which your team can promptly update this document after making a WebSphere system change. An obsolete WebSphere System Tracking Document with inaccurate system information can cause confusion, rework, or even serious production support problems (for example, performing a system operation on the wrong server).

WebSphere Stress-Testing Support Operation

During stress testing, there are two parameter-tuning exercises: parameter tuning for problem avoidance, and parameter tuning for performance. A well-managed tuning exercise is the key to success. In addition, there are both application- and system-related WebSphere problems that may delay stress testing. The WebSphere team needs to work with the testing engineers and application developers to resolve these problems and provide routine support, such as application code deployment.

Operation Framework and Description

This section systematically describes the WebSphere Stress-Testing Support Operation applying WebSphere Operations Framework.

Description

Stress testing is critical before a WebSphere application goes into production. Although there are many objectives for the WebSphere team in promoting, encouraging, and insisting on a rigorous stress test, the primary goal is uncovering and correcting application and system defects to ensure production system stability and availability. The key for a good stress test is that it is done with a realistic load, which is identical to or more strenuous than that of production traffic. Proper testing duration that can reveal time-sensitive defects is also a critical factor of successful stress testing. This is because some defects show themselves only when a system is stable, and others only after a system has been running for a duration sufficient for time-sensitive errors to build up to a noticeable level.

The WebSphere tasks for stress testing are implementing WebSphere configuration changes, assisting in code deployments, helping in testing problem resolution, and performing WebSphere server administration (for example, starting, stopping, or synchronizing WebSphere servers). Most importantly, a WebSphere team that has the subject matter expertise in WebSphere performance optimization and problem avoidance can make recommendations to identify and remove performance bottlenecks. By doing so, they enhance system performance and isolate vulnerabilities, therefore avoiding production problems.

During stress testing, the application testing team may observe the completed throughput and the average response time on each type of request to identify performance bottlenecks. The WebSphere team uses several tools to monitor the system stability and system performance that are related to WebSphere Application Server processes. The monitored system resources include CPU, memory, disk input/output (I/O), network I/O, and others. Also, the WebSphere team monitors the state of the WebSphere Application Servers, including session, thread pool, database connection pool, garbage collection (GC), and Java Message Service (JMS) sessions. Last but not least, the WebSphere team responds to stability and performance issues of the testing environment and participates in problem determination and resolution.

It is not the WebSphere team's responsibility to collect and report application stability and performance data. However, the WebSphere system data that the WebSphere team collects helps validate and improve the stability and performance of the application.

Entrance Criteria

- WebSphere stress-testing environment is built and available.
- Stress-testing criteria are established.
- Projected traffic volume and pattern are gathered.
- Test cases and scripts are ready.
- Load generators are set.
- Stress-testing plan is developed, reviewed, and approved.
- Tools to collect WebSphere system stress data are standing by.
- Tools for JVM diagnostics are installed and tested.
- Tools to collect end-to-end transaction stress data are prepared.
- Performance baseline has been formed, if applicable.

WebSphere Resources

- Primary WebSphere support engineer
- Secondary WebSphere support engineer
- Application testing team
- Environment change-coordination team
- Application development team
- Other infrastructure engineering support team

Activities

- Deploy application code or assist in application code deployment, depending on the service level agreement (SLA).
- Perform WebSphere configuration changes.
- Operate WebSphere servers (start, stop, and synchronization).
- Operate Web servers.
- Collect and analyze WebSphere system resource usage data (for example, CPU, memory, disk space).
- Collect and analyze WebSphere server stability and performance status data (heap, CPU, database connection, thread, session, HTTP request, ORB request, JMS resources, among others).
- Lead or participate in problem resolution.
- Engage IBM WebSphere and Java support (opening IBM PMR tickets, uploading documents, and following up on PMR tickets).
- Analyze Web server stability and performance.
- Perform problem resolutions are related to Web servers or WebSphere plug-ins.
- Perform problem resolutions are related to WebSphere Application Servers.
- Perform post-change review and sign Post-Change Peer Review Document.

Processes

- Stress-testing process
- Change-control process
- Emergency change-control process
- Problem resolution process
- Post-change peer review process

Artifacts

- Stress-Testing Guideline Document (external to the WebSphere team)
- Performance data metrics (external to the WebSphere team)
- WebSphere stability and performance data collection procedure
- Problem Resolution Guideline and Procedure Document
- Post-Change Peer Review Document

Tools

- Deep dive JVM Diagnostic tool (for example, Introscope)
- WebSphere Tivoli Performance Viewer
- Change Management System

External Teams

- Stress-testing team
- IBM WebSphere and Java Support Organization
- Environment change-coordination team
- Application development team
- Other infrastructure engineering support teams (for example, the team that is responsible for the OS support)

Sign-Off Parties

- Stress-testing team

Exit Criteria

- Transaction per second (TPS), total current users (TCU) and average response time (ART) must meet or exceed the SLA. (This depends on the size of the test system compared to the size of the production system.)
- Stress test is signed off by testing team.
- Any major application and system problems uncovered during stress testing are satisfactorily resolved.
- WebSphere team is reasonably confident that the WebSphere application and system are adequately stress tested, meet performance targets, and are likely to be stable in the production environment.

Key Processes and Artifacts Explained

This section explains the processes and artifacts used in the WebSphere Stress-Testing Support Operation.

Problem Resolution Guideline and Procedure Document

The Problem Resolution Guideline and Procedure Document is where you record a structured approach to WebSphere problem resolution. For example, you can provide guidelines on problem resolution engagement and list the Web server and WebSphere Application Server components that you must examine to identify the problem. This document helps you be more consistent in your problem resolution work. In addition, the document must provide guidance for problem communication protocols so that the communication of the problem, especially that external to the WebSphere team, is experienced, constructive, and appropriate.

Common Problems Resulting from Insufficient WebSphere Stress Testing

The quality of the WebSphere engineering work in stress testing determines, to a large degree, how stable your production systems are. Insufficient stress testing may result in numerous production problems.

Profiling the WebSphere application is important. In an environment in which IT constantly tries to deliver early to satisfy business drivers, it is not uncommon that WebSphere applications are not profiled. This may lead to out-of-memory problems and thread or synchronization problems in production, especially when good stress testing is not adequately performed.

Stress testing can be insufficient in volume. When the traffic volume in production and stress testing has substantial gaps, the following problems occur because of application or system defects that may not be detected in a stress-testing environment. As a result, these potential problems can slip into your production WebSphere systems:

- Resource exhaustion that can include high CPU consumption, thread exhaustion, and connection pool saturation
- Process deadlocks
- Hung processes
- GC issues

When these problems occur in the production environment, they can cause serious instabilities and prolonged production outages (and therefore, heavy losses to IT and the business).

Testing data can be an issue. If adequate testing data is available, it is relatively easier to generate high volumes of traffic for stress testing. However, preparing a large amount of testing data is not an easy task. Worse, a frequent challenge prohibiting high volume testing is the backend system testing regions that have limited capacity because of environmental or financial reasons, or both. Large companies with complex IT systems sometimes may have to scrub real production data for testing purposes. This practice may produce unrealistic data that can invalidate the test and cause problems.

WebSphere stress testing can also be insufficient in duration. As a result, application code memory leaks and system anomalies that take time to show are not uncovered through stress testing and cause elusive and nagging instability issues in the production environment. Stress testing the WebSphere system and the application for eight hours or longer helps uncover time-sensitive defects and configuration issues. This kind of stress testing is called a *long duration test*,[2] or a *lingering test*. It's important to run this type of test long enough. However, this type of stress testing requires a large amount of testing data, significantly increases in workload for all the teams involved, and ties up critical testing environments for a long time. Therefore, it is not always possible to perform a long duration test, although it is a highly recommended best practice for achieving high system stability.

2. This type of test is more often seen in testing systems that demand high stability and reliability (for example, in testing new propulsion systems for rockets).

As a matter of experience, a great majority of the defects uncovered are in application code. Some are in WebSphere configuration, especially WebSphere configuration errors and inconsistencies between the stress-testing environment and production environment. The WebSphere Application Server is a set of large, mature, and stable technologies. Occasionally, WebSphere system defects occur and cause stress-testing difficulties and production system instabilities. Usually, there are fixes for these system defects. However, it is impossible to apply, test, and patch WebSphere systems for every fix that IBM releases. A limited number of defects exist as a normal state of the system between major WebSphere system upgrades and patches. It requires a balanced upgrade strategy and the cooperation and support from your business and technology partners to keep your WebSphere systems highly stable and available with the minimum exposure to system defects. Forming the right upgrade and patch policy is a matter of achieving an engineering balance in upgrade strategy and reaching agreement and compromise between the WebSphere team, project management, and application development and support teams. (Chapter 10, "System Upgrade and Product Maintenance Management," has detailed discussion of WebSphere system upgrade strategies.)

You are not the testing manager. You do not control the application testing and application defect resolution. However, you can promote, encourage, participate, support, and monitor the quality of stress testing in the stress-testing environment. Remember, this is your last line of defense against WebSphere application and system defects to maintain your production system stability. Assign experienced WebSphere engineers to the critical stress-testing environment support. They provide daily WebSphere support. Also, they watch stress testing closely, especially when the production date is imminent. You may want to request a concise weekly testing status report from your testing organization and discuss any concerns with project management, the testing organization, and the application support and development teams.

One or two weeks before the production date, you may want to meet with your engineers working in the stress-testing environment, review testing results, and determine whether adequate stress testing is performed in both volume and duration. If you conclude that the stress testing performed so far is not good enough and the problems uncovered are not addressed, you have to formally document and communicate your concerns to project management, the testing organization, application development teams, and your own management.

The document needs to be concise with an appropriate level of technical details so that it is suitable for senior management audiences. It is important to ask your testing organization to review the document and make changes according to their feedback. Such a documented communication is usually the last effort in defense of the WebSphere production system stability before major releases. You have to do a good job at communicating risks. At the same time, it is critical that you work to minimize negative impacts on work relationships when you send this document as a final attempt to address the testing problems. Provide clearly defined risk mitigation suggestions to address the issues. If your document only exposes risks resulting from inadequate stress testing without suggestions for what can be done to mitigate them, it may be considered as negative and unconstructive. This is discussed in more detail later.

Alleviate any perceptions that your testing organization may have about "surprise attack and unilateral communications." This document has to clearly display a positive and constructive attitude. The document can have the following four parts:

1. A **concise overview** of the background of the testing issue under discussion.

2. **Technical issues**, such as problems uncovered during testing, but not addressed (for example, a bug fix that has not been insufficiently stress tested). You must communicate technical issues without providing overwhelming technical details. Too much information drowns out your central message: The application needs more rigorous stress testing to adequately address the problems uncovered. Also, stick with the facts and refrain from sharing your observations and opinions.

3. **Risks to the production environment** (for example, possible instability and outages). You have to be as specific as possible about the risks and their possible impact to the customer experience and your company's bottom line. It may help to assess the risks according to a risk level system, such as HIGH, MEDIUM, LOW, LIKELY, and UNLIKELY. However, it is difficult to predict future events and their severity levels. Be prudent in providing a risk level assessment. Otherwise, your credibility is at risk.

4. **Risk mitigation suggestions**. Include this section, although sometimes it seems impossible to identify any risk mitigation measures. Without this section, your document may be perceived as unconstructive.

This is a highly sensitive document. By documenting and communicating production risks right before a major application release goes into production, you take considerable risks in terms of teamwork, project momentum, senior management concerns, and perceptions from the business. It's not about criticizing others' work, but protecting the production WebSphere environment and the business from risk. However, no amount of teamwork and communication skills can change the sensitive nature of this communication. Be careful and tactful, but never falter from the courage, determination, and professionalism to do the right thing.

The last section of the document must have an accountability clause. The accountability clause must clearly state the responsibilities to enhance accountability. For example, in the accountability clause, you can assert that because of the lack of stress testing, production instabilities occurred and need to be addressed by the application development organization, which decided to substantially reduce the time for stress testing.

As a teamwork consideration and communication-savvy approach, ask the teams involved to review your risk exposure and mitigation document draft. Carefully listen to and seriously consider their input before you officially release the document to the teams and senior management. In addition, you may not have to officially release this document. After reviewing the draft, the responsible team may decide to correct this problem of inadequate stress testing. Therefore, you may not need to make the document publicly available to your IT organization.

Major Challenges for Stress-Testing Environment WebSphere Engineering Support

A stress-testing environment is a busy and tough environment in which to provide WebSphere engineering support. The following are frequently observed challenges:

- Increasingly interconnected WebSphere systems significantly increase the workload of the stress-testing environment and the complexity of managing the environment.
- The stress-testing environment may not be built to perform stress testing for large interconnected WebSphere systems.
- Application code quality issues significantly affect the stress-testing workload and degree of stress-testing difficulties.
- Stress-testing environment support is resource intensive for all infrastructure support teams, including the WebSphere team.

Interconnected WebSphere Systems and Increased Workload and Complexity

The fact that enterprise systems are increasingly interconnected substantially increases the amount of testing work. This is true in the sheer amount of testing work that has to be done, as well as in the high complexity of large interconnected WebSphere systems, for which it is difficult to perform meaningful stress testing. WebSphere application stress testing used to be self-contained within one large WebSphere application suite, but enterprise information systems are more and more interconnected. It is now compulsory to test a WebSphere application with other interconnected systems. This requires communicating, planning, coordinating, and performing stress testing over numerous large enterprise projects, across many technical teams and business organizations. Also, this may involve stress testing many applications with different technologies and network communication protocols. To do a good job in communication, project planning, coordination, and execution within one large IT project is challenging enough. To manage these tasks for many large enterprise systems is a substantially more ambitious undertaking. Some integrated testing tool vendors have started to address this need for testing interconnected systems with promising products and technologies.[3]

However, in the stress-testing space, the industry has yet to witness viable testing tools to help with interconnected systems stress testing. Also, there has to be organizational adjustments and engineering process regeneration in order to support interconnected stress testing. Frankly, before the right organization model, engineering processes, testing technologies, and communication model are in place, interconnected stress testing continues to be a daunting challenge and, at best, inadequately done. There is a price to pay for not doing a good job at such a critically

---

3. Chris Benedetto. "SOA and Integration Testing: The End-to-End View," *SOA World Magazine*, (September 2007). http://webservices.sys-con.com/read/275057.htm.

important task. Often, a seemingly harmless and insignificant minor change in one system may lead to serious problems in other interconnected systems. Worse, such a minor problem may even cause a cascade of failures of interconnected critical WebSphere systems and lead to grave losses for both IT and the business. Chapter 12, "Managing the Stability of Large Enterprise WebSphere Systems," discusses the stability of large and interconnected WebSphere systems.

Stress-Testing Environment May Not Be Built to Perform Stress Testing for Interconnected Systems

Ideally, a stress-testing WebSphere environment needs to mimic production in topology, configuration, and application release level. Often, this is true, at least for one of the multiple stress-testing WebSphere systems. For a large WebSphere project, there are frequently multiple stress-testing WebSphere systems. However, the limiting factor usually comes from the backend testing regions that may not have the capacity to sustain the stress-testing volume identical to that of production. For example, a mainframe database testing region may not have the same capacity as the production system. A WebSphere stress-testing environment designed and built for a given large project may have other enterprise systems interconnecting to it in later development. Therefore, it may not have the necessary new components to conduct the stress testing against these newly added execution paths. For instance, it may be difficult to generate the kind of assembled and serialized complex composite message traffic to stress test multiple interconnected systems. We are confronted with many challenges today in properly stress testing interconnected systems, such as the static and dedicated nature of WebSphere infrastructure, the project management maturity level, and current organization models that dedicate stress-testing environments to different large IT projects. Performing coordinated stress testing in this environment demands changes. You have to embrace creative strategies, innovative thinking, and the willingness to experiment with new technologies and processes.

Resource Intensive for the WebSphere Team

For the WebSphere team, supporting the WebSphere stress-testing environment perhaps is the most resource intensive among all the WebSphere engineering support areas.

Most of the application defects and configuration issues are uncovered and resolved in this environment. This is especially true when rigorous and well-planned stress testing is being consistently performed. The quality of the application code directly affects the human resource consumption of the WebSphere team. Many difficult and complex application defects demand a lot of time from the WebSphere team to resolve. IT finance management practices and work request processes may not always allow the WebSphere team adequate resources to cover the steep cost of supporting low-quality code. Such costs can be consistently underestimated, if not totally hidden because it is difficult to predict code quality and perform project change control based on application code quality. The WebSphere team typically has neither the technical means nor the management privilege to evaluate the quality of the application code and satisfy resource requirements accordingly. In addition, any assessment or communication over application code quality, perceptional or factual, is an extremely sensitive issue. For example, to the application development and support organization, questions about application code quality may sound more like a lack of confidence in its work versus trying to solve the problem.

You have to do both jobs well. First, you have to allocate adequate resources for the critical engineering support of the WebSphere stress-testing environments. Second, while doing so, you have to be careful to not get yourself and your team into any political hot water. Doing the right thing for your team sometimes means having tremendous managerial courage not to tackle systemic issues at that moment and focusing on delivering immediate engineering value to your company.

These large and costly stress-testing WebSphere environments are most likely to be highly utilized in stress testing many parallel application code releases. These are busy environments in which much work is being done. For example, you may find your team supporting many WebSphere stress-testing systems with full redundancy and failover, taking simultaneous stress testing tasks on a 24/7 basis. Occasionally, these large and complex WebSphere environments can be overwhelming, even to the most experienced WebSphere professionals. To orderly manage such a large and dynamic WebSphere stress-testing environment and before you can spend less time fixing the stress-testing environment, you are better off spending more time in the following three areas. If you do a good job in these critical areas, you may find that your WebSphere stress-testing environment support becomes more manageable:

1. Create a good WebSphere system tracking document that records and tracks the WebSphere systems that you have for the large and complex WebSphere stress-testing environment. You can include system information, such as IP address, release level, data center name, OS level, key technical contacts, and server names. You can also use an automated system providing the same capability as that of a hard copy document to track stress-testing WebSphere systems. Develop a WebSphere system work process so that your team makes timely updates to the system tracing document so that it contains accurate system information.

2. A rigid change-control process is absolutely necessary for the stability of WebSphere stress-testing environments. The testers and developers sometimes want to change WebSphere configuration parameters on the fly. Because so much work must be done to the WebSphere stress-testing environment, hundreds of WebSphere parameters have to change, and with so many teams working together in the same environment, working without a rigid change-control process can force everyone to spend a lot of time fixing the resulting mess. The project suffers unnecessary delays because of difficulties coming from testing environment conflicts and instabilities. All changes must go through a careful approval process and all WebSphere configuration changes must be performed by the WebSphere engineering support team. The next section discusses change control in detail.

3. Promote the environment change-coordination team that plans and coordinates all the release testing work and environment changes. With an environment change-coordination team helping out in planning and coordinating stress-testing work, your stress-testing WebSphere support work becomes easier and less error prone, especially in coordination with other technical teams. An environment change-coordination team saves you time and improves the quality of the service delivery.

These stress-testing environments are usually used by a global workforce on a 24/7 basis. When you work with global testing teams and application development teams, you have WebSphere engineering support requests 24/7. This adds to your overall resource consumption. A viable solution is to build a global team with teammates operating from different time zones to better deal this type of WebSphere support requests.

Production WebSphere Systems Stability and Stress Testing

If you want to know how stable your production WebSphere system will be, look closely at your stress-testing WebSphere environment, testing status, and results. You have good reason to watch your testing environments closely, because they are a reliable indicator of your production system stability, or rather instability. If you have no major problems in the following WebSphere areas, you have solid reasons to expect a stable production WebSphere environment.

The WebSphere application has been tested according to a testing schedule with the projected volume and traffic pattern. Be particularly alert about repeated delays in stress tests that usually are good signs of nagging problems. Sometimes, addressing application problems uncovered during system integration testing may leave no time for stress testing. An application release going into production without adequate stress testing likely destabilizes your production WebSphere environment.

WebSphere application defects and WebSphere system issues have been adequately addressed. Testing status reports have been regularly shared and issues clearly communicated. Your WebSphere engineers assigned to work at WebSphere stress-testing environment are confident that adequate testing has been performed and the new application release is unlikely to cause production WebSphere system stability issues. Let's look at best practices in these areas.

Communication

Your WebSphere engineer working in the stress-testing environment needs to quickly communicate critical issues to the WebSphere team member in charge of the production environment (if managed by different engineers) and the WebSphere manager. This allows the team an opportunity to carefully evaluate the production stability impact of these issues and take appropriate actions in addressing any concerns that it may have. This communication and teamwork is especially critical immediately before the production date, when the application code that has been stress tested in the testing environment is migrated to the production environment. If your stability concerns, after repeated and documented communication, are not addressed to your satisfaction, you may want to consider using a risk exposure and mitigation document to share your concerns and inputs. It is important to document and formally communicate your concerns as early as possible before sharing a formal document. The intent is to reduce the impact to the project progress and reduce possible teamwork issues while doing the right thing for the project. Your team may be perceived as constructive if you communicate concerns as early as possible rather than surprising testing and application teams with last-minute concerns. Also, it is a positive thing to share the risk analysis document draft with the affected teams. It helps to maintain work relationships during a trying moment, and this prepares the affected teams for your important communication. If you wait until the last minute to send this document without asking them to review it, they may feel that your communication could have been done earlier. The document sounds more like a surprise attack rather than a positive move to solve stress-testing problems to the affected teams. Be aware of the overall organization involved and communicate critical issues with a genuine intent to be considerate to the other technical teams and improve teamwork. Although it is not easy, you can do a good job if you are committed to both communicating a serious concern in testing while trying to improve work relationships.

Promote Long Duration Stress Tests

Promoting and advocating long duration testing is an effective way to ensure production WebSphere system stability. This type of stress testing can reveal elusive application and system defects, such as slow memory leaks and time-sensitive thread contention. Long duration tests are arguably one of the best ways to prevent hidden problems being migrated with the application release to critical production WebSphere systems. However, it is not easy to perform long duration tests that need a large amount of testing data and use testing resources for a long period of time. The project management and testing teams need persistent encouragement to fully appreciate and support performing long duration tests. Because of the long testing duration, you may consider running long duration tests over weekends.

WebSphere Environment Consistency

It is of paramount importance to keep your stress-testing environment and your target production environment highly consistent in WebSphere configuration settings. Many serious production problems, which result in heavy losses, can be traced back to minor and seemingly insignificant WebSphere stress-testing environment configuration and target production system configuration inconsistencies. Therefore, carefully compare the final WebSphere configuration of your stress-testing environment and your target production WebSphere system right before production deployment. It is equally important to do the same WebSphere configuration comparison after the production deployment to ensure that the WebSphere configuration has not been changed to incorrect settings during the migration operations.

Because of the numerous WebSphere configuration parameters, you need a sophisticated configuration comparison automation program. You can develop this configuration comparison automation program in house to best suit your needs, or purchase commercially available off-the-shelf software.

Develop an effective and practical process to manually inspect the specific WebSphere configuration items that have been changed following a change-management process before and after the configuration change.

WebSphere configuration inconsistencies between production WebSphere system and the stress-test WebSphere system are frequently suspected for serious production problems, and sometimes they are the culprit. Having an established process to both programmatically and manually compare and ensure WebSphere system consistencies helps the technical teams focus their attention in the right direction of problem isolation and resolution, rather than wasting precious time worrying about WebSphere system inconsistencies when there is a production outage.

Strict Change Control

It is difficult to find arguments against the importance of change management in achieving high system stability and availability. However, it is not difficult to come up with actual engineering practices that bypass change management, especially during an emergency or under tremendous project progress pressure. Certainly, no change-control process is perfect. Indeed, it takes time to manage changes in an orderly fashion following established processes. However, if you do not follow change-control processes, your WebSphere environment may become inconsistent, causing you to waste time identifying configuration errors.

Consider using the same change-control ticket for both your WebSphere stress-testing environment and your target production WebSphere environment. This should minimize documentation errors and enhance production system stability.

The worst situation in which you can find yourself is that you are working with business partners who do not follow the change-control process at all because of the uneven maturity level within your IT organization. Have the courage to say no. Insist that change-control processes must be followed. Never hesitate to lead. People are smart and they will appreciate your leadership, follow your example, and diligently perform change control when they learn that following an established change-control process not only makes their life easier, but also makes them more successful in their job.

Future Directions of Stress-Testing Environment Support

In looking at the future work of WebSphere stress-testing engineering support, WebSphere configuration comparison software is a big task. Some of the recent commercial software can only be compared vertically, as different versions of WebSphere configurations of the same WebSphere environment, rather than comparing configurations of different WebSphere environments. One option is to build such configuration comparison programs in house. Building such a WebSphere configuration automation program in house has challenges, too. The WebSphere team usually has the programming talents to design and code its own automation scripts. However, it is challenging to thoroughly test the automation programs and provide technical support for these programs for a large organization with multiple WebSphere teams. After all, the WebSphere engineering support team is not a software development organization. Occasionally, serious production problems do occur, due to incomplete testing of "homemade" WebSphere configuration automation programs. An ideal situation is to buy a WebSphere configuration program that conforms to your company configuration management strategy, and that is also practical and simple to use.

Another big question for the near future is whether to use WebSphere Virtual Enterprise for the design and building of the WebSphere stress-testing environment. Can WebSphere Virtual Enterprise be used for stress tests independent of a production environment that is built by using WebSphere Network Deployment? For example, can you build a WebSphere Virtual Enterprise-based stress-testing environment to share among major applications that achieves higher utilization of WebSphere infrastructure? If you can, should you also build your production WebSphere systems in WebSphere Virtual Enterprise? In other words, can you build WebSphere testing environments using WebSphere Virtual Enterprise, but use WebSphere Application Server Network Deployment to build production WebSphere environments? These are questions and choices that WebSphere managers, consultants, and engineers have to deal with in the near future, if not immediately.

The last area to tackle is how to design, implement, support, and manage an effective WebSphere stress-testing environment for large and complex interconnected WebSphere enterprise applications. There is much work to do in understanding how to design and build a WebSphere stress-testing environment to effectively stress test large interconnected WebSphere systems for composite applications.

Summary

This chapter explored WebSphere stress-testing environment support. It discussed challenges, problems, and best practices in supporting WebSphere stress-testing environments. It described WebSphere operations in configuration change and WebSphere stress-testing engineering support. This chapter emphasized and introduced the importance of stress testing (especially long duration testing). It talked about the relationship between the WebSphere production environment and the WebSphere stress-testing environment. Last, but not the least, this chapter provided some thoughts on the future directions of WebSphere stress-testing environment support. The next chapter covers production environment support.

CHAPTER 8

Production Environment Support

WebSphere production environments are where "the rubber meets the road." This is the final test of your WebSphere organization's technical rigor, the engineering maturity of your team, and the process excellence of your practice. This test is brutally direct and honest and will conspicuously prove the stability and availability of your WebSphere systems. By the same token, the lack of these qualities in your WebSphere infrastructure will become clear.

The WebSphere production environment is not a place where engineering inadequacy can hide. The performance of your production WebSphere environment is similar to the performance of a military organization or of professional athletes. Neither eloquent communication nor suave political skills can make your WebSphere production environment look better. You either succeed or not—both in a measurable and an unambiguous manner.

When your production WebSphere system is consistently stable, your business partners can do what they need to do in providing products and services to the users, either internal or external. If your business partners cannot do their jobs because of numerous WebSphere infrastructure issues, and are therefore questioning when the WebSphere systems are stable, you have a big problem.

Considering the fact that one hour of unscheduled downtime for a large production Web-Sphere environment may translate into millions of dollars in direct losses, frequent WebSphere production fires can cause serious damages to a large corporation's bottom line and dampen the goodwill of its customers. Worse, for interconnected WebSphere systems—which are becoming the trend—one WebSphere production system's instability may cause cascading failures of many other interconnected systems, with snowballing financial impacts and catastrophic consequences. Finally, frequent production instability is both demoralizing and debilitating to the WebSphere team. Instability deprives the WebSphere engineers of the opportunity to develop engineering processes, document systems, and improve skills because they are constantly firefighting.

171

Therefore, the WebSphere team may be trapped in negative cycles of production instability that feed on technical skill inadequacy, the lack of technical documentation, and problematic engineering processes that, in turn, leads to more production instability.

Other than technical factors, achieving stable production WebSphere systems is difficult because today's large IT organization does not live in a perfect world. Many systemic issues, whether they're organizational, financial, or cultural challenges, are beyond the direct control of the WebSphere team. In addition, these systemic problems are aggravated by the sheer size and complexity of the operations of large IT organizations. All these issues make maintaining highly stable large WebSphere systems a tough challenge. For example, one of the major challenges to the stability of large WebSphere environments is application code defects. Although the WebSphere team must be responsible for production WebSphere system stability, the WebSphere team has no direct control over application code quality that significantly affects stability. Also, it is difficult to promptly isolate and correct these application code defects because of the size and complexity of both the operation and organization. WebSphere system stability, the cost of WebSphere system operations, and the workload of WebSphere engineering support usually have a direct relationship to application code quality. For example, when a large application is sourced to a less expensive and less experienced development organization, the application code quality frequently takes a hit at the beginning. As a result, the WebSphere engineering support cost goes up. Sometimes, a WebSphere team can spend up to 90 percent of its engineering time on participating, assisting, and occasionally leading the troubleshooting process for application code defects. For an application with questionable code quality, application code defects can pop up weekly, or even daily, and become a tremendous challenge to WebSphere system stability, a heavy burden to a WebSphere team in terms of workload, and a dire challenge for resource allocation.

WebSphere code deployment or application release management for the WebSphere team can be a set of tough choices in terms of technology, organization, and engineering processes.

The dynamic nature of a large production WebSphere environment makes maintaining stability and availability challenging and complicated. Large WebSphere applications can have many development and testing pipelines with multiple application releases working in parallel. You can have a new release every week to apply application code fixes or to implement new functions and provide new services. A new application release usually requires corresponding WebSphere configuration changes. This change combination further complicates the endeavor for high WebSphere system stability. This is especially true when there are serious production issues. Because both the application code and the WebSphere configuration have been changed, it is more difficult to isolate the production problem and to quickly determine whether the root cause is from application code, WebSphere configuration, or both.

The last challenge for WebSphere production environment is again the size and the complexity of large applications and number of integrated components and systems. Of course, the outcome of changes and operations needs to be predictable, especially in production. Otherwise, it must not go to production. However, because of the limitation of engineering practice and technical capabilities, sometimes it is not easy to predict the outcome of interconnected changes and operations to all the interconnected systems. Chapter 12, "Managing the Stability of Large Enterprise WebSphere Systems," discusses why interconnected changes and operations are difficult to predict. It also discusses why interconnected changes can have a significant impact on stability and can be unmanageable. As a consequence, it is difficult to always avoid operations and configuration mistakes that may seriously affect the normal execution of WebSphere production systems. Working with a number of such large and critical WebSphere production systems, surely we can learn many lessons and share many experiences.

This chapter covers the following topics:

- Lessons learned
- Best practices and experience sharing
- WebSphere Application Release Support Operation
- WebSphere Data Center Switch Support Operation

Lessons Learned

This section discusses some of the most common mistakes in production WebSphere environment support. Any of these problems can significantly contribute to your production WebSphere system stability and availability problems. This section reviews the lessons learned in the following areas:

- Documentation
- Testing
- Configuration
- Tooling
- Capacity planning
- Communication
- Upgrade strategy

Lack of Documentation

In many IT organizations, documentation seems to be the last priority. Daily we see as an industry practice large software systems and large IT infrastructure that are built without adequate, accurate, and updated documentation (or any documentation at all). Even experienced IT leaders frequently fail to understand that the lack of documentation for large IT systems is responsible for many of their quality problems in products and services delivered. An accurate, concise, and promptly updated set of system documentation helps you achieve precise environment tracking, improve the quality of daily WebSphere engineering support, effectively train new members of the team, and promote teamwork and a team-based approach to WebSphere engineering.

WebSphere System Tracking

The WebSphere system tracking set of documentation is good for your WebSphere systems because it allows you to accurately track your large and complex WebSphere environment. If the document is updated in a timely manner, it helps you understand the changes made to your Web-Sphere system. Therefore, you always have precise and updated critical system information at your fingertips. It is not easy to accurately identify the technical details of your critical Web-Sphere systems at any given moment because of their enormous size and complexity. It is equally difficult to follow critical project contact changes and numerous system changes that are constantly occurring for large and dynamic WebSphere systems. This difficulty in precisely differentiating and tracking your large WebSphere system increases the probability of system operation and configuration errors. The WebSphere System Tracking Document is a powerful tool to help you overcome this difficulty. The lack of WebSphere system tracking documentation significantly raises the likelihood of WebSphere system instability.

Application Support Documentation

A clear, comprehensive, and concise document about the WebSphere applications supported is an effective knowledge-management system that powerfully facilitates your daily WebSphere engineering support operations. To expect a WebSphere engineer to remember all of your large and complex WebSphere applications and depend on her memory in performing system operations for these applications is both unreasonable and dangerous. By using a good WebSphere Application Support Document, a WebSphere engineer can quickly identify critical information, such as the business description of the application, WebSphere topology and system layout, system tools, and key application support contacts to perform a prompt and quality WebSphere engineering support job. This is especially true for the WebSphere on-call engineer dealing with production emergencies. The lack of a WebSphere Application Support Document is a major hurdle for the team in its effort to provide high quality WebSphere application support service.

Team Approach

Both the WebSphere System Tracking and WebSphere Application Support Documents promote a team approach to large WebSphere projects. Without these documents, the primary WebSphere engineer takes with him all the knowledge about the large WebSphere project that he has been responsible for when he leaves the team or is unavailable for an extended period of time. Thus, your team may have problems performing a quality job in supporting the concerned WebSphere applications. Usually, a WebSphere team adapting an individual approach to WebSphere engineering support—rather than a team approach—has no technical documentation or other forms of knowledge management systems. In addition, WebSphere teams with no technical documentation for their WebSphere systems usually suffer a high level of system inconsistencies that not only affect WebSphere system stability, but also prevent WebSphere operation automation.

Documentation and Repeatable Processes

Documentation and established, repeatable, and scriptable processes go hand in hand. The simplest possible WebSphere Production On-Call Document goes a long way in growing the quality of your team's WebSphere engineering service delivery. This is because now you have a documented and repeatable process that is the foundation for engineering process optimization. As soon as you have a documented engineering process, it is possible for your team to work on WebSphere engineering process optimization.

A WebSphere team with good documentation practice is likely to be a competitive team because it is proactively performing knowledge management, using a team approach to WebSphere engineering, and every member of the team truly knows all the WebSphere systems and applications that it supports. A WebSphere team that has good documentation tends to be a team of orderly and disciplined engineering practices rather than a group of system engineers who are constantly bogged down in improvised chaos and disorder.

Lack of Testing

In the space of testing, the lack of stress testing, the lack of longer running testing, and the lack of testing communication and reporting are frequently encountered as major issues that affect the stability of the WebSphere production environment. The attitude of a WebSphere team toward testing is usually a good sign of the engineering maturity of the team. A mature WebSphere team understands the importance of testing and tirelessly works with its business partners to achieve testing excellence, while a fledgling WebSphere team finds testing as a last-minute consideration, if it's considered at all.

Lack of Stress Testing

The gravest threat to the WebSphere production system stability is the lack of stress testing. Good stress testing is difficult to achieve. It takes time to prepare test data, tools, get environments ready, and coordinate technical teams participating in the stress test. Usually, stress testing is more likely to be compromised because of intense release schedule pressures. This is especially true when the application code quality or environmental issues prevent the normal progress of stress testing. In this situation, stress testing may become only a reduced number of nominal tests that do not uncover any application code defects or system problems.

Inadequate Testing Load

Inadequate testing load can be a serious problem in stress testing. Frequently, because of backend capacity constraints, financial resource shortage, and environmental limitations, it is not always possible to have the same traffic load as that of the production system during stress testing. This gap in stress-testing load sometimes leads to capacity-sensitive WebSphere system issues in the production environment.

Lack of Long Duration Testing

The ideal stress-testing scenario involves a set of long duration tests with testing length equal to the normal execution length of the application, which is usually five full business days. Long duration tests can reveal time-sensitive system and application issues (for example, a slow memory leak that leads to unpredictable WebSphere system crashes). Yes, long duration tests are expensive in both testing data preparation and tying up critical and expensive stress-testing environments. However, even long duration tests of four to eight hours help expose many time-sensitive defects; therefore, they are highly valuable. The lack of long duration tests may mask elusive system or application defects and cause serious and nagging instabilities.

Lack of Testing Communication

Communication during testing is as important as testing itself for a large IT organization in which many technical teams work together to ensure the quality and stability of critical IT systems. A weekly testing status report is important for the WebSphere team and other technical teams to understand the status, details, and issues of testing. This is especially important before a major application code migration to the production environment or implementation of important WebSphere system changes on production servers. The WebSphere team needs to carefully read the weekly testing status update. If such a communication is not part of your testing organization's practice, the WebSphere manager or senior consultant must require a weekly update on the critical testing status and before every major production release.

Code-Deployment Coordination

Application code deployment can be done by three different teams: the WebSphere team, the application production support team, and the application deployment team.

The application deployment team is a technical team that applies tools and processes and specializes in code migration for many IT projects. The application deployment team can achieve a high degree of automation of application code deployment and a high level of quality consistency because of its specialization. Therefore, it needs to be the preferred approach for application code deployment, especially production code deployment. However, the initial collaboration between the WebSphere team and the application deployment team and the hookup between the application deployment scripts by the WebSphere team and the application code deployment programs managed by the application deployment team can be time-consuming, complicated, and challenging. Before this collaboration and hookup are fully tested, many application code deployment problems can occur for major code releases. These application code-deployment issues can cause major rework and delays, and therefore become a serious threat to production system stability and availability.

A best practice is to use a consistent application code approach for the production environment, stress-testing environment, development, and other testing environments. This consistent approach gives the WebSphere team and the application deployment team an opportunity to fully test automated application code migration in development and testing environments. Code deployment in development and testing environments is good practice on collaboration and hookup between the WebSphere team and the application deployment team to ensure quality before the application code-deployment strategy is used in the production environment.

Configuration Management Issues

WebSphere configuration errors account for a significant number of WebSphere system-induced instabilities. In the production WebSphere environment, the following needs to be avoided.

Dynamic Systems

Key WebSphere systems are dynamic. However, it is still important to try hard to reduce the frequency of configuration changes whenever possible and appropriate. Less frequent configuration changes significantly reduce the probability of configuration and operation errors; therefore, it helps maintain system stability.

Separate Changes

If possible, avoid implementing important WebSphere system changes with major application releases. Combining the application code changes with WebSphere system changes can be misleading and confusing, especially when you have production problems and resulting outages after implementing these changes. If you encounter production system problems, it is more complex and more difficult to isolate the problem. Also, it is more difficult to focus on the problem area because the technical teams do not know whether it is primarily an application issue or a WebSphere infrastructure problem because both have been changed.

Configuration Errors

Configuration errors are among the most difficult system defects to uncover. The key is prevention. WebSphere system configuration errors may damage the WebSphere engineering support team's reputation. Many of them look so ridiculously simple that they seemingly should never occur. Many of your business partners and customers do not fully understand that there are hundreds of configuration items for WebSphere Application Server, and sometimes human error happens, despite the WebSphere team's best efforts. Your business partners and customers may also remember the mistakes that others have made. For example, it does not really matter if you have only one WebSphere configuration error during a three-year period. The first thing a business partner may say next time a production problem occurs is, "The WebSphere team needs to examine whether the WebSphere configurations are correct." It is in your best interest to try to prevent WebSphere configuration errors from happening. You can conduct system audits, peer inspections for system changes, and configuration comparisons between target and source WebSphere environments for intended configuration changes. You can also take advantage of other processes and mechanisms in your efforts to prevent configuration errors.

Environment Inconsistency

WebSphere production-environment configuration inconsistencies to your stress-testing Web-Sphere environment can cause serious production problems and unscheduled system outages. Make sure that your production WebSphere system is identical in configuration to that of your stress-testing WebSphere environment in which the WebSphere configuration and the current production application release have been tested. Because of many configuration parameters, you are better off using a WebSphere configuration comparison program to perform this task. Even if you use an automation program, comparing and then analyzing and interpreting the results can be a time-consuming task. You may want to allocate enough time before the production migration to accurately perform this comparison. Also, without adequate WebSphere knowledge and skills, it is difficult to correctly interpret the differences found. It may not be productive to share a "raw" result data file from the system configuration comparison with your business partners and customers. If you do have to share the result data file from the system configuration comparison, you have to give your business partners and customers the proper knowledge to correctly interpret the findings and carefully walk them through the details. Otherwise, you may spend more frustrating hours explaining what the results data really means, especially those differences that are normal because of environmental settings, but nonetheless may look suspicious to inexperienced eyes.

Lack of Tooling

Not using deep dive diagnostic tooling and an end-to-end transaction monitoring facility may not cause production system issues, but it certainly won't help you promptly identify and fix major production problems.

The lack of a deep dive diagnostic tool capable of looking into the Java Virtual Machine (JVM) and getting performance and troubleshooting data seriously limits the WebSphere team's ability to prevent and resolve problems. Without a deep dive diagnostic tool, it is nearly impossible to identify the root cause of many application defects and system issues that occur within the JVM. As a result, the root cause of many recurring problems cannot be found; instead, the WebSphere engineers may have to depend on a workaround to restore service (for example, periodically recycling the WebSphere Application Servers or blindly adding system capacity).

It is a serious system-stability challenge to not have a good end-to-end transaction monitoring tool that can perform monitoring functions spanning multiple protocols and technologies and precisely reveal the state of a specific transaction. Without such a monitoring facility, it is difficult to know whether the problem is at the enterprise application integration layer (EAI) using TIBCO or the DB2 data store on the mainframe. Of course, there are layers of other system components where the problem may be occurring (for example, a large number of security servers, load balancing devices, firewalls, and Web servers or WebSphere Application Servers, among many others). Chapter 12 talks more about tooling and large system stability.

Capacity Planning

The current practice of capacity planning is all about traditional system resources, such as memory, CPU, disk space, and network capacity. These traditional system resources continue to be important. However, the lack of what I call deep capacity planning is causing problems. *Deep capacity planning* regards thread pool, JVM instances, and database connections, among other resources managed by the middleware (for example, WebSphere Application Server) as essential system resources and performs capacity planning on these "deep" system resources. The lack of deep capacity planning hurts WebSphere system stability. The traditional capacity planning focusing on CPU, memory, disk space, and network bandwidth is still important. However, the need for deep capacity planning is becoming apparent, particularly when you have plenty of overall CPU and memory resources, but your thread pool is saturated and causes an unscheduled outage because of an increase in traffic load.

An argument challenging the notion of deep capacity planning asserts that capacity planning needs to be approached in its traditional role: to be concerned only with the system resources area where the increase of capacity is frequently associated with purchasing recommendation and decisions (for example, system memory, processor, and disk space). In addition, system resources/parameters, such as threads and connection pools, seem to be the concern of performance tuning. This is true in the traditional sense of capacity planning and performance tuning. However, in the brave new world of middleware engineering that tries to support Internet scale data centers of huge but unpredictable workload, the system resources that are exhausted are seldom CPU or system memory or disk space. Instead, the problems usually come from issues such as thread saturation in response to a traffic spike. The WebSphere team and the testing engineers must work together to tune these parameters in problem avoidance and performance enhancement. However, it is a huge challenge in making the right system configuration that ensures the applications have adequate traditional and nontraditional system resources to respond powerfully to today's Internet computing without a dedicated capacity planning team. Such a team has both an enterprise vision of many systems and the specialized tools and processes to monitor, analyze, report, and recommend system resources, such as threads and connections responding to system workload change, while working with the WebSphere team and the testing teams. The need for deep capacity planning is especially acute for an interconnected environment in which WebSphere system A may have a pending change that mandates how WebSphere system B needs to configure its Web container thread pool. Chapter 11, "Critical Work Relationships," discusses the need for deep capacity planning and challenges for the capacity planning team.

Communication Failure

Large IT projects depend on many technical teams working in collaboration and cooperating with each other. To keep the teams synchronized, the right level of communication between technical teams is of paramount importance. Communication failure between organizations can cause serious WebSphere production problems. For example, an interconnected enterprise system increases traffic volume to one of your critical WebSphere systems. The traffic volume changes from a few thousand messages a day to a few million. Without any knowledge of this change, the WebSphere team won't be able to do the testing and system tuning necessary to adequately deal with this significant traffic volume and pattern changes. As a result, your WebSphere system may run out of database connections or Web container threads and become unstable. With WebSphere systems becoming increasingly interconnected, timely and formal interproject and interorganization communication is indispensable for WebSphere system stability and smooth production operations. Chapter 12 provides a solution to overcome this communication challenge.

Upgrade Strategy Challenges

WebSphere upgrades are not simple tasks that merely involve applying a new WebSphere system software release. WebSphere upgrades are complex and involved. This section only covers a few WebSphere upgrade topics. Chapter 10, "System Upgrade and Product Maintenance Management," systematically discusses the WebSphere Production Maintenance Operation that focuses on the details of WebSphere system upgrade management:

- Test the new WebSphere release with the target application code releases all the way from the development and testing WebSphere environment to the stress-testing WebSphere environment for each development and testing pipeline.

- Assist the application development team to identify, plan, and implement any necessary application code changes (for example, replacing deprecated functions).

- Plan and coordinate a WebSphere upgrade through the development and testing pipeline. Amid fast-paced application and system changes, this planning and coordinating job is not trivial.

- Resolve system, application, and integration issues during the upgrade operation.

- Manage possible WebSphere topology changes, WebSphere security changes, and operating system setting adjustments, among other new WebSphere system issues.

WebSphere system upgrades involve a lot of work and affect a lot of teams. You cannot upgrade your system each time IBM makes a new release available, either a major upgrade or a maintenance release. If you do, the entire technical organization has no time to do anything else than constantly perform WebSphere system upgrades. Paradoxically, you cannot delay WebSphere system upgrades too long, either. Each new release will have new system code that fixes known system defects. Prolonged delays of major system upgrades make your WebSphere system vulnerable because existing system defects are always part of any software. Yes, you want to remove known WebSphere system defects. At the same time, you have to remember that all software has a reasonable amount of known defects. If you apply WebSphere upgrades too soon or too often, you may introduce system fixes that are worse than the system defects you are trying to correct. Although there is no simplistic approach to WebSphere system upgrades, you perhaps can use two major WebSphere upgrades a year, and then apply a relevant system fix targeted at a specific system problem identified or required by IBM WebSphere Technical Support Organization.

Applying WebSphere system upgrades too early, too late, too often, or too infrequently may cause grave WebSphere system problems and unscheduled system outages. As the saying goes, engineering is all about achieving the right balance. WebSphere system upgrades demand a thoughtful, diligent, and balanced approach.

Strive for WebSphere Production Operations Excellence

An outstanding WebSphere team and a struggling WebSphere team are likely spending approximately the same amount of engineering hours and performing practically the same set of engineering tasks. Frequently, curious IT managers try to find out what special things highly successful WebSphere teams do to allow them to reach 100 percent stability and availability for their large, dynamic, and critical WebSphere systems. Actually, a successful WebSphere team is most likely conducting exactly the same WebSphere engineering operations—no more, no less. Normally, the engineers of such teams do not dive deep into the application, review the code, or identify defects. They have no secret weapons or special magic tools. They perform the same routine tasks as the other WebSphere teams and face the same kind of daily challenges. However, their performance is markedly different because the way in which they perform the same WebSphere engineering tasks is markedly different. This may not be intuitive to you. However, the methods that make a WebSphere team outstanding are not profound or complex. They are simple things within the reach of any WebSphere engineering support organization if it is determined to achieve engineering excellence in production environments. Still, performing these WebSphere engineering tasks properly is not easy. Here are some insights and experiences coming from real-world WebSphere engineering practice:

- Disciplined, responsible, and enthusiastic team
- Documentation
- Change management
- Empowered application support teams
- Engineering and engagement experience

This chapter does not cover production problem resolution. Chapter 9, "Managing a Production Emergency," covers this topic in detail.

Build a Disciplined and Technical Team

Build not only a highly competitive and capable technical team, but an emphatically disciplined, responsible, and enthusiastic technical force with precision execution.

You need a disciplined team that your company can depend on to manage your critical IT systems. You want to nurture a team culture of responsibility and dependability. You want to develop and encourage a culture of enthusiastically getting the job done and working diligently to serve the customers. If you can build this type of WebSphere team, when an engineering task is assigned, it will be accurately carried out with meticulous planning and unwavering attention to detail. The WebSphere technical job will be executed at exactly the designated time, the designated place, and in the designated manner.

WebSphere engineering support work can be complex or mundane. For example, inadvertently pushing the wrong button can shut down your entire production WebSphere server suite and disrupt its production execution. Using one command, your WebSphere engineer can launch a configuration automation program targeting the wrong data center and, in a matter of a few seconds, completely render your production WebSphere servers in that data center out of service. There are no system work control processes or quality assurance mechanisms that can replace a WebSphere engineer's high sense of responsibility and his determination and enthusiasm to do the job right.

Building a strong WebSphere engineering support team one engineer at a time is the first step to high WebSphere system stability. Substantially and conspicuously reward responsible, enthusiastic, and detail-oriented employees. Publicly recognize those who take the business of your company seriously and swiftly take disciplinary actions against those who do not. Irresponsible and unpunctual system engineers are dangerous to the safety, stability, and availability of your critical WebSphere systems. It does not take many unqualified staff to bring substantial harm to your company. Even if your team has only one or two irresponsible members, your critical WebSphere systems are in grave danger. Quickly take appropriate actions, such as transferring those individuals out of the team to noncritical positions; do this before they bring serious instability to your critical WebSphere infrastructure and cause your company major losses.

The performance of a WebSphere engineering support team is the summation of the quality of all its team members. The human factor is the most important link in your effort to WebSphere engineering excellence, and every member of the WebSphere team counts. You need a highly disciplined, enthusiastic, and responsible team, and it is your first job for high WebSphere system stability to build and strengthen such a team.

Production System Documentation

To reiterate what was mentioned in a previous section, without a set of concise and promptly updated production system documentation, your production WebSphere systems are not stable. This is true for a simple reason. Typically, your WebSphere systems are large, complex, and dynamic, with hundreds of servers, many applications, upstream and downstream components, and tremendous configuration details. Without the aid of documentation as a knowledge-management system for such large WebSphere environments, you do not really know what you have, and you do not really know what you need to do, especially when confronted with an urgent production issue. WebSphere system documentation, which is a seemingly low priority and a boring chore, is one of the first tasks in your quest for high WebSphere production system stability and availability.

Change Control

Change control is not a formality, a bureaucratic process, or a necessary evil. Change control is an all-important assurance to your WebSphere system stability and availability. Good change-control practice is the cornerstone for the quality of the WebSphere products and services that your team delivers. Not following the change-management process seriously violates IT operations for any company that desires to achieve any measure of success in the smooth operation of major IT systems. An unstructured approach to IT system changes leads to nothing but chaos and severe financial losses. Any individuals who won't diligently follow change-control processes and emergency change-control processes must not work in the critical middleware area. Unfortunately, it is occasionally still a fairly common practice to bypass change control in implementing production changes for immature and inexperienced WebSphere teams. Understandably, the WebSphere systems managed by such teams are volatile and unreliable.

Empowered Application Support Team

Empower your application production support team with an appropriate level of access to WebSphere system and WebSphere technical knowledge and skills. Not only does it make your life easier, but it also enhances the overall system stability and the response time to production problems.

If your application production support team has a reasonable level of WebSphere technology knowledge and the right level of access to WebSphere systems, it tends to do a better job as the first line of defense against production problems. It pays to include a number of application production support team members in your WebSphere training program (or even conduct joint technical training). Also, the WebSphere team can offer WebSphere technical training on certain topics to the application support team. In return, the application production support team can offer application walkthroughs for your team to better understand the applications that execute in the WebSphere runtime environment.

Another best practice is granting read access to application production support teams to certain log files. Before you allow such system access, it is important to ensure that the application production support team can correctly interpret what it sees in the log files. Java Enterprise Edition (JEE) consulting and support, in which the WebSphere team can offer application code defect isolation, can be useful to the application production support team depending on the specific financial arrangement and the service level agreement (SLA) between the teams.

Share Your Deep Dive Diagnostic Tool

The basic rationale is the more capable your application production support team becomes, the more likely the WebSphere system is stable. Therefore, open up and share. If you have deep dive diagnostic tools (for example, those from Mercury or Introscope), share them with your application production support team. Show them the tools, help them gain access, and assist them in tailoring the tools to their needs. Having a dedicated group of IT professionals, such as application production support team members, diligently watching your WebSphere systems through a powerful deep dive monitoring tool certainly benefits the WebSphere team.

The following sections introduce three WebSphere engineering operations that are frequently used for WebSphere production environment support: the WebSphere Application Release Support Operation, the WebSphere Data Center Switch Support Operation, and the WebSphere System Monitoring Support Operation. Chapter 9 covers WebSphere Problem Resolution Operation.

WebSphere Application Release Support Operation

Any inconsistencies in the WebSphere Application Release Support Operation will have serious consequences for the WebSphere team. This will likely cause production outages, especially when the deployment is incomplete because of integration issues between the WebSphere scripts used in deployment and the automation tools that the application deployment team specializes in. Deployment difficulties can cause scheduled outage window overrun, which causes the WebSphere system to be unavailable for production operation. To avoid these production problems, carefully plan, test, and execute the WebSphere Application Release Support Operation.

Operation Framework and Description

This section systematically describes the WebSphere Application Release Support Operation applying the WebSphere Operations Framework.

Description

This operation varies by application. For some WebSphere applications, there are more frequently scheduled major application releases that provide new functions to the users, and others may have more releases that fix application code defects. It typically involves prerelease activities, code deployment, post-release activities, and application certification.

Entrance Criteria

- Application is rigorously tested in its release pipeline, which is some (or all of) functional testing, integration testing, ad-hoc testing, and stress testing.

- Application defects and system configuration issues uncovered during testing are resolved.

- Both the primary WebSphere support engineer and secondary engineer concur that this application release is sufficiently tested and free of known defects.

- Five business days before the application release goes to production, the WebSphere manager needs to work with the WebSphere engineers assigned to the WebSphere project to determine whether this application release is safe to migrate into the production WebSphere environment.

WebSphere Resources

- Primary WebSphere support engineer

Activities

- Prerelease activities:

  - Take action to ensure that applications are sufficiently tested and application and system defects are corrected.

  - Perform system comparison to identify any configuration inconsistencies, correct these problems, and verify WebSphere environment consistencies.

  - Make any WebSphere changes required by this release of the application.

- Code deployment. Depending on individual applications, code deployment may be done by the WebSphere team, application support team, or application deployment team.

- For each code release, a WebSphere system consistency inspection and verification must be executed before and after the application release takes place. This inspection guarantees the consistency of the WebSphere environments with respect to WebSphere configurations and OS-level system configurations. This helps troubleshoot any issues that may arise as a result of the application release. The technical teams know that the WebSphere system configurations are consistent, so they can focus their attention on other more likely areas.

- Post-release activities:

  - Check to see whether the correct versions of all applications are installed.

  - WebSphere system executes its normal functions. (The servers start up cleanly and no system errors are found in the log file.)

  - Application correctly delivers functions as expected.

- Application certification. Typically done by the application support team. If any issues arise, the WebSphere team assists in troubleshooting.

Processes

- WebSphere system configuration comparison process
- WebSphere application release management process

Artifacts

- WebSphere application release form
- Application testing status report (external to the WebSphere team)

External Teams

- Application production support team
- Application deployment team

Sign-Off Parties

- Application production support team

Exit Criteria

- New application release is installed.
- Accompanying WebSphere configuration changes are implemented.
- Application production support team certifies the application.
- Application production support team signs off on the application code release.

Key Processes and Artifacts Explained

This section explains the processes and artifacts used in the WebSphere Application Release Support Operation.

WebSphere System Configuration Comparison Process

The WebSphere system configuration comparison process defines when, where, and how your team needs to conduct a WebSphere system configuration comparison. For example, before a major application release, use your WebSphere system configuration comparison program to compare your stress-testing environment where the new application has been tested with the target WebSphere production environment. Analyze any possible differences to determine whether corrections are needed. In addition, this process needs to clearly recommend the communication process of the findings, especially if any discrepancies needing correction are identified by the comparison process.

WebSphere Application Release Management Process

The WebSphere application release management process is all about application release approval and application deployment implementation. Who needs to kick off the application release process, and what is the process to examine the readiness of the new application release and the proper approval procedure? This process answers the questions such as who should do code deployment—the WebSphere team, the application development and support teams, or the application deployment team. The process must give specific technical and procedural details on the critical hookups between teams (for example, how the application deployment team uses its automation programs to call application installation automation programs of the WebSphere team).

WebSphere Application Release Form

The WebSphere Application Release form is a quality-control document that has application release information for a particular application. It can include major changes (for example, new business functions provided by the new release). The primary objective is to document the application release's readiness in terms of testing and stress testing—duration, testing environments, and major problems uncovered and addressed. You may want to include important documents such as problem tickets and change tickets associated with the new release. This document must be reviewed and approved by the WebSphere team, testing team, and application production support team.

WebSphere Data Center Switch Support Operation

Practice makes perfect. Many data center switch support operations are not a result of disaster recovery, but they give the team needed practice. These practices also flush out issues that need to be corrected so that the operation succeeds during real production system outages. These exercises usually have high visibility. Your WebSphere engineers' performance at these operations may affect their reputation and management's perception of them.

A hardware problem, such as main memory failure or hard drive crashes, often makes it necessary to switch to a redundant WebSphere system at a different data center. A data center switch may not help with software issues, unless after a major application release, the backup WebSphere system keeps the previous application release and system configuration for a predefined period of time. In the case when the new release turns out to have serious problems, the production operation can be switched back to the backup WebSphere system.

For large major application releases that provide new functions and services for end users, switching to a previous release is usually impossible because of the extensive changes that have been done irreversibly in interconnected systems and backend data stores.

Operation Framework and Description

This section systematically describes the WebSphere Data Center Switch Support Operation applying the WebSphere Operations Framework.

Description

For high availability and failover, many companies have many WebSphere server redundancies. Some of these are hot-and-hot redundancies, and some of these are hot-and-cold redundancies. It is possible to have a need to perform a switch operation between hot-and-hot redundant servers at different data centers. This is usually to switch the traffic from one or more WebSphere servers to redundant WebSphere servers at different data centers to either test the overall system's capability to deal with catastrophic events or to manage a real production crisis. For hot-and-cold redundancies, as a matter of periodical practice, operational needs, and environment synchronization, there are often scheduled switch operations of production environments between data centers. A switch is a large and complex IT operation to move production operation of critical IT systems to backup or standby systems in a different data center. Switch procedures vary for different applications and can be complex and challenging; thus, the need for regularly scheduled practice. Different applications have different touch points that require different technical teams' participation and coordination between these teams.

Entrance Criteria

- Production environments switch between data centers as an established process for concerned applications and infrastructure components (for example, Web servers and WebSphere Application Servers).
- Detailed production environment switch guidelines are established by the application production support team with WebSphere tasks clearly identified and specified.
- Automation for the WebSphere tasks is already implemented.
- Automation is tested, staged, and ready to be executed.

WebSphere Resources

- Primary WebSphere support engineer
- Primary WebSphere on-call engineer

Activities

- Primary WebSphere support engineer or the primary WebSphere on-call engineer works to clearly identify the switch process.
- Conduct preswitch walkthrough.
- Carefully study switch process documents.
- Participate in technical training on switch automation.
- Attend switch planning meeting prior to the actual switch event.
- Perform configuration comparison between home environment and target environment at different data centers to note any discrepancies that need to be rectified before the switch event.
- Execute the data center switch tasks according to plan.
- Verify that all the assigned tasks are successfully completed.
- Conduct peer change review for all the assigned and approved changes.

Processes

- Data center switch process (external to the WebSphere team)

Artifacts

- Data center switch task guide (external to the WebSphere team)
- WebSphere configuration comparison program
- WebSphere switch task automation program

External Teams

- Application production support team
- Large number of infrastructure, application, project management, and change management teams

Sign-Off Parties

- Application production support team

Exit Criteria

- Successful overall data center switch.
- Target WebSphere system in the target data center is certified.
- Target WebSphere system in the target data center is in production operation.

Key Processes and Artifacts Explained

This section explains the processes and artifacts used in the WebSphere Data Center Switch Support Operation.

Data Center Switch Process

The data center switch process is external to the WebSphere team. However, it should have a description of the steps that the WebSphere team needs to perform in a data center switch operation, along with the procedures for other technical teams. The steps include the high-level enumeration of WebSphere operations, particularly the sequence of these operations in relation to the operation of other teams, and the communication and hookup mechanisms used during the data center switch operation.

Data Center Switch Task Guide

The data center switch task guide is external to the WebSphere team. It provides detailed description of the technical tasks that the WebSphere team must perform during the data center switch operation. In addition, this guide includes instructions for all the other technical teams participating in the data center switch operation.

WebSphere Configuration Comparison Program

The WebSphere configuration comparison program can be part of your WebSphere automation programs. It can either be a vendor application or a "homegrown" automation script that your team designs and codes. This program must be able to compare WebSphere configuration settings between two or more different WebSphere environments (for example, the WebSphere production environment and the WebSphere stress-testing environment). In addition, the comparison results need to be formatted in an easy-to-read format.

WebSphere System Monitoring Support Operation

From the WebSphere Application Server perspective, there are three levels of monitoring:

- The first level is the traditional system monitoring, which focuses on CPU, memory, disk space, processes, and network connectivity.
- The second level of monitoring tracks transactions and real-time user experience, as well as traffic pattern and load changes for the overall systems and selected components.
- The third level of system monitoring employs deep dive diagnostic tools to monitor the JEE application and the JVM (for example, application method invocation and JVM garbage collection), among many other objects to monitor.

All three monitoring mechanisms give the WebSphere team critical capabilities to detect, prevent, preempt, and resolve production problems. Therefore, the quality of this operation affects the stability and consistency of the production WebSphere systems.

Operation Framework and Description

This section systematically describes the WebSphere System Monitoring Support Operation applying the WebSphere Operations Framework.

Description

Overall system monitoring work is not the responsibility of the WebSphere team. The WebSphere team provides information about the WebSphere Application Server and the Web server monitoring specifications that need to be monitored. There needs to be a common set of company-wide system parameters to be monitored for the WebSphere Application Server and Web servers.

Entrance Criteria

- Overall monitoring strategy is established.
- Enterprise monitoring teams are engaged.

WebSphere Resources

- Primary WebSphere support engineer

Activities

- Provide detailed WebSphere monitoring specifications.
- Provide detailed Web server monitoring specifications.
- Assist the monitoring team with WebSphere monitoring testing.

Processes

- WebSphere and Web servers monitoring process

Artifacts

- Apache and IHS Web server monitoring requirements
- IPlanet Web Server Monitoring Requirements
- WebSphere Application Server Monitoring Requirements

External Teams

- Application production support team
- Enterprise monitoring team

Sign-Off Parties

- Application production support team
- Enterprise monitoring team
- WebSphere engineering support team

Exit Criteria

- Provide the WebSphere and Web server monitoring specifications documents to the monitoring team.
- Successful WebSphere and Web server monitoring implementation and testing.

Key Processes and Artifacts Explained

This section explains the processes and artifacts used in the WebSphere System Monitoring Support Operation.

WebSphere Application Server Monitoring Requirements

The WebSphere Application Server Monitoring Requirements Document contains WebSphere Application Server information, files to monitor, threshold values, and Java processes to monitor. Include paging information for your team and the problem queue name of your team for your problem tracking system.

Web Server Monitoring Requirements

The Web Server Monitoring Requirements Document contains Web server information, files to monitor, threshold values, and the Web server processes to monitor. Include paging information for your team and the problem queue name of your team for your problem tracking system.

Looking into the Future

Looking into the future, production problem resolution processes, visualization of large interconnected WebSphere systems, as well as dynamic WebSphere Virtual Enterprise-based WebSphere systems are some of the major directions for WebSphere production environments.

Chapter 12 discusses the visualization of large interconnected WebSphere systems. Dynamic WebSphere Virtual Enterprise is covered in Chapter 13, "WebSphere Engineering Going Forward."

Many of the large IT infrastructure teams are organized by products or a group of similar products and are aligned with major line of business (LOB) or business divisions. For example, you may have a WebSphere engineering support team and a DB2 engineering support team for your customer-care department that manages call centers and customer information for your company. Considering the size and complexity of the technologies supported, this dedicated support organization model that is based on a product is suitable for WebSphere, DB2, MQ, AIX, and other products. However, it does present challenges for critical production problem resolution.

During production problem resolution, each infrastructure product team has visibility only to its own system state and system data because of security setup and organization division. A frequent concern is that other infrastructure teams, without the necessary domain knowledge, may not correctly interpret the system state and system data. Given such opportunity to access system data outside of their own domain, it is possible that their incorrect interpretation may bring misleading perceptions, incorrect directions, and inconveniences to the technical team responsible for the product.

When confronted with a tough production problem, the technical teams involved may get defensive if asked to share system artifacts, such as error logs or monitoring tools. Therefore, precious time may be lost in excessive yet careful communication of system states and data, especially during major production problems that have serious consequences.

Can you find the right organization model, a workable process, and a smart solution to mitigate this difficulty? As an example, can you select the right mix of professionals from different teams to form a special task force to create synergy between teams?

Can you use an improved Pay for Performance (PFP) process and an innovative post-problem resolution (a procedure to motivate all teams to focus on the fast resolution of the problem), regardless if it is WebSphere, DB2, network, or the application?

Most importantly, can you devise the right incentive plan to encourage the right kind of business behavior to focus on doing whatever is necessary to solve a problem? The objective is to emphatically encourage the technical teams to work shoulder to shoulder, proactively providing inter-team assistance, and collaborating in solving production problems.

Summary

There is always more to do to have your WebSphere production environments reach a new level of stability and availability, regardless of how mature your team is and how well you are doing today. Because of the inconsistent practice level of WebSphere engineering in the IT industry, for some companies, the urgent task of improving WebSphere engineering is not in achieving an admirable level of process consistency and engineering excellence. Instead, the focus is on moving the WebSphere team out of the firefighter-level of practice. When your WebSphere system reaches a reasonable level of stability, it is possible for your team to have the time needed to create repeatable processes, develop system and support documents, focus on technical training, and build a world-class WebSphere practice. If you make a commitment today and follow the basic WebSphere engineering best practices outlined here, you will gradually stabilize your WebSphere systems and lay the foundation work to move on to the next level of WebSphere engineering maturity:

1. Develop and document a minimum set of WebSphere engineering processes. This initial set of documents is best if blessed with practicality and simplicity. For example, you will see a huge difference in your production on-call work, even if you have an on-call document that is only a few pages long.

2. Adopt or follow a change-control process for all of your WebSphere production changes and some critical testing environments, such as pre-production stress-testing environments. Be rigid and inflexible in following change-control processes and emergency change-control processes.

3. Rigorously follow your WebSphere standards and build consistent WebSphere systems.

4. Focus on building a disciplined, enthusiastic, and highly technical team. Insist on technical strength and professional excellence in hiring. As a leader of an organization, your first job is to use people who work with you and your team. Without effective control of your team, you do not have a job. However, do not let company politics or organizational dynamics become the dominant hiring factor. The performance of your team is the summation of the quality of all its members. For IT infrastructure production support, especially for a critical area such as WebSphere engineering, one unqualified worker drags down the performance of the entire team.

5. Promote, encourage, participate, support, and insist on rigorous and diligent testing, as well as stress testing all major application code releases and all WebSphere system changes before allowing them to migrate into production WebSphere environments.

When you no longer spend most of your time fighting production fires, and after you achieve a reasonable level of WebSphere system stability, the following could be your next endeavor in your pursuit for WebSphere engineering excellence:

1. Enhance your on-call rotation, on-call responsiveness, and on-call service quality.

2. Examine and optimize your production configuration change processes.

3. Develop user experience, transaction, in-depth JVM monitoring, and deep dive diagnostic capabilities.

4. Design, build, and deploy WebSphere systems of high availability and scalability (for example, take advantage of WebSphere clustering to enhance resiliency for critical WebSphere infrastructure).

If you can successfully implement these improvements, your WebSphere system stability will be high. It is completely possible to achieve 100 percent system stability and availability.

Chapter 9 systematically works through managing a WebSphere production emergency.

Managing a Production Emergency

Do you sometimes feel that your WebSphere team is guilty until proven innocent? Do you sometimes feel that people wrongfully blame the WebSphere team for production issues? If you feel this way, you may be right. Many serious system and application issues can first manifest themselves as WebSphere system anomalies, even though for the majority of the cases, you can eventually prove that the WebSphere system is not the root cause of the problem. For example, a corrupted database table may cause Java Database Connectivity (JDBC) connection pool saturation. An application code defect that jams a huge number of large objects into the memory may express itself as Java Virtual Machine (JVM) garbage collection (GC) difficulty and, consequently, a JVM crash. An intermittent network-connectivity problem may look like the Web server plug-in is malfunctioning and cannot communicate with the WebSphere Application Servers. Before you can identify the real root cause, you have a serious production problem on your hands.

The system integration job is difficult. Often, complex environments lead to complex problems because many moving parts can affect your WebSphere systems. Typically, if an application and its environment stabilize (for example, when it does not have many significant application, network, or business function-related changes), the number of problems is few and its severity is usually low. A large enterprise application can be dynamic because mergers and acquisitions can cause changes in requirements. The new business drivers may add new applications or expand existing applications, causing significant and constant changes in your applications and infrastructure and forming a highly dynamic environment. Worse, almost all these changes and moving parts are well beyond your direct control. In the aforementioned examples, you have no control over the database. You do not know what developers add into a new release of application code. You do not monitor or manage the network. However, if any of these critical areas have a problem, it can affect the stability and availability of the WebSphere systems. In addition, the root cause of a nagging instability may be elusive. This may cause interruptions to your system's availability that may extend over a prolonged period of time. As a result, the business may suffer heavy losses. When this happens, you have a production emergency.

This chapter systematically discusses how to skillfully deal with a production emergency and defines a structured approach that covers the entire spectrum of production emergency management. For example, this chapter discusses how you can decide the severity of the problem, invoke a critical situation, mitigate customer experience, perform documentation, and conduct post-problem resolution.

The first group of the focal points for managing a critical production outage is given in the following list. These areas cover the full cycle of production emergency management, from evaluating and reporting the severity of a production problem to post-problem resolution, including the introduction of the WebSphere Application Server Problem Resolution Support Operation:

- Evaluating and reporting production problems
- Mitigating customer impact
- Managing progress
- Performing WebSphere Application Server Problem Resolution Support Operation
- Conducting post-problem resolution

The second group of the critical areas for dealing with a production emergency includes managing communication, work relationships, and the WebSphere team. These jobs are not "soft" or optional; they are of paramount importance. If you do not succeed in managing these areas, you will fail at managing a production emergency:

- Communicating effectively and enabling teamwork
- Working with IBM
- Managing the WebSphere team
- Building a strong business reputation

Evaluating and Reporting Production Problems

One way to prevent a production emergency is by managing a production problem in a timely fashion and not allowing it to become a high-severity production emergency. If a high-severity production emergency does occur, it is critical that your WebSphere team and other appropriate technical teams are alerted of the situation so they can immediately work on the problem to minimize loss.

ENHANCED MONITORING AND ALERTING

User experience monitoring, end-to-end transaction monitoring, and the capability of monitoring system resources within the JVM need to be put in place to anticipate outages. The monitoring of traditional system resources, such as CPU, memory, disk space, network, and processes, continues to be important, while more monitoring and alert capabilities are needed. For example, if you have a monitor in place with certain levels set for measuring the heap size, you can be alerted when the heap size goes beyond normal levels. This alerts the WebSphere engineers to look for the cause before an outage occurs. The establishment of enhanced monitoring and alerting helps minimize the length of outages, if not eliminating some.

Therefore, it is crucial to accurately evaluate the severity and quickly report or escalate a production problem. This helps your organization quickly engage the right resources and enact the right processes to give the production problem adequate attention. For example, if a serious problem is incorrectly declared a low-severity issue, the problem resolution process may allow for several days to resolve this type of problem. You may not engage the adequate technical resources to manage the problem upfront. Changes in severity yield differences in solution time because of factors such as management focus. Severity reported to assisting organizations may influence how soon they respond to the problem. Consequently, an underreported problem may deteriorate and cause extensive damage to your company's bottom line. Conversely, over-escalating a problem draws resources away from existing projects and possibly affects the rollout of critical updates.

It is true that sometimes the initial reporting has to be revised when more information becomes available. However, frequently a serious production problem is not reported correctly and the delay incurred often leads to a costly production emergency.

Production problem evaluation and reporting issues are complex, and you need to look at the causes, solutions, and best practices.

Determine the Severity

Let's assume that you have three levels of problem severity: yellow, red, and purple. Yellow is the least severe and purple is the most severe. When you have a minor production problem, the severity decision can be simple. For example, it is not difficult to send out a yellow alert for inadequate disk space or an ephemeral memory spike. However, it can be a complex decision when sending out high-severity alerts. It is not always straightforward because many factors need to be considered.

Availability

For a typical large WebSphere environment with clustering and server redundancy, it may be possible to use system availability to determine the production problem severity. Say that you have one application that is deployed on 10 nodes, and each node has 20 JVM instances. Then you can define the severity according to the number of JVM instances that remain available when the WebSphere system experiences unscheduled outages. For example, if 40 JVM instances (or 25 percent of the total JVM instances) are not available and the overall system is still functional with reduced response time, a red alert must be sent out. If 100 JVM instances (or 50 percent or more of the JVM instances) are not consistently available, a purple alert needs to be sent out.

Interconnected Systems

Availability-based severity determination is straightforward, but it does not apply to all situations. For example, on WebSphere system A, you may have a noncritical component malfunctioning intermittently. However, the overall WebSphere infrastructure is consistently available. Therefore, you issue a yellow alert.

However, to an interconnected WebSphere system B, this abovementioned minor anomaly seriously affects an important batch job. As a result, it causes many critical transaction failures. To the interconnected WebSphere system B, this is clearly a severe production problem, and a red alert needs to be sent out.

For a large interconnected WebSphere system, it is difficult to precisely predict the impact of one system to another. Therefore, a low-severity production problem for one system may escalate to a high-severity problem on an interconnected system. It is a difficult job to trace problems between interconnected WebSphere systems or between WebSphere systems and other enterprise systems. This is because, with the current gaps in technologies, IT organization structure, and business processes, it is possible but not easy to fully understand the interdependency of interconnected systems.

Although it is not easy to do, you still need to try to assess the impact of one production problem to the interconnected systems to determine problem severity.

Dollar Amount

The actual or potential financial loss to a business can determine the severity of a production problem. Especially for transactional systems, dollar-amount-based severity determination is feasible.

However, for some types of WebSphere systems, this may be difficult (for example, a customer portal where a customer or potential customer browses for information).

It is difficult to attach a dollar amount to an outage, but customer service may provide metrics for problem severity determination.

Customer Service Failure

For the WebSphere system that directly serves the customer, it makes sense to determine production problem severity by measuring customer service failures.

Any interaction with the customer that failed is a customer service failure. For example, if a customer cannot get a requested Web page, this constitutes one customer service failure. If a customer cannot get the loan application to appear online within a predefined time, this is another customer service failure.

You can use quantified customer service performance to measure problem severity. In other words, you can use the number of customer service failures to determine the severity of a production problem based on a unit of time (for example, per minute or per hour).

Critical Systems

An internal WebSphere system that is used by a few hundred employees to perform authorized vendor lookup differs from an online system used by 20 million customers. Business criticality can be used to determine the severity of a production problem. Even a relatively minor production issue can be treated as a high-severity problem for a highly critical system.

Unstructured Problem Evaluation and Reporting

It is difficult to develop a matrix that is applicable to all situations. However, a concise and practical guideline must provide guidance and reference to the WebSphere manager and on-call engineer in determining the severity of a production problem. Nevertheless, it may not be possible to develop a formula including all the aforementioned factors and make it applicable to all production problems. Experienced assessment on a case-by-case basis is still an important means to determine production problem severity.

Improvised problem evaluation and reporting leads to inconsistencies in assessing and reporting problems.

Underreporting

The reluctance to report a serious production problem as a high-severity issue is understandable, but it can be damaging. No one wants to have a high-severity problem on his record. However, failure to report it in a timely manner causes severe production problems and can be costly.

More Loss

The reluctance to report a high-severity problem may lead to delays in applying critical resources to deal with the problem. This may cause your company substantially more damage.

For instance, a potentially high-impact WebSphere application problem seems to have a root cause in the application code. However, the application development team does not agree to report it as a high-severity problem. As a result, only a yellow alert is sent out. The technical teams have many high-priority tasks to take care of and may not immediately work on a low-severity problem. Thus, there is a delay in applying critical technical resources. Several hours later, the situation becomes worse. It is clear that you need to upgrade the problem's severity. However, the application development team disagrees that this warrants a purple alert. Therefore, only a red alert is sent out after a long discussion. However, at this point in time, the production problem has lost its best window of opportunity to be contained and quickly resolved. Now the problem rapidly deteriorates into a system-wide high-impact production outage and causes the company tremendous loss.

Hide a Problem

Your reluctance to report a high-severity problem may be interpreted as an effort to hide a serious problem. This may leave lingering negative effects to your reputation. Any meaningful work relationship is based on trust and respect; without both, the WebSphere team has a dubious future.

Causes

Performance concerns sometimes drive the WebSphere team and other technical teams to try to quickly fix a serious problem without declaring high severity. However, often these problems are not something that you can fix quickly.

The lack of process and leadership can get in the way of correctly determining and reporting a high-severity production problem.

The inability to fully understand the problem can cause both complacency and improper problem assessment. This is true especially when a different team seems to own the production problem. For example, when the application development team looks like the owner of an application code issue, the WebSphere team may feel that it is not the responsible party of the problem; therefore, it fails to pay enough attention to a potentially serious production problem.

Finally, delays and inaccurate assessments occur when the technical teams fail to keep an open mind. Here are two examples:

- The WebSphere team may refuse to report a high CPU utilization as a red-alert issue because it has a solid configuration quality assurance program. Even though signs indicate possible WebSphere configuration issues, the WebSphere team insists that it is not a WebSphere system issue that needs a red alert. However, the best WebSphere team may occasionally make a configuration mistake that causes a production issue.

- By the same token, in another case, the application development team may flatly refuse to consider that the application code may be the issue, because there have been no application code change for several months. Even if there have been absolutely no application code changes, changes in transaction mix and traffic pattern may touch off an application code defect that has been in the system since day one.

It is important to keep an open mind, follow established processes, define triage leadership, and focus on resolving the problem.

Overreporting

Overreporting the severity of a production problem is as bad as underreporting, with many serious consequences.

Damages

You may be perceived as panicky or losing control when you inappropriately report a production problem with high severity. Your management and the technology community may question your judgment, confidence, and your fitness for critical positions.

High-severity problems have greater management attention and organization focus. Much time and energy is spent in attending meetings with senior management and crafting carefully drafted status reports. High resource consumption may not be what you want at a time when you have an urgent production problem to deal with.

Reasons for Overreporting

Unfortunately, the dominant IT culture nowadays is still one that rewards firefighting rather than engineering precision and process excellence. Because objective financial evaluation of IT service is not mature enough to provide fact-based and quantitative performance management, your act in fire fighting is a good way to boost the reputation of your team.

Competition for senior management attention and visibility can be another cause for exaggerating a problem. When there is little effective means to factually evaluate WebSphere teams for their technical service output in a dollar measurement, competing for senior management attention is a useful way to get ahead. A high-severity production problem usually gets more senior management attention and visibility; therefore, it may be the motivation for unmerited reporting of high-severity problems.

Invoking an IBM WebSphere Critical Situation Status

An IBM WebSphere Critical Situation is a heightened support status for a highly critical production problem that has lasted for an extended period of time with unsustainable loss to the business. An IBM WebSphere Critical Situation must be only invoked for a severe problem.

There are three major considerations to think about before you invoke an IBM WebSphere Critical Situation.

Intensified Resource Consumption for IBM and Slower IBM Response

Securing more IBM technical resources and management attention may be one of your major objectives of escalating a production problem to a critical situation status. Sure enough, IBM applies more technical resources because of the severity of a critical situation. However, you must be aware that an IBM WebSphere Critical Situation is a level of support that causes greatly intensified resource consumption for IBM, and it eventually translates into higher cost for you in using the WebSphere technology. In addition, the IBM technical support staff has to spend more time on reporting and attending meetings with its senior management. On one hand, more technical IBM resources working on one problem certainly would help. On the other hand, this also introduces more internal communication and coordination work, which sometimes does not directly translate into a better and faster IBM response. Finally, IBM asks for additional data and information, which causes an additional load on your WebSphere engineers.

Negative Visibility

Senior management attention, like everything else in corporate life, has two sides. It may bring more resources to help you work on the problem. However, it may also make a problem in your area visible to offices higher up. Senior management attention to a serious problem for which you are responsible may not lead to the kind of visibility that you are looking for. In addition, a widely publicized problem in your area may produce a lingering negative perception for your team and immediately affect your project's momentum.

You need to escalate your production problem to the critical situation status only when it is completely necessary for solving a high-severity and high-impact production problem.

Best Practices

Problem severity determination is not an easy task, but the following tips may help.

Leadership Team

Designate a leadership team to determine the severity of the production problems. A triad of the WebSphere manager, the application production support manager, and the application development manager must meet and make severity recommendations. Timely reconvening of the meeting to revise the problem severity must be built into your problem-management process. Usually, the application production support manager has the final say on determining the production problem severity. However, because of the degree of complexity of the problem and technical specialization, other teams may have significant feedback in the final evaluation. For example, if the problem is primarily a WebSphere infrastructure-related issue, the WebSphere team may better understand the impact and scope of the problem, and it is in a better position to help determine problem severity. As a best practice, maintain well-documented processes to manage production problems, including guidelines on how to determine the severity of a production problem. These processes make clear the roles and responsibilities of the problem determination process, and speed up production problem resolution.

Documented Matrix

Documented matrix of production problem severity evaluation may not cover every possible situation, but it needs to provide relevant reference over a significant number of production problems.

The availability of such a document as a useful guide during production emergencies may make the management of production problems more predictable.

Consistent Problem Reporting Format and Process

Develop a structured problem-reporting system and business process. Improvised problem reporting does not help with consistent assessment of a production problem's severity. For example, if one WebSphere team sends out a quick email, another WebSphere team compiles a Word document, and the third WebSphere team uses a spreadsheet, the quality of your problem severity reporting and evaluation is not good. Your problem report needs a fixed format for all the production problems and must be used by all WebSphere teams.

Problem Statement

For high-severity production problems, you need a concise and well-written problem statement as part of your problem reporting documentation.

A problem statement is a crisp description of the production problem. It needs to include information about the time, location, events, and anomalies that occurred. In addition, it needs to estimate the resulting impact to the business and IT. A good problem statement forces you to think logically and helps form a good direction for problem resolution.

Problem statements can be easily bypassed. Under pressure to do something immediately to stabilize the production system and restore production execution, the WebSphere team may simply overlook the need for a good problem statement. The WebSphere engineers and consultants may plunge immediately into activities identifying the root cause and achieving a possible solution to the problem. However, without a good problem statement, it is possible that you may work in the wrong direction without fully understanding the problem.

The WebSphere Operations Framework may help. For example, the activities check list of the WebSphere Application Server Problem Resolution Support Operation includes "identify the problem and form a concise, but clear and accurate, problem statement." If you follow the operations framework, your management of a critical situation may be more consistent, with better results.

In the problem statement, it is not a good idea to include suggestions for responsible teams and solutions. References to responsible teams may be misinterpreted as accusations. Talking about unmerited solutions is not only misleading, it also may smother the innovative and creative thinking needed to solve a tough and complex problem.

Customer Experience Mitigation

Critical situations in WebSphere environments can cause a prolonged production instability that has immense financial implications. For large mission-critical systems, such as stock-trading systems, mortgage application generation, or popular online auction systems, a one-hour unscheduled production outage can translate into millions of dollars lost, if not tens of millions of dollars for large systems. Money is not all that is at stake. The far more lasting damage is to the goodwill of the customers. Therefore, during prolonged production instability, Maintaining a level of production operation and mitigating customer experience is a difficult but important task. The measures discussed in this section may help with customer experience mitigation.

Recycling JVM

Recycling JVM is often used to resume system operation and achieve service restoration. The application of recycling JVM may be more successful if your WebSphere system has failover and redundancy. For a critical WebSphere system, horizontal clustering is often an appropriate topology. Vertical clustering can allow you to recycle JVM instances separately to maintain a level of production service. For WebSphere systems with horizontal clustering, it is possible to have minimal or no impact on the customers in some cases, because you can recycle the JVM instances after quieting the traffic to the cluster that is to be recycled.

It is critically important to produce and capture heap dumps, thread dumps, and sometimes core dumps, along with other necessary diagnostic data, when you recycle JVM to obtain documents for root cause analysis. To be able to produce good documents for root cause analysis and problem resolution, you want to consider the following.

Have a version of JDK that allows the generation of heap dumps and thread dumps. Testing whether a certain JDK would produce heap dumps and thread dumps needs be part of your system upgrade process. Being unable to produce heap dumps and thread dumps because of JDK defects makes you lose much precious time and significantly slows you down in identifying and addressing the problem during a production crisis. This is because if the current JDK does not allow you to produce dumps, you have to upgrade JDK. The JDK upgrade must be tested and stress tested before moving to production. Testing a new version of JDK with a particular release of application code is a time-consuming task. It is not something that you want to do when you have a production emergency to deal with.

In addition, you have to make sure that, as a normal practice, you have adequate disk space to generate diagnostic data, such as dumps. These dumps can be large files. Therefore, without enough disk space, the dump generation may either fail or become incomplete with truncated files that are useless to IBM in troubleshooting.

You need to have a process in place for the JVM recycling that includes and requires document generation, especially for critical production issues. Having a process for recycling JVM during emergencies helps the system engineer consistently produce the documents[1] needed for root cause analysis.

For mainframe WebSphere systems, proper automation to generate Supervisor Call (SVC) dumps help in emergencies. In addition, the WebSphere engineers have to understand the compression process before uploading the heap dump, Java dump, and SVC dump to IBM and its

---

1. In IBM-speak, *document* means data files generated for troubleshooting (for example, the Java heap dump, the Java threads dump, and the operating system core dump).

impact to data format conversion in order to prevent delays caused by format conversion or compression.

DOCUMENT COLLECTING ON THE MAINFRAME

SVC dumps are OS-level dumps that contain a summary dump, control blocks, and other system code, but the exact areas dumped depend on how the dumps are requested.

For some types of system instabilities, recycling is highly effective (for example, if a slow memory leak induced a JVM crash). However, for many system anomalies, recycling JVM is not an effective way to restore production service. For example, regardless of the JVM heap size, if the application code allows an unbounded data structure instantiated with thousands of large records fetched from a database, the JVM memory may quickly be saturated. Then, GC may take too long and, as a result, the JVM crashes. In this case, you may have to recycle the JVM quickly (perhaps, every five minutes) to remain at a minimum level of production service before you find a permanent fix or identify another effective way to mitigate customer experience (for example, reducing the system load).

System Load Can Be a Critical Factor

Production problems are typically difficult to identify. Heavy system load does not always trigger a serious production problem, but sometimes it does. Frequently, WebSphere system load is a critical factor.

As a rule, production code and its related system configuration is rigorously tested through the development and testing pipelines. The production problem caused by an application code defect that slips through a diligent testing process is sometimes induced by a heavier production system load than what is in the stress-testing environment or, by the same token, caused by a different traffic pattern (for example, a different transaction mix). System load may not be the root cause of the instability. Other problems, such as slow-downs on the backends or communication bottlenecks, are possible root causes. However, the severity of system instability is likely to have a direct relationship to system load. Therefore, reducing system load may be an effective means of mitigating customer experience.

Reducing System Load

Reducing system load may help reduce the severity of the instability and mitigate customer experience for load-sensitive system problems. Therefore, it must be vigorously pursued when appropriate. Have a plan for production emergencies that provides concrete steps in reducing system load to minimize customer impact. This is especially a good practice if monitoring indicates areas of abnormalities, such as unusual load spikes.

The plan needs to identify nonessential traffic that can be stopped during production emergencies. For example, the plan can include shutting down a performance-monitoring tool that generates considerable traffic. The plan needs to also clearly identify low-priority jobs that cause considerable system load and temporarily stop their traffic.

You can also develop an Application Operations Document that provides concrete recommendations for rebalancing and better scheduling batch jobs around the critical system components that may come under stress. In addition, in the Application Operations Document, provide a list of batch jobs that can be appropriately postponed during production emergencies to reduce system load.

A benefit of reducing system load by stopping nonessential and low-priority jobs is that it makes isolating the offending traffic and the source relatively easier.

Increase Capacity

For an instability that is load sensitive, increasing capacity is often a highly effective means to reach a reasonable level of production operation before the root cause of the instability is isolated and effective problem resolution provided. However, by increasing capacity before the root cause of the problem is clearly identified, you take serious risks because this increased capacity may effectively mask the root cause of the problem.

One of the risks is misleading the troubleshooting effort in the wrong direction. Capacity can be added by making changes to system configuration (for example, adding vertical JVM instances). If the significantly increased JVM resource substantially reduces the severity of the problem or even completely eliminates the phenomenon of the instability, there may be the perception that the instability is caused by inappropriate system configuration settings.

The second risk of increasing system capacity is that it may make problem isolation and root cause analysis more difficult, if not practically impossible. When the system is less stressed, exception and error-message generation tend to decrease. Thus, increasing system capacity may make it difficult to trace the problem. For example, there may be fewer or no error messages in the log files. In addition, the Java heap dump and the thread dump may contain reduced amounts of evidence leading to the root cause of the problem. All of these could delay the troubleshooting process.

The last risk is the possible reputation loss of the WebSphere team. Substantially increased WebSphere system resources may mask a serious problem. If the increased system capacity is considered a final fix of the instability problem, rather than a customer-mitigation measure, the WebSphere team's technical competence may be questioned; therefore, the WebSphere team may suffer lingering reputation loss.

You have to carefully consider the specifics of each critical situation, evaluate the pros and cons in increasing capacity on a case-by-case basis, and strike a balance between root cause isolation and customer-experience mitigation. What's more, you may want to team up with system architects and the capacity planning team to work on the possible increase of capacity. Whatever you do, you always want to do what is best for the customers, the employees, and the shareholders in terms of their long-term interests. Consider taking some of these measures:

- **Increase traditional system resources**. The term *traditional system resources* refers to CPU, memory, disk space, network bandwidth, I/O, and paging, among others. These system resources are traditional against "deep" system resources at the WebSphere Application Server and Java internal level, such as the JDBC connection, Web container threads, JMS listener, and JVM instances. System resources provide the system capacity for processing. For example, without an adequate amount of JVM resources, your WebSphere Application Server system may crash under a heavy load. Therefore, you need to capacity plan all system resources. Traditional system resources, such as CPU and memory, are typically resource capacity planned, and therefore likely to be adequate. However, during a load-sensitive instability, these traditional system resources can become stressed and in need of extra capacity. In addition, adding more CPU and memory is not only intended to provide relief, but also paves the way for adding nontraditional system resources, such as more JVM capacity, when necessary.

- **Add JVM instances, especially in vertical clustering**. This substantially increases the overall system-processing capability for load-sensitive problems. Adding more JVMs allows the WebSphere Application Server to use more system resources and increases the overall processing capacity of the WebSphere system. This is a highly effective way to stabilize the system to a level of acceptable operation for certain type of problems, such as gradual overall system load increase. Adding more JVM instances also buys time for root cause analysis and problem resolution.

  The addition of new JVM instances needs to be substantial. Consider increasing close to 100 percent capacity. For example, if you originally have four JVM instances in a vertical cluster, consider adding another four and configure eight total JVMs. A large number of production problems are system load sensitive. Therefore, adding more JVM instances can be a practical way to make your system less volatile; therefore it is a powerful mitigation of the customer experience. As long as this addition of JVM capacity is carefully tested and downstream components are carefully tuned against this increased JVM capacity, this will at least not introduce any additional harm. Adding JVM instances in vertical clustering is particularly suitable for frontend traffic load increases or pattern changes. However, vertical clustering requires that the JEE application supports vertical clustering. Also, although adding additional JVM instances to a vertical cluster is a rather simple system configuration change, extensive testing needs to be performed in all the downstream areas before vertical clustering can be introduced into production. (These tests are discussed later in this chapter.)

- **Remove system bottlenecks**. Identifying and removing system bottlenecks is again not removing the root cause, but better tuning the system under stress to achieve a less unstable system and mitigate the customer experience. This type of tuning can be considered problem avoidance tuning. This is especially necessary if you plan to increase JVM capacity or other WebSphere Application Server-level system resources. Among many possible system bottlenecks, you may want to carefully look at your TCP queue settings that are OS-level parameters, database listener, and connection pool settings. For this type of change, you need to work with your OS engineers and capacity planning team to find the best configuration. You do not want increased upstream system capacity overwhelming downstream components. Any of the system tuning changes must be stress tested before they are introduced into the production environment.

JVM Setting Change

Be careful about adjusting and changing JVM settings during production emergencies. Most of these settings are where they are after long years of production operation and many testing efforts. They may appear strange to a new team member or even to an experienced IBM WebSphere support engineer. However, they are there for a reason. Adjusting these tried-and-true settings, such as heap size, may create unexpected results that may further complicate the problem and delay root cause analysis and problem resolution. Unless a JVM setting is identified as a clear and direct root cause of the instability at hand, leave it as an actionable item for the future endeavor of system optimization.

Shut Down Problematic Components

When possible, bringing down problematic components helps reduce volatility, but it is not an easy task. Shutting down the problematic components requires that you know which components to shut down. Unfortunately, sometimes you know, and sometimes you do not. What's more, every now and then, you cannot afford to shut down the problematic component.

The nontraditional resources, such as a thread pool, JDBC database connection, JMS connection pool, MQ connections, JMS listener ports, and the JVM heap, are not consistently the targets of production-grade monitoring today. The coarse-grain monitoring of traditional system resources, such as CPU and memory, is too high level to identify the problematic component. For example, the traditional monitoring can only tell you that a Java process is using an abnormally high amount of CPU, but it won't tell you which component within the JVM is the problem. The industry must come up with a standard practice of providing production-strength nontraditional system-resource monitoring.

Even if you are fortunate enough to know which component is the problem, you may not be able to shut it down. You cannot shut down a key component for long, because you depend on its normal function to maintain a level of production operation before you can find a permanent fix. This is especially true for a highly critical component or system that many client applications use (for example, the customer data application that is used by 40 other mission-critical applications of a large insurance company). If the problematic component is used by all the client applications or a significant number of them, you surely cannot afford to shut down this critical component without severely affecting many customers.

To identify and shut down a problematic component to mitigate the customer experience, your WebSphere system must be prepared with the right design. For example, you can get the system ready by designing and implementing a dedicated JVM cluster for each client application. The advantage is that you can positively identify and shut down any component without bringing down all 40 client applications and causing a system-wide meltdown. Of course, the price that you have to pay for the segmentation is an increased cost of support and an increased cost in hardware and software acquisition. For very critical WebSphere systems (for example, the system record application that holds all the customer information of a large investment company), it makes good sense to spend money on a dedicated JVM cluster for each client application than to see your entire online operation go down when your system record application is undergoing a serious and prolonged outage for an instability that is difficult to identify and mitigate.

Route Traffic Away from Problematic Component

To route traffic away from the problematic component is easy to say, but it's difficult to do without proper WebSphere system design and enhanced monitoring capability. First, you may not know which stressed component is the real problem and which stressed component only expresses the problem. Worse, you may not know the origin, destination, and volume of traffic going through your system's components. If this is the case, consider both the aforementioned JVM segmentation design and enhanced nontraditional system-resources monitoring. If you do not have the proper technical architecture or the monitoring capabilities that allow you to shut down the problematic components or route traffic away from them, take action to address these deficiencies as agenda items for your post-problem resolution.

All capacity increase recommendations must be tested. A recommendation to fix a stability problem remains a recommendation until it is proven, validated, and improved through carefully planned and rigorously executed tests that need to at least include the following:

- **System test**. Conducted against the entire system based on system and functional requirement specifications. You have to work with the testing organization to ensure the recommended fix works with the rest of the system.

- **Regression test**. Uncovers software bugs that cause anomalies in functional programs. Regression testing is extremely difficult to perform when there are many client applications that may themselves be large systems interconnected with many other applications and systems. Sometimes, a seemingly innocent change in a client application can cause a complete meltdown of the host system. Therefore, conduct regression testing in a testing environment that is as realistic as possible before introducing the change into production as a fix.

- **Stress test**. Puts a WebSphere system with proposed configuration changes and the application code that it may contain as part of the overall fix under a load higher than that of normal production. If the system operates satisfactorily under this load, you can expect the production system to be stable, especially after issues revealed during testing are adequately addressed.

- **Ad-hoc test**. It is impossible for any structured testing to cover all possible execution paths and functions of the application or application suite executing within the WebSphere Application Server to validate the solution. The random nature of ad-hoc testing helps uncover otherwise unexpected problems. In addition, experienced ad-hoc testing focused on interesting areas can be a highly effective way to prove the recommended solution.

For large and complex WebSphere systems, implementing a recommendation without due testing, even for a severe and urgent problem, is highly risky. It may introduce more problems into your WebSphere system and make your critical situation worse by increasing complications and delays. You are better off controlling your urge to act immediately on the recommended fixes by trying them out in production. Instead, follow established processes to perform rigorous testing, working with the testing organization to turn these recommendations into effective and safe solutions through testing, carefully performing change control and emergence change control, and then implement the solutions into your production environment.

Managing Progress

During a production emergency, what you need from your WebSphere team is intense but orderly work.

First, you must work on the production problem with intensity and enthusiasm. Your job is to keep the critical WebSphere infrastructure stable and available. When a production problem occurs, regardless of the root cause, you must give it all your best to help your company stabilize the production system and restore production operation. Remember that you, as the WebSphere manager or senior consultant, are expected to work on the problem with a high level of intensity and dedication. During a production emergency, any deviation from impeccable professional commitment and a high sense of responsibility eventually costs your team or yourself.

Second, you must work in an orderly and calm manner. A serious production problem requires orderly work executed with calm confidence. Working in an orderly manner frequently means following established processes.

Follow Established Processes

Under the pressure of a production emergency, it is particularly important for all of those involved, including the WebSphere team, to diligently follow established processes. Otherwise, disorder surely occurs. As a result, the troubleshooting and problem resolution work suffers and slows.

Engagement

The normal engineering support engagement process must be followed. For example, if the normal process to engage WebSphere engineers involves sending a message to the WebSphere team's on-call pager, a page needs to be sent to engage the WebSphere team. In such a case, engaging support engineers without following the process, especially requests directly from senior management that bypass the engagement process, needs to be discouraged because it may cause confusion and delay the engagement.

Problem Reporting

Your team needs to closely follow the problem reporting process. If the process is that your on-call engineer needs to send out a structured problem report to the team, it should then be done. Assisting with a high-severity production problem is not a good excuse for not following the process, because without the appropriate problem reporting, it is more difficult for the management team and technical teams involved to understand and assess the problem.

Documentation

A problem documentation process must be followed. For a complex problem, a concise but clear problem statement needs to be carefully written, and a chronological problem-resolution journal must be kept. For a complex and prolonged production problem, without a written problem-resolution journal, the technical team and management find it difficult to track and manage many of the changes considered, tested, or introduced. Documentation of a severe production problem is not optional; it must be done with discipline.

Communication and Teamwork

Without following an established communication process during a production emergency, serious confusion and teamwork issues may occur at an inconvenient time. For example, according to the established process, your application production support manager is supposed to send out a daily problem status update. If you do not follow this process of centralized communication, and send out unilateral messages that have not been reviewed by the leadership team, it is likely that your message may contain contents that they disagree with, are contradictory, or even offensive to them. Thus, the propagation of your messages may cause major problems.

Troubleshooting Data Collection and Upload for IBM

Generating and sending troubleshooting data to IBM can take as long as two to four hours, depending on the size of the documents. Without carefully following the process, frustrating rework may occur and become a major showstopper in obtaining IBM technical support. During a production emergency, there is a tendency to deviate from standard processes and not generate heap dumps, thread dumps, core dumps, and other diagnostic data in a rush to restore service. This makes you lose the most critical data for troubleshooting. During an emergency, different teams, including management, may have different opinions about collecting data for troubleshooting; however, the WebSphere team needs to stick to the process, carefully generating, collecting, and transmitting data to IBM for troubleshooting.

Change Management

Not following a change-control process can lead to several serious issues. First, it is next to impossible to orderly execute changes without rigorous change management.[2] More production problems may occur if you do not follow a change-control process. Second, bypassing change managers while dealing with a production emergency may not be appreciated. You may lose the support of your change-management organization when you really need their assistance and support. Third, not following an established change-management process during a production emergency may be interpreted as a sign of weakness. Such a perception may cast a shadow on your suitability for critical posts. Finally, many companies are serious about their change-control process. Not following established change-control processes and causing heavy losses is frequently a valid reason for immediate involuntary severance.

Testing

If you introduce system or application changes to production without testing, the outcome of such "fixes" is unpredictable. All proposed fixes must be tested, especially stress tested, when they can be validated and improved before going to production. By not following the proper process and testing of your solutions, your production WebSphere system may become even more unstable. (Chapter 6, "Functional and Integration Testing Environment Support," and Chapter 7, "Stress-Testing Environment Support," discuss testing.)

Senior Management Participation and Leadership

Senior management brings experience, leadership, and the ability to mobilize more resources during a production emergency. However, for senior executives and managers, the direct management of technical teams on what and how they should do may not be the best practice.

Disastrous Case

Under the pressure to restore production service, the onsite senior manager may order the WebSphere team not to "waste" time producing data for troubleshooting. However, if the WebSphere team does not take the time to produce diagnostic data, the technical teams, including IBM, has almost nothing to work on in order to get to the root cause of the problem. This is like completely wiping clean a crime scene that leaves the detectives with little information. In addition, it may not help your career to start a public debate with your senior management about what to do during a production emergency. If the WebSphere team follows senior-management instruction, the critical troubleshooting data is lost. Without using this troubleshooting data to find the root cause, the problem won't be fixed, and it may recur.

---

2. *Change management* is a service-management process. It controls and manages the service requests to make changes to IT infrastructure. The objectives of change management are to realize the full benefits of the change while minimizing the risk of disruption to the services provided by the infrastructure. Change managers are responsible for the change-request process and approve or disapprove change requests.

Too Many Captains and Not Enough Crewmen

It is not rare to see one or two WebSphere engineers "guided" simultaneously by three or more managers, including senior managers or executives. One senior executive told the WebSphere engineers not to generate the heap dump to save time by quickly recycling the JVM. The Web-Sphere manager instructed the engineers through private channels that the heap dump must be produced. Adding to the confusion, a third manager is loudly spelling out his speculation-based analysis and asking the WebSphere engineers to comb through the system log file to verify his technical insight. In this case, there are too many captains and not enough crewmen.

Assign a Peer Manager to Assist with Production Emergencies

Assigning a peer manager to assist with production emergencies is a highly sensitive move and often ineffective during a production crisis. First, the WebSphere manager in charge and his engineers may feel that this is a sign of lack of confidence from senior management. Second, for a difficult technical problem with a history in a large and complex environment, the peer manager has much to learn before being able to provide intelligent feedback. This learning curve takes time to overcome, and the time latency is not good for quickly solving the problem. Third, dealing with a production emergency is trying enough, and having to deal with a peer manager makes the challenging situation more complex—now the WebSphere manager does not only have a tough technical problem, she also has to deal with office politics and peer relationships, which is the toughest relationship to manage in a corporate setting.

Give Workers a Chance to Do Their Jobs

If a senior manager does have experienced and practical feedback, by all means, she is welcome to provide it. In addition, the senior managers are valuable assets in helping the teams make difficult decisions. However, do not try to take over the technical details. Leave the WebSphere engineers alone. Let the WebSphere manager run her team. Trust your engineers and respect your frontline managers. Give people a chance to do their jobs. You are much better off managing a production emergency by enabling and empowering your teams, rather than being disruptive and interfering.

Frequency of Meetings and Status Reporting

When you have a production emergency, you have to focus on managing many tasks and solving technical problems. However, there are constant distractions.

One such stressful distraction is constant requests for a status report from senior management. It is not an easy job to report a complex technical problem and progress. It takes much time and effort to get a status report drafted with the right content, have it reviewed for accuracy, and approved by different teams. Sometimes, the technical teams can spend more time writing these reports than actually working on the problem. Management at all levels needs to exercise restraint during a production emergency and not send a barrage of status report requests to the technical teams. One centralized status report a day is good enough in most situations. If a senior manager has a need for immediate update on the progress and up-to-the-minute status of the problem resolution effort, the best way is to directly plug into the meetings and activities.

Another problem is attending a large number of meetings. In an effort to understand the status and manage the progress, there can be a lot of meetings. However, too many meetings may distract the team from working on the problem. Senior management needs to depend on quick calls and short conversations to get what it needs, rather than calling one meeting after another. One status meeting a day may be adequate in most cases.

Separate Meetings

Although you do not want to have too many meetings that distract the technical staff, for the following situations, consider having separate meetings with specific purposes in mind. More meetings take more time. However, these meetings may be worthy investments that help you quickly solve the high-severity problem.

Separate Managers from the Technicians

First, separate management status meetings from technical discussions. The management status meeting needs to be short. It is all about progress, problem status, actions to take, changes to propose, and major roadblocks. It is not a place to discuss technical details. Technical discussions can be long meetings where the technical teams work together to set directions for problem resolution. The intent is to separate the management discussion from the technical discussion so both can proceed smoothly.

Separate Operators from the Technical Task Force

It is a best practice to separate the ongoing operations support activities from the technical discussion. Often, there is an urge to pull all the technical resources into one big room with the hope that the synergy created and information shared quickly leads to an effective fix. Unfortunately, during a production emergency, the production operation is not only intensive, but also has higher priority over technical discussion. Therefore, the technical discussion can be interrupted so often that it becomes difficult. This costs you precious time in finding a fix for the complex problem. You need to keep operations away from the technical discussion. Assigning liaisons for production operation and technical discussion can help keep the communication free and clear.

Dedicated Daily Testing Meeting

You need to have a separate daily meeting on the testing of the proposed solutions. Every proposed solution must be tested—especially stress tested—for validation and improvement before it can be introduced to production. Therefore, during a critical situation, the testing organization has a tremendous amount of urgent work to do. The testing environments and testing engineers are valuable and critical resources during a production emergency. The appropriate application of this resource and the right priority of testing are important in reaching an effective fix. A separate daily meeting that focuses on testing strategy, resources, and priority may help.

WebSphere Application Server Problem Resolution Support Operation

To provide WebSphere engineering support during a production emergency is a tough job that demands balanced approaches. In addition, you have to provide technical support consistently in a high pressure environment. For example, you have to quickly restore service to your critical production system and collect diagnostic data that sometimes takes a significant amount of time. You have to be systematic in your triage effort and not exclude significant system components while finding the root cause of the problem and providing an effective resolution. To provide top-quality WebSphere engineering support in this challenging environment, it helps to follow a systematic framework of best practices.

Operation Framework and Description

This section systematically describes the WebSphere Application Server Problem Resolution Support Operation applying the WebSphere Operations Framework.

This operation is a structured response to issues reported at various engineering phases of WebSphere engineering. However, it is during a WebSphere critical situation when experienced management of a problem is needed most. This operation provides a systematic approach for even seasoned WebSphere managers and WebSphere consultants who lead and participate in the problem resolution process. This operation may occur during different phases of the support life cycle.

Entrance Criteria

- Issues, especially those of high severity, are reported in supported WebSphere environments.

WebSphere Resources

- WebSphere manager
- WebSphere engineers
- IBM WebSphere Application Server technical support
- IBM Java technical support
- IBM premium support

Activities

- Identify the problem and form a concise, but clear and accurate, problem statement.
- Narrow and isolate the problem from the symptoms:
  - Network
  - OS

- Loan balancers
- Security server
- Web server
- WebSphere Application Server
- Application code
- MQ
- Databases
- Interconnected enterprise systems

- Document the problem with the sequence of events that led to the problem (Event Tracking Document).
- Analyze the problem:
  - Check whether anything has recently changed in the environment.
  - Is this the first time that the problem was seen, or it is a recurring problem?
  - Which environment is affected?
  - Has the problem been in the stress-testing environment?
  - Is the problem reproducible in the stress-testing environment?
- Check the logs associated with all the components that are suspected to contribute to the problem.
- Check whether any other systems or applications have encountered a similar problem, especially if these systems or applications are located in the same data center.
- Conduct extended research on the issue (for example, search internal knowledge bases and external discussion repositories based on errors and keywords found in the logs). Often, you can find feedback and recommendations from other WebSphere professionals who have suffered a similar problem. Search the IBM error depository and other resources, such as Java problem discussion databases.
- Use the IBM Support Assistant, IBM Support site searches, and other self-help tools offered by IBM.
- Escalate the issue to IBM by opening an IBM Problem Management Record (PMR) and monitoring the PMR electronically.
- Collect and upload all necessary documentation for IBM according to IBM PMR instruction; (for example, collecting IBM Must-Gather data to attach to the opened IBM PMR (collecting Must-Gather data can be automated via IBM Support Assistant).
- Collaborate with other application and infrastructure teams, as well as IBM, to arrive at the technical solution.

- Implement the solution in testing, especially the stress-testing environment, and test thoroughly to make sure that the solution is sound and the problem is actually resolved.
- Be certain to implement only one change at a time. This is important to determine the root cause in both the testing and production WebSphere environments.
- Exercise collaborative communication in progress status updates, root cause analysis reporting, and solution recommendations.
- Follow the change-control process and emergency change-control process, and obtain formal and official approval for all changes to be made.
- Implement the solution in the production WebSphere environment.
- Document the solution and put it in a central repository to make it a reusable asset for later reference.
- Close the problem with concurrence from all teams involved.
- Conduct post-problem resolution if needed.

Processes

- Problem resolution process
- Change-control process and emergency change-control process

Artifacts

- Problem resolution check list
- Problem Resolution Activity Diagram Document
- IBM WebSphere support Web site
- IBM ESR Web site
- IBM Must-Gather Web site
- IBM Support Assistant

External Teams

- Depending on the nature of the application, this may include application production support teams, application development teams, technical teams from IBM, other vendors, and other infrastructure teams.

Sign-Off Parties

- Application production support team

Exit Criteria

- Successfully resolve the problems.

Key Processes and Artifacts Explained

This section explains the processes and artifacts used in the WebSphere Application Server Problem Resolution Support Operation.

Problem Resolution Process

The problem resolution process is a process that your WebSphere team follows in production problem triage and problem resolution. It defines who leads the triage effort, who attends the triage effort, and who participates in the problem resolution process. This document outlines resource engagement and management escalation procedures. The problem resolution process must provide quick and clear guidance during a production emergency as to the structure, the leadership, and the team members and their roles and responsibilities.

Problem Resolution Check List

The Problem Resolution Check List is a list of system components that you check for evidence of anomalies during the triage effort; for example, infrastructure components such as network, LDAP servers, operating systems, and so forth. It needs to also include application items, such as the application log file and proper file changes, among others. This check list can be different from one WebSphere system to another, as well as application to application. However, it ensures the completeness of your triage and troubleshooting effort. When you have a production emergency and are under high pressure to restore production service and quickly isolate the root cause, being complete and thorough is not easy to do without a documented process to follow.

Problem Resolution Activity Diagram

The Problem Resolution Activity Diagram Document provides a step-by-step sequence for triage efforts. This document clearly spells out the problem resolution activities for each WebSphere application that you support.

Post-Problem Resolution

Post-problem resolution is a series of meetings to revisit the events of the production emergency, finalize the root cause, explore improvement opportunities, and form actionable items. To have a productive post-problem resolution, the key is preparation.

Preparation

Preparation can be divided into two interwoven parts: documentation and consensus building. This involves drafting the Post-Problem Resolution Document, reviewing the document, meeting with the main stakeholders to discuss the document, and finalizing the document. It is a process that gradually leads to a high-quality Post-Problem Resolution Document with an agreement on its major contents, or an agreement to disagree on some points needing further discussion.

Documentation

The document needs to include four sections:

- Section 1 needs to be a concise problem description. It must contain the basic information of the problem, time, location, and what happened.

- Section 2 can be a concise chronology of what has been done about the problem in service restoration and problem resolution.

- Section 3 is the all-important root cause analysis. Use neutral language in this section. If IBM provides a root cause analysis statement, quote IBM.

- Section 4 recommends actionable items to prevent the problem from recurring.

The document needs to be concise, but formal and official. It is important to conspicuously mark the document as Draft For Review before all the parties reach a level of agreement on its contents.

This document needs to be first reviewed by at least one more member of the WebSphere team who is familiar with the production problem. Ideally, the document needs to be internally reviewed by a few WebSphere team members, including senior management, depending on the severity of the problem.

Consensus Building

You can call an informal meeting of a smaller scale to discuss the Post-Problem Resolution Document. The objective of this premeeting is to discuss any possible differences, build consensus, and avoid major confrontation at the formal full-scale post-problem resolution meeting.

The senior management and the technical community have no stomach to see teams engage in public fights. Instead, you are expected to work as a team to prevent the problem from recurring. Working hard to reach an agreement and working with each other is not only in your best interest, but in the collective best interest of all the teams involved.

You need to update the Post-Problem Resolution Document with the feedback from this pre-post-problem resolution meeting. Send the draft to the teams involved for review. You may have to update the document a few more times until it is ready for presentation at the formal post-problem resolution meeting.

Post-Problem Resolution Meeting

Now your document is ready for the post-problem resolution meeting. You have to make sure that you are ready, too. Be prepared to be calm, friendly, and professional.

Post-Problem Resolution Is Not a Political Tool

Do not use post-problem resolution as a political tool. Whomever you have an issue with during the process of managing the production emergency, you can address your grievances at a different time and location. This is a high-visibility meeting with many key people attending. If you do not bring your best intentions to the meeting, they will know, and they will not like it.

Yes, accountability is important. It needs to be clear who should take action and make improvements. However, your focus must be on helping the teams figure out how to prevent the problem from recurring. The slightest hint of finger pointing will surely touch off resentment, confrontation, and even hostility because during a post-problem resolution, attendees may be understandably more sensitive than they usually are. In the final analysis, any accusatory remarks will not only hurt the receiving party, but will hurt you even more because it damages your image as a professional.

Team Review of the Final Recommendation

All the parties involved must review the final recommendation of improvement opportunities. Before this document can be published, you need to adhere to a patient review and approval process. The process may take some time, but it's worth it.

You particularly need to ask those who are responsible to make improvements to review and comment on the Post-Problem Resolution Document. Before such a review and approval process is done, try to keep the document as private as possible. For example, you may want to send the document to the application development manager only (for him to review the recommendations on application code quality), instead of sending the document to a large number of audiences.

There isn't anything more destructive to work relationships than unilaterally broadcasting a Post-Problem Resolution Document without giving the responsible party a chance to review and provide feedback. This is because a Post-Problem Resolution Document without the final review and approval process sometimes contains misleading information that can cause confusion and resentment.

Follow Up

You have to check on the actionable items. You have to ensure that the proper work is done and the problem is not going to recur. This task may sound deceptively simple. Actually, it can be quite complex, depending on who is responsible for the improvement opportunity.

Do Not Push

In corporate life, the only one that you can push hard is yourself. You may be able to push your WebSphere team sometimes, but not always. Pushing a business partner or a peer team is a bad idea.

The first problem is that you may not be successful in achieving your objectives after all the pushing. For example, the Post-Problem Resolution Document points out that the application code has a defect in its logging component. Your resident JEE expert codes a simple prototype and makes a convincing case by demonstrating the fix to the application developers. However, the application development team determines that this fix needs to be tested and deployed with the next release, which is two months from now. You become anxious about the problem and escalate to the application development executive. The application development executive may agree with his managers that this code fix needs to come in with the next release. Then, your push fails.

Second, even if the code change is made promptly after you push, your action is still rather questionable. The application development manager should have all the motivation in the world to fix a code defect. If he decides not to do that, there has to be a reason. Often, the reason for delaying a code fix has to do with the resources needed to fix the defect and the priority of new business functions that must go into providing a set of new functions to the customer. The application development manager has to prioritize needs, and usually the business need for new functions wins, especially when it is possible to provide a workaround solution for the code defect. If the application development manager is forced to make the code fix, the work relationship suffers, because he may remember this stressful experience working with you.

Is this the ideal situation? Absolutely not. If you allow these code defects to pile up, sooner or later, the WebSphere application becomes fragile or even too brittle to be useful. However, this problem stems from the systemic issue of fast-changing business needs and the orderly engineering execution of IT. This intrinsic latency of IT is aggravated by the difficulty of the business in understanding technology and its engineering processes. Therefore, pushing the application development team does not achieve much; instead, it makes a big dent on the work relationship.

Influence

The most powerful influence is by example. The best way to influence your WebSphere team, is to set a good example. The same goes for influencing your peer teams. If your WebSphere team is taking responsibility, working hard on your improvement items, providing timely updates, the other teams are more likely to follow suit.

Of course, you can always ask for a status report and honestly share your concerns, working with your peer teams one at a time. In addition, you can ask the post-problem resolution manager or a member of the senior management to do the same inquiry.

You can formally share your concerns in a written communication about the possible risk for a recommendation that has not been carried out. However, this is perhaps about as far as you should go. It is all right to be passionate about what you do while recognizing what is appropriate to do and the need to reconcile yourself to the imperfect, complex, and sometimes seemingly chaotic world of IT.

Communication and Teamwork During a Production Emergency

During a critical production emergency, your job as the WebSphere manager or senior consultant can be summarized with two words: mobilizing and motivating. Mobilizing is all about urgently allocating the right amount of technical resources with the right skills to engage in the right tasks. Motivating is about forming a converged technical force to solve the problem through skillfully managing communication and teamwork.

Communication: A Powerful Tool During a Production Crisis

During a production emergency, your communication performance significantly contributes to your overall success. The quality of your emergency situation communication or the lack of it conspicuously displays the level of your technical skills, the maturity of your management ability, and your characteristics, caliber, and potential as a technology leader.

Disciplined Communication

A critical production emergency is a serious matter during which both written and verbal communication must be disciplined. Resist the urge to send any messages that are not carefully prepared. This is not easy, especially when the WebSphere team is the target of blame, but it is possible if you try.

Do not get into a defensive posture and spend a lot of time and energy arguing for your team or yourself. You do not have to get the story right. Eventually, no amount of blame or accusation can alter the facts of the root cause and the responsible party. If any incorrect information from anyone is causing confusion and is misleading to the problem-resolution efforts, you can certainly carefully clarify. However, do not respond quickly, early, or frequently.

Do not become emotional. Instead, send a carefully prepared, reviewed, and improved message that is of impeccable professionalism, as well as factual, positive, and constructive.

Internal Review

The internal review of an important message is a best practice. The collective wisdom and experience of a team is always of a higher magnitude than that of yours as an individual. Get the key members of the team to review important messages. Encourage constructive criticism so as to improve the message. You may be surprised how much better your message becomes. Your message is most likely to become more rounded and balanced.

Open and Honest

You have to be careful, but at the same time, try to be open and honest. Remember that this is an internal message to your management, business partners, and peer technical teams. Caution and prudence are all good, but do not let your message sound like a legal document from an overzealous attorney, because it may be taken as a sign of distrust or a defensive posture. Neither is good for teamwork.

Centralized Status Communication

You need to discourage premature status updates, especially to senior management. You should not support unilateral communication (for example, communication without consulting the other teams about the communication content). A centralized status communication during a production crisis is a best practice. For example, you can send out a problem status update daily after getting the key teams and key individuals to review the message.

However, it is difficult not to respond to the request for a status update from your own management. Of course, if you must send messages to your management unilaterally, you can add a disclaimer to the message such as "not reviewed by peer team," "intermediate," or "subject to change." However, some senior managers may be confused or offended by verbiage such as this in an update sent to them:

- Your management may not understand that you are trying to avoid unilateral communication. They may be confused as to what you are trying to convey by adding these disclaimers.

- Your management may take these disclaimers as an excuse for the lack of due diligence on collecting and verifying important information.

- Your management may take this as your evading responsibility for your own messages.

- The worst possibility is that your reminder may be interpreted as an indication that you do not trust your management. Nobody likes distrust, but it is particularly hurtful to senior managers who usually have—or at least perceive themselves as having—excellent people skills, especially at building trust-based relationships.

Adding a disclaimer depends on your relationship with your management. If you have a close work relationship with your management and your management understands what you are trying to convey, adding a disclaimer or reminder is fine. Otherwise, you may want to concisely mention at the end of the update that you have not had time to ask your business partners (for example, the application development manager) to review this update because of time constraints. This kind of straightforward explanation about the unilateral communication is more natural and easily understood.

Collaborative Communication

You may not know how your production support manager responds to a communication. People are different and teams have different focuses and perceptions. What appears to you as complimentary may be totally inappropriate to another team. The best way to work with your business partners and peer technical teams on important issue communications is to ask them to review your message and provide feedback. This is collaborative communication. Although this is an effective means of communication during a production crisis, there are two areas that you have to watch out for to cut down on confusion and teamwork issues.

First, do not let collaborative review of messages slow you down. When you have to communicate in a timely manner to grasp an opportunity to fix the problem, just communicate. Communication techniques and best practices should not stand in the way of your solving the problem quickly. When you have solid reasons to take a risk in communication, take a risk.

Second, your exercising collaborative communication does not give you a right to ask for reciprocation. To ask your business partners to share with you an email to be sent to their management or the technical communication about the production emergency brings about many problems. For example, your peers may think that you are not trusting or you are interfering with their work. Do what you think is the right thing, but do not ask or expect reciprocation.

Fight a Production Fire by Working as One Team

A critical production emergency can bring a tremendous amount of pressure and may become a stressful moment in your work relationships and teamwork. However, it can also present a wonderful opportunity for the WebSphere team to build better work relationships with business partners and improve work relationships with peer technical teams.

Opportunities for Improved Relationships

A production emergency can be a good opportunity to improve teamwork and build long-lasting work relationships. "A friend in need is a friend indeed." A crisis may give the WebSphere team a rare opportunity to help those in need of assistance and start a rewarding work relationship. For example, the WebSphere team can change the configuration to mitigate the customer experience, and then help the application development executive isolate a difficult application code defect using its deep dive diagnostic tools. Another example involves testing. You, the WebSphere manager, have more exposure to production problems than the testing manager. When you feel that a high- severity production problem may be related to testing issues, keep the testing manager informed so that she is prepared to deal with the issues. In case the production problem is caused by a flaw in testing strategy, you may want to work with the technical teams involved to help improve the testing plan while articulating your appreciation and support for what the testing team does for improving system stability.

The WebSphere team, as an IT middleware infrastructure team, has exposure to many WebSphere applications. The WebSphere managers and engineers usually have experience managing difficult production emergencies. Be proactive and do whatever you can to help. When you see many changes are introduced into the critical testing environment without careful documentation, document the changes and help to manage testing activities in an orderly manner. When you realize that a change manager is not part of the task force, propose to engage a change manager that brings discipline and experience to the problem resolution. Carefully study the anomalies and compare them to the problems that you have experienced with other WebSphere applications. Share the results of your research.

Doing a good job is not enough. You need to challenge yourself to do what is well above and beyond your call of duty. Your business partners and peer teams will remember your dedication and contribution. You will earn their respect, which is the foundation of any meaningful relationship.

Shared Business Interest

You have to remember and remind the teams that any success or failure managing the production emergency is collective. All the technical teams are in the same boat because they are on the same project. If you do not contain the production problem and find a permanent fix, you will all fail. This is your shared business objective that sometimes is forgotten.

Whenever you have an opportunity, remind your team that you are the greatest resources for each other. To fully take advantage of these priceless resources, you must work as a team. Teamwork is the key to winning, and everyone is expected to be a team player.

No Blame

Blaming anyone, either explicitly or implicitly, is damaging to the business. People are intelligent. They can see through the most subtle and implicit finger pointing. Blaming slows everyone because it creates resentment between teams and team members, and it distracts everyone from focusing on fixing the problem.

Blaming triggers defense mechanisms that have nothing to do with working on the production emergency. The worst kind of accusatory campaign during a production crisis can force everyone to perform complex and sophisticated covering of their tracks. Everyone has to take a huge amount of time and energy to play the defense attorney. Then, your problem resolution efforts will, most likely, be derailed.

Focus on the problems, not teams or team members. It is not really a production code issue, a database issue, or a WebSphere Application Server issue. It is a production problem for all the technical teams.

Do the Right Thing with an Awareness of the Long-Term Work Relationship

Teamwork techniques are important, but focusing on the job is a must. Managing work relationships in a large corporation is important. However, always have the courage to openly and honestly express a professional opinion. In addition, during production emergencies, work relationship considerations must never be the obstacle for you to take the right action for your company.

However, always have the strategic view of a long-term work relationship. Even when you take actions that may affect a key work relationship, careful consideration and preparation must be made to minimize the impact. You have to work on preparatory measures and get ready to mend the relationship. In no case should you stretch the relationship to the extent where trust and teamwork may be difficult to rebuild.

Focus on solving the production problem while bearing in mind that if you have a myopic approach to work relationships in a corporation setting, you won't go far in your career. The culmination of the art is to do both jobs in a balanced manner: you must fix the instability and strengthen work relationships to be successful.

Working with IBM During a Production Emergency

During a critical situation, as the WebSphere engineering leader of your company, it is your job to mobilize all the resources to help your company overcome the problem and restore the production service of your WebSphere system. Other than your WebSphere teams, the IBM technical support organization is the most important resource available to you, especially WebSphere technical support and the Java technical support organization. However, skillful collaboration and teamwork with this awesome technical force is needed to help with achieving problem resolution and system stability.

Generating and Uploading Documents

During a production emergency, it is critical to correctly generate and quickly transmit the troubleshooting data, or documents, as they are known in IBM technical jargon.

Without these documents, IBM WebSphere technical support can do little to help. Also, the documents, such as heap dumps and core dumps, are large documents, so it takes considerable time to generate and upload them. Time is in short supply when you have a production emergency. Finally, the process of generating and transmitting documents is not trivial, and can be error prone. Generating and uploading documents sounds simple, but it frequently becomes the showstopper for fast problem isolation and timely problem resolution.

To do a good job at generating and uploading documents, you have to do the following jobs well.

Get the Process Right

Usually, you want to collect the documents and send them to IBM when you open the PMR. In that case, your WebSphere team needs to make a judgment as to what documents are most likely necessary (which Must-Gather must collect). It's probably a good idea to write a script to collect the most common documents for your environments. For specific situations, IBM may communicate a special process for generating and collecting documents by PMR, email, or both. Your team must carefully read and thoroughly understand the process. It is better to spend the time upfront to be completely clear about the process than to repeat the time-consuming job. Clarify anything that you do not completely understand immediately. Request a phone number from IBM and call to clarify instead of waiting for an email response.

It is particularly important to ask for and confirm the process if the document upload involved data format transformation or compression (for example, reformatting the documents from EBCIDC to ASCII and using the mainframe "terse" program to compress the documents before transmitting). More than once, IBM has been unable to read a document that is formatted incorrectly or compressed by using an inappropriate program. As a result, even four to five hours can be lost, with each hour accounting for a few million dollars lost to your company.

Watch the Transmission

The transmission of documents can take several hours, depending on the speed of your Internet connection and the size of the files. Sometimes, after all the troubles that your team has gone through, IBM can do nothing to help because the documents transmitted are truncated.

Watch the transmission and ensure that the documents are uploaded in their entirety. This, of course, is a tedious job when your engineer finally finishes generating the documents at 2 AM and then has to stay up for another two or three hours to ensure that the documents are uploaded.

Still, during a production crisis, you have to do what you have to do. You have to watch the process and ensure the successful transmission of documents to IBM.

Confirmation

Call IBM WebSphere Application Server technical support immediately after uploading the documents and confirm the following:

- IBM received the documents that you uploaded.
- IBM confirms that these are the needed documents.
- IBM verifies that the documents are not corrupt or truncated.

Ask IBM to provide the following information:

- A tentative time for IBM response. You are better off having this information ready because this question may be asked many times in the next 12 to 24 hours.
- Are any other documents needed by IBM? This is asked so that you can get ready to generate and upload.

Get IBM Personnel to Perform This Job

Sometimes, after all due diligence on both the IBM side and that of your team, correct documentation generation and timely uploading can become an issue. IBM is powerless to help without the correct documents. For your team, complaints about the lack of the right process from IBM may become increasingly pronounced.

At this point, the best practice is to remove the WebSphere team from the process and ask for IBM onsite technical personnel to perform document generation and transmission. As part of the production emergency process, familiarize yourself with the application and approval process to give IBM personnel the appropriate security access they need to perform document generation and transmission. This application process of security access for nonemployees can be lengthy, and you want to be armed with the knowledge of how to speed this up during a production emergency.

You need to fix any problems in document generation and uploading so that your team is not slowed the next time this happens.

Onsite IBM Support

During a high visibility production emergency, such as a WebSphere critical situation, understandably, it is management's focus to ensure that adequate technical resources are being applied to deal with difficult problems. Often, IBM technical support personnel working on the issue are required to travel to the main site of your company to join the technical teams in a "war room." This actually may not be the best practice in today's IT marketplace of globalization and workforce diversity.

Traveling to Your Site

In today's IT marketplace, every large company, including IBM, is trying to build a global workforce of diversity to better serve its customers, get stronger employee satisfaction, and achieve higher shareholder values. For example, the IBM technical support organization may have a Level 1 WebSphere support in Hyderabad taking initial feedback, who then escalates the PMR to a Level 2 WebSphere support in Raleigh, who works with a Java technical support engineer working in London. It is possible but difficult to fly the IBM WebSphere support from all over the world to your company's site. Worse, production emergencies are not predictable. It is not possible for the IBM technical support organization to make travel plans for your production emergencies ahead of time. Everyone understands the hassle of impromptu travel arrangements and how it interrupts work and family life.

Of course, these last-minute travels across the world are expensive. As a business partner, you want to help reduce the technical support cost of IBM whenever you can, because more cost-effective IBM technical support may eventually mean cost savings to your company.

The most significant loss to you is the lost time and productivity degradation when IBM personnel travel to your site. Even within the continental U.S., it could take an entire day for the IBM technical support to travel to your site, and that is one day lost for your team. If your IBM technical support has to fly from Europe or Asia to a U.S. site, it could take at least 20 hours. The time spent on the trip won't be productive, regardless of how eager the IBM technical staff is. The IBM technical support is busy getting to and from airports, struggling through security with laptop and bags, and worrying about the getting to the right gate on time at unfamiliar terminals. In addition, while the IBM technical support is flying, he is completely isolated from the teams and the ongoing troubleshooting efforts.

Your Main Site May Not Be the Most Productive Environment for IBM Technical Support

Finally, your IBM technical support engineers arrive at your site. However, they are not in the best working environment where they can be the most productive. They may or may not be able to use their troubleshooting tools to do their data analysis. These powerful software tools are usually installed on their high-end UNIX workstations, which they cannot take with them. They may not have direct access to some of the IBM software facilities that they need to do their job because of your company's security setup. You may suddenly find that security regulation exception requests are never something that can be approved quickly and easily because of legal reasons, even during a highly stressful production emergency (for example, complying with laws protecting private customer information). Of course, your critical IBM onsite resources have to spend extra time to familiarize themselves with their new work environment, where connecting to a printer and printing a WebSphere Application Server topology diagram can become a huge and time-consuming challenge, or even impossible altogether if they are not allowed to access your company's network.

The fact that IBM technical support has traveled across the world to help your company is encouraging to all the teams involved. It makes a resonating item on the status update to the business, too. For example, you can tell the business leaders that IBM technical talents are on site providing technical support and use this as evidence of your technology partner management performance. However, it is a highly ineffective and costly way to use your critical technical resources during a crisis when you cannot afford not to make the best use of your best technical talents, including IBM technical support. Always carefully explain the pros and cons about IBM sending onsite technical support, as well as the risk, which is likely continued delays in problem isolation and resolution. By the end of the day, your performance as a technology leader in your company is evaluated by how well and how fast you can fix the problem. A show of IBM onsite support sometimes is important; however, the right use of IBM resources to solve the problem as soon as possible is always critical and needs to have higher priority.

Communication Collaboration

Usually, the WebSphere team manages the communication with IBM technical support. This is done through IBM PMR, email, and telephone conversations. The WebSphere team carefully studies the IBM feedback and when necessary, shares IBM feedback with the other technical teams.

Managed IBM Communication

The WebSphere team should review IBM feedback and make an experienced decision whether to share it with the other technical teams. This is a best practice for good reasons.

IBM feedback, at this juncture, may not yet have a recommendation, but it contains more detailed requests for more technical information for analysis and troubleshooting. Without specific technical training, it is not easy to understand what the IBM feedback really means. It is appropriate for the WebSphere team to filter this and decide whether it helps to share specific IBM feedback with the task force.

These critical situations are all about complex and challenging problems. In addition, the IT environments that the WebSphere team works in, as well as the WebSphere engineering practices in your company, may be far from perfect. IBM feedback, if not put in the right context, may lead the technical teams in the wrong direction and derail your problem resolution efforts. For example, your JVM heap size is 2GB. IBM has recommended the JVM size be reduced to one-fourth its current size. It is a perfectly correct recommendation, but not a good one for you at this moment during a production emergency. This is because your application code is not perfect and it loads large objects into the heap at initialization. In addition, you know that the current large JVM heap size setting has been there for two years without causing a problem; therefore, it is unlikely to be the problem. If you follow the IBM recommendation, you have to allocate resources to test a smaller JVM heap size with the application. Regardless of whether the testing is successful, it is unlikely to solve your problem, but only distract your teams from finding the real problem. In this case, you may want to hold the IBM communication, and explain the context of the problem to the teams and the management to prepare them to better understand the IBM recommendation and then share the IBM feedback.

IBM has absolutely top technical talents and great IT professionals. However, IBM technical support may make a recommendation that can be improved upon. Your WebSphere team needs to discuss, validate, and improve such feedback, working with IBM shoulder to shoulder, before it can be shared with the technical community of your company.

For the WebSphere team and for your company, managed IBM communication adds value and is the right thing to do. However, during a critical situation, this may or may not be possible and you have a whole new kind of challenging communication management job to do.

Direct IBM Communication

During a severe production emergency, such as a critical situation, IBM technical support personnel may directly participate in meetings and may even be onsite working with the technical teams of your company in troubleshooting and problem resolution. Although this is a tremendous help to your teams, it can also present new challenges and even issues in teamwork and collaboration with IBM technical support.

IBM feedback on a technical issue, especially during a technical crisis, carries enormous weight. It often builds immediate momentum for action along the recommended direction. It also has a lingering effect. The IBM recommendation keeps pulling the minds of your technical community back to the recommended direction for a considerable period of time to come.

Of course, IBM technical support personnel have broad and profound WebSphere Application Server and Java technology knowledge and skills. The WebSphere teams of your company may know more in the following areas:

- Detailed knowledge about your large and complex WebSphere infrastructure and WebSphere application or application suite
- The long and complicated history of the technical problem (for instance, in the previously example, how the JVM heap has grown over the years, the changes of the ownership of application development, changes in business drivers, as well as the extensive testing work conducted so far)
- The large and complex IT organization and business organization of your company, as well as relationship and organization dynamic issues that are relevant to the technical problem that you are dealing with
- The large suite of engineering and business processes and procedures of your company (for example, the change-control and emergency change-control processes and production fix promotion and testing procedures)

A technical problem, especially a critical technical problem with a complex history in a large IT organization, is never a pure technical issue. It has important project management dimensions, dynamic organization impacts, and process considerations. If the technical problem is taken out of this complex context, the recommendation provided may not be a practical solution. During normal times, the IBM technical support team and your WebSphere team can work together to provide and improve a solution. However, IBM technical support is now directly participating in the troubleshooting and problem resolution, and as a result, your WebSphere team may not have the usual window of opportunity to add value.

Hold an in-synch meeting between the IBM technical support personnel assigned to the critical situation and your WebSphere team before important meetings. This gives you a chance to share information about the history of the problem, the relevant specifics of the WebSphere environment and idiosyncrasies of the applications, the political landscape, and the company processes that you have to follow. The meeting objectives are to be in synch with IBM technical support on important topics and recommendations and to seek agreement on major technical issues and critical situation management concerns.

Ask the IBM team resident in your company, including IBM Premium Support, to actively participate in the critical situation work and play the liaison between your WebSphere team and the IBM technical support personnel. The IBM team working in your company knows your WebSphere system well, understands the history of the problems, is aware of relevant organization issues, and is familiar with the processes of your company. In addition, the IBM team working in your company also has in-depth knowledge of the large IBM organization and has members who are part of the IBM technical support team. Therefore, it is in a perfect position to deal with any possible complex conversations, to promote teamwork, and to strengthen work relationships.

Should there be any post-problem resolution process in identifying and implementing improvements, the IBM technical support personnel, your resident IBM team, and the WebSphere team must work closely and carefully to devise strategies to help with the process and collaboratively draft and finalize the all-important root cause analysis report.

Grow the Relationship with IBM and Get Ready for the Next Problem

To best manage your relationship with IBM, you must have the right expectations.

Fast IBM Response

A critical situation is never a simple technical problem, but typically a complex and elusive problem with many factors involved. To provide solutions for such problems, there are large WebSphere infrastructure and applications that IBM technical support personnel must work to understand. There are usually long histories of the problem that IBM technical support personnel must learn. Also, there is a huge amount of troubleshooting data in the format of uploaded documents that IBM technical support has to successfully download from the FTP server, decompress, and transform into the right format, and use a number of tools to process. Then, they must carefully analyze the result, draft and compile a report, get proper review and approval when needed, and communicate the recommendation to you. All this will take time.

Sometimes, after all the work that IBM technical support has done, it is possible that IBM technical support may not have any feedback for you. Instead, IBM technical support may give your WebSphere team another set of instructions for more data collection before any recommendation can be made. For example, the Java heap dump may be truncated and does not provide enough data for troubleshooting and needs to be regenerated and resent. Yes, it is a critical situation. Indeed, it is an emergency. Still, before all of this work is done properly, the IBM technical support team cannot provide useful feedback. You have to understand this and help educate the task force built for the critical situation to guard against impatience and unreasonable expectations.

No Feedback from IBM

Your frustration is understandable when IBM technical support has no feedback at all after all the work that you have done to provide troubleshooting information. However, this is possible sometimes, especially in the case in which no critical troubleshooting documents are produced, or are produced incorrectly. Specifically, if you have not provided a good Java heap dump, a Java thread dump, an OS level core dump on the distributed platform, and a SVC dump for the mainframe, it is difficult for IBM technical support to provide effective assistance. As a result, IBM may have no feedback for you.

It is possible that occasionally IBM does not find evidence of problems in the documents that you provide for troubleshooting; therefore, it cannot provide useful feedback.

Understand that IBM wants to help you succeed in using IBM WebSphere Application Server products and if it can help at all, it absolutely will.

In addition, keep in mind that you have direct access to your WebSphere systems and IBM does not. When it is not possible for IBM to provide technical assistance based on the provided documents, it is your job to figure out how you can share available information to help IBM help you. For example, you can share with IBM the findings from your deep dive diagnostic tool, such as Introscope. This constructive move may give IBM new data to help with the problem and allow your WebSphere team to work together with IBM technical support in searching for an effective solution in the fastest manner possible.

Team Management During a Critical Situation

During a critical situation, it is not uncommon to see intensive research and testing efforts being carried out around the clock. The workload for the WebSphere team dramatically increases; therefore, there is a need for experienced resource management and intensified caring for the team to avoid work-related safety issues.

What's more, increased work means increased expenditure and consequently budgetary challenges that need careful management, even when you are focusing on dealing with a critical technical problem.

The team under stress is more sensitive to the influence of example from its leadership. How you carry yourself during an emergency is critically important to the morale and productivity of your team.

Guard Against Applying Too Many Resources

As the WebSphere manager or senior consultant, your first job in dealing with a critical production emergency is to engage adequate resources of the right kind to work on the problem. What are adequate resources is a key question. On one hand, you need to mobilize your team to deal with a serious production emergency. On the other hand, you have to provide normal WebSphere engineering support to all the projects that you have committed to and carry out the normal business processes for supporting a large number of production WebSphere systems. In addition, you have to consider the length of the critical situation. It could last days, weeks, or even months for a highly complex and elusive problem.

Assigning too many WebSphere engineers to work on the critical situation stresses the WebSphere team and drains its strength as a sustainable source of engineering support. This hinders the effectiveness of the WebSphere team in supporting the WebSphere engineering work for troubleshooting and problem resolution efforts.

Assigning too many WebSphere engineers to work on a production outage actually can hurt the image and business reputation of the WebSphere team. Rather than appreciating the focus and enthusiasm of your team in helping with a major problem that your company is suffering, a harmful perception may develop that the WebSphere team simply has too many people. Another possible perception is that the leader of the WebSphere team is panicking under pressure and applying excessive resource allocation that has no practical merits.

Assigning adequate resources, but the least possible, to support the critical situation usually is a balanced approach.

Form a Support Rotation Plan as Early as Possible

As soon as you realize that this production emergency may drag on for an indefinite period of time, form a support rotation plan. This is a useful way to get the team prepared in both time allocation and mentality to provide the extra support needed for dealing with the critical situation. Ask as many WebSphere team members to participate in forming the support rotation plan as possible. The team can always come up with good solutions when they put their heads together. As the leader of the group, you may want to offer your contractors extra hours so that they get extra pay; the same suggestions can be made to team members in the areas where overtime pay is required by law. A collectively made emergency support rotation plan tends to get the support and the commitment of the team.

Caring for the Team Under Stress

Your team does not care how important you are unless they know how much you care. Production emergencies are difficult times. The stress is high, the work hours are long, and the work is hard. During such times, be attentive to the team, especially for prolonged production emergencies. Guard against possible safety or injury issues. This helps you maintain the morale of the team and avoid liability or legal complications. Even under the pressure of a production emergency, the safety of your employees needs to be your first priority:

- Pay for the hotel expenses of individuals working around the clock so that they can up catch up on some sleep. This helps avoid accidents and costly system operation error.

- Pay for a taxi for those who are too tired to drive home safely.

- Production emergencies can stress your team. Try to help them better manage work-related stress. For example, invite a teammate to take a coffee break. Ask an engineer who has just braved a difficult meeting to have a short walk around campus.

Take care of your team, especially when the going gets tough. Remember that a small, genuine kindness goes a long way in mobilizing your team to help you get over the problem. During emergencies, do not panic, do not become snappy, and do not lose your own balance. Continue to treat your team with trust, respect, and attention. Then, you may find that the problem starts to resolve itself.

Manage Financials During a Critical Situation

The extra work needed during a critical situation costs extra money. For example, a month-long production emergency can translate into a mobile phone bill of over $1,000 for a senior WebSphere engineer. There are extra expenditures to pay salaries for contractors and overtime payment for employees, when applicable. Meals, hotel rooms, and late-night taxi rides all cost money. If it turns out to be an application code issue, but not a WebSphere system issue, JEE application consulting assistance from IBM has to be paid for if your company decides to use IBM JEE application expertise.

Make a realistic estimate and formally communicate this extra cost to your senior management and customers upfront. Obtain official approval for unusually high expenditures incurred during the critical situation. You need to engage established processes of your company and get the funding needed through normal channels. When the critical situation is ongoing, it is easier to get verbal agreements on the extra costs. However, when it is over and you're confronted with large bills, your senior management and customers may have slightly different opinions about the extra costs. Make your life easier by choosing to do a little extra work upfront and secure prior approval for the extra costs while the critical situation is ongoing.

Disciplined Internal Communication Within the WebSphere Team

The appropriate way to communicate during a critical situation may be counterintuitive. Communicating early and often may not be the best idea. Control your urge to send many messages to the team. Stop calling your team members, who are working on a problem, every 15 minutes. Let your WebSphere engineers focus on solving the tough problems, not dealing with numerous anxious emails or phone calls.

Develop a structured process on progress reporting and problem status tracking. Do not panic, but steadily follow that established process for status updates and problem reporting during a production emergency.

Your example has incredible influence over your WebSphere team during crises. If you are calm and confident, the team tends to be calm and confident. Then it can focus on solving the problem rather than worrying about the possible consequences and fallout of the problem.

Can you keep a sense of humor during a grave production outage? If you cannot, start to develop one. Can you maintain impeccable professionalism during a crisis? If you cannot, start working on it. Regardless of what industry you are in, a critical situation is not an excuse to abandon common courtesy and professional decorum. Under the pressure of a critical situation, those who are preoccupied by fear are unable to think about anybody else but themselves, and as a result, they won't take care of their teams. Remember that a critical situation is a high-visibility event. Your management is watching how you interact with your team and business partners. Your employees are acutely aware of what you are doing. Your management style has a direct relationship to the performance of your team. How you behave under pressure leaves an impression on your technical community about who you are.

Building a Strong Reputation for the WebSphere Team

Business reputation has a direct relationship to business prosperity. As the leader of the WebSphere team in a large IT organization, take every possible opportunity to build a strong reputation for the WebSphere team and project an image of a well-trained, confident, highly capable technical force that is helpful and pleasant to work with. Treat the WebSphere team as a brand name and grow a positive image whenever you can. A high-visibility critical situation presents a good opportunity to promote the WebSphere team if you can do a good job in the following areas.

Confident, Professional, and Disciplined Verbal Communication

Of course, good written communication is equally important in building a strong team reputation, but here, the focus of discussion is verbal communication. During a production crisis, there are plenty of important opportunities to talk (for example, introducing a technical solution that the WebSphere team recommends). If you can speak with confidence and authority, it helps with both the team image and the resolution of the problem.

Have Faith in Your Team

Trust your team or the extended team of a task force that will do a good job and isolate the problem. Have faith in the hard work that you are doing to resolve the issue. Believe in the determination and technical capabilities of your organization. Confidence is neither optimism nor pessimism; it is a resolved expectation for a positive outcome. You want to make sure that people understand that you have complete confidence in the team and the problem will be resolved.

Get Prepared

Confidence can come from good preparation. If you know what you are going to talk about, you will be more relaxed and confident in your presentation. You have to work up to really knowing the details of a complex production issue. A short document with four sections can be useful in helping you get prepared:

- Problem statement.
- What have the teams been doing?
- What have been the findings so far?
- WebSphere team recommendation.

Think from the Perspective of Your Audience

Certainly, it is difficult to correctly predict how the other participants of a large meeting will react to your proposal. However, carefully thinking through their work, their concerns, and their objectives helps you be better equipped to deal with possible situations and reactions. Thinking from the perspective of your audience gives you more confidence because you are better prepared. Let's take the application development team as an example.

- **Work**. Identify the code defect and provide a permanent fix.
- **Concerns**. If the production problem is escalated to purple alert state, it may affect team performance record.
- **Objective**. Fix the code defect as soon as possible without escalating to the purple alert state.

Armed with this analysis, you may want to talk more about the deep dive JVM diagnostic capabilities that the WebSphere team has and refrain from making a recommendation to escalate the severity of the problem. As result, it is likely that you have a far more relaxed presentation without the application development team opposing you. It is important to have a cooperative and smooth meeting because a confrontational and emotional exchange does not help the image of the WebSphere team.

Modesty and Patience

Always speak with confidence and authority about technical issues. However, this does not mean refusing to listen to different opinions. It does not mean that you can interrupt others, and everyone must treat the solution that you propose as absolute truth. Under the pressure of production emergencies, it is not rare to see otherwise civil professionals interrupting others, snapping out commands, and even yelling at each other.

Listening to different opinions is not easy when you have a mature and thoughtful idea about what to do with a production crisis and you are not allowed a chance to speak. However, it is possible if you realize how important it is to listen carefully and really hear the different message. At a critical moment, different opinions and a full discussion of these opinions lead to much more balanced solutions and is a powerful insurance policy to avoid disastrous mistakes that come from omnipresent uniformity and a lack of diversity in opinion.

Be respectful of different opinions. Recognize that your teammates and their opinions are as important and valuable as your own. Do not interrupt others. If you interrupt others accidentally, apologize, and politely yield. When you try to express an opinion, use terms such as "in my mind" or "I hold the view" to ensure that people understand that you are aware of other opinions and you recognize and respect different opinions.

If after all your efforts, the teams still cannot reach a consensus, you may want to adjourn with an encouraging remark such as "Let's have a short break. When we come back, I am sure we can figure something out working as a team." It is important to be constructive at all times. Your positive energy is contagious and sets an example.

Remember that you are trying to do a job and promote a professional image for the WebSphere team. Being modest and patient helps because many people, including your senior management, do not like impulsive employees or mean corporate bullies.

No Speculation

Meetings dealing with a severe production emergency are not good places to engage in speculation-based technical possibility discussions. There is nothing more damaging to the technical authority of your team than sharing speculation. It discredits your feedback and reduces the weight that your team carries.

Feel free to conduct whatever discussion you like about the technical possibilities of the root cause to a problem. However, this type of discussion must be done behind closed doors with the WebSphere team members only.

Whenever you participate in a formal meeting, your feedback must be carefully prepared, your argument must be supported by solid facts, and your recommendation must contain the appropriate level of technical details. Resist the urge to be part of any discussion that is not based on hard evidence, facts, and valid data.

Take Responsibility for Your Problems

Take full responsibility for your problems. Taking responsibility is a three-step procedure: First, emphatically agree to take full responsibility for your errors. Second, clearly express regret for the problem that the WebSphere team caused. Finally, make a commitment in identifying and implementing improvements to prevent the problem from recurring.

In corporate life, there are all kinds of creative ways to dodge responsibility. However, people will figure you out. If you do not like taking responsibility, you will find your responsibilities dwindling. If your WebSphere team makes an error, take responsibility for it or, in the long run, you will not be successful because you will lose the trust and respect of your company's technology community.

Yes, the situation in which your team made an error may be complex. Sometimes we all make mistakes. However, do not excuse yourself. Always express regret for the problem that your team has caused. Also, keep in mind that how you express regret may become a legal issue if an external client is affected. Then, you may want to work with your legal counsel on when to say what.

When it is proven that the WebSphere team has made a mistake, what people want to see is that appropriate actions are taken and that the same mistake will not be repeated. As long as the mistake is not one that indicates a conspicuous lack of professionalism, willful violation of established processes, and unforgivable negligence, senior management understands that sometimes problems do occur. It is rare that any team member will be penalized for an innocent mistake. Therefore, focusing on identifying improvement areas and actionable items is better than worrying about what will happen to you and your team.

Summary

As the critical middleware of large and complex IT systems, the WebSphere Application Server can be the manifesting point of numerous system and application problems. Many of them originate from other upstream and downstream system components. It is also possible that the trouble spots are buried deep in the JEE application code contained in a WebSphere Application Server.

During a critical moment of a production emergency, as the WebSphere manager or senior consultant in charge, you have to engage the right level and the right kind of resources. You have to keep the team motivated and focused on resolving the technical problems. You have to take effective measures to mitigate customer experience and minimize your company's losses.

While working to perform progress management, you have to adhere to change-control processes and participate in change management. You have to carefully manage communication with many teams, management, and strategic partners, such as IBM. During the full course of the production emergency, you have to work diligently to promote teamwork and strengthen work relationships.

Finally, you want to skillfully conduct rigorous post-problem resolution and timely follow-up to prevent a recurrence of the problem.

You have to do both well—you have to "walk the walk and talk the talk." You have to "walk the walk" by skillfully leading the WebSphere team in restoring service, identifying the root cause, and providing and implementing the problem resolution. You have to "talk the talk" by effectively managing the communication and work relationship between teams, with management, IBM, and within the WebSphere team.

Managing a production emergency is not easy. However, for a battle-hardened WebSphere engineering professional, there could not be a better opportunity to fully use your business acumen, teamwork skills, technical insight, abundant experience, and the confidence of a world-class technology leader to serve your company, which urgently needs your services.

System Upgrade and Product Maintenance Management

The WebSphere system upgrade strategy and practice are deciding factors in WebSphere system stability.[1] There is also a direct relationship between the productivity and efficiency of the WebSphere team and the need to support multiple versions and releases of WebSphere software.

The lack of a strong software-currency program substantially increases the cost of support and operations. Using out-of-date WebSphere software that is either out of active IBM technical support or has many known system defects may lead to serious production problems. What's more, supporting many different releases of WebSphere Application Server software can be resource intensive.

At the same time, it is equally untenable if you do too many WebSphere system upgrades. Just like any other software, WebSphere Application Server maintenance releases need time to mature and stabilize. If you upgrade your WebSphere systems too soon for a given maintenance release, it may cause serious issues in your critical testing and production environments because of the defects introduced in the new release.

In addition, a system upgrade for large WebSphere environments is a large project in itself. It significantly affects the WebSphere team and many other technical teams with regard to workload. There are financial considerations for all the teams involved.

Last, but not least, a large amount of WebSphere planning engineering work, such as roadmaps and upgrade strategies, must be accomplished before an orderly system upgrade can happen. The same is true for various WebSphere process engineering tasks (for example, system build standards, engineering processes, and the design, development, and testing of new automation programs).

---

1. Upgrade Strategy for WebSphere Application Server V6.0 Release, (March 8, 2006), IBM Software Group.

This chapter covers the following topics on WebSphere system upgrade management. These discussions are also applicable to WebSphere product maintenance:

- Major issues and challenges of system upgrade
- WebSphere planning engineering
- WebSphere process engineering
- WebSphere system build standards
- WebSphere Application Server Product Maintenance Operation

Major Issues and Challenges of System Upgrade

The WebSphere system upgrade challenges include gaining approval from your business partners, enforcing system build[2] standards, scheduling upgrade tasks, and achieving a balanced approach in upgrade frequency. A workgroup needs to be formed to review the roadmap, define a migration strategy, and formalize communication.

Gaining Approval and Support from Business Partners

Gaining approval and support from major business partners for the WebSphere system upgrade can be a challenge. The WebSphere system upgrade is a large project that affects many technical teams and project schedules. Typically, the following teams' participation is needed for a system upgrade:

- Application production support team
- Application development team
- Environment change-coordination team
- Testing team
- Project management team
- Other infrastructure technical teams

Because of the differences in priority and focus of these technical teams, it is not always easy to gain approval and support from all of them. You need the support of all the teams involved to move forward with your WebSphere system upgrade project. The rejection of the system upgrade project from one team is enough to derail the initiative or significantly delay the upgrade project.

Often, the proposal to upgrade a large WebSphere environment substantiates a real financial aspect that your business partners must consider. A WebSphere system upgrade, although a resource-intensive project, may be considered part of the normal business-as-usual infrastructure work and require no additional funding. This may be true for the WebSphere team and all the

---

2. System build or WebSphere system build is a shortened form of WebSphere Application Server system build. In this book, system build and server build are used interchangeably.

technical teams participating in the project. Therefore, resource consideration, as a priority setting against WebSphere system upgrade, is understandable.

Usually, IBM end-of-support timelines are given as main business drivers for a WebSphere system upgrade. With such end-of-support deadlines far in the future, a WebSphere system upgrade is frequently a hard sell. With the WebSphere technology maturing and stabilizing, the technological differences between major releases are shrinking. The application development team may not have as urgent a need for a new release as before for new technologies that used to come with new releases.

All these difficulties in pushing a system upgrade highlight the necessity to help your business partners fully understand the advantages of adhering to WebSphere build standards and the importance of an effective and disciplined software-currency program.

Adhering to WebSphere Application Server Build Standards

It seems that everyone needs to agree to adhere to WebSphere Application Server build standards in a system upgrade. However, in the real life of large IT organizations, this is frequently not the case.

When new WebSphere Application Server build standards make it necessary to change application code and the way it is deployed, the resistance from the application development and project management teams can be anticipated. Prolonged debates about WebSphere Application Server build standards, project progress, and development team priority can turn bitter and cast a lasting shadow on the work relationship between teams.

For example, your WebSphere Application Server system build standards may make it mandatory for a large application to support clustering. However, the Java Enterprise Edition (JEE) application has a serialized messaging design and implementation that does not work well with multiple Java Virtual Machine (JVM) instances. It takes time to redesign the messaging components and recode, test, and implement the application changes. The application development team may have neither the extra budget nor the time needed to cover the additional work necessary to enable the application for clustering. Understandably, project management does not like delays, either. However, on the other side, the WebSphere team may become concerned about building and delivering a major WebSphere infrastructure without the necessary redundancy for availability and failover. Also, a single WebSphere JVM does not have the capacity to handle any traffic spikes.

With these conflicting motivations and priorities, the WebSphere Application Server build standard discussion can become difficult.

Scheduling Difficulties for a Highly Dynamic Environment

The WebSphere environment for a large enterprise application is a busy place. It is not unusual to have multiple development and testing pipelines with the WebSphere Application Server at the center of the infrastructure. You may also have a large pre-production and production WebSphere

Application Server cluster. All of these can easily translate into numerous physical server clusters and JVM instances for only one WebSphere application suite.

Worse, you may have many such large WebSphere environments to upgrade. In addition, the development and testing pipelines are engaged in constant developing and testing of many application releases in parallel to provide new business functions and capabilities. They are so dynamic that there are many changes in both applications and infrastructure constantly flowing through these WebSphere systems.

The WebSphere team is not the only team working in these environments; a large number of other technical teams work in them, too. WebSphere system upgrade affects all of them to a certain degree. To coordinate all these technical teams and schedule WebSphere system upgrades for hundreds of servers is not an easy task.

Upgrade Only When Upgrade Is Needed

Generally speaking, to have a strong program of software currency is good. Apparently, system-wide release consistency speaks greatly of the leadership and discipline of the WebSphere organization at your company. A highly consistent middleware environment almost always draws out an approving nod from the senior executives of your IT organization.

However, at the same time, a cookie-cutter approach to the system upgrade strategy for a large company with thousands of WebSphere applications can sometimes be perceived as a single-minded pursuit of nominal software consistency. Some may even suspect that you put "face work" to look good on paper ahead of the company's real business priorities.

For example, say that you insist on using a large amount of technical and financial resources to upgrade hundreds of WebSphere Application Servers supporting a large JEE application. However, the WebSphere application will be sunset before IBM support for this release expires. Your technical business partners and the leaders of the line of business (LOB) may question your motivation or your business acumen, or both. People are smart. They will eventually get it that your vigorous but unmerited pursuit of a WebSphere system upgrade for a particular application is nothing but a self-serving act wrapped up in eloquent arguments for system consistency and software currency. The same concern may come from your own WebSphere teams as soon as your WebSphere managers and engineers realize that they are doing an enormous amount of work that ends up just serving your need to look good before senior executives.

To avoid such an imbalanced approach to a system upgrade, carefully consider the business drivers of the WebSphere application and respect the input from the LOB and various technical teams involved. Also, carefully listen to your own WebSphere teams and then derive a thoughtful solution through an inclusive decision-making process.

Never do a WebSphere system upgrade to make your software currency program look good to your managers and the IT community. When you have solid business reasons not to do a WebSphere system upgrade for a particular application, have the managerial courage to do the right thing for your company. When your heart is in the right place, your WebSphere engineering decisions are smarter. In the long run, your priority in making the best possible decision for your company pays off. Allocating considerable resources and upgrading a large WebSphere infrastructure without solid business rationales brings negative business impacts and reputation losses to the WebSphere organization and its leaders.

WebSphere Planning Engineering

As discussed in Chapter 1, "Organization Models and Choices," WebSphere planning engineering has four major tasks in planning and strategizing, including evaluating existing WebSphere systems and devising migration strategies and plans.

Form Conversion Strategies and Plans

Forming conversion strategies and plans for converting to WebSphere technologies from legacy systems and other middleware systems is the first task for a conversion job. Evaluating target systems on various platforms and forming conversion strategies and plans gives your WebSphere organization a strategic view of the direction for the WebSphere engineering work. It helps the WebSphere team understand where it can add more value in the critical middleware area of your company. This may also include the conversion strategies and plans to move off or move into a certain platform (for example, moving WebSphere Application Servers into the mainframe computers or distributed platforms, according to your company's business drivers and overall infrastructure optimization strategy). Alas, many WebSphere organizations do not have a long term view of its work and may think that strategies and plans as such do not help with their success and prosperity. This thinking cannot be more wrong. The first step to winning WebSphere engineering work is to have a solid strategy and plan. Victories belong to those who are prepared, and two artifacts may help:

- **WebSphere Application Server Conversion Strategy Statement and Plan**. Explains the business rationale of conversion to WebSphere technologies, as well as the financials, selection criteria, and a high level conversion plan for your company.

- **Target systems inventory and timetable**. Comprehensive list of target systems and a rough-grain conversion timetable.

WebSphere Systems Upgrade Strategies and Plans

Forming upgrade strategies and plans can be an annual exercise to evaluate the existing WebSphere systems and provide guidance to migration strategies, plans, and roadmaps. Although still high level, WebSphere planning engineering needs to provide concrete guidance in a system upgrade.

Unambiguous recommendations need to be made regarding the frequency of WebSphere product maintenance, the timelines of major system upgrade, and a definitive system upgrade roadmap. Utmost care and diligence must be given to the timelines of major system upgrade, frequency of system maintenance, and the language used to describe the proposed strategies and plans. For example, an erroneous description of a specific WebSphere Application Server release as "not allowed technology" can cause many technical teams to waste time and financial resources prematurely working on a WebSphere system upgrade. The following deliverables may help with creating system upgrade strategies:

- **WebSphere system upgrade and maintenance strategy statement**. For example, you can state that the WebSphere system has two maintenance upgrades a year. You may inform the IT community that the next major WebSphere Application Server system upgrade must be finished before a specified deadline for the WebSphere Application Server system to be supportable.

- **WebSphere system upgrade roadmaps**. Technology road mapping itself is becoming an elaborate science with distinct phases and dedicated tools and formats. For the Web-Sphere system upgrade roadmap, it is usually a layered bar chart as a development phase deliverable.

- **WebSphere systems inventory.** A comprehensive inventory of all the WebSphere systems that must be upgraded.

Industry Trends and Emerging Technologies Evaluation

Impromptu and improvised emerging technology evaluation is a serious problem in this area of WebSphere planning engineering work. Without dedicated resources systematically evaluating industry trends, emerging technologies, and forming introduction strategies and plans, your Web-Sphere organization's performance in working with new technologies will be inconsistent. A quarterly evaluation of new technology on the discussion agenda for the leadership technology planning meetings is a good mechanism to keep important emerging technologies on the radar screen of the organization.

Collaboration between the WebSphere team and the application development organization on JEE standards is important. They can devise joint strategies and plans to convert parallel technologies to JEE and WebSphere Application Server and provide guidelines for JEE development work.

WebSphere Process Engineering

WebSphere process engineering has four major areas of work: standards, processes, automation, and WebSphere Application Server and Java best practices. All of these areas contribute to the WebSphere system upgrade. Because of resource considerations, you can have one WebSphere team that does both the planning engineering and process engineering. However, it helps to remember that these are separate functions.

WebSphere Application Server Build Standards

WebSphere server installation standards are the foundation of consistent WebSphere systems across your company. The quality of the WebSphere installation standards affects the stability of your WebSphere systems and the efficiency and productivity of your team. The contents of the WebSphere server build standards are covered later in this chapter. This section discusses some of the major considerations of the WebSphere server build standards work.

WebSphere Standard and Process Team

The WebSphere standard and process team needs to have a group of experienced senior WebSphere engineers and consultants of diverse WebSphere engineering work experience.

The WebSphere standards and processes are not a set of arbitrary technical decisions; they are a comprehensive summary of the state-of-the-art WebSphere engineering experiences, lessons learned, and best practices of your company. In addition, it is a reflection of the technical and business reality of middleware environments in which your WebSphere systems operate.

WebSphere standards and processes are like the legal code of a nation. The existence of laws is not to create a new reality of the society. Instead, it is a formal and enforceable recognition of the actualities of the concerned societal life in a given area. Those who make the laws need to represent sections of the society where the legal code is intended.

The same goes for WebSphere standards and process work. Without WebSphere professionals of diverse backgrounds, the WebSphere standards and processes delivered may be narrow and limited in their usefulness. Also, there may be substantial gaps between the official WebSphere standards and processes and the actual WebSphere systems and WebSphere engineering practices.

For example, if the WebSphere standards and process teams are made up of primarily WebSphere professionals with experience and exposure to dedicated WebSphere environments on distributed platforms, the WebSphere standards and processes produced may be difficult to apply to very large shared WebSphere environments on mainframes.

Ideally, the WebSphere standards and process teams need to have senior WebSphere professionals with diverse WebSphere engineering experience in the mainframe, distributed platforms, dedicated environments, and shared environments.

WebSphere Standards and Process Consistency

WebSphere standards and standard related processes need to be enforced system-wide.

First, this is a difficult job for a large and dynamic company with a long history of fundamental changes, such as mergers, acquisitions, business regeneration, and reorganizations.

Second, for such a large company and its large and complex WebSphere systems and applications, it is harmful to take a dogmatic attitude toward standards and process consistency. Of course, both the leadership and the technical teams need to constantly focus on system-wide WebSphere standards and process consistency. At the same time, you also have to guard against standards and process consistency hype, exaggerations of differences and gaps, and conspicuous gesturing about standards and process consistency. Unfortunately, in the corporate life of a large company with a lengthy history of drastic changes, sometimes, such vocalization and gesturing for system consistency may not lead to serious, meticulous, and detailed work to achieve consistent WebSphere systems and engineering practices. Rather, they are sometimes merely moves to please senior executives or a subtle way to compete for positive managerial attention.

Nevertheless, it is usually possible to tell who is working hard to make your various WebSphere systems consistent. Ask the WebSphere manager or senior consultant who has been talking about system inconsistencies to give you the details of three examples of inconsistencies, system configurations, standards, or processes that she wants to fix. Reward those who can relate to the technical details of inconsistency problems with more responsibilities because they want to help solve the problems. Reprimand those who cannot identify inconsistency problems to fix but have been pointing a finger at apparent inconsistency problems in areas for which others are responsible.

You have to fully realize that standards and process consistency is critically important for system stability, operation efficiency, and organization coherence, while some reasonable process and procedure variations between WebSphere teams absolutely are needed for a large or very large company because of the size and complexity of its operations. You have to insist that standards-related processes, such as WebSphere system build, system configuration, and security settings, need to be consistent across all WebSphere systems and applications. WebSphere engineering processes and procedures related to system build, system configuration, and security settings of different WebSphere teams must be consistent.

At the same time, some differences in processes and procedures between WebSphere teams may be reasonable and necessary, especially those pertaining to domains specific to certain WebSphere applications. For example, a new team member may not have production responsibilities for the first three months for a WebSphere team that supports your Customer Care System, which is large, complex, and highly critical, with millions of active users. The new WebSphere team member needs roughly three months of training and mentoring to safely provide production support to such key WebSphere systems, where two hours of unscheduled downtime may translate into tens of millions of losses for your company. However, the same long training period before taking on production responsibility may not make sense at all for another WebSphere engineering team in charge of a different set of small internal applications. The WebSphere engineering work of a large company is too large, too diverse, and too complex to adopt a tight cookie-cutter kind of process consistency approach. Spare no effort to achieve a high level of system, processes, and standard consistency, as long as it is reasonable, practical, and flexible in meeting the myriad of middleware engineering needs of the many projects and applications of the a large IT organization.

WebSphere Standards Collaboration and Review Process

WebSphere standards work, for the purpose of producing a widely acceptable and practical standards document, should be the collaboration between WebSphere process engineers and WebSphere service engineers. Without these WebSphere professionals working together, the work product delivered is nothing but a pile of official-looking documents.

The WebSphere standards need to be relatively stable. However, there should be a review process with reasonable frequency to accommodate the changes and developments in the reality of WebSphere engineering in your company so that important revisions and additions can be made to the WebSphere standards.

A good balance of standards stability, standards regeneration, and revision is important. A highly dynamic and constantly changing WebSphere Application Server Build Standards Document does not serve the function of an official standard document. A static and stale WebSphere Application Server Build Standards Document is equally harmful because it hinders your WebSphere team to adapt and meet business drivers and fast-changing technologies.

WebSphere standards need to be a strong cornerstone of stability and consistency to your WebSphere engineering work. At the same time, it should not be allowed to become a hindrance to the IT business by any means. It is not easy to achieve the right balances in WebSphere engineering. It takes much work to get it right.

WebSphere Standards Should Stay Ahead of the Curve

WebSphere system inconsistency often comes from the lack of server build standards, especially for new technologies (for example, WebSphere Virtual Enterprise).

WebSphere standards are not something that can be formed on paper only. The WebSphere engineers need a test bed to drive out new engineering practices for a new WebSphere technology. Therefore, the lack of real-world projects that use a new release of WebSphere Application Server may not give WebSphere process engineers a necessary real-world engineering environment to work on WebSphere standards for the new release.

What's more, WebSphere standards work must stay ahead of the curve in terms of adopting new technologies or releases. Therefore, the early availability of a project using the new release as a proof of concept or pilot for system build standards is useful. It provides a real project with real problems and challenges and often leads to real solutions in the form of standards and best practices. It gives the service engineers an opportunity to participate in the standards work as well, working along with the process engineers.

As you can expect, when the service engineers realize that the WebSphere standards are the results of their own work collaborating with the process engineers, you may no longer need to push the standards and sell them to service engineers. Chances are that the service engineers will be interested in trying out their own ideas and be highly motivated to put their own standard work product into engineering practice.

Enforcing WebSphere Standards and Exception Request Process

WebSphere standards must be enforced. The enforcement can come in three ways—an automated build process, an effective system audit process, and a good exception request process:

- An automated build process helps make the WebSphere systems consistent. If all the WebSphere systems are built using the same server build automation, the basic system conformity is ensured.

- A periodic system audit and exception report shared with the organization and the management is a good way to motivate WebSphere managers and engineers to take action and move their system off the list of WebSphere standards violators.

- A practical and effective exception request process discourages frivolous WebSphere server build exception requests and ensures proper documentation in order to seek senior management approval and help later with managing the accountability of the exception tracking.

Server Build Process and Automation

Working with a large technology for a large company is never easy. The WebSphere Application Server build process sounds simple. However, in real life, it is a challenging area of WebSphere engineering work. At minimum, there are five significant areas of server build process and automation work where you, as the WebSphere manager or senior consultant, have to do a good job:

- Organization choices and the division of responsibilities between teams
- Server build or upgrade scheduling and coordination
- Server build automation
- Server build validation and verification
- Quality assurance

Organization Approaches

The first choice is whether to have a dedicated WebSphere system team in charge of all WebSphere topology design and system build. This system team does topology design and system build for many WebSphere project support teams that directly interact with the project management, provide daily WebSphere engineering support, and system operations.

WEBSPHERE SYSTEM TEAMS

A *WebSphere system team* is a WebSphere Application Server engineering support team that focuses on system design and system build. When you separate the system design and build functions from engineering support, WebSphere project management, and system operations, you have a WebSphere system team and a WebSphere project team. If one WebSphere team provides end-to-end WebSphere engineering services from design all the way to project management and system operations, then you have one WebSphere engineering support team: the WebSphere team. A *WebSphere project support team* is a WebSphere Application Server engineering support team that is responsible for WebSphere Application Server project management, daily engineering support, and system operations.

In this book, when there is a separation of design, build, and operations, the terms *Web-Sphere system team* and *WebSphere project support team* are used. If only one Web-Sphere Application Server engineering support team performs all system design, system build, and system operations functions, the term *WebSphere team* is used.

The advantages are easy to see. With one dedicated WebSphere system team, it is easier to maintain system consistency and enforce installation standards. However, the disadvantages of this approach are equally conspicuous because of the following risks:

- It can be difficult for a system team to learn all the different systems of a large company and be highly effective.

- It can add another layer of dependency for a WebSphere project support team that has to accomplish system design and system build in a timely manner, because it is directly responsible to project management for making acceptable progress.

- The separation of system design and system operation functions may result in a Web-Sphere system that is difficult to support in real-life engineering. Worse, a WebSphere system designed by a system team that is responsible for topology but does not have to "eat its own dog food" and run the system built according to the topology may not work in real engineering practice.

- The same difficulty may be true for system build. A dedicated WebSphere system team may build a WebSphere system that is defective or difficult to use in real-world engineering practice because the WebSphere system team does not have to live with the systems that it builds.

The risks come from the separation of major WebSphere engineering tasks. There are three major areas of WebSphere engineering tasks: system design, system build, and system operations. An organizational structure separating these major functions may have more drawbacks than benefits because of size, complexity, and historical reasons (for example, WebSphere system configuration gaps due to the company's history of many mergers and acquisitions), and thus your WebSphere systems are inconsistent in system configuration, engineering processes, and knowledge management.

The WebSphere system teams may be a group of highly trained, experienced, and hard-working professionals. However, resource contention, the need for complex build job coordination and communication, accountability, and responsibility issues between the dedicated WebSphere system team and the WebSphere project support team are tough obstacles for such a dedicated WebSphere system team. For the WebSphere project support team in charge of the project, scheduling installations with a dedicated system team may be difficult because of different priorities coming from many peer WebSphere project-support teams needing the same service, resulting in disagreements about resource availability and build schedules. The WebSphere system teams may not connect with the projects directly by design because of single point of contact; thus, they may appear consistently disconnected from project management and may not have the opportunity to fully understand the urgency of project plans and deadlines that come only by working with the projects directly, so delays in system build may occur frequently.

Many times, the scheduling and coordinating may be near impossible because of the differences in priorities and competition for resources. This may lead the WebSphere project support team responsible for the project to perform the build function themselves instead of waiting for an available date from the dedicated WebSphere system team. The frustrating negotiation and challenging coordination between the teams frequently may cost more time than having the WebSphere project support team itself do the system build. This model of separating system design and build work from the WebSphere project support team may consistently cause serious teamwork and work-relationship issues between WebSphere project support teams and a dedicated WebSphere system team. There are usually enough tough challenges to deal with, even for experienced senior WebSphere managers and engineers.

An effective way to organize is to concentrate system design, system build, and system operation into one WebSphere team for one large LOB or for one large business division. The advantages are high accountability, practical topology design, and timely delivery of system builds, as well as better work relationships between teams.

However, nothing is perfect. With this organization model, you have to have system and process consistency management. Otherwise, before long, you will have different WebSphere systems supported by different WebSphere teams that are costly to maintain, operate, and upgrade.

Server Build and Upgrade Scheduling and Coordination

Server build scheduling and coordination differs, depending on the organization model of the WebSphere teams. If you do have a separate WebSphere system team, schedule your server build or upgrade work with your system team, project management, and several other technical teams: for example, the operating system team, the environment change-coordination team, the application support team, and the change managers, among others. If one WebSphere team is responsible for system design, system build, and system operation, you can form a virtual system subteam within the WebSphere team to perform the system build job. Using this subteam structure, rotate your team members to share the system work. You have the benefit of training the entire team on the WebSphere system work to develop a technically well-rounded team and share the system workload across your team.

Here are some of the most common problems encountered in system build scheduling and coordination. Each problem is discussed and best practices are offered.

Drawback of Informal Server Build Communication

This section is about how a WebSphere team communicates server build order. How this communication is done is a mark of engineering maturity and experience.

The most elementary form of server build order is verbal communication. Because of the inaccurate, ambiguous, and incomplete nature of verbal communication, the result is almost invariably a large amount of reworking, if not complete rebuilding, of the intended WebSphere system. Using this primitive form of build order communication, the WebSphere system can be built on the wrong hardware or in the wrong data center.

A marginally better form of build order is an improvised written server build request (for example, an email or Word document). The form of server build order is still unsatisfactory, but better in terms of quality than verbal communication. At least the server build request is a document. The downside of improvised documents is that they are almost always incomplete and inconsistent.

A mature system build order is an official document with consistent format and complete and accurate contents. Such a build order usually contains the following information. The work product facilitates the scheduling of an accurate, complete, timely, and quality system build or upgrade. (Refer to Chapter 5, "Server Build," for the details of the WebSphere Application Server Build Request and WebSphere Server Build Operation.)

- Server build request
- Software requirements
- Hardware requirements
- Server security access requests
- OS requirements
- WebSphere installation specifications
- WebSphere global security requests
- JEE security-enabling specifications
- Web server specifications
- Server port assignments
- Infrastructure engineers assigned
- Change-management information
- Monitoring requirements

Ambiguous Division of Labor

If one WebSphere team does all its system design, system build and upgrade, and system operations, you do not have a problem with division of labor. However, if you have a dedicated WebSphere system team that does WebSphere system builds and upgrades, you are better off if you have a clearly understood, carefully defined, and documented division of labor.

Which team should be responsible for the server build and upgrade progress management? To achieve a single point of contact from the WebSphere organization perspective, the WebSphere system team usually does not have direct project and customer contact. This approach may lead to major issues for the project progress and accountability with quality issues. With this organization model, progress management frequently causes frustrating internal haggling between WebSphere project support teams and the WebSphere system team. One way to overcome this is to let the WebSphere system team directly participate in the scheduling of WebSphere system builds and upgrades with project management. This holds the system team responsible for delivering the WebSphere systems according to the project plan and avoids layers of lengthy and difficult negotiations for scheduling system builds and upgrades.

The WebSphere system team needs to be responsible for delivering a validated and certified system and should be held accountable for addressing any build quality problems. It is easy to launch a server build automation script and lay down the binary. The real job is to deliver a working system. The challenges of WebSphere system build or upgrade are scheduling, coordinating, solving problems, and delivering a working WebSphere system free of defects. The system team needs to be held responsible for resolving any build problems and performing a carefully documented build validation and certification process. A WebSphere System Build Acceptance Form can ensure the quality of the WebSphere system delivered, better manage build progress, and reduce the stressful finger pointing between teams when problems occur.

Lack of Environment Change Coordination

The WebSphere system build and upgrade is not only a job for the WebSphere organization. It involves many infrastructure teams and application support and development teams that may belong to different organizations. These teams may not have an effective and established channel of communication and coordination. A dedicated environment change-coordination team that helps with planning, scheduling, and coordinating WebSphere system builds and upgrades for large WebSphere environments immensely increases the efficiency and quality of the WebSphere system build and upgrade job.

Lack of Effective Means to Track a Large WebSphere Project

For a very large project, it is difficult to track and manage numerous WebSphere systems. You may want to develop a document to help track and manage these large technical environments.

A WebSphere System Tracking Document is a helpful WebSphere project document. It divides WebSphere systems into the following separate sections according to environments:

- Development
- Component integration testing
- System integration testing
- Stress testing

- Training
- Quality assurance
- Production

Each section needs to provide detailed system information. This document must be updated immediately after a system build, upgrade, or another significant system change. Also, an automated format of a WebSphere System Tracking Program is good to have, but it should not replace the WebSphere System Tracking Document. The WebSphere System Tracking Document must have a system journal that carries any and all system changes. (Chapter 7, "Stress-Testing Environment Support," and Chapter 8, "Production Environment Support," describe the usage of WebSphere System Tracking Document for different areas of WebSphere engineering work.)

Server Build Automation

IBM provides WebSphere Application Server software with the basic building blocks for automation. It is your choice whether to create a WebSphere system build automation program or purchase such a program. If you decide to create a server build automation program in house, evaluate whether you can provide timely production technical support to address production build issues. Also, you have to think through the level of testing for production-grade server build automation. WebSphere system build anomalies can be difficult to isolate and can cause serious problems.

WebSphere Security Standards and Security-Related Processes

As a WebSphere manager or senior consultant, there are three areas of WebSphere security standards and process work for you: the WebSphere security work team or task force, major work products, and WebSphere security related processes.

You need to have a WebSphere security work team. This must be a team or task force led by a WebSphere engineer and corporate information security consultants.

There are a number of WebSphere security-related work products: WebSphere Application Server Security Guidelines focus on WebSphere Application Server security, and WebSphere Application Server Build Standards have important sections dedicated to various security topics at various levels. (For a more detailed discussion, see the next section, "WebSphere Application Server Configuration Standards and Processes.")

Finally, you need to have a number of WebSphere security processes. These are carefully documented, approved, official processes to request access, install WebSphere Application Server binaries, add and delete user IDs, group IDs, job codes, root access, and exception request processes.

Server Configuration Standards and Processes

Server configuration standards need to be part of the WebSphere standards. Because of a large number of WebSphere configurable items, it is necessary to automate the configuration process.

Using WebSphere configuration automation, it may take only a few minutes to configure a Web-Sphere Application Server suite that may otherwise take days.

The quality of the configuration automation progress is critical, as is production support for this program. WebSphere configuration errors are notoriously difficult to identify and may cause serious and elusive production problems. (See Chapter 5 for more information on WebSphere Application Server and Web Server build and configuration operation.)

WebSphere and Java Best Practices

Forming and communicating a WebSphere and Java Best Practices Document is a major engineering task for the WebSphere engineers. In collaboration with enterprise architects and application development teams, the WebSphere engineers create the important JEE Best Practice Guidance Document for your company.

The early forming and sharing of WebSphere and Java best practices with the application development teams of a large project can save the WebSphere team much time and trouble later. Otherwise, the WebSphere team may be forced into supporting substandard application code and nonstandard WebSphere configuration.

On the business side of work, any JEE consulting work, even if your team has this capability, must be an authorized and funded activity. If so, it may be an acceptable practice to provide code samples and prototypes. However, your WebSphere team may not serve your company's best interest in writing all or part of the application code for a project. This may lead to tangled roles and responsibility problems, as well as accountability issues for production problems.

Rather than doing the actual design or coding for the application, the WebSphere process engineers need to deliver a WebSphere and Java Best Practices Document upfront. It needs to state what is encouraged and discouraged in JEE code implementation for your enterprise architects, software vendors, and application development teams as part of a communication package for new projects.

WebSphere Application Server Build Standards

A WebSphere Application Server Build Standards Document is the crystallization of your Web-Sphere process engineering. It is one of the core competence and focus areas of WebSphere process engineers. A WebSphere Application Server Standards Document reflects your company's WebSphere engineering practice. Although the details of these standards differ between companies, they typically cover the following areas.

Naming Convention

There is no best naming convention, only an agreed-upon naming standard. A system-wide consistent naming convention goes a long way to help with automation, reducing operation errors, and enhancing system consistency and system build quality. Usually, WebSphere process engineers try to make the naming convention descriptive of the systems represented. However, the simplicity requirements of the naming convention may not always support the intent of being descriptive. As a result, the naming convention often may not be descriptive enough, regardless of the intention for readability. What's more, your naming convention needs to apply for both large dedicated WebSphere environments and large shared WebSphere environments.

Application Server

Application server standards are mostly related to JVM settings (for example, JVM IP caching, JVM log rotation, garbage collection settings, and JVM monitoring and PMI settings).

File System Layout

File system layout standards define where to put the WebSphere Application Server system binaries, property files, log files, application-specific files, tools (such as scripts), and resource drivers.

Operating System Security

Operating system security standards are typically related to user identifiers, group members and identifiers, WebSphere job codes, user profiles, and various WebSphere related OS-level security guidelines (for example, the usage of SSL and root access).[3]

Application Server Security

Application server security standards form acceptable practices in managing numerous security or access identifiers and group identifiers, the use of WebSphere global security, the choice of enterprise security information system and repository, certificate management, application security requirements, messaging and connectivity security, and WebSphere operation security.[4]

TCP/IP Port Assignments

TCP/IP port assignments ensure structured port number assignments and their orderly usage. Again, attention and consideration need to be given to the differences between dedicated WebSphere system and large or very large shared WebSphere systems. The former tends to use less port numbers. However, in a shared environment, there may be more JVMs for smaller applications that use a large number of ports.

Web Server and Plug-In

Web server and plug-in standards include all the previous topics pertaining to Web servers and plug-ins.

---

3. WebSphere Application Information Center, "Securing Applications and Their Environment," (2007), IBM Software Group.
4. Ibid.

WebSphere Application Server Product Maintenance Operation

The primary objectives of this operation are to achieve a well-prepared WebSphere system upgrade or maintenance, assurance of system compatibility between various components of the overall WebSphere system, adequate testing, and the cooperation and coordination of many technical teams.

Operation Framework and Description

This section systematically describes the WebSphere Application Server product maintenance operation applying the WebSphere Operations Framework.

Description

IBM constantly makes progress on WebSphere Application Server products by making new editions generally available. IBM regularly releases fixes and upgrades correcting known software defects and providing new functions and capabilities. Therefore, it is important and necessary for the WebSphere team to keep the WebSphere Application Server infrastructure up to date. This ensures that you have reasonably current WebSphere Application Server system software, reduce the number of known system defects, and maximize stability and availability.

Entrance Criteria

- Identify WebSphere system upgrade or product maintenance as specified by your system upgrade roadmap and product maintenance plan.
- Or identify a product maintenance need by researching IBM scheduled WebSphere Application Server vulnerability alert reports and IBM HTTP server releases, including IBM HTTP server vulnerability alert reports. Then, evaluate the risks and opportunities for applying the maintenance.
- Or identify a mandatory WebSphere Application Server product maintenance as required to continue IBM technical support.
- Confirm with IBM WebSphere Technical Support on the product maintenance or upgrade.
- Following the WebSphere system upgrade communication plan, discuss and present the importance and necessity to implement the WebSphere system upgrade or maintenance.
- Successfully test and certify the WebSphere Application Server release or FIXPACK.
- Upgrade plan or maintenance plan is established, reviewed, and approved by the management of all the technical teams to be affected.
- Develop or update, test, and certify WebSphere server build process and maintenance process.
- Automate these processes or update existing automation, if needed.

- Form detailed work plans within the WebSphere team for each application that is to be affected.
- Establish a backout plan for critical systems.
- The approval of the WebSphere manager for the work plan and backout plan signals the start for the WebSphere system upgrade or maintenance work for a given application.

Resources

For high profile and very large WebSphere system upgrade projects, you may want to build a fairly large virtual team to get the job done or obtain a reasonable resource allocation from your dedicated WebSphere system team. For large upgrade projects, the WebSphere manager needs to work closely with the team and business partners throughout the entire process of the project:

- WebSphere engineers
- WebSphere system team (optional, depending on the organization approach taken)
- WebSphere manager
- Environment change-coordination team (in charging of scheduling)

Activities

- Research and identify WebSphere Application Server fixes or patches that are needed to perform a scheduled upgrade or to resolve a known system defect.
- Test WebSphere Application Server upgrades, fixes, or patches in testing environments and collect necessary data.
- WebSphere team proposes the WebSphere system upgrade plan to customers and technical business partners.
- Draft and propose WebSphere system upgrade implementation plan.
- Negotiate timeframe with all involved, led by the environment change-coordination team.
- WebSphere engineers, either a dedicated system team or the primary support engineer of the project, execute the plan, and generate the WebSphere system upgrade report:
  - Ensure system prerequisites are met by using a prerequisite checking utility or manual examination.
  - Perform system backup.
  - Execute the update or maintenance scripts or perform manual installation.
  - After the update plan is executed, inspect the following items, and validate that they are correct:
    - WebSphere file system ownership and permission
    - WebSphere configuration backup

- • WebSphere version, IBM HTTP server version, and JDK version
- • Start and stop the Deployment Manager, node agent, server, and applications
- • Check WebSphere logs to validate that the system is running cleanly and no error messages occur
- Verify the update or maintenance by using any report tools that you may have and generate WebSphere system upgrade report.
- If the dedicated WebSphere system team performs the upgrade, this system team should produce a WebSphere Application Server System Work Acceptance Form. The WebSphere project support team reviews the form, examines the system delivered, and accepts or rejects the delivered WebSphere system.
- Update the WebSphere System Tracking Document.
- Update the WebSphere Application Support Manual.

Processes

- WebSphere system work process. (Chapter 5 provides details of this process.)

Artifacts

- WebSphere System Upgrade Check List.
- WebSphere System Tracking Document.
- WebSphere System Work Acceptance Form. (Chapter 7 provides details about this document.)

External Teams

- Application production support team
- Environment change-coordination team
- Operating system support team
- IBM WebSphere Technical Support Organization

Sign-Off Parties

- WebSphere team
- Application production support team

Exit Criteria

- WebSphere system is delivered and accepted after a formal system validation and verification process

Key Processes and Artifacts Explained

The following explains the processes and artifacts used in the WebSphere Application Server Product Maintenance Operation.

WebSphere System Upgrade Check List

The WebSphere System Upgrade Check List is a check list used before a WebSphere Application Server system upgrade to a target WebSphere Application Server release. It includes all the necessary software and hardware perquisites, as well as integrated software compatibility. For example, you may use the document to ascertain that the Web server you use supports this particular WebSphere Application Server release. This is a simple document, but will likely help you avoid major trouble. For example, it helps you avoid the embarrassment that may occur when your company finds out the hard way that your current Web servers do not work anymore after your WebSphere Application Server upgrade because of overlooked compatibility issues.

WebSphere System Work Journal

The WebSphere System Work Journal records any and all changes made to the WebSphere systems. At a minimum, it needs to include the following information:

- Time and date
- WebSphere engineer name
- Project name and server name
- Concise description of the changes made

WebSphere System Work Acceptance Form

The WebSphere System Work Acceptance Form ensures the quality of the system upgrade or maintenance work. It formally documents the WebSphere system delivery date, validation results, and verification process. The WebSphere project team may use the form to accept a WebSphere system build or reject a defective delivered WebSphere system.

Summary

If you take care of the following five areas, your WebSphere system work should be predictable in quality. This quality consistency significantly contributes to your overall WebSphere system stability and availability:

- Set of well-rounded and balanced WebSphere system build standards
- Effective and efficient division of roles and responsibilities for WebSphere system work
- Documented, repeatable, and clearly understood WebSphere system work processes, along with a number of key system work documents (for example, a WebSphere System

Work Document, a WebSphere System Upgrade Check List Document, and a Web-Sphere System Work Acceptance Form)

- System work tools, especially system work-automation programs (for example, Web-Sphere system build and system configuration automation programs)
- Availability of a minimal set of WebSphere system documentation, such as a Web-Sphere System Work Journal and a WebSphere System Tracking Document

This chapter also explained how to build consensus and support for WebSphere system upgrade. The next chapter systematically examines how to manage key work relationships.

Critical Work Relationships

The WebSphere Application Server is the central integration point for infrastructure components, such as DB2, load balancers, or MQ. What's more, WebSphere provides the execution environment for Java Enterprise Edition (JEE) applications. Therefore, the WebSphere Application Server touches many systems as a focal point of large IT projects.

From an organizational perspective, the WebSphere team typically operates within a large modern IT organization that is a complex technosocial ecosystem. In such a large organization, no team or individual can achieve success independently because of the complexity and scale of the operation. Every team must depend on the other teams to perform its jobs. The survival and prosperity of the teams are interdependent. Therefore, the WebSphere team needs to work hard on building, maintaining, and strengthening work relationships with key business partners and peer technical teams.

The stability of these critical work relationships is indispensable to the WebSphere systems' stability. For example, the WebSphere team depends on upfront collaboration with the enterprise architecture team to select the right application vendors. The right vendor selection helps with WebSphere system stability if the vendor software is supportable within your company's standard WebSphere build. It is difficult to operate substandard WebSphere systems needed by a JEE application that does not conform to your company's WebSphere standards. As a consequence, overall WebSphere system stability suffers.

Good work relationships are important, but they are not easy to manage. The technical teams share the same objective: making the project a success. However, for a specific event in a specific context, the short-term objective and focus of these teams may differ. As a result, at a given point in time, the technical teams may hold different views or even conflicting opinions over critical issues. For example, a critical WebSphere application has a nonstandard application code-deployment process that the WebSphere team knows is resource intensive because it can use no standard deployment tools for this application. The WebSphere team wants to sunset this non-standard process. However, to achieve this objective, it needs the full cooperation and support of the application development team and the application production support team. To these two application teams, the application code deployment standardization proposed by the WebSphere team saves resources for the WebSphere team, but it does not present them with any benefits other than additional work. What's more, after the standardization, these application teams are responsible for application code deployment as the enterprise standard practice dictates. This only means more work to these application teams, who already suffer from the lack of resources. Therefore, these application teams have strong opinions against this standardization effort and resist the changes that the WebSphere team proposes. As a result, the application deployment standardization project does not move forward.

Diversity in opinion is unavoidable, but it's also necessary because it helps you make balanced decisions. You must carefully listen to different opinions and give them serious consideration. Nevertheless, the team has to reach a timely consensus to push the business forward. Every team must seriously try to resolve the differences that inevitably develop and work diligently to reach timely decisions to get the job done.

According to Mick Marchington and his coauthors, "Mutually beneficial relationships may be the aspiration of network thinking and, where it is undertaken across organizations' employing staff with shared value systems and priorities, there may be a good prospect of anticipated benefits materializing."[1] The key to good work relationships is the understanding of the mutual benefits, partnerships, and collaborations.

Therefore, the WebSphere team has two equally important jobs. One is to constantly deliver quality WebSphere services, and the other is the constant improvement of work relationships. Delivering WebSphere engineering results must be achieved with work relationship considerations. It is easy to emphasize either, but it's difficult to strive for a balance between both.

In simpler language, delivering WebSphere services while damaging work relationships is not a successful engagement; it is a miserable failure. Delivering WebSphere services without improving work relationships is, at best, only half of a success story. Only when you deliver WebSphere services *and* improve work relationships can you claim total success. Going back to the previous example, the WebSphere team can work with executives to enforce the enterprise application code deployment standards. The WebSphere team can unilaterally set up a deadline of sunsetting the nonstandard application deployment process without the application team's agreement, but with the approval of senior executives who want to see standard engineering processes across the company. It's likely that the WebSphere team will successfully avoid the application code-deployment chores. However, this adds tremendous stress to the application teams that simply have neither the skills nor the resources to take over the application code-deployment job. As a consequence, the relationship between the WebSphere team and these application teams suffers.

1. Mick Marchington (ed.) et al., *Fragmenting Work: Blurring Organizational Boundaries and Disordering Hierarchies* (Oxford University Press), Chapter 12.2, "Fragmenting Work."

This chapter discusses how the WebSphere engineering support team can manage critical work relationships with the following teams:

- Enterprise architecture team
- Testing organization
- Application development and production support teams
- Capacity planning team

Enterprise Architecture Team

The enterprise architecture team has a unique job. As Stephen S. Bonham observed, it translates a set of business drivers into technological solutions:

> Where an EBA (Enterprise Business Architecture) helps guide the business initiative stream, the EIA (Enterprise IT Architecture) helps guide the acquisition and deployment of technology. But before any purchases can be made, they need to be associated with a business need. These needs come in the form of approved business initiatives. When a business idea is presented to the IT architectural committee, the EIA is used to help establish the risks that might be involved if the initiative is allowed to proceed.[2]

In some enterprises, IT has the power to build infrastructure as a technology need that is determined to be necessary, although the immediate business drivers are not yet identified. For example, the need to better monitor critical systems to stop the high costs of outages can be justified as a part of a technology need. For such enterprises, the enterprise architecture team is responsible for driving new initiatives for technology needs.

DEFINING ENTERPRISE IT ARCHITECTURE

Enterprise IT Architecture (EIA), according to Stephen S. Bonham, includes Enterprise Information Architecture, Enterprise Technical Architecture, and Enterprise Application Architecture.

Relationship of Interdependency

Enterprise architecture teams need the WebSphere team and its expertise to construct solutions that have WebSphere-centered IT infrastructure as part of its major system components. WebSphere teams depend on the enterprise architecture team to exercise technical influence early on to ensure that the solution is based on a standard technical approach. As a result, the solution can

2. Stephen S. Bonham, *IT Project Portfolio Management* (Artech House, 2005), Chapter 5, "Architecture Management."

be optimally supported within the standard IT infrastructure. The success of a WebSphere-based IT initiative depends much on this critical work relationship between the enterprise architecture team and the WebSphere team.

Areas of Collaboration

The lack of collaboration between the enterprise architecture team and the WebSphere team may result in tremendous difficulties for the initiative in working well within your company's standard IT infrastructure. It may bring about disastrous consequences for both teams. For example, say that an agreement with a vendor is already signed when the WebSphere team discovers that the purchased vendor solution is practically impossible to support within the standard WebSphere environment. It is important for the WebSphere team and the enterprise architecture team to work together. The following sections discuss the areas of collaboration necessary between the enterprise architecture team and the WebSphere team.

Vendor Selection

In the search for vendors, the enterprise architecture team creates design documents and generates a Request for Information (RFI) document, which is an invitation for suppliers. Through a bidding process, the enterprise architecture team submits a proposal on a specific product or service. It also submits a Request for Proposal (RFP) document, which is a standard business process that collects a supplier's capability information and pricing. Nowadays, it is often better to buy application software rather than build it. The WebSphere team needs to be deeply engaged in any initiative upfront, before major business agreements are made. The WebSphere team must assist enterprise architects to fully evaluate the solutions against enterprise WebSphere standards, roadmaps, policies, guidelines, and engineering practices.

Proof of Concept

A WebSphere team needs to work with the enterprise architects to encourage Proof of Concept (POC). The best form of POC comes from testing and real-world volume stress testing. These tests help validate RFP responses and the solution's consistency toward enterprise policies, standards, and guidelines, including security, upgrade policies, mapping to your release management, and migration strategies. The lack of POC frequently leads to surprises in later stages. It is in the best interest of your large and critical WebSphere-based project to advocate and support a solid POC process. The enterprise architecture team and the WebSphere team have vested interests in encouraging a rigorous POC project before business agreements are reached.

Early Engagement in Design

WebSphere engineers need to be engaged at the define level to support the architecture-specific requirements for WebSphere that flow to the conceptual system design and high-level and low-level execution architecture design documents and other related work products.

SIX SIGMA STYLE IT PROJECT MANAGEMENT

"Define" refers to the first of the phases used in a Six Sigma IT project management that features define, measure, analyze, improve, and control phases.[3]

WebSphere Strategy

Enterprise architects need to be aware of major strategies for WebSphere engineering, preferably all of them (if possible) with an appropriate level of detail, and how they affect business in both business-as-usual engineering support and design and build work for critical IT initiatives.

The WebSphere team needs the enterprise architecture team's full collaboration in support of its processes and standards at all phases of an initiative or business-as-usual operation and change. Collaboration between the enterprise architecture team and the WebSphere engineering team is the key to success in a large IT organization.

What an Enterprise Architect Needs to Do

Both the enterprise architecture team and WebSphere engineering support team must fully understand their interdependency and make a conscious effort to help each other. For the enterprise architect team, the following helps achieve this early collaboration:

- Timely communication to the infrastructure organization and WebSphere engineering support team of the need for collaboration on new initiatives.
- The enterprise architecture team may want to use its considerable influence to secure needed financial resources for the WebSphere team to engage as Subject Matter Experts (SMEs) or participate in POC projects.
- Strongly encourage and promote a stress-test-based POC.

Why the WebSphere Team Needs to Be Flexible

The WebSphere team must display a greater level of flexibility in performing a reasonable amount of voluntary or informal consulting as WebSphere SMEs when the engagement process of a large company is not fast enough to allocate the financial resources in supporting the SMEs' functions. The WebSphere manager must understand that the willingness to play the SME role voluntarily pays off handsomely. It saves the WebSphere team from suffering a tremendous amount of difficulty and costs in supporting nonstandard infrastructure or engineering practices. For the WebSphere team, it is cheaper to help out upfront, rather than to fix the stressful mess

---

3. Greg Brue and Rod Howes, *SIX SIGMA: The McGraw-Hill 36-Hour Course* (McGraw-Hill, 2006).

when it is too late. For example, say that the WebSphere team is at the table as WebSphere SMEs to evaluate a vendor application. The WebSphere team then learns that the development and testing environments that the vendor uses are JBOSS systems. In addition, the vendor is found not to be diligent at performing stress testing. The WebSphere team can share its concerns upfront over the lack of a WebSphere stress-testing environment and avoid dealing with the messy situation that results from the lack of stress testing performed on WebSphere systems before the vendor deploys its application releases into the WebSphere production environment.

Testing Organization

This section discusses the importance of testing and the work relationship between the WebSphere team and your testing organization: the roles that the testing organization can play, the collaborations between the WebSphere team and your testing organization, and considerations in building close work relationships in your testing organization.

All-Important Testing

Testing is critical to the success of any engineering discipline, including IT. However, its importance has yet to be fully recognized. Of course, the support engineers know the value of testing. However, some application sponsors may not want to pay to perform good testing. For those companies in which the funding for new applications is coming from business sponsors, testing is an expense that must be ardently negotiated. For example, it is not rare to see application development executives and project managers circumvent testing under the pressure of deadlines in order to deliver. Inadequate testing, especially for stress testing, can cause a volatile system and unscheduled system outages. For a large corporation's mission-critical systems, in some cases this can result in tremendous business losses, both in revenue and customer experience. Testing needs to be done in one of two ways. You either pay upfront by taking the time to do thorough testing, or you pay a lot more by using your production system and real customers as test subjects. Using your customers as beta testers has a long-term impact on your company because this negatively affects your customer experience, reduces customer satisfaction, and eventually erodes your customer base.

Testing is a reliable indicator of the maturity of an IT organization. Experienced WebSphere teams are committed to testing excellence. This is because they know that, without testing—especially vigorous stress testing—there is no WebSphere system stability.

Testing is the critical life-support system of large and dynamic IT applications. Through the development and testing pipelines, the WebSphere production environments are constantly being provided with high quality application code to provide new business functions to satisfy your customers' growing needs.

Testing is the vigilant defender of your production systems. In a business-as-usual operation, testing uncovers application code defects and system configuration errors, preventing them from moving into the production environment and becoming WebSphere system stability issues.

During production emergencies, your testing organization works around the clock to validate and improve solutions before they can be safely applied in the production environment.

If high WebSphere system stability is important to you, your testing organization is your most important ally and a critical business partner. To survive this tough WebSphere job, you need to build close work relationships with your testing organization. You must ensure that your WebSphere team works in close collaboration with your testing organization to improve WebSphere engineering work for your company.

Planning and Change Coordination

Testing coordination has long been recognized as a dedicated and critical function. According to Info-Tech Research Group, "Different problem or enhancement work may be happening concurrently, making testing coordination very complicated."[4] Besides the critical testing role, the testing organization usually fulfills this important environment change-coordination and management function for testing activities, using technologies such as IBM Rational ClearQuest® as an IBM-recommended best practice. According to the IBM Rational White Paper from 2006:

> Communication and coordination are enhanced by enabling development and testing teams to share the latest test plans, test cases, and test results. Projects that span locations and time zones can be managed more effectively through comprehensive metrics and reports. Whether teams are collocated, distributed, or outsourced, Rational ClearQuest software provides the flexibility and scalability required to support enterprise-wide development and testing needs. This allows teams to realize the cost benefits of leveraging distributed and outsourced resources while mitigating communication and coordination risks.[5]

This role arises from the need to perform the complex job of scheduling and coordinating the code migration and testing work in the development and testing environment of multiple pipelines. (Refer to Chapter 6, "Functional and Integration Testing Environment Support," and Chapter 7, "Stress-Testing Environment Support," for descriptions of the testing environments and pipelines.) The same planning and coordination role is also needed for the critical pre-production stress-testing systems. The environment change-coordination function includes the following for all development and testing environments:

- Manage and schedule code migrations and new releases into each development and testing environment of each pipeline.

- Manage the communication about environment availability to all infrastructure, application development, and testing teams.

- Coordinate with the infrastructure, development, application development, and testing teams to resolve any test-environment issues to ensure the successful execution of the testing schedule.

---

4. Info-Tech Research Group, "A Guide to Software Maintenance Improvement" (Info-Tech White Papers 2006).
5. IBM Rational, Streamline and Speed the Delivery of High-Quality Software Applications" (October 2006).

- Act as the primary liaison and escalation point to the proper organization's senior management for system testing and environmental issues (for example, the infrastructure team or the testing organization).

- Securing, masking, sanitizing, and conditioning testing data for stress testing and performance testing. Often, this time-consuming job is overlooked until it is too late.

Areas of Collaboration

Your work relationship with your testing organization goes beyond the benefits of the testing and environment change-coordination services it provides. The WebSphere team and testing organization have a close work relationship as a converged technical force in the following areas.

WebSphere System and Application Tuning and Optimization

As part of the preparation for production, the WebSphere system and the application go through tuning for problem avoidance and optimal performance. Both of these are primarily done in the pre-production stress-testing environment. The WebSphere team, application architects, and the application development team, as well as stress-testing teams, work together during this important tuning exercise.

This WebSphere environment is a large set of WebSphere servers mimicking the production WebSphere server suite. Many teams work simultaneously in the same stress-testing environment. In addition, during this tuning exercise, many changes are made. Sometimes it can be difficult to manage and track the configuration changes. Without a rigorous change-control process, chaos may result. You need to work with your testing organization and establish a change-management process. A change-control process is an official document of change-management policies and procedures, and it is usually aided by an automated change-control system.

In addition, there should be a single point of responsibility for configuration changes. Usually, the WebSphere team is the only team responsible for implementing WebSphere configuration changes. Otherwise, serious confusion can result. Your production WebSphere servers' configuration may be different from your stress-testing WebSphere servers configuration. These system differences can cause serious stability problems.

Lastly, configuration change confusion and the lack of systematic control in the critical stress-testing environment can result in serious tension between the WebSphere team and your testing business partner, hurting your relationship with the testing organization. You need your testing organization's agreement and support to allow the WebSphere team exclusive WebSphere system configuration access to all the WebSphere systems in all the development and testing pipelines.

System and Application Defect Isolation and Correction

It is important to work with your testing organization and recreate production failures in your stress-testing environment. This gives you an opportunity to isolate defects and test fixes. Your fix needs to be rigorously tested because it may introduce unintended effects with unpredictable results that cause further problems. Only testing and stress testing can validate whether a fix is effective and sound before it can be improved and then implemented in the production environments.

For large mission-critical applications, it is necessary to have multiple stress-testing environments identical or similar in physical layout to the production environment. These WebSphere systems must be identical in basic WebSphere topology and WebSphere configuration to production systems (for example, they must have the same number of horizontal clusters) to provide a realistic stress-testing environment. At the same time, these WebSphere systems can be different from the production systems in physical server system resources and capacity (such as CPU speed and the size of memory, as well as in backend testing regions that are too expensive to duplicate).

For critical systems, one such stress-testing environment must be reserved as a dedicated system for reproducing production problems and testing solutions. Therefore, this stress-testing environment needs to be identical to production in the application code release and WebSphere system configuration. The stress-testing environment is a busy place where many releases are rigorously tested, usually in a 24/7 fashion. Work with your testing organization to keep the reserved stress-testing environment identical to production. The availability of this environment helps you isolate defects and test fixes when you have serious production problems.

Of course, it is not always possible to keep a stress-testing environment completely identical to production, mostly because of the limited availability of costly backend systems. Still, you must make the stress-testing system similar to your production system in overall layout and identical in configuration. (For more discussions on testing, refer to Chapters 6 and 7.)

Testing Strategy and Priority Setting

It is a challenge to decide on testing strategy and set priorities. A joint strategy can help achieve the balance between quality and progress management.

Testing is important, but it isn't easy. Testing environments can be costly to build and operate, especially the stress-testing and performance-test environments because they have to be identical to production in WebSphere topology and configuration. Stress testing can be long and may demand a large amount of testing data. Testing technology tools, such as a load generator and monitor, must be acquired and testing engineers appropriately trained. None of these are easy to obtain for good testing.

With testing, the most precious asset is time which seems always to be in short supply. Meeting a deadline often has a higher priority than testing. Because of the pressure to deliver the new business functions, the choice of high testing intensity to avoid possible losses resulting in unscheduled downtime is not always the most favorable consideration. You also have to work with the testing organization to communicate the risks and benefits of each possible alternative, along with risk-mitigation suggestions so your business leaders can make a well-informed and balanced decision.

Unilateral communication about the lack of testing to the business, without the collaboration of your testing organization, harms your relationship with the testing organization.

Test Planning

You need to work with your testing organization in test planning and technical support resource allocation.

Today's important testing environments are used in a 24/7 fashion. Testing is resource-intensive work and requires good planning for all the teams involved. Periodically, joint planning sessions attended by the WebSphere team and testing organization can help allocate adequate WebSphere resources to better support testing efforts.

Last-minute requests for WebSphere support can stress the WebSphere team. For example, say that it is 5:30 PM on a Friday evening, and your team is ready to leave for the weekend. Then a request comes in and your team has to provide WebSphere support for a stress-testing job that runs overnight. This type of request can strain a work relationship. A joint planning session may help reduce the tension between teams resulting from these last-minute WebSphere support requests.

Inclusive Technical Training

When you schedule WebSphere technical training, if possible include a limited number of seats for the testing teams, along with production support teams, application architects, and developers. This facilitates communication between the groups, so members from different groups feel more comfortable collaborating.

If your key business partners have a degree of WebSphere technical competence, it helps them to do their job better; for example, they can more skillfully perform an authorized WebSphere operation, such as recycle a Java Virtual Machine (JVM). Of course, your team may have a reduced overall workload, because an enabled business partner can help himself instead of calling the WebSphere team for technical assistance.

Most importantly, WebSphere knowledge helps your key business partners understand your positions and the limitations of important WebSphere technical issues. As a result, it becomes easy to develop a rapport because you all "speak the same language." For example, the partners may better understand why you need a standard build to promote a high level of system automation.

Environment Change Coordination

A WebSphere team usually supports many large projects with the same line of business (LOB). You acutely feel the pain if you do not have an environment change-coordination team. Scheduling, planning, coordinating teams to implement changes, certifying the changes and environment readiness, handing over important tasks and processes—all these critical jobs suffer without an experienced environment change-coordination team. As a WebSphere manager or senior consultant, it is your job to proactively support the work of your environment change coordination team.

Critical Situation Communication

What should be the right level of communication with your testing organization during a critical production situation? Answer: Keep a communication channel open with the testing organization and adequately communicate important issues.

It may sound strange to engage the testing organization for production issues. However, this is actually a best practice. The testing organization knows both the application code and the infrastructure system. Therefore, it can provide valuable information and insight into production problems and help with triage and problem resolution.

In addition, adequately communicating the serious production problem status alerts the testing organization to get critical stress-testing environments and testing engineers ready for production problem recreation and isolation.

Communicating serious production problems that involve heavy losses is always tricky. At the critical moment of serious production problems, a strong relationship and solid trust between the WebSphere team and the testing organization will prove to be valuable to the teams and your company.

Understanding Testing and the Testing Organization

Your relationship with your testing organization can be the most significant work relationship to your system stability and the quality of the WebSphere engineering services delivery. You'll want to constantly nurture this important relationship. Meanwhile, it is crucial that you are reasonable in your expectations of your testing organization. Even the best testing organization has limitations. It must operate within technical, technological, and resource constraints.

Knowing the Limit of Testing

It is absolutely impossible to test all the combinations of real-time execution of a new solution. Testing excellence rests in striking the balance between the reward of exhaustive testing and the constraint of limited financial and human resources. To expect your testing organization to catch every possible application code defect and system configuration error is neither realistic nor reasonable. If you closely look at testing reports, you can see that most defects are routinely uncovered and fixed. You have to recognize that without your testing organization, your production environment becomes volatile, and your WebSphere team is going to be stressed.

Environmental Constraint

When talking about the stress-testing environment and production environment being identical and consistent, it means that they should be the same in terms of WebSphere topology and system configuration, such as the number of vertical clustering and the Web container thread setup.

What's more, system consistency between stress-testing and the production system may have a time factor of which you have to be aware. The stress-testing environment is expensive and often highly utilized. After testing the current application release, the system configuration may be changed to test the next application release. Your production system configuration must be the same as the system configuration of the stress-testing environment that was used at the time when the current application release was tested in the stress-testing environment. Not all projects have the financial capabilities to keep a dedicated stress-testing environment that is identical in system configuration to the current production system.

In other words, there are several levels of production and stress-testing environment consistency. One is that the WebSphere topology and system configuration have to be identical. The other is that the overall environment, including the hardware and backend, is interconnected. Your overall stress-testing environments may not be completely identical to your production environment in the following three areas because of costs and technical difficulties:

- **Physical hardware**. It is costly to duplicate production system hardware. Frequently, the stress-testing environment uses less powerful hardware in terms of the speed of the CPU and the size of memory.

- **Backend systems**. Mainframe testing regions and other expensive backend systems that are the same as production's backend systems may not be available.

- **Interconnected systems**. It is impossible to duplicate the entire interconnected system, especially those that are large, complex, and costly.

This environmental constraint is particularly true in testing an interconnected WebSphere system. It is not possible to build an interconnected stress-testing environment. Therefore, the testing organization has to depend on innovative testing technologies to simulate a large interconnected technical environment. However, the richness of interconnected systems interaction still remains difficult to simulate in testing, especially in stress testing. Recent breakthroughs in testing technologies and methodologies can help out. Solstices testing technologies is one of the new products that makes end-to-end integrated testing of a large interconnected environment possible. As more new technologies with more capabilities, such as Solstices, appear on the testing landscape, the testing organization has more new tools and processes to close the gaps.[6]

In addition, because of the SOA paradigm shift, extensive changes to applications and infrastructure will continue to change the tools and testing requirements.

Support Your Testing Organization

It helps to understand these constraints and limitations. However, these limitations and constraints do not in any sense diminish the paramount importance of a world-class testing organization. Meanwhile, be aware that every day, your testing organization is adding new capabilities and new directions by adopting breakthrough technologies and innovative processes.

The WebSphere team benefits from the good work of the testing organization in many ways. It helps you reach high WebSphere system stability; therefore, it frees your team from fighting fires. Only then can you focus on improving your technical skills, achieving greater engineering excellence, and enjoy a better work/life balance. Most importantly, your testing organization saves your company millions of dollars on a daily basis by dramatically reducing unscheduled downtime and considerably improving the customer experience.

---

6. Lori Gipp. "Getting the Most Out of Integration Testing," (11/24/2005), http://www.ebizq.net/topics/soa/features/6510.html.

To build a strong work relationship, fully appreciate the work of your testing organization and be supportive, especially when issues arise. Yes, sometimes, things happen. Your testing teams won't catch every possible defect, regardless of how hard they work. When problems occur in production, be a solid supporter of your testing organization. You need to help by educating your technology and business communities on the wonderful work that your testing partners do, as well as the challenges and constraints that they have to overcome to get the job done right.

Application Development and Production Support Teams

The relationship between the WebSphere team and the applicant development and production support team is not simple. It is a relationship of mutual dependency and collaboration, and as with all relationships, it has its fair share of stress, anxiety, and even suspicion and distrust. Your job as the WebSphere manager or senior consultant is to develop the collaboration and cooperation with these teams, while skillfully reducing stress and anxiety, and preventing suspicion and distrust. First and foremost, you have to understand that you depend on the application teams to do a good job as your first line of defense in your constant battle for high WebSphere system stability and availability.

First Line of Defense

The WebSphere team provides and supports the execution environment for the JEE application. The quality of the application design and coding work directly affects the stability of the WebSphere system. Without a top-notch application development team that understands your company's WebSphere standards and the JEE best practices for WebSphere, your WebSphere system is unstable. JEE consulting, WebSphere best practice sharing, code review, WebSphere standards education are all good areas of assistance that the WebSphere team can do to help the application architects and developers do a better job of being the first-line defender of WebSphere system stability.

The WebSphere team depends directly on the application production support team for daily operation and problem notification. The production support team watches the production status of the application and takes some WebSphere system operation actions when appropriate (for example, recycling a sick JVM). The production support team engages the WebSphere team about serious problems. This arrangement is not only good for timely management of a production problem, but it also helps reduce the WebSphere team's resource consumption.

Respect-Based Relationship

Any healthy relationship is based on genuine mutual respect. Why do the application teams respect and depend on some WebSphere teams? How does the WebSphere team gain respect from the other teams? There are three answers to these questions:

- **Build a capable WebSphere team**. It is important that you try to hire the best WebSphere engineers available. It helps to have senior-level JEE development talents as

WebSphere team members. This makes the communication about complex and difficult technical problems much easier when working with the application teams.

- **Do a good job and add value**. You have to keep your systems free of defects, such as configuration errors, so that your application development and support business partners can do their jobs well. During production emergencies, you have to work hard with the application teams to solve problems. A capable and hard-working team earns a good business reputation that helps with work relationships.

- **Develop and acquire powerful deep dive tools that allow you to look into the JVM and the application code to identify issues**. This technical capability helps you back up your technical insight with solid facts; otherwise, no matter how correct your comments, they are nothing but speculation. Using deep dive diagnostic tools is critical because your application teams depend on you to identify application issues during a production emergency.

Outstanding technical competence and capabilities lead to mutual respect and interdependencies, upon which an amiable work relationship can develop and grow.

Focus on Doing a Good Job and Be an Unsung Hero

To maintain and grow positive work relationships, focus on the job, take responsibility, share credit, and be aware of the relationship impact in your interteam communication. This section gives several examples of how to do this.

Say that you have a technical and highly experienced WebSphere team; you have powerful deep dive diagnostic tools; and your team works diligently to help with a production emergency. You have found an unbound data structure in the logging logic of the application code. This application code defect is causing a classic case of memory saturation, resulting in a Garbage Collection (GC) thrashing and JVM crash. Now you have to communicate your findings to the technical teams involved. How you communicate this directly affects your relationship with the application teams.

Do Not Vie for Positive Visibility at Others' Expense

This is easy to say but hard to do, because we all yearn for positive visibility. In our eagerness to gain positive attention, we may not be aware that our communication may bring negative attention to others and affect the critical work relationships that we want to nurture. For instance, you may decide to maximize the benefit of positive visibility for your team by sending the following email to all teams involved, letting them know that your team has found a major application code defect and helped save the day:

> In the application code, my team found several instances of a large data structure holding more than 10,000 large objects in the JVM. This is a classic case of an unbounded data structure. IBM WebSphere Support has researched this finding and agreed that this is the root cause of the production outage that we have been suffering. Please see the attached email from IBM and a Word document with more technical details that my team has drafted. Please let me know if you have any questions about this communication.

It seems that this is just a factual, straightforward, and professional message about finding an application code defect. However, from a critical relationship-management perspective, this message has problems:

- Your emphasis on claiming credit and broadcasting your team's achievement is obvious. You are really saying, "Look at me and my team: We are heroes." Although this may be true, the management and your business partners may appreciate modesty. A better strategy is to do your job well and let others take care of the performance evaluation.

- Your application development team cannot find anything critical to say about this message. However, the developers may not like it at all. Although you did not mention them in your email, you clearly placed the root cause and responsibility of the production outage on the application developers. Although this may be true, is it your job to unilaterally decide on root causes and assign responsible parties?

- The language of "classic case of unbound data structure" can be interpreted as an overt accusation against the developers. It seems that you are highlighting the inexperience of the application development team that, as you depicted, does not know how to avoid a typical and possibly rudimentary memory-management issue by wrapping a bound surrounding the data structure.

Share the Credit Skillfully

Let's improve the previous email by removing some harsh-sounding language while sharing the credit with the other teams involved:

> Working with the application development team, we found in the application code several instances of a large data structure holding more than 10,000 large objects in the JVM. This seems to be a case of unbounded data structure. IBM WebSphere Support has researched this finding and agreed that these large data structures may have an intrinsic relationship with the problem that we have been seeing. Please see the attached email from IBM and a Word document with more technical details. Please let us know if you have any questions about this communication.

This email sounds better in the sense that the credit is shared and the focus is on teamwork. The email uses language such as "we" and "us," instead of "me" or "my."

However, as the WebSphere manager, you are still talking about application code defect. Will it be better if the application development manager talks about his own problems? Why not just send your finding to the application development manager and let him decide what to do?

Private Message or Face-to-Face Meeting

Sometimes a private message is the best option. The following is an email from the WebSphere manager to the application development manager on the same issue:

Hello, Kerry. My team found a few large data structures holding more than 10K of large objects in the JVM. I know that you are working hard on the production problem, and this large data-structure finding may be useful to you. Can you look at the attached Word document that contains technical details of the finding? IBM WebSphere Support thought that these large data structures look interesting. Please let me know what you think.

The following are the benefits of the private email:

• There is no mistake that your only intention is to help.

• Your respect for the application development manager is more than adequately expressed. You are not giving an implicit command: "Here is the problem—fix it." You point out a possible problem area and let her be the ultimate decision maker.

• This email normally won't cause any sensitivity on the part of the application development manager. However, you never know. Some inexperienced application development managers with an exaggerated ego may still think that you are interfering. In this case, a face-to-face meeting may be a better route to disseminate the WebSphere team findings.

Recognize Your Team

It is understandable that your instinct is to send out a broadcast email about the good work that your WebSphere team is doing. Everyone wants to be recognized for their contribution. However, if you choose to send out a private message to your application development manager, it is possible that your critical contribution may not be recognized. The application development manager may instead emphasize the work that his team does to provide a timely fix for the bug. The teams may be more focused on solving the production emergency rather than taking the time to give recognition.

It is always better to focus on doing a solid job rather than vying for visibility. An unsung hero is often the real hero. However, a real concern is that your team may become dissatisfied by not being recognized for their contributions. You can certainly recognize the WebSphere engineers who make the important contributions and copy your team and your management. This dispels resentment that your team members may have against the application development team, who might inappropriately take full credit for your team's contribution. Such resentment, if not managed, may hinder development of the critical relationships that your team depends on to do its job well.

Develop a Different Perspective

In relationship building, try to think through the issues from a different perspective. This is an essential skill. How skillful you are at doing this may make or break relationships. This section discusses many interesting examples of this skill.

Copy Senior Management

When you copy your senior manager on a critical message to the application support manager, all you intend to do is to provide an update to your manager. However, your application production support manager may take this as a politically motivated escalation. In an effort to "get the story right," he may start looping in his senior leadership team. If you had put yourself in his shoes and then thought through your message, you probably would not copy your manager, which prevents a messy round of ugly escalated emails.

WebSphere Configuration

Another example is WebSphere configuration. Even the best WebSphere team sometimes makes a mistake in WebSphere configuration and causes a serious production problem. Production problems can be complex and their root cause can be elusive. When such a mysterious production problem arises, your application team managers may start getting anxious that the WebSphere configuration is the problem again. Therefore, the application development executive or production support manager may ask the WebSphere team to verify that the WebSphere configuration settings are correct.

Unfortunately, the WebSphere team may feel this is nothing but speculation and finger pointing that hurts its reputation. However, if you make an effort to approach the issue from the perspective of the application teams, you may find that they are only doing their job and trying to fix the problem; they don't intend to start an interdepartmental war.

With this understanding, to reduce the anxiety of the application teams about WebSphere configuration issues, you may want to develop processes to verify that the production WebSphere environment is correctly configured, and it is consistent with the WebSphere configuration of the pre-production stress-testing environment. This process of WebSphere configuration assurance must be used before and after a major application code migration and WebSphere configuration change.

Fix Code Defects

The WebSphere team sometimes feels that, whenever there is a WebSphere infrastructure issue, the application teams are excited about taking action and fixing the problem. However, when an application defect is uncovered, suddenly, all the excitement about fixing problems dies.

Over time, this "double standard" can cause two problems. The JEE application with many kludged solutions that "work around" the known problems can become fragile and brittle. From time to time, these known defects will cause production issues and substantially increase the WebSphere team's workload. The WebSphere team certainly has reasons to be concerned about this practice, and its concern may turn into resentment when the application teams initiate discussions on the root cause responsibility for some of these known application code defects with the WebSphere team.

Do the application developers want to fix all the code defects? Absolutely. However, they are under constant pressure to design and develop new code to meet the fast-changing business drivers. Between fixing a problem for which there is a temporary solution and delaying the roll-out of a new function, they may not have a choice but to focus on the latter.

The application teams are closer to the business than the WebSphere team is. Therefore, they may better understand the priorities and pressures of the business. Without having such a close contact with the business, the WebSphere team may be oblivious to the pressing situations where fixing the code defects takes a low priority.

To be completely objective, fixing any production problem is not easy. However, sometimes, it may be easier to fix a configuration error than to redesign and rewrite a piece of JEE code. This may explain why the application developers so eagerly look for a WebSphere fix for a known problem.

Do not let the reluctance and hesitation of the application teams bother you. Try to understand their situation. However, never give up asking them to commit resources to fixing code defects, because if there are too many known defects, when you do have a problem, it is difficult to isolate and identify its root causes. Sometimes, you have a mysterious problem that occurs once, leaves no trail, and does not recur. For this kind of problem, you may never find out what exactly happened and which team is responsible.

Take One for the Team

When it is impossible to determine the root cause of a serious production issue and the teams get into a long and increasingly ugly discussion on accountability, have the courage to take responsibility for the sake of minimizing the team relationship impact.

Nobody wants a big production outage on their performance record. However, a prolonged conversation on which team should take the high severity problem ticket puts a lasting dent on the work relationship that you work hard to nurture.

In addition, your senior management does not want to hear eloquent debates about which team should take the production problem ticket. Instead, they want to see teams work together to focus on preventing similar problems. Sometimes, just take one for the team and move on.

A stable work relationship with your production development and support teams is highly valuable. It helps you form a converged team working in tandem in many areas to achieve a shared business objective: a more stable WebSphere environment and application. When problems happen, you are able to work closely with your production development and support teams and quickly identify the root cause and resolve the problem, promptly restore production, and be more effective in preventing the problem from happening again. This is why work relationships are so critical and why you must work hard to improve them.

Seek Feedback

Surely, we all have a need to better understand ourselves in order to grow and improve. You sometimes may want to solicit feedback and suggestions from your application teams to improve your work and work relationships.

A good way to do this is to formally seek feedback on both your technical service delivery and communication performance. Technical service feedback focuses on the quality of the products and services delivered. Communication feedback focuses on teamwork and relationship.

It is important to immediately and formally seek feedback when you clearly feel that your application development and production support teams are unhappy about certain issues. This gives them a chance to channel any possible negative impressions or resentment into productive energies to help the WebSphere team make improvements. You can also ask them to provide feedback to your management when necessary.

Use carefully designed official documents to seek feedback on your team's performance in technical service, communication, and teamwork.

It is natural for anyone to talk many times about a negative experience. These complaints cause reputation damage to the WebSphere team. This structured feedback process ensures that the WebSphere team can learn from the feedback and protect the team's reputation. A formal feedback process gives the application developers or application production support managers a formal channel to share their concerns. After spending the time and energy to share their concerns, there are usually fewer comments in the community about the grievance against the WebSphere team because the formal feedback process provides an effective channel to share concerns. People may feel that they have adequately addressed their concerns and there is no need to constantly talk about their experience.

Capacity Planning Team

The work relationship between the WebSphere team and the capacity planning team is evolving and unclear. New technologies, interconnected systems, and composite applications expand capacity planning. There will be changes. However, we do not yet know what these changes will be, especially in the roles and responsibilities of the WebSphere team and the capacity planning team. Changes are needed in the following areas:

- Capacity planning of WebSphere Virtual Enterprise-based dynamic WebSphere systems
- Transactional system resources and capacity planning, especially those of interconnected systems and composite applications
- New tools and the mechanism of deep dive system-capacity monitoring and planning (for example, diagnostic and monitoring tools from Tivoli, Wily, and Mercury)

Virtualized IT Infrastructure Capacity Planning

In this area, the capacity planning team continues its usual focus on traditional system resources, such as CPU, network bandwidth, disk storage space, and main memory. However, capacity planning work faces new challenges; there are more questions than answers at this point.

One of the problems that WebSphere Virtual Enterprise intends to address is low system-resource utilization of the traditional WebSphere environments. Usually, you see about 10 percent of system resource utilization. However, how does the capacity planning team derive the intended overall system utilization rate, given a set of WebSphere Virtual Enterprise-bound applications targeting a specific virtualized WebSphere environment?

Will the capacity planning team determine the WebSphere Virtual Enterprise health policies because problems such as excessive memory utilization are areas of system monitoring pertaining to health policies and capacity?

Will the capacity planning team provide a resource-utilization ceiling for service-level optimization for the overall WebSphere Virtual Enterprise systems or the upper limit details of fine granularities for each application executing in the WebSphere Extended Deployment?

Will the capacity planning team drive capacity planning or server optimization, or only play the role of a major participant?

What kind of understanding about the WebSphere Virtual Enterprise-bound applications should the capacity planning team have to produce meaningful capacity plans for such dynamic operation environments?

Does the capacity planning team have the kind of diagnostic and monitoring tools that no longer only track the physical server level resources utilization and anomalies, but also dive deep into the WebSphere applications to lead the kind of capacity planning for dynamic operations of the WebSphere Virtual Enterprise?

Virtualized IT infrastructure, based on WebSphere Virtual Enterprise, demands that you fundamentally rethink your roles and responsibilities. You may have to think of new ways to collaborate—and even new models to organize—to work optimally in a dynamic technical environment. Survival and prosperity belong to those who are agile, adaptive, and change. The capacity planning team may have to learn more about grid computing, autonomic systems, and the WebSphere Virtual Enterprise. The WebSphere team may have to bravely go into new areas of capacity planning on transactional capabilities and application server system resources and become ready to provide an extra service by working with the capacity planning team.

Another dimension is the increasing interconnectivity of critical WebSphere systems and the challenges that it brings to capacity planning. These interconnected WebSphere systems are providing plumbing for composite applications of Service Oriented Architecture (SOA). SOA has a major impact on the direction of capacity planning. Failover and disaster recovery also have a different context in the future, because the distributed SOA components allow more flexibility in the overall system architecture and operation, and therefore affect capacity planning as well.

Nontraditional System Resources

Today, more and more enterprise systems are interconnected. This brings about several tough challenges (for example, identifying effective ways of communicating major changes, instability insulation, optimal organization models, and new capacity planning).

Traditional Capacity Planning Is Inadequate

It's clear that traditional capacity planning, which focuses on CPU, memory, network capacity, and disk storage space, is severely inadequate to effectively manage the capacity-planning needs of interconnected systems. A volume increase or traffic-pattern change of one interconnected system can cause serious system stability issues for another interconnected WebSphere system. Interestingly, you may find that, often, WebSphere systems that have unscheduled outages because of significant volume increase or traffic pattern change actually may cause no CPU or memory-capacity problems. An interconnected system with ill-communicated changes of new functions may cause sudden spikes in transaction volume. A large batch job of an upstream application may substantially alter the traffic pattern. These unexpected changes in an interconnected system may cause thread pool saturation and stressed database-connection pooling, which results in serious outages. However, at this point, thread pool is not the concern of capacity planning. Furthermore, these WebSphere Application Server-level resource issues may not have direct manifestation in traditional system resources, such as CPU and memory monitored by the capacity planning team. Actually, it is possible that nobody is really watching these critical resources at the WebSphere Application Server level.

Challenges

Both the WebSphere engineering support team and the capacity planning team face challenges in fulfilling the capacity planning service at the WebSphere Application Server level in an interconnected environment.

The first challenge is organization. It might be difficult for both the WebSphere team and the capacity planning team, working in a large IT organization, to develop the kind of visibility and reach the kind of communication level needed to understand and define the capacity issues between interconnected systems belonging to different sections of the same LOB, or even between different LOBs.

The second area of challenge is the tools, knowledge, and skills in which the capacity planning team needs to work on interconnected capacity planning at the level of WebSphere Application Server and major messaging systems, such as MQ. The capacity planning team needs access to deep dive diagnostic tools from Wily or Mercury to collect and analyze capacity data. Significant knowledge in WebSphere and Java technologies and skills are necessary. This interconnected capacity-planning function should concern itself with the concurrency of user access and transaction volume measured by transaction per second (TPS), collaborating with the testing organization, the WebSphere engineering support team, and other teams.

The last challenge is how to take full advantage of new technologies, such as IBM Tivoli Application Dependency Discovery Manager (ITADDM), to visualize and abstract large and complex interconnected systems, in terms of WebSphere Application Server and messaging systems.

Visualization allows you to ignore irrelevant details and focus on the key facts of the large and complex interconnected systems. Vital facts and data revealed can be further captured by using quantitative tools, such as IBM Tivoli Composite Application Manager (ITCAM), to drive out the vulnerabilities in the capacity of the interconnected systems and provide a quantitative foundation for corrective actions.

In the new world of dynamic WebSphere infrastructure and large interconnected WebSphere systems that support SOA, WebSphere systems capacity planning has a new meaning. It is not clear yet how capacity planning will evolve in terms of organization, process, and technology. However, it seems certain that capacity planning will go through significant changes. Tighter collaboration and closer cooperation between the WebSphere team and capacity planning team are necessary to figure out how to work together. It is likely that the WebSphere team will play a greater role in capacity planning going forward.

Summary

In working for a large corporation, you sometimes have to zoom out. You have to look at what you are doing with a greater reference and broader framework in terms of space and time. Then you can find a wider context to evaluate what you are doing, and you may develop a completely new perspective.

You may realize that your work as the WebSphere manager or senior consultant is not just getting one project after another done for your company. Instead, it is a journey of professional growth and personal maturity. Your relationship with your critical business partners is that of fellow travelers. You can choose to closely work with them toward a collective win or distract yourself from focusing on the job by engaging in endless infighting.

Your performance needs a suitable platform that is as big as your heart. If you have your business partners, their objectives, their careers, and their successes in your heart, you can work with them to render the most splendid performance of a lifetime in pursuing WebSphere engineering excellence.

CHAPTER 12

Managing the Stability of Large Enterprise WebSphere Systems

The WebSphere team's ultimate objective is to provide resilient WebSphere Application Server infrastructure of high stability and availability. With WebSphere and Java Enterprise Edition (JEE) technologies rapidly maturing, achieving high WebSphere stability primarily depends on the maturity of your technical management practices and innovative deployment of WebSphere technologies. How you manage system stability is critical, and how you motivate your entire team decides whether you can achieve your stability objectives. What's more, you need to find innovative ways to manage changes in response to the new challenges of an increasingly interconnected environment. This chapter explores the following topics:

- Balanced strategy to manage instability
- Incentive plan for high system stability
- Change management in a large interconnected environment

Strategies for Managing System Instability

There are three approaches to deal with system instability. The first approach may not sound like an approach at all because system instability is unmanaged or under-managed. In the worst case, no rigorous problem-reporting mechanism exists, there is no official post-problem review process, no scheduled problem statistics compilation and reporting, and little or no senior management attention. It is understandable that sometimes the IT infrastructure engineering organization may feel that many stability factors are beyond its direct control (for example, application code quality). Therefore, it may wonder how much it can do to help improve system stability. Although it is true that many factors leading to instability are not the direct responsibility of the IT infrastructure engineering organization, the lack of attention to system stability can be harmful because it does not encourage a range of proactive activities that the system managers and engineers can carry out to enhance infrastructure stability.

A second and more effective approach is to manage each production instability problem on a case-by-case basis. This approach is direct and effective. When applying this approach, it is frequently possible to identify the root cause of the instability, and design and implement a resolution. This is a useful way to manage system stability, especially as a tactical approach. However, when misused, this approach can cause serious problems.

The third approach is addressing not only the symptoms that are the manifestation of the problems, but the systemic issues that cause these problems. This approach is based on the understanding that system instability is more of a painful symptom rather than the infirmity itself. As a metaphor, many medical conditions can lead to acute pain. For example, appendicitis can cause devastating pain. If the treatment choice is to keep giving the patient painkillers, the problem won't go away and the patient won't get healthy. Infrastructure system instability may be a symptom of organizational dysfunction, the lack of engineering process, work relationship and communication issues between teams, and the need for innovative technology deployment. Without fixing these broad systemic problems, your system instability may recur in various forms.

You must focus on each case of infrastructure system instability and fix its root cause. It is equally important to develop a comprehensive strategy that corrects the deeper and broader root causes of instability.

Therefore, when you have a production stability problem, drill down to the definitive root cause. You must clearly identify improvement areas and take appropriate actions. Try everything possible to prevent the problem from recurring. You must maintain a constant focus on improving system stability. In short, persistent managerial and technical attention to problem management must be exerted.

Focusing on managing problems is absolutely necessary to maintain any level of system stability. However, in your pursuit of stability, a thoughtful and balanced strategy is needed. For example, when dealing with each stability problem on a case-by-case basis is overused, it can seriously affect the entire infrastructure engineering organization. This is especially true when it is used not as a tactical solution to system stability, but as the only solution. Nevertheless, you must focus on stability by systematically managing stability problems.

Focus on System Stability

As the leader of a WebSphere engineering organization, you must focus on many key areas (for example, system stability, employee satisfaction, and the efficiency and productivity of your organization). Among all these areas, arguably WebSphere infrastructure stability is your #1 job. Your WebSphere team must provide your company with a capable and stable WebSphere infrastructure. Otherwise, it fails in performing its most fundamental responsibility. It is unacceptable to indulge in inaction and not work to achieve high system stability. There must be consistent focus and constant management attention on system stability. Structured and careful effort to manage system stability is compulsory. Your team must tirelessly grow infrastructure system stability and the following may help:

- Form an effective problem-resolution process.
- Adopt a rigorous problem-reporting mechanism.
- Establish an official post-problem review process.
- Regularly compile and publish stability statistics.
- Conduct periodic senior management review of stability issues.
- Analyze stability problems; identify and correct systemic issues.

Dealing with Instability, One Problem at a Time

Managing system stability issues one at a time is a powerful way to reduce production problems. The focus needs to be on the following four areas:

- **Events**. Details of events leading to the anomaly
- **Impact**. Impact to the customer and company
- **Root cause**. Analysis and isolation of the root cause
- **Actionable items**. Actions made to improve stability

This approach ensures that the root cause is isolated and enhances accountability. It enables the teams to recognize improvement opportunities, and it enforces the implementation of actionable items for correction and improvement. All in all, it is a useful way to prevent the problem from recurring. If you desire any degree of system stability, you must make good use of this methodology. All high severity system instability problems need to be rigorously reviewed one by one.

Nevertheless, you have to be careful not to inappropriately apply this approach. Otherwise, you can run into issues. The first possible misuse is thinking that this approach is the only way to deal with system instability. The second potential misuse is over-applying this approach.

Look Beyond Individual Problems

When you ask WebSphere managers if the WebSphere team is merely fixing the symptom or really working on the illness itself in managing system instability, almost every WebSphere manager will tell you that the illness itself is being addressed. Furthermore, the WebSphere manager will also tell you that the root cause has been identified and proper actions are being taken to prevent a reoccurrence of the problem.

However, dealing with each problem one at a time and getting to the root cause for each problem may not be enough. You may have to develop a broader vision and more inclusive methodology to address deep issues from which these stability problems arise. This vision and methodology enable you to look beyond the root cause of each individual problem and find out what are common and generic to many of your problems. Doing this helps you identify and manage systemic problems—the real hotbed that keeps generating stability challenges.

For example, say that you have several simple, but important, WebSphere configuration changes during an authorized change window on a Saturday night. You carefully go through the change-control process to get proper approval. You diligently walk the on-call WebSphere engineer through the changes assigned to him. On Friday, you remind him of the changes before you leave the office. You are promised he will do a good job. Finally, you ask the backup on-call WebSphere engineer to be on standby just in case. After all this preparatory work, unfortunately, the WebSphere changes are not performed within the allotted authorized window of time, but much later. As a consequence, a huge system outage occurrs that costs your company a tremendous amount of money.

After an official post-problem review, the root cause is determined. The primary WebSphere on-call engineer overslept and did not perform the changes within the authorized time. As a result, proper human resources actions are taken against the responsible employee.

Realize that this must not be the end of the problem review process. Now you need to look beyond the direct root cause and identify deeper issues, especially those systemic to your WebSphere organization. For example, you may want to explore why a trusted and experienced WebSphere engineer suddenly lost his sense of responsibility. Was it because your highly confidential plans to offshore 50 percent of WebSphere engineering work were leaked? Maybe this engineer had been spending long and stressful hours looking for a job. Was this why he was so tired and overslept? Perhaps many other WebSphere engineers were equally concerned and were also working on their resumes and job interviews. Without fixing the concerns of WebSphere engineers, this particular problem may be fixed while other stability problems continue.

Actualize the Mean

Anything good that is pushed to the extreme can be harmful, because it suggests a deviation from the mean. Case-by-case stability problem management is a powerful approach when appropriately used in a thoughtful manner, considering both reward and risk. Conversely, overdependence on this problem-management approach can cause imbalances. For example, senior executive attention is valuable and necessary to reduce production problems. However, like everything else, too much senior executive attention can lead to various problems.

Stressing the whole organization. Because of the high frequency and high visibility of problem reviews, everyone struggles to come up with the best possible report before the deadline just because of the senior executive's attention. Several members of the technical staff and managers have to get ready to participate in problem-review meetings with the senior executive to discuss these complex technical problems. The first- and second-line managers have to fully grasp many technical details before they can help review and improve the report and attend the problem-review meeting with senior executives. This frequently involves asking many questions to the already tired WebSphere engineers who are working on intensive and challenging technical support engagement regarding the problem.

For a number of reasons, frequently participating in high severity production problem-review meetings is a stressful activity for anyone, regardless of caliber or experience:

- The sensitive root cause and accompanying accountability issue can be a major part of the discussion. These are not relaxing topics. The apprehension of being identified as the responsible party for a high severity production problem with heavy losses can make anyone tense.

- For highly complex production issues, you simply cannot be perfectly prepared for all the possible questions from the senior executives, business representatives, and technology vendors. However, you look bad if you cannot address every question.

- When the senior executives are reviewing high severity problems frequently, it may become an increasingly popular practice for the teams to emphasize avoiding the blame for a stability problem and thus dodge problem tickets instead of focusing on solving problems and preventing their recurrence.

Sometimes it is impossible to find out who is responsible for a complex production problem. It is natural that nobody wants to be responsible for a production problem ticket that is perceived not to be within his area. This reluctance to take undue responsibility and the aversion of wrongly assigned problem tickets are understandable. However, when a large gathering of technical staff and managers spend many hours in a nonstop meeting pushing a production ticket to each other, you know that you have pressed your system stability methodology too far, and that something has gone wrong with your problem-resolution approach.

Distracting the senior executives. When these reviews become frequent, they can add a tremendous workload to the senior executives and significantly distract them from the strategic work that they need to do. They have to frequently prepare for a formal discussion on many complex stability problems that cover wide areas. This time-consuming job may drag them away from their primary responsibility of developing a long-term and holistic view of these problems, which is managing the strategically significant aspects of these stability issues so that the systemic root causes of instabilities affecting the entire system and organization are identified and addressed.

However, I must emphasize that there are two exceptions to the constant application of senior executive attention.

The first exception involves ongoing production problems that are of high impact to the system and company. You need daily senior executive attention to these high-impact production problems until they are resolved. For example, a system-wide network meltdown demands the focused attention and participation of the senior managers of your IT organization. The second exception is when your infrastructure as a whole has serious and frequent stability problems. Before the general stability of your critical systems is improved to a minimal acceptable level, senior executives have no choice but to work on the immediate system stability issues on a daily basis. Before your IT infrastructure is generally stable, it is difficult for senior executives to allocate time to work on strategy.

Work on What Is Strategic

Without addressing the long-term issues, pressing and immediate problems keep popping up. For each production problem, you need to have both a vertical view and a horizontal view. The vertical view is to manage the production problem one at a time. The horizontal view is to find out, pertaining to the problem at hand, the general characteristics and systemic issues that cause the instability. For every stability problem, you must look at it from four different perspectives with intent to uncover the underlying cause for this and other stability problems:

- Organization
- Engineering process
- Critical work relationship (Chapter 11, "Critical Work Relationships," covers this topic.)
- IT culture

Organization

Possible organizational issues that can lead to WebSphere instability are an incorrect organizational model, organizational instability, hiring and training challenges, and inappropriate incentive planning.

The wrong organization model can make WebSphere products and services delivery difficult and problematic. For example, a multilayered support model with a Level 1, Level 2, and Level 3 WebSphere technical support structure may actually slow the problem-resolution process because of the latency caused by the communication of complex technical problems between each layer of WebSphere support (discussed in Chapter 1, "Organization Models and Choices").

Organizational instability is another hotbed for system stability problems. An existing organization has powerful and important internal mechanisms that may be lost in seemingly strategic but often myopic organizational design exercises. IT organizational stability has a direct relationship to infrastructure stability. For example, it takes as long as 12 months for a WebSphere engineer to learn a large and complex WebSphere system. The WebSphere team has important internal and external work relationships. All of these relationships take years to build, but they can be destroyed in just one day. Be prudent about organizational changes and organizational designs. Do not try to reorganize yourself because of a problem. Instead, fix the problem. Reorganization should be a last resort in a corporate environment where the resentment and fatigue from ill-understood and fast-paced organizational changes are steadily growing, while the stability of a large IT system is declining as a result. During the post problem-resolution phase, you may want to seriously look at your organization and devise a practical strategy on embracing positive changes while maintaining a level of organizational stability for your WebSphere teams amidst inevitable organizational dynamics that are typical of a large corporation.

A questionable hiring strategy and the lack of technical training can take your team directly to instability. Is your hiring practice relationship-oriented or technical skills-based? Do you hire those who are talented in WebSphere engineering or those whom you know and trust? The dilemma sometimes can be between your effective control of the organization and its technical competence. By not exercising effective control of your WebSphere organization on behalf of your company, you fail as a manager. Building a technical team with technically less desirable but trustworthy members leads to team technical incompetence. A hiring practice that emphasizes only technical skills or only trustworthiness eventually leads to serious system instability because of lack of effective control of the team or technical skills challenges. After you suffer a serious WebSphere production problem, you need to think about whether you have a balanced approach in your hiring practice.

WebSphere engineers need to constantly renew their knowledge and skills through technical training. In addition, technical training is a strong motivator for maintaining high morale. You must have a disciplined, structured, and innovative technical training strategy. You must diligently work to implement technical training programs for your team, as discussed in Chapter 2, "Building a World-Class WebSphere Team Through Hiring and Training." Otherwise, your WebSphere system won't be stable. WebSphere technical training is an important area to examine in order to identify improvement areas dealing with systemic instability issues.

Engineering Process and Critical Work Relationships

WebSphere engineering process defects can cause serious system stability problems. Process-induced instability is possible during any WebSphere engineering life cycle. For example, a flawed engagement process may lead to inadequate resource allocation. Without enough resources working on a project, there is no product and service quality to discuss. As a result, an inferior WebSphere infrastructure and system outage may occur. This book offers an exhaustive discussion on each operation of WebSphere engineering, and it provides food for thought in identifying improvement opportunities, especially during post-problem review. The same goes for critical work relationships.

IT Culture

If the dominating IT culture for your organization rewards fire-fighting rather than engineering discipline and process excellence, stability issues tend to occur and recur. If you richly reward good firefighters rather than talented system engineers and technical managers who keep the critical IT infrastructure stable and prevent production fires from occurring, it is difficult to keep your WebSphere infrastructure stable. You must transform a heroic fire squad to a team of WebSphere engineers that embraces tight standards, consistent processes, and operational excellence. Only then can you achieve high system stability. However, this transformation needs basic but fundamental changes as conditions.

The first condition is that you have to quantitatively measure technical service quality and output. The inability to provide solid service performance numbers can lead to chronic resource shortages for the WebSphere organization and unrealistic project progress pressure that are directly responsible for many production fires. You have to explain to your customer the details of technical services. Making "black box" charges brings you neither customer satisfaction nor sufficient resources to do the job.

Second, you must have the ability to quantitatively measure performance by objectively evaluating the quality and output of a WebSphere engineer or team. Otherwise, system volatilities may provide the rare—if not the only realistic—opportunities to see a WebSphere engineer or manager's technical skills and leadership capabilities. These instabilities may become the only venue for the WebSphere team to be recognized and rewarded accordingly. Under such circumstances, do not be surprised if that WebSphere engineer or team has little motivation to work and keep their systems highly stable.

The third condition is that your WebSphere systems need to reach a minimum level of stability before a culture change is possible. This is because when your WebSphere infrastructure is suffering from frequent instabilities, you have to depend on those who can help you stabilize your systems, and you have to reward your fire squad for their help.

Changing IT culture to promote high system stability is necessary. However, it requires systemic improvement in the overall IT environment in which your WebSphere organization operates. Without the ability to quantitatively measure technical services, objectively evaluate performance, and reach a minimum level of system stability, an IT culture change will not be something that you can successfully tackle in the near future.

Linking Stability to Compensation

In the workplace, the ultimate motivation is financial compensation and incentive. Therefore, your greatest motivator is your incentive plan. For the revenue side of the house, it is relatively easier to form a fact-based incentive plan and objectively measure a division's performance. For example, a large electronics company may have four divisions. Each division has an annual revenue target of $1 billion. At various levels, the incentive plan can be directly tied to the revenue target and evaluated accordingly. The right incentive plan encourages the right business behavior. Linking system stability numbers with incentive payment encourages a large set of management and technical practices that lead to high system stability.

However, this linkage is complex and has many challenges. For example, how do you manage the incentive distribution fairly among those who have direct production responsibilities and those who have support roles, but are not immediately accountable for production stability? In addition, this linkage requires a solid foundation in organizational alignment, process excellence, and engineering maturity.

Incentive Plan

An incorrect incentive plan encourages incorrect business behavior. If you do not link system stability to financial incentive, you may never have strong system stability performance, because your managers and technical staff are not motivated to perform the work needed for high system stability. Even if one or two WebSphere teams achieve high system stability without the right incentive plan, the strong performance is ephemeral and local to those teams; it does not pervade the whole organization.

For example, say that you have several WebSphere teams. The average WebSphere stability performance is about 60 unscheduled production system outages per year, with 10 problems of high severity, 20 in medium severity, and 30 in the low severity category. A high-severity problem can last for two hours, which causes more than $1 million lost per hour in revenue. A medium-severity problem can last for one hour with about $500,000 lost per hour. A low-severity problem is a system anomaly causing no customer impact.

You have an outperforming WebSphere team that manages many large, complex, and dynamic systems, just like the other teams. This team has had only one or two unscheduled production outages each year for the past two years. Therefore, this team has achieved virtually 100 percent WebSphere infrastructure stability. However, if the incentive plan for this team does not link to its system stability performance, this outperforming WebSphere team will inevitably become like the other teams. This is true for many reasons.

First, this outperforming WebSphere team and its manager may have serious work-relationship issues. When the performance difference is relatively small, an outperforming WebSphere team encourages all. However, when the performance gap between teams is substantial, the outperforming team may become an embarrassment to everyone else because they aren't performing up to this team's level.

This team's existence and its high performance constantly reminds senior management that it is possible to better handle the company's system stability. Because these senior managers are not motivated by the right incentive plans to promote production stability, regardless of what they say, they are not genuinely interested in taking on a huge amount of work to significantly drive up system stability. They know for sure that their financial rewards have little to do with the company's system stability performance; therefore, they have no reason to make the outperforming team an example for other teams to follow. Instead, they may try to quietly make this team and its performance invisible to both IT and the business.

It may irritate the other teams to know that the outperforming team constantly provides a stark contrast to their own performance, which is considered normal. Therefore, the majority of peer teams won't like this outstanding team; therefore, work relationships may be tense despite the best teamwork efforts.

Finally, the WebSphere manager may have relationship issues with his own team. To keep virtually 100 percent stability is not easy. The entire team must work to maintain this level of performance. However, when this high performance is not rewarded by financial incentives and the

WebSphere manager continues to demand the same level of commitment for system stability, the team may have a hard time finding valid reasons to respond positively.

Although substantially contributing to the bottom line by saving your company $30 million a year for two years, the outperforming WebSphere manager and his team are consistently not paid for performance. Worse, the team has serious relationship issues with just about everyone in the organization (perhaps with the exception of the business, which is pleased with the team's performance, but makes no decision regarding an IT team's promotions or financial incentives). To pour salt on the wound, several senior managers may try to make this outperforming team and its performance invisible. The WebSphere engineers may no longer be enthusiastic in pushing hard on system stability without being rewarded. What do you think this WebSphere manager is going to do? Remember, with all of his professionalism and intentions to do the right thing for the company, he has come to the workplace to make a living, not to fight an apparently losing war against everyone.

Most likely, this WebSphere manager will shift his focus to obtain high visibility assignments, instead of working to make his systems so stable that they are invisible. Perhaps he will pay more attention to what senior management wants to hear and work to figure out how to act before the executives, instead of concentrating on smoothly running his critical WebSphere systems. Don't be surprised if he stops pushing himself and his team about maintaining high system stability and availability! Why should he brave all this extra hard work and increasingly nasty relationship issues without being rewarded for great performance?

Challenges in Implementation

Directly linking system stability performance and incentive plans is a powerful means to motivate management and the technical teams to do the right thing and help the company's bottom line. However, an attempt to implement this linkage may be met with resistance.

Lack of Confidence

The success of anything starts with the confidence that it can be done and a determination to get it done. However, some IT managers may not have high confidence in high system stability. Without these managers' genuine support, you won't be successful in implementing the important linkage between pay and system stability performance. These seasoned managers have valid reasons for disliking this linkage.

With their extensive knowledge and long years of exposure to IT problems, many experienced managers may have the view that it is not possible to reach a high degree of system stability. They understand the discrepancy between the fast-changing business drivers, the need for orderly IT execution, and the devastating consequences of this discrepancy in IT work quality. They are fully aware of many deep-rooted systemic issues of IT, such as the intangible nature of technical service and the perennial IT challenges between resource shortage and project progress pressure.

The concerns of these IT veterans and their lack of confidence are fully understandable. However, never underestimate the power of capitalism in its reward for performance and business success. Such rewards, when appropriately applied, release explosive creative energy and persistent innovative enthusiasm. The skillful and proper use of a financial incentive can move mountains. In addition, the WebSphere technology is maturing. WebSphere engineering is gradually moving into a sophisticated era of process consistency, system standardization, and experienced practices of winning IT methodology. The timing is right to tackle WebSphere infrastructure stability. Today, it is completely possible to reach 100 percent stability and availability if the WebSphere systems are in the right hands, with the right talents following the right engineering processes and belonging to an IT organization motivated and encouraged by the right incentive plan.

Nevertheless, this lack of confidence may bring a real concern (such as being held accountable for something that is perceived as impossible to achieve). Therefore, many managers may worry about their lost income if the linkage between system stability performance and financial incentive is formalized; they may stubbornly resist the establishment of this linkage.

General Fairness of the Linkage

Accountability is never comfortable, especially for those who have little confidence in achieving the performance desired or required. To move out of the comfort zone of collective low performance can be unnerving. It is particularly unnerving when you know that your pay will soon be tightly coupled with your volatile WebSphere systems.

You can certainly stage a tough fight to resist the change. You can also retreat to a position where there is no direct linkage between tough system stability numbers and your total compensation. For example, you may want to work for a department that manages the engagement process, or another department that does business support for the organization.

This raises a question of fairness. If you link the pay with system stability performance, are you being unfair to those who have direct system stability responsibilities? In your organization, why would anyone want to take a job with tough production responsibilities that often involves working long and stressful hours and then be penalized in pay for system stability issues?

Thus, general fairness within an organization is also an issue in the implementation of the incentive and system stability linkage for an infrastructure engineering division in general and for a WebSphere organization in particular.

Production-Oriented Organization

There are two enterprises in the world in which there is little fluff: competitive sports and war. In both, your capabilities to get the job done are tested beyond any fuzzy logic. In sports and war, you either win or lose, and your competence or incompetence has a direct, conspicuous, and serious consequence.

These two enterprises have another outstanding characteristic. The entire organization is streamlined toward a single-minded purpose: winning. Should an IT infrastructure engineering division, such as a WebSphere organization, adopt the same kind of structural focus and organizational orientation? Yes, it should. However, how can you achieve this and what is winning? What does winning mean to a WebSphere organization?

System Stability and Availability

Sometimes, the complexity and size of a large IT infrastructure organization obscures its key functions and critical objectives. Let's not be mistaken. Providing capable and resilient Web-Sphere infrastructure of high stability and availability is the business objective of the WebSphere organization. Winning means consistently provides highly stable WebSphere infrastructure. The WebSphere teams need to focus on achieving this objective, and all the organization's departments must be streamlined toward supporting this objective.

Streamlined Toward Supporting System Stability

Many departments appear to be of equal importance and exist in a parallel fashion with the IT infrastructure organization: business support, HR representatives, engagement service, and project management, among others. Align all of these departments toward supporting the Web-Sphere teams and other technical teams in their work to design, build, and operate capable Web-Sphere infrastructure of high stability and availability.

All these departments are logistical units of an army that enables the frontline soldiers. Their only reason to exist is to support the technical teams, who are the foot soldiers fighting on the front lines. The relationship between the technical teams and these supporting units must not be one of equal organizations existing in parallel. Instead, all the IT units must take supporting the frontline technical teams as their first and only priority. Doing this achieves the stability and availability performance goal.

However, if you have ever worked for two weeks in any IT establishment of large corporations, you may start wondering how this priority setting is possible. The answer is simple, but powerful—use the right incentive plan for the entire organization.

Build System Stability into Every Stakeholder's Incentive Plan

Build system stability into every stakeholder's incentive plan, including all the WebSphere engineers, all the team members of other technical teams, and all the staff members of the supporting units.

This plan focuses everyone, regardless of position or division, on achieving the organization's key objective: providing capable WebSphere-centered IT infrastructure of high stability and availability. For example, if the WebSphere team suffers a high severity production problem, the engagement engineer, finance officer, HR representative, process engineer, project manager, and design engineer may all lose a portion of their incentive payout, along with the WebSphere engineers. This linkage effectively motivates the supporting units to help the WebSphere team achieve high system stability.

For example, with this linkage, the engagement engineer understands that incorrect Web-Sphere resource estimates and allocation can eventually harm him in the form of bonus payment reduction or other losses in financial compensation because the resource issue may lead to Web-Sphere infrastructure instability. The HR representative is as anxious as the WebSphere manager to hire the best in the market in the fastest manner possible because he knows that the WebSphere team does better by adding qualified team members. As a result, his income increases. The project manager is less likely to rush the WebSphere team through complex engineering tasks because she is aware that mediocre work may lead to WebSphere instability, and that is extremely bad news for her checkbook.

If a business leader refuses to link his incentive plan to the revenue of his department, it will be generally considered unacceptable. The same should be true for the IT leaders of an infrastructure engineering division. If you are serious and confident about performing your most fundamental job well, which is providing a stable and capable IT infrastructure, link your incentive plan to your system stability performance. It is critical to link the incentive plan of all senior managers and executives to short-term system stability performance and long-term system stability strategies. This fundamentally changes the IT managers' behaviors. This forcefully encourages them to use the right kind of people and build the right kind of teams to deliver on the promise that is the designing, building, and operating of highly capable and stable IT infrastructure for the company.

Be tactful with a gradual introduction of the linkage. For example, you may start with a relatively small percentage of the incentive plan linked to system stability at first and gradually increase the percentage of the linkage to a significant proportion. Also consider setting incremental stability performance targets for each team against its own record. These slow and incremental strategies of introducing the linkage may give you a better chance to fine-tune the linking mechanism and reduce anxiety and resistance. However, the overall strategy should not change. People must be paid for performance. Their performance is measured by hard numbers. You have to implement this linkage to achieve fundamentally higher system stability. Align your entire organization toward winning. Focus everyone on supporting the war against system instability. Motivate all the departments to give the highest priority to production stability and availability. When you have the right incentive for everyone in your organization, you see the right business behavior from everyone. When a large organization refocuses itself with a newfound explosive positive energy to focus on the essential job of providing resilient IT infrastructure, there will be nothing in the world as easy as achieving 100 percent stability and availably for your large, complex, and powerful WebSphere-centered IT infrastructure.

Change Management in a Large and Interconnected Environment

In a large interconnected environment, one WebSphere system can be connected to hundreds of other systems. You do not know when what change from which interconnected system will hit your WebSphere infrastructure and cause a problem. It is possible that one or two systems among hundreds of interconnected systems have a change that affects your WebSphere system in significant ways. For example, a low-risk change in system X may cause a severe production outage in system Y, for which you are responsible. Worse, you may not be aware that system X even has a change because it is a large system managed by a different team that belongs to a different line of business (LOB).

To know what changes will affect your systems, you must overcome many challenges to be informed and get prepared for the pending interconnected changes:

- Lack of organization support
- Lack of process
- Lack of relevant technology

Organization Support

The first area in filling the gap in support of interconnected change management is to improve interproject communication. This can be done by taking advantage of the organization's strength by assigning a designated interproject communication function. However, who is the best candidate/team to take on this function?

Intuitively, the WebSphere managers may be the first on the candidate list to carry out this interproject communication function. Because many projects use WebSphere infrastructure, the WebSphere teams have wide visibility to a large number of projects and applications. However, the WebSphere teams have limited exposure to business logic and application component details; therefore, they may not understand the interaction between interconnected systems as some other technical teams do, such as the application development team. The application development manager knows more of the application code details and the business rationale of the application. However, the application development manager does not work in the production environment where the applications are interconnected. The application production support manager works in the production environment. He well understands how the applications are interconnected. In addition, the production support manager has strong motivation to keep the production environment stable; therefore, he is more likely to go the extra mile to perform the critical interproject change communication. Nevertheless, he does not work in the development and testing phases of the current application code release. To effectively manage interconnectivity between applications, work needs to be also done at development and testing life cycles to prevent problems in the production environment. This leads us to evaluate a candidate that has visibility of all the environments: the release manager. Your release manager's work area covers development, testing, quality assurance, and production life cycles. Among the release manager's vast work areas, release policy, release planning, roll-out planning, and communication strategy, there are good tools, mechanisms, and the window of opportunity to implement policies, guidelines, and plans for managing interconnectivity. In addition, the release manager can play the following critical roles between interconnected projects and applications.

Facilitator

The release manager can serve as the liaison officer between interconnected systems and applications to ensure different business units are educated about the time and scope of the delivery of new products and updates that may affect them. The release manager can use tools, such as roll-out planning and communication strategy, as formal communication mechanisms.

Architect

The release manager can help with new processes and guidelines that define resilient and robust interfaces between system and applications. For example, the release manager can guide the application using large-scale caching for short-term data independence or alternative execution when the interconnected system is experiencing problems and becomes unavailable.

Coordinator

The release manager can be the coordinator working together with disparate applications, projects, and technical teams to ensure that the production release of one application coordinates with the changes in release and configuration of other interconnected systems. The release manager must have both a vertical view of the project that she is responsible for and a horizontal view of the applications and projects interconnected to her project.

From an interconnected perspective, although the release manager's focus is to ensure the new release of her application or project does not negatively affect other interconnected applications and projects, she must have a strong motivation to ensure that communication and coordination happen. The instability of the interconnected applications and systems will eventually backfire on the projects that the release manager is responsible for. In addition, organizational means, such as a properly structured performance plan that includes measuring how the release manager copes with interconnected applications and systems and interproject communication to minimize the negative impact of interconnectivity.

The identification of the responsible party for interconnected change communication and coordination is a good first step. To guarantee the effectiveness of this function, there is a need to establish process and support mechanisms.

Process Support

The release managers of interconnected applications and systems should have established processes and support mechanisms to manage interconnected changes.

Change Management

In your change-control process, you can add an interapplication impact analysis and approval step. For an interconnected application, your change managers or change-control board needs to consider asking the application to provide the following document along with the major change, whether it is a new application release or update. Call the document Interconnected Impact Assessment Document, and it needs to include the following:

- Application name
- List of interconnected applications
- For each interconnected application, you can have the following:
  - Application name
  - Impact (yes/no)

- Severity (low/medium/high)
- Description of the impact
- Impact communicated to the application (yes/no)

Release Management

For each affected application, the release manager must require a document from the application development team called the Interconnected Application Release Document, which includes the following details:

- Application name
- List of affected application components
- For each affected component, you can have the following:
  - Component name
  - Severity of impact (low/medium/high)
  - Volume change (yes/no)
  - Volume change description
  - Traffic pattern change (yes/no)
  - Traffic pattern change description
  - Stress testing (yes/no)
  - Stress-testing description

You must describe volume change at the application component level. This is because even though the total volume may not change at the application level, significant volume changes local to an application component can still make a serious stability impact. This document helps the release managers work with change managers to approve/disapprove a new release or update as a change request.

Senior Management Review

For critical enterprise applications, such as the system record of a large insurance company, a senior executive review needs to be conducted against major release and update. This is because such applications or systems are interconnected with many other enterprise systems; therefore, the stability impact of possible issues may have wide enterprise impact. This is also to take advantage of the fact that senior executives have broad exposure to a large number of enterprise applications.

Technology Support

Today, the interconnected enterprise systems are large and complex. They defy the most experienced and the most talented in developing a holistic picture of the complete environment of a large system. It is difficult to quickly identify and isolate a problem caused by interdependencies of such large and complex systems.

Seeing the Big Picture

It is important to see the big picture of a large interconnected enterprise system. It lets you understand where the servers, applications, and components are and how they interconnect. Without seeing this picture, it can be difficult to understand the impact of the changes of one system to another. In addition, when you have a problem, seeing the big picture helps you quickly identify and isolate the problem.

To help your WebSphere teams overcome these challenges with large, interconnected systems, IT infrastructure and application discovery technology becomes a necessary enabler, especially when such technology has the capability of large-scale visualization. System visualization can enable WebSphere system engineers to quickly identify a large number of logical resources and their physical mappings. These mappings include networks, operating systems, storages, interfaces, systems, applications, and components.

The visualization enables triage and troubleshooting for large, interconnected systems. For example, it may take several hours for a large group of system and application support professionals to figure out that a network issue caused a dozen critical systems to fail at the same time. However, with visualization of enterprise systems and graphical presentation of error conditions, at the system management console, the technical teams may immediately see that all the affected systems reside in the same data center; it would be easy to find out that, at this particular moment, a certain segment of the data center is suffering a network issue that is affecting these WebSphere servers.

The visual presentation needs to have the proper abstraction to provide the big picture while hiding unnecessary details with the capability to zoom out. Meanwhile, it needs to have the capability to zoom in to provide more details for a portion of the interconnected entity (for example, the configuration of the WebSphere Application Server).

Understanding Interdependencies

System and application discovery technologies should give you a comprehensive, but manageable, view of a highly complex and large system by abstraction that hides unnecessary details. Thus, it helps to discover and understand interdependencies, interrelationships, and interactions between interconnected systems, applications, and components. Without understanding these interdependencies and interactions, it is impossible to prevent a change for one system from affecting the other interconnected systems.

Furthermore, large-scale visualization-based interdependency discovery capabilities help you quickly recognize tell-tale patterns and reveal relationships between interconnected systems and the applications and their supporting infrastructure, therefore providing unprecedented insight into otherwise seemingly unrelated system phenomena.

For example, say that you have spent two days troubleshooting Web server and WebSphere Application Server communication issues that have affected many large WebSphere applications. Many efforts have been made to examine the Web server plug-in program without making much progress. Only accidentally, your WebSphere teams working for different LOBs have found that all of these Web servers and WebSphere Application Servers reside on the same network segment in one data center. The network team is called in and quickly uncovers a network connectivity issue, provides a solution, and fixes the problem. If you had IT infrastructure and application dependency discovery technology based on large-scale visualization, you would have been able to see with one glance that all the malfunctioning servers are sitting on the same network segment. Then it would not have been difficult to identify the network problem and fix it within a few hours.

Uncovering Configuration Drift

A simple configuration error can cause a serious outage. Often, a stability problem is caused by nothing more than a single configuration error or inconsistency. Unfortunately, the error can hide deep in thousands of configuration items of large systems that have many components, making it difficult to isolate. System and application discovery technologies can help.

After the components are discovered, components can be compared. This useful comparison can be done between the stress-testing environment, production environment, and production environments between data centers to identify any unintended configuration change or configuration drift. In addition, the visual presentation shows the interdependencies between components to help with the impact assessment. A visual presentation of configuration drift can be a powerful help for problem preemption, prevention, and correction.

Without powerful and mature system and application discovery technologies, identifying configuration drift is difficult and resource intensive. Given that manual comparison of configuration drift is almost impossible, the WebSphere team may have to depend on a script-based comparison strategy. Such script programs take time to develop, test, and implement. In addition, the analysis of the results is usually time-consuming and demands both experience and expertise to interpret correctly.

It does not matter if the system and application discovery technology chosen is based on Web services, the deployment of a set of cooperative scanning agents, or an agent-free discovery engine. It is important to have this much needed technological capability to keep your large interconnected WebSphere system stable.

Summary

Technology is not the ultimate driver for achieving high stability of large interconnected WebSphere systems. The business needs of your company require your large and critical WebSphere infrastructure to be resilient and stable. In addition, today IT does not only support the business; often it is the business itself. For example, a company's online system may have more sales than those generated from all its branches. A corporation that has a fragile and brittle IT infrastructure sits on a time bomb. The cascading failure of the IT infrastructure may bring significant financial harm to your customers, shareholders, and employees.

As the WebSphere manager or senior consultant, you have to work diligently on system stability with a tactical focus and a strategic vision. You have to work with your human resource business partners to devise the right incentive plan and provide the vital link between compensation and system stability performance. You have to develop a true enterprise view of the interconnected systems, in terms of change management and production problem prevention.

Again, the business is the driver of system stability. You have to be aware that this business need will be fulfilled one way or another because, without it, the survival and continued prosperity of your company is at risk. The interesting question is not *if*, but *who* will satisfy this need for system stability.

Working as a technology leader for a company is tough. You will always have competition. You cannot neglect large-system stability because it is so critical to your company. If you do not focus on system stability, someone else will. If you have not developed a long-term stability line of attack, others may fill that vacuum for your IT organization. If you do not work on infrastructure architecture resiliency, someone else can step in and provide that badly needed vision for your company.

Chapter 13, "WebSphere Engineering Going Forward," invites you to look at the near future and see where WebSphere engineering is going and examine its new challenges and opportunities.

WebSphere Engineering Going Forward

WebSphere technologies have reached a high level of maturity and capability where new products are being built on top of the WebSphere Application Server in support of Service Oriented Architecture (SOA). What is the future of WebSphere engineering? Is it the continued development of WebSphere engineering as a rigorous engineering discipline? Should it regenerate itself to accommodate the expansion of the brand new technologies, such as WebSphere Enterprise Service Broker? Will it keep evolving as an IT methodology for deploying the WebSphere Application Server, the premium execution environment for JEE applications? With these questions in mind, this chapter discusses new challenges and opportunities in three main areas: providing infrastructure for SOA, infrastructure virtualization, and Service Science Management Engineering (SSME).[1]

This discussion focuses on technical skills, organization models, and the WebSphere engineering process. In addition, instead of providing definitive conclusions about future directions, this chapter includes thought-provoking questions and gives insight into the future of WebSphere engineering.

Providing Infrastructure for SOA Solutions

This section discusses WebSphere technologies that provide an end-to-end IT infrastructure plumbing for SOA strategies. You will find a survey of these technologies and possible new technological directions. After reviewing the skills needed from a team-building and technical

---

1. According to IBM:

> Service Science or Service Science, Management and Engineering (SSME) is a growing multi-disciplinary research and academic effort that integrates aspects of established fields like computer science, operations research, engineering, management sciences, business strategy, social and cognitive sciences, and legal sciences.

training perspective to support these technologies, you explore the organization structure to effectively support these technologies.

WebSphere Infrastructure Technologies Supporting SOA

The WebSphere team provides infrastructure plumbing for SOA applying WebSphere technologies. These technologies are IBM WebSphere Service Registry Repository (WSRR), IBM WebSphere Enterprise Service Broker, and IBM WebSphere DataPower® SOA Appliances.

WSRR provides registries for both metadata and service descriptions. It stores, manages, and queries service metadata, such as properties, relationships, classifications, and service artifacts, such as physical documents, logical derivations, and GenericObjects. WSRR publishes, finds, enriches, manages, and governs service. It encourages reuse, enhances connectivity, enables SOA governance, and helps with service optimization. WSRR is the master repository where service and related information are stored, found, and managed. WSRR covers the full engineering life cycle of a service, from creation to decommissioning. WSRR is critical to better manage and govern services.

Enterprise Service Bus (ESB) is an architectural pattern for service-oriented application integration. Be careful not to confuse the generic ESB with IBM WebSphere Enterprise Service Bus (WebSphere ESB). The former ESB is an architecture pattern, while the latter, WebSphere ESB, is a product. Notice this difference and understand that ESB is not a product. ESB reduces the interface complexity, quantity, and magnitude. ESB helps achieve the virtualization of participants' location and identity, conversion between different transport protocols, transformation of message formats, promotion of Quality of Service (QoS), and distribution of business events between disparate sources. ESB helps take care of the integration logic and allows the technical teams to focus on solving the business problem to apply the technology.

IBM WebSphere ESB is a product that supports the ESB architectural pattern. More specifically, WebSphere ESB is for Web services integration. WebSphere ESB delivers Web services connectivity, Java Message Service (JMS), and services integration. It features integrated, interactive, and visual development tools, supports many vendor solutions, and can be dynamically reconfigured to meet changing business drivers. It integrates well with the WebSphere infrastructure; for example, it can take advantage of WebSphere Application Server's clustering and failover capacities. WebSphere ESB provides a basic requirement of SOA.

Another new technology that you can use to build ESB is IBM WebSphere DataPower SOA Appliances (DataPower). DataPower redraws the boundaries of middleware into dedicated and specialized superior performance SOA appliances, featuring hardened security and enhanced integration. There are high performance costs for XML and cryptography processing, and DataPower directly addresses these performance costs while providing innovative new features. DataPower can be used as a security gateway, to implement ESB, and for sophisticated logging, auditing, and Web services management.

To build IT infrastructure supporting your company's SOA strategy, these new technologies require new technical skills and new thinking when providing your team with technical training.

Technical Skill Set and Training Considerations

A middleware engineer who builds WebSphere infrastructure to support SOA must have two areas of technical knowledge and skills:

- Foundational technical knowledge of XML, Web services, and SOA
- Product-specific technical knowledge and WSRR, WebSphere ESB, and DataPower skills

Foundation

A solid foundation for learning new WebSphere technologies supporting SOA is important. Those practitioners who do not have the technical knowledge foundation of XML, Web services, and SOA won't fully understand the specific technical products they will work with in building WebSphere infrastructure for SOA. They may know how to perform a specific job, but they do not understand why the job has to be done in certain ways. For example, without knowing that some XML parsers use computing-intensive recursive traversal algorithms in parsing out an XML document, a WebSphere engineer may not fully appreciate the value of DataPower. As a result, he cannot correctly estimate and recommend its utilization in a specific SOA solution design. You cannot build lofty buildings on a shaky foundation. The same is true for building technical strength to support your company's SOA strategy. The basic technical knowledge foundation and skills include XML, Web Services, and SOA.

XML is a good place to start the learning process. It is the platform of Web services. A WebSphere engineer can start with the following XML fundamentals:

- HTML and XML and their usage in e-business
- Rules of a well-formed XML document
- Document Type Definition (DTD) and XML schema
- XML namespaces and the management of the symbol space
- XML Path Language (XPath)
- XSL and XML document transformation
- XQuery and its usage and syntax
- XML development tools

Although the WebSphere engineers may never need to write XML code or XML Java applications, the next level of XML learning needs to focus on XML parsers because they are the heart of XML document processing and XML applications. The following knowledge and skills of XML parsers can be helpful:

- XML parsers used in Java applications
- Simple API for XML (SAX)

- Document Object Model (DOM) API
- Creation of XML documents from Java objects
- Architecture of XML application
- Conversion of structured data into XML documents

XML is one of the basic platforms for Web services. Web services learning or training can be done through a phased approach. The first phase covers Web services basics, and the second phase focuses on advanced skills. The content for the first phase of Web services learning includes the following:

- Web services architecture
- Basic Web services protocols
- Simple Object Access Protocol (SOAP)
- Web Services Description Language (WSDL)
- Universal Description, Discovery, and Integration (UDDI)

The second phase of Web services learning may cover some of the same topics as the first phase, but at an advanced level. You can select some of the following contents to structure your advanced Web services training program:

- Web services and its usage in enterprise applications
- WSDL and its testing
- JEE Web services programming model
- Web services packaging and deployment
- SOAP message handlers
- SOAP programming model
- SOAP over JMS and ESB
- Web services security, XML signature and encryption
- WS-Security elements by WebSphere
- Web services transaction

A WebSphere engineer must understand many aspects of SOA while focusing on providing WebSphere infrastructure connectivity for your company's SOA strategy. The following SOA basics can serve as a SOA entry point:

- Business and technical value of SOA
- Principles and characteristics of services within SOA and various service types
- Difference between SOI and Enterprise Application Integration (EAI) approaches
- SOA analysis and design methodologies

- Programming models and standards that support SOA realization

- Support of Web services to the realization of SOA solutions

- SOA governance

Product-Specific Training

Armed with a solid foundation of XML, Web services, and SOA, you can start product-specific technical training for your team. For a WebSphere engineering support team, the training needs to include WSRR, WebSphere ESB, and WebSphere DataPower. The following technical training classes (or equivalent) are a good start:

- **IBM WebSphere Service Registry and Repository for Administrators**. Among the prerequisites of WebSphere Application Server skills is a high-level understanding of Web services and SOA. Without prior knowledge of Web services and SOA, it is difficult for a WebSphere engineer to fully take advantage of this training. Therefore, it is important to follow this sequence of learning: XML, Web services, SOA, product-specific technical training. This class covers the following:
  - Use WSRR in a standalone or high-availability configuration
  - Design an appropriate IBM WebSphere Application Server topology for WSRR
  - Design and implement a suitable service registry configuration to work with a local or remote database installation
  - Determine governance enablers and Web UI elements and customization
  - WSRR service promotion through technical environment
  - Fine grain security model enabling and management

- **Introduction to IBM WebSphere Enterprise Service Bus**. This course teaches the features of IBM WebSphere ESB, the key architecture components of the product, and the support, testing, and deployment of integration artifacts to IBM WebSphere ESB. This class covers the following:
  - SOA enabling of end-to-end business integration
  - ESB concept and its advantages in service-oriented integration (SOI) and SOA enabling
  - IBM WebSphere ESB product and its capabilities supporting SOI and SOA
  - WebSphere ESB architecture and its relationship to WebSphere Application Server
  - Key characteristics and benefits of Service Component Architecture (SCA)
  - Mediations and integration capabilities of WebSphere ESB
  - Service requestors, providers, and methods to interact with WebSphere ESB V6
  - WebSphere ESB system administration

- **IBM WebSphere DataPower System Administration**. This course teaches the functions and benefits of an IBM DataPower SOA appliance as a middleware solution platform in terms of high performance, tight security, and managed integration. This class covers the following:
  - Basic administrative tasks on the DataPower appliance
  - Upgrade firmware
  - Manage user accounts and domains
  - Manage load balancer groups and clustering
  - Performance monitoring using service-level monitoring and the IBM Tivoli Composite Application Management (ITCAM)
  - Services problem triage and resolution using WebSphere DataPower problem-determination tools
  - Manage logs, including using external locations

WebSphere Product Support Responsibilities and Hiring Considerations

Four core WebSphere products are used to build a SOA infrastructure: WSRR, WebSphere ESB, WebSphere Message Broker, and WebSphere DataPower. Among these products, what WebSphere products need to be best supported by the WebSphere Application Server engineering support team? What hiring strategy helps build the best WebSphere team to support these technologies?

WSRR and WebSphere ESB are WebSphere Application Server-based technologies. The WebSphere team is best positioned to support them. This is especially true when you consider the significant amount of engineering tasks to support WSRR and WebSphere ESB are related to the WebSphere Application Server. In addition, it reduces teamwork and communication issues if the WebSphere team supports both the WebSphere Application Server infrastructure and WSRR and WebSphere ESB.

WebSphere Message Broker may be best supported by a dedicated enterprise application integration team because of the heterogeneous nature of the type of integrations that it supports.

WebSphere DataPower is a new product. One approach is to assign the WebSphere DataPower support to the engineering team that uses this technology (for example, a technical team that does enterprise application integration and applies WebSphere DataPower in its major projects). The disadvantage of this approach is the difficulties that it introduces to use WebSphere DataPower as a central piece for SOA governance. Perhaps the WebSphere team or a dedicated team must manage all WebSphere DataPower devices as a better organizational model. Web server and application servers may eventually become appliances with minimum configuration chores. These Web server and application servers can quickly be put together as commodities to meet the time-to-market challenge of designing and building IT middleware. The increasing popularity and critical application of high performance and dedicated appliances, and the disappearing boundary between middleware and operating systems, are exciting and promising areas that the WebSphere team wants to get involved with early as a technological direction and strategic posture.

Because these are new technologies, not many WebSphere professionals on the market have extensive experience in WSRR, WebSphere ESB, and WebSphere DataPower. Therefore, consider candidates with the following skills and provide formal technical and on-the-job training:

- XML and Web services
- SOA and SOA governance
- WebSphere Application Server

An ideal candidate has development experience in XML, Web services, and WebSphere Application Server system exposure. This candidate has the fewest technical training needs. After introducing her to your company's SOA strategy and governance structure, she can be quickly trained in WSRR, WebSphere ESB, and WebSphere DataPower and start adding value.

Both as a hiring requirement or as a means of technical training, IBM XML and related technology certifications and SOA certifications are valuable. The process of learning and passing tests to obtain these certifications requires candidates to systematically study and understand the details of the concepts, architectures, technical models, processes, and tools of these technologies and to form a solid technical foundation for more learning and practice. Here are three of the IBM technical certifications on XML and SOA for your reference:

- IBM Certified Solution Developer: XML 1.1 and Related Technologies
- There are two IBM technical certifications on SOA: IBM Certified SOA Associate and IBM Certified SOA Solution Designer. For the purposes of hiring and training, WebSphere system engineers work with the WebSphere infrastructure to support SOA. The entry-level IBM Certified SOA Associate is sufficient, unless you are trying to hire and train an architect-level WebSphere professional.

Virtualization and WebSphere Engineering

Infrastructure virtualization is a major trend that addresses many issues. This section looks at some major issues and trends for large WebSphere infrastructures. In addition, it discusses what WebSphere engineering must overcome to help build the next generation of virtualized WebSphere IT infrastructure.

Major Issues and WebSphere Virtual Enterprise-Based Solutions

One of the top issues confronting IT leaders worldwide is to continue growing utilization and sharing of infrastructure resources.[2] In a typical WebSphere environment built on WebSphere

2. Bart Jacob, et al., "On-Demand Operating Environment: Managing the Infrastructure (Virtualization Engine™ Update)" (IBM Redbook, 2006), IBM.

Application Server ND technology, WebSphere system resources are dedicated to particular applications or projects. Hence, individual resources are sized and provisioned to handle the peak load. This static structure leads to unused capacity and the inefficient use of resources, with most servers being underutilized. It is common that less than 10 percent of the WebSphere server suite is used, while other servers may be overloaded. WebSphere Virtual Enterprise enables you to create a dynamic, virtualized, goal-based environment for hosting your enterprise applications. This environment can adapt to varying traffic levels and allocate server resources as necessary to help meet the performance goals of your applications. Applications are installed to dynamic clusters, which can be dynamically resized within the virtual pool of resources. The application placement controller is the component that is responsible for making placement decisions based on current load levels and user-defined performance goals.

The second challenge is infrastructure optimization. There are increasing trends of server consolidations for IT infrastructure. It typically involves purchasing and deploying fewer servers, but using more powerful machines. This is partly driven by the rapidly changing marketplace and the need to reduce application and infrastructure complexity and system management overhead. Server consolidations typically require more sharing and more effective use of underlying computing resources. As a result, it requires the software and software platform to accommodate sharing and more effective resource utilization. Adopting new technologies, such as WebSphere Virtual Enterprise, is especially important because static WebSphere infrastructure depends on redundancy to reach a high level of scalability and failover, which helps with server proliferation.[3]

Complex integration is the third area of concern for IT organizations. There is increasing complexity involved in integrating various components into a large WebSphere system. There are many components and systems to integrate, relational databases, messaging systems, Web services, and legacy systems. This integration requires a more centralized and easier-to-manage middleware platform. The WebSphere Virtual Enterprise has both the powerful integration capabilities and extended management functions.

In an IT organization, systems and applications increasingly rely on each other to obtain information and complete the business logic. For example, to process a customer loan application, the loan-processing logic needs to know the detailed customer information, so the loan application needs to access the customer information system. Although the software components are designed and implemented to be decoupled from each other through asynchronous messaging or Web services, they still affect each other through the load placed on the system, their capacity, and availability. There needs to be a middleware system, such as the WebSphere Virtual Enterprise, that monitors the system performance, and dynamically allocates the resources as demands vary for large and complex interconnected systems and applications while isolating system instability and unavailability. This dynamic resource allocation capability of the WebSphere Virtual Enterprise provides a great level of resiliency for the interconnected WebSphere systems to better manage capability issues and peak loads that are difficult to predict in a large and complex interconnected environment.

3. Adam G. Neat, *Maximizing Performance and Scalability with IBM WebSphere*, (Apress, 2004).

In a static WebSphere environment, all the application processes compete for the resources, and there is no distinction between the applications' priorities. As a result, a few noncritical but problematic applications can disrupt the entire WebSphere operating environment; this affects the critical applications that need high priority and no disruptions. The WebSphere Virtual Enterprise addresses this problem through goal-directed infrastructure and dynamic operations. It helps to ensure that workloads, such as user requests, are classified, prioritized, queued, and routed to servers based on application service policies that, in turn, are tied to business goals. This goal-directed infrastructure implements a strategy in which business goals are defined in the operational environment as service policies (for example, the response time). The requests are categorized by the definitions of transaction classes (for example, a particular URI). This ensures that the important applications get more resources when needed. The on-demand router of the WebSphere Virtual Enterprise is the point of entry for HTTP requests into a dynamic operations environment. It performs request classification based on user-defined rules, ensures that more important requests flow through to the backend more quickly than less important requests, and dynamically routes requests to application servers and dynamic cluster members running in the application server tier.

Last but not least, system complexity and management overhead is troubling. With the ever-increasing complexity of the infrastructures and applications, the required resources and engineering time spent supporting the WebSphere applications are increasing. It is important to monitor the real-time status of the system, and to be alerted when anomalies occur so you can proactively provide the corrective actions. The WebSphere Virtual Enterprise provides an extended management capability to view system status and perform health checks in real time, in a simplified administrative console view. As an option, the WebSphere system can function to generate correction recommendations or automatically correct error conditions in a supervised or autonomic computing mode. That is, the WebSphere Virtual Enterprise provides action recommendations or takes action based on the configuration and circumstances where erroneous system conditions are detected; it does not require human intervention.

The WebSphere Virtual Enterprise features can significantly contribute to the resolution of the previously discussed difficulties and issues, and these features provide support to the work along major IT infrastructure trends and strategic directions. This analysis sheds light on how the WebSphere Virtual Enterprise affects WebSphere IT infrastructure. However, to effectively and efficiently design, build, and operate WebSphere Virtual Enterprise-based systems, efforts need to be made to update WebSphere engineering. Now, let's look at this WebSphere engineering process and framework regeneration and how to make it work well with the WebSphere Virtual Enterprise.

WebSphere Engineering Challenges and Opportunities

The WebSphere Virtual Enterprise is a powerful platform for building next-generation WebSphere IT infrastructure with simplified but extended infrastructure management, dynamic operation, increased system utilization, and high availability. There are also exciting opportunities for significant cost savings, especially in extended management, better scheduling, more effective prioritizing, and enhanced Quality of Services, system consolidation, and higher system utilization. IBM has come a long way to bring about the innovative WebSphere Virtual Enterprise technology. As a WebSphere engineering professional, you have both opportunities and challenges to deploy this technology in designing, building, and operating WebSphere Virtual Enterprise-based IT infrastructure.

For a large IT organization, or within one large line of business, the financial relationships between business and IT and between different divisions of IT organizations are complex and complicated. To mingle several large lines of business to share a common enterprise middleware infrastructure for their large and critical IT applications is challenging in terms of the funding model and IT organization financial practices, but it's not impossible. The funding model has intrinsic reasons to exist the way it is today. However, strong incentives exist for changes with the emergence of a new technology with better mechanisms to assist in fact-based accounting information on infrastructure utilization and engineering support services. A new technology can make positive changes in the IT organization and the underlying relationships that dictate a sizable company's complex IT funding practices.

Savings in hardware resources, server consolidation, and infrastructure optimization give strong incentives for IT managers to adopt the WebSphere Virtual Enterprise. It is always important to save on hardware expenditures, even amidst the trend of hardware commoditization. This is important as IT organizations reduce underutilization and nonessential hardware. It also enables a "no hardware growth" strategy, where IT can soak up all the underutilized infrastructure resources, such as CPU and memory, and apply them to new applications. Software and human resources also have increasingly more weight in overall IT budgetary consideration and the total cost of ownership (TCO) of technology. Fewer WebSphere servers to manage translates into human resource savings. IT management and lines of business will stop tolerating low utilization (for example, distributed WAS servers are generally reaching only about 10 percent of their capacity). This, along with other potential rewards, may motivate IT managers to introduce the WebSphere Virtual Enterprise as part of the middleware infrastructure optimization plan.

Particularly interesting is the WebSphere infrastructure for nonproduction environment support. Large and critical initiatives frequently have many development and testing pipelines to speed up the implementation of new business functions. Therefore, many WebSphere servers exist at the development and testing environments, where the utilization is lower than approximately 10 percent, because of the nature of development and no-load-testing environments. The server proliferation of development and testing environments may be a good area in which to bring in the WebSphere Virtual Enterprise. For example, you can add more development environments on the same hardware. The WebSphere systems can be turned on only when they're actually used. This works well for a "follow the sun" model where development cycles are complementary across strategic global sites.

A shared WebSphere computing environment for numerous mid-sized and small applications is another candidate for introducing the WebSphere Virtual Enterprise.

One more area for introducing the WebSphere Virtual Enterprise is a large dedicated WebSphere infrastructure that contains a suite of applications for focused functionality, such as consumer credit decisions. This needs to include both production and development and testing environments.

These areas are ideal for adopting the WebSphere Virtual Enterprise technology. With the continued maturing in engineering practice and technical management, we will see more sweeping infrastructure changes in virtualized IT WebSphere infrastructure. This new dynamic WebSphere infrastructure needs to be systematically managed with a new generation of WebSphere engineering.

WebSphere Engineering Regeneration

The current WebSphere technical management maturity and engineering practices are a systematic response to the challenges of making a large and dynamic set of technologies work for several large and critical WebSphere projects. To work on a number of such large WebSphere projects with a new dynamic WebSphere middleware infrastructure requires continued development of WebSphere engineering practices and processes. For example, to manage multiple pipelines of code migration through many development and testing environments on the same WebSphere infrastructure for one large WebSphere project is difficult, but it can be executed well within the current WebSphere engineering practice. The degree of complexity in managing multiple pipelines of code migration for multiple large and complex WebSphere projects on the shared WebSphere Virtual Enterprise infrastructure demands a new set of WebSphere engineering best practices, framework, processes, and standards.

WebSphere engineering needs to be updated and helpful to WebSphere professionals working on the WebSphere Virtual Enterprise. You must guard against any "pure" technology philosophy in current or future WebSphere engineering work. Instead, WebSphere engineering is not only technology, but WebSphere technical management, WebSphere project management, WebSphere engineering standards and processes, and organization, communication, and culture areas of work. Middleware in general—and WebSphere in particular—have developed to a critical juncture where such service science-oriented thoughts are an indispensable factor to a winning middleware engineering strategy. To work with the WebSphere Virtual Enterprise, you need to update and regenerate WebSphere engineering in the following areas:

- **Server installation planning**. You see plenty of work in upgrading WebSphere engineering to the WebSphere Virtual Enterprise suite. For example, how do you plan capacity for a dynamic WAS environment?

- **Server build**. The WebSphere Virtual Enterprise executes on top of WebSphere Application Server ND. This involves extra installation work. Also, installation verification may take on a completely new meaning.

- **Configuration**. You will have more activities in configuring priority polices and health policies.

- **Stress-testing and testing environment support**. You may have to quickly build and tear down WebSphere testing environments to test different applications.

- **Code migration**. You may have to consider how you want to manage and use the WebSphere Virtual Enterprise application version-control facility.

- **WebSphere environment orientation**. Different WebSphere environments have different emphasis and features. You may need different tool sets targeted at different environments.

Updated WebSphere engineering best practices provides a useful framework for engineering processes, operations artifacts, such as automation tools, performance metrics, system management, and monitoring strategies, among others, for WebSphere Virtual Enterprise deployment.

SSME and WebSphere Engineering

SSME intends to realize the synergy of current work in computer science, operations research, industrial engineering, business strategy, management sciences, and social and cognitive sciences, among others, to develop the skills and services systems required in a primarily service-based economy.

From the perspective of SSME, WebSphere engineering must never exist as an isolated discipline that deals only with engineering processes and technical details. Instead, WebSphere engineering must combine multiple disciplines to form a new IT engineering discipline that increases the understanding of value co-production in sociotechnical systems.[4] Eventually, this deep understanding of services system-oriented WebSphere engineering will lead to more systematic approaches to WebSphere engineering innovation. As a result, engineering innovations will positively affect WebSphere products and services delivered in terms of productivity, quality, and rates of growth and return.

SSME emphasizes an integrated services system of several equally important components: technology, people, processes, communication models, and cultural values. This is a marked departure from the "technology as primary focus" approach that has been prevalent in IT. SSME encourages a better understanding of services systems and, especially, the development of services systems. For example, SSME principles can be applied to determine the development of the current WebSphere systems into a virtualized and dynamic technical environment. In addition, if you are provisioning the WebSphere Virtual Enterprise-based dynamic IT infrastructure, from a SSME perspective, your job is not done after you accomplish the design and build of WebSphere systems. Along with the WebSphere Virtual Enterprise infrastructure build, according to the new multidisciplinary approach of SSME, you may also have to provide the following deliverables (of course, the same applies to WebSphere ESB, WebSphere DataPower, and other new WebSphere technologies):

4. "The term **co-production** is an idiom to explore the ways in which technical experts and other groups in society generate new knowledge and technologies together. More specifically, some use it to conceptualize the dynamic interaction between technology and society." Wikipedia, 2008, "Co-production."

- New WebSphere engineering processes and related artifacts that cover the full WebSphere engineering life cycle
- One or more organizational models for the WebSphere team to optimally support dynamic WebSphere systems
- Reference models for effective communication and best practices for IT culture changes to help technical teams function effectively in a new technical environment

Engineering Processes

The SSME approach to IT products and services makes it necessary to ship engineering processes—or at least a framework—together with the introduction of new technologies. For example, state-of-the-art technology, such as the WebSphere Virtual Enterprise, will certainly force process reengineering. The capacity analysis of the WebSphere Virtual Enterprise-based infrastructure will certainly differ than that of WebSphere Application Server ND-based systems. The resource-consumption accounting and hosting charge calculation are more likely to require new tools and new processes. If a technology infrastructure provider can provide a comprehensive set of engineering processes, standards, and automation, the WebSphere engineers working for an IT organization can focus more on designing, building, and operating WebSphere infrastructure, and they may become more successful. As an option, the WebSphere engineers will have to design and implement engineering processes in WebSphere engineering regeneration for the full WebSphere engineering life cycle, as indicated in the previous section.

Organization Model

The right organization model for a new technology is every bit as important as the new technology itself. This builds the right sociotechnical systems for the optimal coproduction between groups within IT. In addition, SSME recognizes the critical interdependency and interaction between the organization and the technology in delivering a dynamic, holistic, and developing services system.

Inappropriate organization models and the resulting organizational issues can substantially hinder the introduction of the new technologies that your company's business strategy demands. For example, deploying the WebSphere Virtual Enterprise can increase system utilization, consolidate servers, and reduce infrastructure costs. For a corporation that has been going through many mergers and acquisitions, there is frequently an ongoing need for organizational integration. Sometimes, significant organizational segmentation does exist. A segmented organization suffers from organizational silos. Interest groups usually form along the alignment of historical company affinities or localism that favors certain strategic sites. As a result, political dynamics may become a significant factor, if not a hindrance, in introducing a new technology that the company wants. As an example, building a large and shared dynamic WebSphere infrastructure requires many different teams to work together. Without a genuine spirit of focusing on the enterprise view and enterprise priorities, even building a modestly sized shared virtualized environment may become too ambitious an undertaking. Therefore, having innovative organization models that can help effectively utilize the WebSphere Virtual Enterprise technologies by over-coming organizational segmentation are valuable deliverables.

The availability of organizational reference models specifically engineered for a new tech-nology makes needed organizational changes less strenuous. Besides, such a change is necessary to provide optimized engineering support for a shift in IT infrastructure technology. With the right organizational model, the resulting integrated technology package will have a far better chance for success than a legacy "bare bones" technology-only solution. Because services sys-tems can deliver greater technological and business value and success, it represents opportunities for the service provider, who could be an IT organization of a Fortune 500 company or a multi-national technology vendor. However, the deliverables for an integrated services system come with costs. Later, this chapter discusses who should provide the services system deliverables that have nontechnical components. To achieve this objective of providing services systems, many questions need to be answered:

1. Can the traditional human resources representatives play the role of organizational expert for technological paradigm change? In other words, do we need technologists who are also experts in organization and organizational changes?

2. What methodology drives out the appropriate organization with the introduction of a new technology needed to support business strategy?

3. Technologies change rapidly. What are the right relationships between organizational change and technological change?

4. Can system stability be maintained and grow during both rapid technology changes and organizational changes?

Communications Model and Culture Change

The corporate communications model and cultural change are indispensable for a major shift in the enterprise computing paradigm. Technology alone does not bring about positive changes—people do. SSME views people, processes, systems, communication, and culture as an intrinsi-cally interconnected ecological system. A services system emphasizes the importance of the relationships between organizations as well as that between people and technical systems.

For a services system to be successful in making positive changes, the most critical element is people. People are change agents. However, they are intentional agents. They support or resist change. To introduce a new services system composed of new technologies, processes, and organizations, a communications model and a cultural change that facilitate and motivate the team must be carefully designed, implemented, and executed. The deliverables need to be impor-tant tasks for technology providers. For example, how do you communicate new initiatives that bring significant changes for various teams that all work in and depend on a large shared virtual-ized infrastructure? What mechanisms do you have available to make people collaborate better when working on an interconnected dynamic enterprise infrastructure? Collaboration is never easy. What new mechanisms and processes can you deliver to help?

You may have to stop the practice of building only WebSphere infrastructure and start delivering WebSphere services systems in order to help your customer succeed in adopting new WebSphere technologies to meet business challenges. Your WebSphere infrastructure may have to be a new package, including technology artifacts, organizational models, engineering processes, communication, and culture change contents. For example, will you continue to see infrastructure architects, WebSphere engineers, project managers, and WebSphere managers in the next generation of large WebSphere projects? Will you also start to see technology organization consultants, communication experts, and corporate cultural analysts all work as a multidisciplinary team? Perhaps how you answer these questions will make or break your effort at building a competitive WebSphere team that can survive and prosper in tomorrow's challenging IT workplace.

Provider of Services Systems

The introduction of a new technology, such as the WebSphere Virtual Enterprise, will bring about the task of WebSphere engineering process regeneration. For example, the system resource needs analysis of WebSphere Virtual Enterprise-based systems will most certainly be different. The human resource consumption estimate for production support is most likely to require new tools and processes. A critical question is this: Who will provide the nontraditional components for services systems? In other words, who will design and test organizational models, engineering processes, communication recommendations, and cultural change best practices?

Technology companies have every motivation to embrace SSME and deliver nontraditional components that a services system demands; this helps the new technology's deployment succeed, with more predictable and consistent results with fewer cost overruns. If technology companies leave the engineering to their customers (IT organizations) it may take their customers a long time to figure out a new set of WebSphere engineering processes. The risk to technology companies such as IBM is that while the IT organizations adopting the technology try to update their engineering processes to manage the new technology, many problems can occur and slow the introduction of the new technology urgently needed by the business. This reduces the likelihood for the new technology's success. It also significantly increases the overall cost of technical support for the technology provider.

Many technology companies such as IBM have wide exposure to the entire spectrum of technologies and various sections of industries. With the release of every major new technology, they can provide appropriate critical elements of services systems, such as a complete IT methodology and engineering process package. These packages help their customers—usually IT organizations—integrate people, processes, and systems for the technological paradigm shift. Technology companies know the technology. Many of them know how to apply the technology, especially those with a large consulting practice, such as IBM. However, their customers still know best how to apply new technologies to support the business strategies in the specific technical and business context of their companies.

IT organizations have the resources, experience, and expertise to design, develop, and implement services systems. After all, IT organizations have been actively applying organization design, communication mechanism improvement, and cultural best practices to support business strategy and the technological changes. Of course, with the advent of SSME, IT organizations can certainly benefit from a more systematic approach to providing services systems. For example, corporate cultural changes can be designed to enhance communication and collaboration between teams working on a large services system that many divisions use. However, starting from scratch and delivering complete services systems with rigorous nontraditional components, such as organizational models and communication mechanisms, has significant costs. For instance, additional talents have to be brought on board, such as organization experts and corporate communication consultants. Extra costs are incurred to design, develop, and deliver the artifacts needed (for example, a new interteam change-management process and supporting documentation systems). Besides increased costs, another concern is the quality and consistency of services systems delivered. These IT organizations know the technology landscape of their companies. However, confronted with a fundamentally new technology and methodology, such as a SOA and WebSphere infrastructure technologies that support SOA, these IT organizations have a significant learning curve.

The best approach is a hybrid model where the technology vendor provides general guidance and generic framework for the new technology, and the IT organization designs and implements the artifacts for the new technology paradigm (according to its own specific situation and business needs). For example, while shipping various technologies to support SOA, the vendor provides the framework of full SOA service life cycle of model, assemble, deploy, and manage; the vendor also supplies SOA governance, management models, best practices, general guidance on roles, processes, policies, metrics, and checkpoints for a SOA project. In addition, the vendor makes artifact templates available and gives concrete examples to help the IT organization systematically design and implement its SOA strategies, policies, guidelines, organizational models, and engineering metrics and processes. This approach reduces the technology vendor's costs and helps ensure the technology's success, because the technology will be easier to use and the IT organization's implementation will be more predictable and consistent across the middleware industry (with experienced guidance from the technology vendor).

Summary

This chapter explored what to do to obtain the technical skills to design, build, and operate a WebSphere infrastructure for SOA solutions. It examined how to build a future WebSphere organization to better support fast-evolving dynamic WebSphere technologies. This chapter discussed the technical knowledge and skills in XML, Web services, and SOA as the building blocks to learn and deploy WSRR, WebSphere ESB, and WebSphere DataPower. Then it examined issues that can be dealt with using the WebSphere Virtual Enterprise and challenges that the WebSphere team must overcome to effectively use this technology to build the next-generation WebSphere infrastructure. Finally, this chapter looked into the possibilities of SSME and the potential applications in WebSphere engineering.

WebSphere professionals worldwide have come a long way in WebSphere engineering, but there is still a long way to go. The industry is moving into the brave new world of dynamic Web-Sphere technologies. New technologies are being used to build enterprise IT WebSphere infrastructure to support SOA. In addition, new thoughts and innovative systems of thinking, such as SSME, promise tough new challenges and exciting new opportunities.

The main challenge is that WebSphere professionals again have to provide high quality WebSphere products and services amidst fast-changing business drivers and rapidly developing technologies. The new opportunity is to advance and innovate WebSphere engineering and build world-class WebSphere teams that deliver WebSphere enterprise infrastructure of industry-leading performance.

Index

X-Y-Z

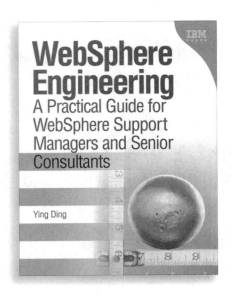

FREE Online Edition

Your purchase of **WebSphere Engineering** includes access to a free online edition for 45 days through the Safari Books Online subscription service. Nearly every IBM Press book is available online through Safari Books Online, along with over 5,000 other technical books and videos from publishers such as Addison-Wesley Professional, Cisco Press, Exam Cram, O'Reilly, Prentice Hall, Que, and Sams.

SAFARI BOOKS ONLINE allows you to search for a specific answer, cut and paste code, download chapters, and stay current with emerging technologies.

Activate your FREE Online Edition at
www.ibmpressbooks.com/safarifree

> **STEP 1:** Enter the coupon code: HABJIXA.

> **STEP 2:** New Safari users, complete the brief registration form.
> Safari subscribers, just log in.

If you have difficulty registering on Safari or accessing the online edition, please e-mail customer-service@safaribooksonline.com